Amplifying the Curriculum: Designing Q[illegible] Learning Opportunities for Multilingual L[illegible] 2nd Ed.
AIDA WALQUI, GEORGE C. BUNCH, & PEGGY MUELLER, EDS.

Reading, Writing, and Talk: Teaching for Equity and Justice in the Early Grades, 2nd Ed.
MARIANA SOUTO-MANNING, JESSICA MARTELL, & BENELLY ÁLVAREZ

When Teaching Writing Gets Tough: Challenges and Possibilities in Secondary Writing Instruction
ANNAMARY CONSALVO & ANN D. DAVID, EDS.

Equitable Literacy Instruction for Students in Poverty
DORIS WALKER-DALHOUSE & VICTORIA J. RISKO

Reading and Relevance, Reimagined: Celebrating the Literacy Lives of Young Men of Color
KATIE SCIURBA

Teaching With Arts-Infused Writing Pedagogies: Freedom Dreaming for Educational Justice
KELLY K. WISSMAN, ED.

A Cyclical Model of Literacy Learning: Expanding the Gradual Release of Responsibility
ADRIENNE MINNERY & ANTONY T. SMITH

Educating African Immigrant Youth: Schooling and Civic Engagement in K–12 Schools
VAUGHN W. M. WATSON, MICHELLE G. KNIGHT-MANUEL, & PATRIANN SMITH, EDS.

Pose, Wobble, Flow: A Liberatory Approach to Literacy Learning in All Classrooms, 2nd Ed.
ANTERO GARCIA & CINDY O'DONNELL-ALLEN

Teaching Climate Change to Children: Literacy Pedagogy That Cultivates Sustainable Futures
REBECCA WOODARD & KRISTINE M. SCHUTZ

Widening the Lens: Integrating Multiple Approaches to Support Adolescent Literacy
DEBORAH VRIEND VAN DUINEN & ERICA R. HAMILTON

Connecting Equity, Literacy, and Language: Pathways Toward Advocacy-Focused Teaching
ALTHIER M. LAZAR, KAITLIN K. MORAN, & SHOSHANNA EDWARDS-ALEXANDER

Writing Instruction for Success in College and in the Workplace
CHARLES A. MACARTHUR & ZOI A. PHILIPPAKOS

Black Immigrant Literacies: Intersections of Race, Language, and Culture in the Classroom
PATRIANN SMITH

Teens Choosing to Read: Fostering Social, Emotional, and Intellectual Growth Through Books
GAY IVEY & PETER JOHNSTON

Critical Encounters in Secondary English: Teaching Literary Theory to Adolescents, 4th Ed.
DEBORAH APPLEMAN

[illegible] and Using Children's Literature for Inquiry and Engagement
ERIKA THULIN DAWES, KATIE EGAN CUNNINGHAM, GRACE ENRIQUEZ, & MARY ANN CAPPIELLO

Core Practices for Teaching Multilingual Students: Humanizing Pedagogies for Equity
MEGAN MADIGAN PEERCY, JOHANNA M. TIGERT, & DAISY E. FREDRICKS

Bringing Sports Culture to the English Classroom: An Interest-Driven Approach to Literacy Instruction
LUKE RODESILER

Culturally Sustaining Literacy Pedagogies: Honoring Students' Heritages, Literacies, and Languages
SUSAN CHAMBERS CANTRELL, DORIS WALKER-DALHOUSE, & ALTHIER M. LAZAR, EDS.

Curating a Literacy Life: Student-Centered Learning With Digital Media
WILLIAM KIST

Understanding the Transnational Lives and Literacies of Immigrant Children
JUNGMIN KWON

The Administration and Supervision of Literacy Programs, 6th Ed.
SHELLEY B. WEPNER & DIANA J. QUATROCHE, EDS.

Writing the School House Blues: Literacy, Equity, and Belonging in a Child's Early Schooling
ANNE HAAS DYSON

Playing With Language: Improving Elementary Reading Through Metalinguistic Awareness
MARCY ZIPKE

Restorative Literacies: Creating a Community of Care in Schools
DEBORAH L. WOLTER

Compose Our World: Project-Based Learning in Secondary English Language Arts
ALISON G. BOARDMAN, ANTERO GARCIA, BRIDGET DALTON, & JOSEPH L. POLMAN

Digitally Supported Disciplinary Literacy for Diverse K–5 Classrooms
JAMIE COLWELL, AMY HUTCHISON, & LINDSAY WOODWARD

The Reading Turn-Around with Emergent Bilinguals: A Five-Part Framework for Powerful Teaching and Learning (Grades K–6)
AMANDA CLAUDIA WAGER, LANE W. CLARKE, & GRACE ENRIQUEZ

Race, Justice, and Activism in Literacy Instruction
VALERIE KINLOCH, TANJA BURKHARD, & CARLOTTA PENN, EDS.

Letting Go of Literary Whiteness: Antiracist Literature Instruction for White Students
CARLIN BORSHEIM-BLACK & SOPHIA TATIANA SARIGIANIDES

continued

For volumes in the NCRLL Collection (edited by JoBeth Allen and Donna E. Alvermann), the Practitioners Bookshelf Series (edited by Celia Genishi and Donna E. Alvermann), and other titles in this series, please visit www.tcpress.com

Language and Literacy Series, *continued*

The Vulnerable Heart of Literacy: Centering Trauma as Powerful Pedagogy
ELIZABETH DUTRO

Arts Integration in Diverse K–5 Classrooms
LIANE BROUILLETTE

Translanguaging for Emergent Bilinguals
DANLING FU, XENIA HADJIOANNOU, & XIAODI ZHOU

Before Words
JUDITH T. LYSAKER

Seeing the Spectrum
ROBERT ROZEMA

A Think-Aloud Approach to Writing Assessment
SARAH W. BECK

"We've Been Doing It Your Way Long Enough"
JANICE BAINES, CARMEN TISDALE, & SUSI LONG

Summer Reading, 2nd Ed.
RICHARD L. ALLINGTON & ANNE MCGILL-FRANZEN, EDS.

Educating for Empathy
NICOLE MIRRA

Preparing English Learners for College and Career
MARÍA SANTOS ET AL.

Reading the Rainbow
CAITLIN L. RYAN & JILL M. HERMANN-WILMARTH

Educating Emergent Bilinguals, 2nd Ed.
OFELIA GARCÍA & JO ANNE KLEIFGEN

Social Justice Literacies in the English Classroom
ASHLEY S. BOYD

Remixing Multiliteracies
FRANK SERAFINI & ELISABETH GEE, EDS.

Culturally Sustaining Pedagogies
DJANGO PARIS & H. SAMY ALIM, EDS.

Choice and Agency in the Writing Workshop
FRED L. HAMEL

Assessing Writing, Teaching Writers
MARY ANN SMITH & SHERRY SEALE SWAIN

The Teacher-Writer
CHRISTINE M. DAWSON

Every Young Child a Reader
SHARAN A. GIBSON & BARBARA MOSS

"You Gotta BE the Book," 3rd Ed.
JEFFREY D. WILHELM

Personal Narrative, Revised
BRONWYN CLARE LAMAY

Inclusive Literacy Teachings
LORI HELMAN ET AL.

The Vocabulary Book, 2nd Ed.
MICHAEL F. GRAVES

Go Be a Writer!
CANDACE R. KUBY & TARA GUTSHALL RUCKER

Partnering with Immigrant Communities
GERALD CAMPANO ET AL.

Teaching Outside the Box but Inside the Standards
BOB FECHO ET AL., EDS.

Literacy Leadership in Changing Schools
SHELLEY B. WEPNER ET AL.

Literacy Theory as Practice
LARA J. HANDSFIELD

Literacy and History in Action
THOMAS M. MCCANN ET AL.

Teaching Transnational Youth
ALLISON SKERRETT

Uncommonly Good Ideas
SANDRA MURPHY & MARY ANN SMITH

Transforming Talk into Text
THOMAS M. MCCANN

WHAM! Teaching with Graphic Novels Across the Curriculum
WILLIAM G. BROZO ET AL.

Critical Literacy in the Early Childhood Classroom
CANDACE R. KUBY

Inspiring Dialogue
MARY M. JUZWIK ET AL.

Reading the Visual
FRANK SERAFINI

ReWRITING the Basics
ANNE HAAS DYSON

Writing Instruction That Works
ARTHUR N. APPLEBEE ET AL.

Literacy Playshop
KAREN E. WOHLWEND

Critical Media Pedagogy
ERNEST MORRELL ET AL.

A Search Past Silence
DAVID E. KIRKLAND

Reading in a Participatory Culture
HENRY JENKINS ET AL., EDS.

Teaching Vocabulary to English Language Learners
MICHAEL F. GRAVES ET AL.

Bridging Literacy and Equity
ALTHIER M. LAZAR ET AL.

Reading Time
CATHERINE COMPTON-LILLY

Interrupting Hate
MOLLIE V. BLACKBURN

Playing Their Way into Literacies
KAREN E. WOHLWEND

Teaching Literacy for Love and Wisdom
JEFFREY D. WILHELM & BRUCE NOVAK

Urban Literacies
VALERIE KINLOCH, ED.

Envisioning Knowledge
JUDITH A. LANGER

Envisioning Literature, 2nd Ed.
JUDITH A. LANGER

Artifactual Literacies
KATE PAHL & JENNIFER ROWSELL

Change Is Gonna Come
PATRICIA A. EDWARDS ET AL.

Harlem on Our Minds
VALERIE KINLOCH

Children, Language, and Literacy
CELIA GENISHI & ANNE HAAS DYSON

Children's Language
JUDITH WELLS LINDFORS

Storytime
LAWRENCE R. SIPE

Amplifying the Curriculum

Designing Quality Learning Opportunities for Multilingual Learners

SECOND EDITION

Edited by
Aída Walqui, George C. Bunch,
and Peggy Mueller

TEACHERS COLLEGE PRESS
TEACHERS COLLEGE | COLUMBIA UNIVERSITY
NEW YORK AND LONDON

Published simultaneously by Teachers College Press, 1234 Amsterdam Avenue, New York, NY 10027 and WestEd, 730 Harrison Street, San Francisco, CA 94107

Front cover design by adam bohannon. Illustration by CSA Printstock / iStock by Getty Images.

"I Lost My Talk" by Rita Joe is printed with permission from the Estate of Rita Joe.

"Theme for English B" by Langston Hughes, from *The Collected Poems of Langston Hughes,* is reprinted with permission from Alfred A. Knopf.

Library of Congress Cataloging-in-Publication Data is available at loc.gov

ISBN 978-0-8077-8714-4 (paper)
ISBN 978-0-8077-8715-1 (hardcover)
ISBN 978-0-8077-8311-5 (ebook)

Printed on acid-free paper
Manufactured in the United States of America

Contents

Preface

In the Preface to the first edition of this book, published in 2019, we argued for a shift from *simplification* to *amplification* as the guiding principle for the education of students classified as English Learners. We maintained that enhancement and elaboration of content and language, instead of reduction and restriction, were particularly important for English Learners, and indeed all students, to meet the more rigorous content standards and assessments that had recently been adopted in many states, especially since these standards increased the literacy and English language required to access the core curriculum. More broadly, we argued that such shifts were necessary to offer students deep, rigorous, and well-supported opportunities to learn in order to become critical and contributing citizens in the 21st century. Thus, we situated the shift toward amplification in efforts not only to increase access to academically rigorous work for English Learners, but also for civic and democratic participation in communities, the nation, and the world.

We drew on our own experiences as educational professionals over several decades—first as classroom teachers ourselves and later as teacher educators, professional development providers, curriculum developers, educational researchers, and scholars of language and literacy issues in education. When we began collaborating 15 years ago, we realized that we shared visions, practices, and commitments in our work across the varied geographical, grade level, and linguistic contexts in which we had worked with K–12 students, teachers, and educational leaders. We also realized we had been grappling throughout our careers with a similar set of problems:

- Deficit views of what language learners can do both intellectually and linguistically as they develop their home and additional languages;
- Reductive pedagogical approaches based on these assumptions that often leave some students without access to high-quality, intellectually rich, discipline-based curriculum and pedagogy;

- The relegation of content-area instruction for students classified as English Learners to language teachers who typically lack the appropriate content and pedagogical content knowledge in the disciplines they are teaching;
- Guidance for teachers that emphasizes discrete "strategies" or "methods" for English Learners that do not cohere theoretically and are disconnected from the key practices in the various disciplines; and
- Teachers being viewed and treated merely as the *deliverers* of curriculum developed by others rather than as *designers and implementers* of lessons, units, and instructional materials themselves.

As we contemplated the invitation from Teachers College Press to produce a second edition, it was clear that the rationale for the first edition remained as valid as ever. In far too many settings, simplification continues to be the preferred response to the education of multilingual learners, and especially students classified by their schools as English Learners. (In the second edition, we use the broader term *multilingual learners* to refer to students from homes where English is not the predominant language, and *English Learners* for those who are officially classified by their schools, following state and federal policy.) In fact, we realized that the need to amplify learning opportunities was even more crucial given the events that had occurred since the publication of the first edition.

The first edition was written before the onset of the global pandemic in early 2020 that upended public education and society more generally for several years, with disproportionate and lasting impacts on multilingual learners and their families. Unfortunately, as students have returned to school in person and as concerns about "learning loss" during the pandemic still reverberate, we find that multilingual learners are often assigned individualized, remedial, uninspired assignments, either via worksheets or monotonous computerized learning modules. In other cases, activities that in a well-designed and implemented learning sequence should take only a portion of one class period get stretched out into days of slow-moving instruction—in other words, the opposite of what we might imagine would be helpful to ignite students' interest in school and invigorate their learning.

The first edition was also written before a number of monumental societal events that have challenged productive civic discourse inside and outside of schools, exacerbated political divides, and increased the vulnerability of students from immigrant families and other racialized minorities. It was written before the murder of George Floyd in 2020, which reignited the Black Lives Matter movement and a national reckoning on the legacies of racism in the United States, only to be followed by a backlash that has included attacks on a wide range of efforts by educational institutions to promote diversity, equity, and inclusion. It was also written before widespread efforts on the part of an incumbent president and his supporters to discredit and invalidate the 2020 election that he lost, including the January 6, 2021, attack on the United States Capitol by a mob of protestors attempting to keep the president in power. And the list goes on. As we write, we are experiencing profound political divides over the U.S. role in death and destruction in Gaza, Israel, Lebanon, and elsewhere in the Middle East. And we are witnessing an even stronger effort than we wrote about in the first edition, by members of both major political parties, to publicly vilify immigrants and craft increasingly harsh immigration policies, for millions already in the United States and others seeking to enter the country.

We mention these events to make the point that we are in greater need than ever of an educated populace that reads critically, listens carefully, thoughtfully considers multiple perspectives, and communicates diverse perspectives with both clarity and nuance—both to those whom they already agree with and to those whose perspectives may differ from their own. With this in mind, we have included in the second edition a sharper focus on how teachers can choose the kinds of texts and learning activities that will engage multilingual learners, and all students, in dialogues with each other, their teacher, and indeed the texts themselves, in order to build the kind of critical reading, informed debate, and consideration of alternative viewpoints necessary for our communities and democracy to flourish.

The second edition also features a number of other important additions and revisions. First, we are delighted to be joined by coeditor Peggy Mueller, who herself brings multiple years of experience as an educator, scholar, and policy analyst. We include new chapters focusing on two important contexts that we referenced but did not adequately explore in the first edition. One new chapter explicitly addresses how tenets, lesson architecture, and learning activities discussed in the introductory chapters can be applied to elementary school contexts, providing examples at various grade levels. Another, written in Spanish, delves into amplifying the curriculum in students' home languages. We have also updated, revised, and/or expanded the other chapters, providing multiple new examples of units, lessons, and learning activities, including brand new chapters on amplifying the curriculum in science, English Language Arts, math, and social studies classrooms. This new edition also features an updated model of teacher expertise, as well as recent examples from our work with both preservice and inservice teachers.

Other fundamental aspects of the book remain the same. It is still written for current and future teachers across the subject areas, with our original focus on the high school and middle school levels augmented in this edition with attention to elementary contexts. It is also intended for those who support teachers in preparing for and carrying out this challenging and rewarding work, including preservice teacher educators, providers of professional learning opportunities for inservice teachers, educational leaders, other curriculum and instructional materials developers (including open-source initiatives and textbook companies), and those who design assessments.

Given the large numbers of multilingual learners attending schools throughout the United States, the language and literacy demands across the subject areas, and the fact that disciplinary instruction can serve as an ideal context for language development, it is still the case that the development of English for academic purposes cannot be the sole responsibility of English as a Second Language teachers. This responsibility has to be understood as belonging to every teacher, in every discipline. The good news is that, as the discussion and examples throughout the book demonstrate, the kinds of amplification we argue for, while particularly crucial for students classified as English Learners, are also helpful for all students, including those who speak only English and former English Learners who have been reclassified as fluent English speakers. Further, multilingual learners, including those classified as English Learners, bring all the necessary capabilities to participate in instruction with such goals *right now*—if units, lessons, and instructional strategies are designed in ways that allow them to leverage their capacity. In other words, it is not the case that English Learners are not "ready" for deep learning, but rather that learning environments as often conceived currently are not ready to maximize English Learners' potential.

The central goal of this edition remains to prepare teachers to design instruction that provides access to and support for multilingual learners to engage in conceptually rich and analytically challenging disciplinary content—while simultaneously developing the language and literacy inherently connected to this content. In articulating the ideas outlined in the book, we build on theory and research in learning, language development, disciplinary literacy, pedagogy, and teacher preparation.

Most of the examples come from lessons and units created with and for classroom teachers by Aída's QTEL team, all of whom themselves are experienced teachers and inservice teacher educators, building on Aída's work on the development of ambitious, well-supported invitations for English Learners to develop their academic potential. Other chapters are written by colleagues who are not part of the QTEL team, but whose work as teachers, teacher educators, and scholars has drawn from and aligns with QTEL.

We can still say from our own professional experience that, despite the challenges, engaging in the design of the kind of amplified learning tasks, lessons, and units described in this book—those that are simultaneously inviting, challenging, and supportive for multilingual learners—is not only possible, but also inspiring and rewarding.

Acknowledgments

In crafting the original volume and engaging in the extensive additions and revisions for the second edition, we are appreciative of the hard work, patience, and good cheer among all the chapter authors throughout the many rounds of conversation, drafting, revision, and editing that we collectively undertook. The chapter authors worked on their own chapters and reviewed others, all while also working full time on other professional learning and design endeavors. Their dedication to sharing lessons learned with educators nationwide propelled them to work diligently and graciously through reviews and multiple drafts to arrive at this publication.

We are pleased to welcome Peggy Mueller as a coeditor for this edition. The original version of this book could not have been completed without her work as a trusted, thoughtful, and meticulous "behind the scenes" editorial colleague to help us enhance our arguments, gain coherence, stay organized, attend to details, and generally maintain our sanity. For the second edition, she again magnificently read and reread every word of multiple drafts of the manuscript, her unfailing eye helping us see through redundancies and inconsistencies and considerably strengthening the book's coherence.

At WestEd, we thank Ursula Wright, Senior Vice President of K–12 Systems, for providing institutional support for the completion of the second edition. Thanks also to Patricia López-Hurtado for her essential assistance formatting all the tables and figures for the first edition, and Danny Torres for his ongoing assistance on both editions.

We again extend sincere thanks to Emily Spangler, our editor at Teachers College Press, who supported the idea for the original book from its inception, patiently encouraged us to complete it, enthusiastically invited us to consider a revised edition, and guided us in seeing it through to completion. We realize how wonderful it is to have editors who are aware of the importance of fanning the fire just right, so that it keeps going without the threat of extinction. Emily's feedback always includes an ideal combination of encouragement and critique, and both editions have benefitted immeasurably from her suggestions.

We also want to thank colleagues and friends who carefully read one or more chapters during the development of the original and/or revised volume and who gave us thoughtful, honest, and helpful feedback. These "critical friends" (critical both in the sense of providing critique and also in the sense of being essential to a successful outcome) include Cindy Pease-Alvarez, Kathi Bailey, Sarah Beck, Pía Castilleja, Hongying Chen, Amanda Kibler, Tatyana Kleyn, Nora Lang, César Larriva, Alicia Rusoja, Jeremy Shonick, Guadalupe Valdés, and Natalia Verástegui. Special thanks also to the teachers, administrators, and other colleagues and leaders who read chapters and provided feedback as they participated in preservice teacher preparation courses, QTEL institutes, and other professional learning initiatives across the country. It has been inspiring to hear you talk about how the book has helped your efforts to amplify instruction for multilingual learners, and we appreciate your feedback regarding how to make the book even more inviting and helpful for teachers and administrators who are in a position to do this work.

Finally, on a personal note, we again wish to express deep appreciation to family, friends, and colleagues for their patience, understanding, and support during the many hours it took us to complete the original project and this revised and expanded version.

Amplifying the Curriculum

Part I

FOUNDATIONS FOR AMPLIFYING THE CURRICULUM

CHAPTER 1

Educating Multilingual Learners

George C. Bunch and Aída Walqui

This book shows how teachers, ideally working together, can design high-quality, intellectually challenging, and well-supported learning opportunities that move from *simplification* to *amplification* as the guiding principle for the education of students who come to U.S. schools from homes where English is not the dominant language. Improving the education of multilingual learners, including those classified by their schools as "English Learners," is not only an act of advocacy for this particular population. It is also in society's collective self-interest to include this large and growing segment of the U.S. population in efforts to strengthen the public education on which our economic vitality, civic health, and participatory democracy rely. Fortunately, challenging, engaging, and dialogic learning opportunities also provide optimum contexts for language and literacy development. And multilingual learners bring to the table a wide range of linguistic and cultural resources that make them not only ideally prepared for the kind of learning increasingly needed for the challenges of our time, but also essential actors in efforts to create a more equitable and just society.

Identifying students who need English language support to succeed in regular content-area instruction in English—along with addressing their specific needs—was mandated by the U.S. Supreme Court over 50 years ago (*Lau v. Nichols*, 1974). Federal policy, and most states, school districts, and schools, use the term English Learners to describe students identified as in need of such support.[1] However, there is currently much discussion and debate surrounding terms used to refer to students who come to school speaking languages other than English (Kanno et al., 2024). The terms *multilingual learner* and *emergent bilingual* have been suggested by some as an alternative to English Learner to emphasize the importance of students' continuing development of language and literacy in their home languages as well as in English (García & Kleifgen, 2018). Such arguments have led to awareness of the importance of languages other than English in students' linguistic repertoires, as well as an awareness of the fact that learning English is not the *only* goal that students from multilingual backgrounds have. However, using these terms as a replacement for English Learner also presents potential ambiguity or confusion. For example: Do students ever *stop* being "multilingual learners"? Does that term include students from English-dominant families who are learning languages other than English in school? When does an "emergent bilingual" actually *emerge* as bilingual? (Kanno et al., 2024).

In this book, we use the term *multilingual learners* to describe all students who come to school speaking home languages other than English, whether or not they are officially classified as English Learners by their district. We use English Learners to refer more specifically to students who have been classified as such following district and state guidelines in accordance with federal policy. As students enroll in school in the United States, this process usually involves first a home language survey to determine if languages other than English are spoken in the home and then an assessment to determine students' English language skills in speaking, listening, reading, and writing. Students are then tested annually. Based on their scores, along with other criteria that vary by state and sometimes by district, they are either determined to remain an English Learner and thus continue to receive mandated services, or reclassified as "Fluent English Proficient" and monitored for several years but not necessarily provided with additional support. Later in this chapter, we will have more to say about this classification process and the problems underlying it.

Although both the Supreme Court's decision and U.S. federal education policy require equitable access to core content-area instruction for students classified as English Learners (Kanno, 2021; Umansky et al., in press), neither the courts nor the federal government have stipulated exactly *how* these students should be supported, leaving those decisions up to states, districts, schools, academic departments, and individual teachers. Unfortunately, the preparation and support provided for multilingual learners in general and those classified as English Learners in particular have often ended up restricting access to both content learning and language development in ways that diminish—rather than enhance—their opportunities to learn important subject matter, enrich understandings, engage in careful analysis, and advance compelling arguments (Gamoran, 2017; Kanno, 2021; Umansky et al., 2020). At the same time, such reductive approaches deny English Learners opportunities to develop the language and literacy resources needed to communicate effectively with a variety of audiences for a variety of purposes in an increasingly complex and interconnected world.

In contrast to the ways that instruction has often been *simplified* for multilingual learners in the past, in this book we present a vision for how teachers and other educators can design activities, instructional materials, lessons, and units that *amplify* opportunities for those learning English as an additional language. The learning designs that we present for teachers in this book engage multilingual learners with rich, meaningful, and challenging language and content in ways that support their disciplinary learning and analytical thinking, allow their voices to be heard, and challenge them to develop the kind of civic discourse and reasoning necessary to participate in and contribute to the democratic life of their communities and the world.

At the same time, because the approach we lay out is designed to support students wherever they currently are in their academic and linguistic journeys, it is applicable to teachers' efforts to design learning opportunities for *all* students, including speakers of nondominant varieties of English and others who may be identified as in need of language and literacy support. Moving from reduction to elaboration is important to support *all young people* in developing the multifaceted and sophisticated communicative and academic competencies they need to navigate a range of challenges facing our local, national, and global communities.

AMPLIFYING THE CURRICULUM

In this book, we offer the following advice to those responsible for the education of multilingual learners—content teachers, English language development specialists, administrators, curriculum developers, teacher educators, and professional development providers: *Amplify, don't simplify!* (Walqui & van Lier, 2010, p. 38). Drawing on definitions of amplification that include "enhancement," "elaboration," "augmentation," "extension," and "expansion"—and theories of learning and language development where these concepts are paramount—we present a vision and blueprint for designing classroom instruction for multilingual learners, and for all students. We elaborate the rationale for amplification, provide guidance for designing it, and share examples of what it looks like in practice. We include examples adaptable for multilingual learners from a wide range of English proficiency levels, in both elementary and secondary contexts, with illustrations from across multiple subject areas, including one chapter focusing on home language instruction in Spanish.

Instruction cannot be amplified in the classroom without careful consideration of the fundamental goals of instruction and how those goals are to be manifested through the organization of learning activities, lessons, and units. Effectively educating English Learners, or any students for that matter, must go beyond the implementation of discrete instructional strategies, no matter how compelling those individual strategies are, and must consider the larger curriculum. But to be clear, *curriculum,* as we use the term in this book, does not refer to something that is merely handed to teachers for them to follow.

Ultimately, we argue, classroom teachers are the most important curriculum developers, both in terms of creating their own materials and adapting those created by others, and so we envision teachers as the most important audience for this book. At the same time, because many teachers have never been asked to participate in designing curriculum, they may feel overwhelmed, not knowing where to begin. Thus, we have written this book also for those who work closely with teachers: preservice teacher educators, professional developers, coaches, and school administrators. We also write for those engaged in curriculum design at larger scales, who continue to play a critical role in influencing the education of English Learners: district-level curriculum developers, commercial and open-source publishers, governmental and nongovernmental organizations, assessment specialists, and educational researchers involved in curriculum development.

In the chapters that follow, we invite readers to join us and the other authors through the journey of designing challenging, interesting, relevant, interconnected, and valuable learning opportunities for multilingual learners across various subject areas. Throughout, we pay particular attention to how teachers can create opportunities for students to engage in critical dialogue with each other, their teacher, and the texts, phenomena, and problems they are engaging in (Kibler et al., 2021; Walqui, 2024). We also discuss how teachers and others involved in developing lessons and units can choose relevant, challenging, and important texts to invite their students to engage with and develop scaffolds to help multilingual learners navigate those texts.

Before proceeding, it is important to point out that there are numerous cognitive, social, and economic benefits of bilingualism in the 21st century (Callahan & Gándara, 2014; National Academies of Sciences, Engineering, and Medicine [National Academies], 2017; Office of English Language Acquisition, 2020; Orellana, 2009; Valdés, 2003), and students' home languages can serve as an important resource for their learning in school (García & Kleifgen, 2018). We are heartened that states such as California and Massachusetts rescinded their "English-only" restrictions for schools a number of years ago, and we support efforts to prepare teachers for leveraging students' home language resources even when the teachers themselves do not speak those languages (García & Kleyn, 2016). At the same time, the fact is that most multilingual learners in U.S. schools still receive content-area instruction and assessments predominantly in English. Because this is unlikely to change in the foreseeable future, most chapters in this book focus predominantly on examples where English is the medium of instruction. Nonetheless, the tenets and designs featured throughout the book are also applicable to contexts that include instruction in languages other than

English and so will be of use to teachers in a range of bilingual settings. In Chapter 5, which is written in Spanish, the language spoken by the vast majority of students classified as English Learners, we focus explicitly on what amplifying the curriculum might look like in classrooms conducted primarily in students' home language.

THE PLAN FOR THE BOOK

The chapters in Part I lay the groundwork for the curricular illustrations that follow. After presenting a rationale for our approach and a description of multilingual learners in this introductory chapter (Chapter 1), we describe tenets that ground our vision of amplification in Chapter 2, along with classroom examples that illuminate those tenets. Chapter 3 presents design features to guide the development of lessons, units, and the broader curriculum.

Part II presents illustrations of specific units, lessons, and learning activities that provide opportunities for students to encounter important concepts, engage in complex analysis, and use and develop a range of literacy and language practices. Written by educators who collectively have experience as classroom teachers, preservice teacher educators, providers of professional development, and curriculum developers, the examples are based on materials, activities, and lessons that we have seen teachers across the United States use successfully with multilingual learners from a wide variety of backgrounds. Each of the chapters in Part II guides the reader through the process of identifying key concepts that the unit will explore: selecting high-quality texts, problems, or phenomena for students to grapple with; developing tasks that will guide students' analysis; facilitating students in developing relevant language and literacy practices; and organizing all of the above into coherent instructional sequences, lessons, units, and larger curricular scopes and sequences.

Part II begins, in Chapter 4, with a chapter by Lyn Westergard describing how teachers can design learning opportunities for multilingual learners in elementary classrooms by asking them to analyze and create stories with a critical social meaning. Chapter 5, written in Spanish by Aída Walqui and Viviana Galdames, describes activities for courses at the elementary or secondary level taught in Spanish to students who speak Spanish either as a home language or an additional language. Those chapters are followed by subject-specific chapters focusing on English-medium instruction in secondary schools, many of which could also be adaptable for the upper elementary grades: Chapter 6 (English Language Arts, by Mary Schmida); Chapter 7 (Mathematics, by Leslie Hamburger and Haiwen Chu); Chapter 8 (History, by Daisy Martin and George C. Bunch); and Chapter 9 (Science, by Tanya

Warren). Chapter 10 presents examples from a unit designed for an important subpopulation of multilingual learners: beginning-level English Learners who have recently arrived in the United States, sometimes called "Newcomers." Collectively, the chapters in Part II illustrate the notion that critical engagement starts in elementary classes and continues through secondary schooling and beyond.

In Part III, the book concludes with two chapters exploring the promise of amplified curricula through the eyes of students who have experienced it and teachers who have implemented it, as well as the teacher preparation and professional learning needed to enact it. Chapter 11, by George C. Bunch, Heather Schlaman, Sara Rutherford-Quach, Shirley Feldman, and Aída Walqui, shares the voices of teachers and students in three different states engaged in a unit developed using the tenets and design features described in Chapters 2 and 3, discussing findings from the first widespread implementation of the approach. Chapter 11 also discusses the most recent work implementing this approach with teachers in a wide range of contexts. In Chapter 12, we discuss what teachers can do immediately to begin moving to amplify the curriculum, as well as how educators in teacher preparation and professional development settings can work with teachers to design the kind of amplified instruction described throughout the book.

* * *

The remainder of this introductory chapter (Chapter 1) is organized into two main sections. The first situates our vision for quality learning for multilingual learners in the context of the competencies required for them to thrive in the 21st century. The second part provides an introduction to students often classified as English Learners and discusses the benefits and liabilities associated with that label. We conclude Chapter 1 by re-emphasizing how, given demographic shifts likely to continue, improving the education of English Learners helps unleash not only their potential for individual success, but also their contributions to a more vibrant, equitable, and sustainable world.

LEARNING FOR THE 21ST CENTURY

If both students and society are to thrive in the 21st century, learners will need to develop a range of competencies. As Mehta and Fine (2017) point out:

> Successfully navigating twenty-first-century adult life requires far more than basic academic knowledge and skills. On the personal front, adults need to be able to navigate among plural identities, to confront complex ethical questions, and

> to make informed decisions in the face of uncertainty. On the civic front, they need to be able to articulate and advocate for their perspectives, to engage in productive dialogue across ideological divides, and to decide among imperfect options. On the professional front, they need to be able to tackle open-ended problems in critical, creative, and collaborative ways and to engage in ongoing learning that allows them to adapt to the needs of a rapidly changing job market. (p. 11)

The competencies necessary to succeed in the world described above, and the goals of instruction that prepare students for this world, have been referred to by different terms, including *deeper learning, 21st-century skills, college and career readiness,* and *next generation learning* (Chow, 2017, p. v; Pellegrino & Hilton, 2012). Research on success during the early years of college has demonstrated the importance of understanding key concepts and "big ideas" of core content areas, but also of developing cognitive strategies, student ownership of learning, and the ability to navigate complex institutions (Conley, 2017, p. 205; Pellegrino & Hilton, 2012). Meanwhile, research on workplace settings has highlighted the need to communicate and collaborate with diverse colleagues, to solve problems of increasing complexity, and to adapt to ever-changing contexts (Heller et al., 2017). Finally, a number of scholars have highlighted the importance of interaction, dialogue, culture, and criticality in learning itself (Kibler et al., 2021; Lee et al., 2020; Mercer et al., 2020; Nasir et al., 2020; Walqui, 2024).

The movement that resulted in current state standards such as the Common Core and Next Generation Science Standards arose out of the belief that the emphasis on basic skills that had gripped U.S. educational policy and practice on and off throughout its history was not sufficient to deal with the challenges of our times. It is true that many past reform efforts also challenged the idea that basic skills should be the primary goal of U.S. public education (Ladson-Billings, 2006; Oakes, 1985; Tyack & Cuban, 1995). There are, however, two critical differences in the 21st century. One is the "rapid and irreversible transformations to the landscape of modern life" that make these competencies even more necessary today than in the past (Mehta & Fine, 2017, p. 13). And the second is that *everyone*—not just those in the "elite" classes—is called upon to use such competencies: in the workplace, in civic spaces, in social networks, and even at home (Pellegrino & Hilton, 2012). We live in such rapidly changing times that we cannot fathom the jobs that will be available when those currently in elementary and middle school will seek them. What skills inside and outside of the workplace will be needed in this new landscape? While many are impossible to predict, certainly the ability to observe critically, ask questions, understand diverse points of view, advance arguments, and negotiate solutions will be among them.

Of course, in a democratic society, preparing students to be successful in higher education and enabling their development for productive careers are not the only goals of public education (Gutmann, 1987; Noddings, 2013). We also need to consider how young people develop the ability to work together with those who may have different backgrounds and views than they do, in the interest of a common good. There are both present and future dimensions of developing civic reasoning and discourse: providing opportunities for children and adolescents to engage *right now* in the important discussions, debates, and actions surrounding current community, national, and global issues, as well as preparing them for *future* democratic decision-making and engagement (Lee et al., 2021, p. 2).

An important part of preparing students for current challenges is providing them with a strong foundation in the disciplines traditionally emphasized in school. Scholars and educators have increasingly emphasized how engaging multilingual learners in the practices at the heart of the disciplines is essential both for their academic preparation and their opportunities for language development, whether it be in mathematics and the sciences (National Academies, 2018a), history and social studies (Bunch & Martin, 2021), or English language arts (Brooks, 2020). As will be clear in the examples throughout this book, we agree that grounding curriculum for multilingual learners in high-quality disciplinary instruction is key for their preparation for higher education and careers, their language and literacy development, and their contributions to communities and society.

But Westheimer (2024) poignantly challenges us to consider what might distinguish classroom teaching and learning in a democratic society compared with a totalitarian regime. Walking into classrooms in both contexts, one would probably see young people engaging in rigorous lessons in mathematics and science, reading and writing, and history. But what, ideally, would be *different* in schools in countries that were preparing students for a democracy? Westheimer (2024) proposes some important questions:

> Do students in democratic countries learn how to participate in public decision making (the kind of participation that is required for democracy to function properly)? Are they taught to see themselves as individual actors who work in concert with others to create a better society? Are they taught the skills they need to think for themselves and to govern collectively? (pp. 11–12)

Unfortunately, classroom environments that foster the rich learning necessary for development of the 21st-century competencies described above have been scarce throughout the history of U.S. public education, particularly for students from racialized, immigrant, and low-income backgrounds (Noguera et al., 2017). Schools' provisions of opportunities for students to develop active citizenship have also been inequitably distributed. Westheimer (2024) points out that, where classroom-based initiatives do exist that "sharpen students' thinking about issues of public debate and concern," they are disproportionately available to already high-achieving students, often from economically privileged backgrounds (p. 14). The result has been called a "civic opportunity gap" leading to disparate opportunities for practicing democratic engagement in schools (p. 14). In fact, data show that, while students overall have shown low levels of civic knowledge over the past 2 decades, gaps based on race, ethnicity, and income have become even more alarming (Lee et al., 2021, p. 3).

An inequitable curriculum, of course, exacerbates societal inequities, with more affluent students having opportunities to further develop "problem-solving" competencies often associated with "managerial classes" while others are given "rule-following tasks that mirror much of factory and other working class work" (Mehta, 2014, quoted in Noguera et al., 2017, pp. 83–84). This arrangement replicates long-standing power differentials, maintaining the status quo of who has access to higher-level jobs (Anyon, 1980; Bowles & Gintis, 1976). It also denies those presumed to be "managers" opportunities to develop multifaceted perspectives and civic responsibility, while withholding opportunities for future "workers" to engage in the kind of intellectual and literacy practices that will lead to substantial and enduring participation in the full range of opportunities available in 21st-century life.

Evidence suggests that shifting school practices toward those that support deep learning can benefit all students. For example, Noguera et al. (2017) report that schools adopting practices to promote deeper learning (including inquiry-based learning and groupwork; performance-based assessments; curricula relevant to the world beyond school; and supports for reflection, collaboration, and professional development for teachers) had better outcomes across a wide range of indicators (academic performance, attendance, student behavior, dropout rates, graduation rates, college attendance, and perseverance) for low-income and minority students than schools serving similar student populations that did not implement these practices (Noguera et al., 2017).

Furthermore, when the lens on civic knowledge and participation is widened to include participatory movements, social action, and engagement in civic discourse on social media (as opposed to only more traditional measures such as knowledge of government institutions, political parties, and voting, which of course are important too), it becomes clear that students of color and those from immigrant backgrounds, including multilingual learners, are eager to engage vigorously in the issues of the day (Mirra & Garcia, 2017).

QUALITY LEARNING IN THE CLASSROOM

The changes needed to amplify the curriculum on a large scale will not happen automatically or easily. Much attention has been placed, legitimately, on the obstacles that hinder the implementation of the kind of quality instruction that will be needed to radically improve the education of multilingual learners. Some of the variables, such as state standards and testing requirements, district policies and funding, and school administrative decisions, are outside of the individual classroom teacher's control and must be undertaken at the school, district, or even state or national level (Bryk, 2015; O'Day & Smith, 2016; Umansky et al., 2020). However, if schools are going to have any chance of moving toward more intellectually substantive and socially relevant practices for all students, it will be teachers who ultimately make it happen. This book, therefore, is about what teachers *can* do, directly within their sphere of influence and with the support of others, as they envision, plan, and enact quality instruction for multilingual learners and for all of their students.

Our model of promoting quality learning for multilingual learners shares features with—and adds to—those of others calling for opportunities for deep learning for all students. As Lampert (2017) argues, if students are going to be expected to "learn deeply" (master core content, collaborate with others, communicate well, and develop "academic mindsets"), then what teachers are asking them to do in classrooms must align with these goals. Unfortunately, students in many American classrooms are still expected to learn predominantly by listening to the teacher and reading textbooks, or, increasingly in some settings, completing individualized assignments, whether online or via paper and pencil, none of which engages them in discourse or dialogue with others. In contrast, "deeper learning" requires "deeper teaching" (Lampert, 2017, p. 149; Walqui, 2024).

Such teaching, which may be quite different from the classrooms that teachers themselves experienced as students and which they may unwittingly replicate (Lortie, 1975), must center on goals that are more "intellectually and socially ambitious" (Lampert, 2017, p. 150). These kinds of learning activities and talk are often quite different from what most students are used to doing in school, but they are consistent with theory and research about how best to support student learning (Bransford et al., 1999; Mercer et al., 2020; Nasir et al., 2020; National Academies, 2018b).

Meanwhile, as schools and teachers contemplate the kinds of citizens they are helping their students become, Westheimer (2024, pp. 80, 99) offers a wide range of ways teachers can promote this vision:

- drawing on their own and their students' interests, passion, and knowledge to focus on students' own questions;
- encouraging students to evaluate core subject matter in substantive ways (rather than as "facts" that they are asked to regurgitate);
- creating contexts in which students can analyze and discuss various viewpoints, including those that are controversial;
- grounding instruction in local contexts; and
- encouraging participation in community projects that encourage personal responsibility, engaged participation, and critical analysis.

Our conception of quality learning, introduced in Chapters 2 and 3, shares many of the same goals as those described above. With a particular focus on multilingual learners, we offer a vision—and a map—for how teachers can design curriculum that provides opportunities for students to engage with each other and the teacher in learning through participation in conceptual, analytic, and language practices in disciplines across the curriculum (Valdés, Kibler, & Walqui, 2014). The tenets and lesson architecture that we present are also conducive to the kind of instruction that has been recommended for promoting the civic reasoning and discourse necessary for the development of young people for democratic participation (Lee et al., 2021, pp. 4–6). These include learning activities that allow students to

- weigh multiple points of view;
- examine the origins of their own beliefs and ideologies;
- engage in opportunities for discussion and engagement;
- voice their diverse perspectives;
- draw on their interests and experiences;
- gather, analyze, and evaluate the reliability of information from a wide range of sources; and
- use disciplinary knowledge and insights to explore the complexity of social phenomena.

The learning designs that we feature in this book contrast sharply with traditional classroom instruction where the teacher does most of the talking; students are expected to listen quietly, read silently, and complete individual writing assignments; and teachers ask the questions and students answer them. They also contrast with many forms of "individualized" computer-based modules, and with classroom instruction in which multilingual learners, even if they are asked to "participate," are expected to reply with one-word answers or use sentence frames that constrict their ideas into conventional "academic language" (Bunch, 2014; Grapin & Llosa, 2024; Wang et al., 2021).

Multilingual learners need opportunities to develop their own voices and to be adept at listening to the voices of others. By amplifying the curriculum, teachers can create learning spaces whereby students, including multilingual learners, have opportunities to *dialogue* with each other, with their teacher, and with the ideas, problems, and texts at the center of instruction (Kibler et al., 2021; Mercer et al., 2020). The learning activities and lessons that we describe in this book include all the features of dialogic activity described by Kibler et al. (2021, p. 5). They are intellectually purposeful, adaptive to specific students and classroom situations, respectful of students and the communities from which they come, and responsive to larger societal contexts. Furthermore, there is evidence that this kind of dialogic learning provides multiple advantages for individual students: engaging them, helping them learn the subject area being taught, and advancing their cognitive development more generally (Resnick et al., 2015). Importantly for multilingual learners, interactive and collaborative engagement also presents essential opportunities for language development (Seedhouse & Walsh, 2010; van Lier, 2004).

But amplifying the curriculum is not only aimed at providing opportunities for interaction that benefit individual students' academic progression and language development. The lessons and learning activities featured in this book also provide opportunities to engage in the kinds of *critical* dialogue so necessary to address injustices in our communities and world today. The framework and activities we present can serve as ideal sites for what Kibler et al. (2021) describe as *critical dialogic education*: that is, classrooms designed to foster equitable participation, attend to the needs of vulnerable and marginalized populations more explicitly, and engage students in conversations and actions aimed at disrupting power dynamics, including those based on race, class, and gender (see also Aragón et al., 2024; Brooks, 2020).

In sum, the model of amplifying the curriculum that we present in this book is informed by theories of how quality learning takes place, how language is implicated in that learning (Bruner, 1996; Vygotsky, 1962, 1978), and the role of critical dialogue in education for democracy and justice. Therefore, the book does not present a list of discrete teaching strategies or activities to be replicated *ad hoc* in classrooms, but rather a principled *framework* for designing learning opportunities for multilingual learners and other students, with many examples of activities that could reside within that framework depending on a multitude of contextual variables. Collectively, the activities are designed to promote students' consideration of powerful ideas that are interconnected and discussed critically through interactions that engage everybody in sustained intellectual conversations and academic work.

WHO ARE MULTILINGUAL LEARNERS?

As mentioned at the outset, we have joined many researchers and some schools and districts in using the term *multilingual learners* to refer to students who come to school from homes where languages other than English are predominantly spoken. In schools, many of these students are officially classified as English Learners, a term that is fraught with multiple meanings, underlying complexities, and dilemmas relevant to prospects for the education of this population (Kanno et al., 2024; REL West, n.d.). The over 5 million students in U.S. schools officially designated by their schools as English Learners come from different geographic, demographic, linguistic, educational, and socioeconomic backgrounds (Office of English Language Acquisition, 2023; REL West, n.d.). And the range of their developmental stages of English is considerable. In fact, the National Academies of Sciences, Engineering, and Medicine (2017) concluded that "a defining characteristic" of English Learners is the diversity among them (p. S-1).

Demographic Diversity

Multilingual learners include young people who arrived in the United States from countries around the globe, some very recently (including in the middle of the school year) and some years ago. Some arrived with their families, others with distant relatives, and still others by themselves, as "unaccompanied minors." Contrary to common assumptions, the majority of students classified as English Learners were born in the United States and are, therefore, U.S. citizens. Others are protected by the U.S. government as refugees, some hold work or family visas, and others are without legal papers. The U.S. Supreme Court ruled over 3 decades ago that all children and youth, regardless of immigration status, have a right to public education while living in the United States (*Plyler v. Doe*, 1982). Yet many immigrant families face continuing—and recently increasing—fear and uncertainty regarding their status and safety.

Multilingual learners also vary with regard to their prior education. Some have had high-quality previous schooling, but many have attended underresourced schools (either in the United States or other countries), and some have had interrupted or even no previous formal education due to war, economic crises, frequent migration, or other circumstances barring them from access to school. They also vary considerably in terms of their parents' socioeconomic status, educational levels, and literacy backgrounds (REL West, n.d.). Finally, it is not uncommon for multilingual learners and their families to travel back and forth between the United States and other countries, pursuing economic opportunities or attending to family needs, over the course of one or more academic years.

Nationally, Spanish is spoken at home by a large majority of students classified as English Learners (75%), while hundreds of other languages are spoken by smaller numbers of students (National Center for Education Statistics [NCES], 2024). Perhaps surprising to many teachers, most students classified as English Learners were born in the United States. Among English Learners born outside of the United States, over 40% were born in Mexico, with smaller but significant percentages born in China, Korea, the Philippines, Haiti, other Latin American countries, Europe, and Africa (National Academies, 2017).

English Language Proficiency

Multilingual learners also have widely different proficiencies in English. Among those classified as English Learners, some have newly arrived in the United States, speaking virtually no English, and others appear to speak fluent English but are still designated as English Learners due to reading and writing or other academic challenges (Brooks, 2020). Even after being reclassified as "fluent English proficient," multilingual learners' English may differ slightly from that of monolingual English speakers, as is almost always the case, even with highly proficient bilinguals (Valdés et al., 2011). Effective instruction will look different for multilingual learners at different places along the continuum of their English language development (Valdés et al., 2005), but the principles, approaches to developing curriculum, and structure of lesson design advocated in this book apply to all.

As we will discuss shortly, it is important for teachers to understand that the bureaucratic categories, English language proficiency "levels" that students are assigned by schools, and criteria for exiting the English Learner designation are the result of imperfect tests, classification procedures, and accountability mandates that may not be valid indications of what students can actually do in the classroom with appropriate curriculum and scaffolding (Poza & Brooks, 2024). Beyond the idealized progressions through different language proficiency "levels," individuals are undergoing the "extraordinarily complex" process of developing an additional language (Valdés et al., 2011). In fact, some scholars have argued that language instruction and assessment should focus on how learners become productive "users" of more than one language, rather than solely on how they develop particular internal linguistic systems (Cook, 2007; Kibler & Valdés, 2016). As Valdés et al. (2011) have put it, the goal of learning a second language from this perspective "is not to become like native speakers of the language but to use the language to function competently in a variety of contexts for a range of purposes" (p. 23).

Although many debates continue among scholars about the nature of developing additional languages and the best conditions to support that development, Valdés, Poza, and Brooks (2014) point out important areas of agreement:

- Language acquisition is not linear.
- It is highly variable and individual.
- The highest attainment for most does not result in perfectly balanced bilingualism.
- Formalized language instruction does not necessarily lead to language development.
- Developing additional languages is "a slow and time-consuming process." (Valdés et al., 2011, p. 17; see also VanPatten, 2003)

These understandings, as Valdés et al. (2011) point out, have profound implications. English Learners will need to use English for school learning before they have fully acquired the linguistic system, and their teachers must learn to support students' content area learning during this process.

The Limits of Assessment and Classification

It is thus important for teachers to understand that the information they receive from schools and districts, both about students' English Learner classification in general and about their language proficiency "levels" in particular, are at best approximations—and at worst distortions—of what students are capable of doing with their developing English language resources. Standardized tests continue to dominate efforts to classify language learners, place them in courses, and measure how teachers and schools are doing in educating them (Valdés, Poza, & Brooks, 2014; Poza & Brooks, 2024). Yet problems have persisted in assessing both the content learning and language development of multilingual learners, leading experts on testing to question the validity of such assessments (Cumming, 2008; Valdés et al., 2011; Rolstad & MacSwan, 2024).

The fact that "proficiency levels" that schools assign to students whom they classify as English Learners may distort what students can actually do leads to a larger point about the English Learner classification itself. It, too, is a construct based largely on testing, not only on students' English language proficiency but often also on students' ability to demonstrate their knowledge of subject matter on standardized tests given (in most states) in English. And the classification has the power to assign services to those designated as English Learners that may in some cases be helpful but that also may lead to "exclusionary tracking" whereby students' assignment to one or multiple English language development classes removes their opportunity to enroll in core content classes (Umansky et al., in press).

Challenges and Opportunities for Multilingual Learners

Moving beyond the "basics" to include opportunities for dialogue, problem solving, and intellectual and civic engagement presents language and literacy challenges for all students, but especially for those called upon to engage in these new practices in a language they are in the process of developing (Bunch et al., 2014; Duhaylongsod et al., 2015; Fillmore & Fillmore, 2012; Lee et al., 2013; Moschkovich, 2012). But the heightened language and literacy *demands* represent simultaneous *opportunities* for language and literacy development. These opportunities suggest that the primary challenge for educators is not to find ways to eliminate the demands but rather to support multilingual learners in meeting them (Bunch et al., 2012).

The good news for teachers is that multilingual learners bring a wealth of resources (Ruiz, 1984) that can allow them both to flourish in the kinds of classrooms called for by the new standards and to participate actively in complex and dynamic 21st-century communities—when these resources are acknowledged and leveraged. As Gándara (2017) has argued, when the skills they bring to the classroom are viewed as resources and opportunities for development rather than deficits to overcome, students from immigrant families are especially well-suited to thrive in the kinds of instructional environments advocated for in this book. In addition to the advantages of bilingualism mentioned earlier, multilingual learners often bring nuanced perspectives on history and politics by virtue of their multicultural and multinational backgrounds; belong to cultures that value collaboration; share the motivation, resilience, and self-reliance often exhibited by immigrant families; and have experience with intercultural communication and teamwork (Gándara, 2017, p. 133).

The families of multilingual learners also have what Yosso (2005) calls "community cultural wealth." Yosso describes the various kinds of "capital" (Bourdieu, 1973), often unrecognized and untapped by schools, that members of communities of color have developed in response to marginalization in the United States:

- *Aspirational capital* to maintain hope for the future even in the face of daunting obstacles;

- *Familial capital* that leverages community knowledge and traditions for emotional support and for educational and professional advancement;
- *Social capital* that helps leverage community networks;
- *Navigational capital* to negotiate institutions that are often not designed with their needs in mind; and
- *Resistant capital* used for challenging inequitable structures in order to transform them. (pp. 78–81)

All of these can serve as resources for supporting multilingual learners in navigating the competencies required in the 21st century and the kinds of learning opportunities described in this book.

Multilingual learners also bring communicative resources that, albeit different from those of their teachers and classmates from dominant groups, can be used to engage effectively in learning activities and demonstrate their understandings when teachers recognize them as resources (Valdés et al., 2005). Such resources include the following:

- Students' home languages (García & Kleyn, 2016)
- Their still-imperfect but developing English (Valdés et al., 2011)
- Nondominant varieties of English such as Chicano and African American English (Fought, 2003; Green, 2004)
- "Informal" English commonly used when discussing ideas and working on problems even by scholars at the highest levels of academia (Bunch, 2014; MacSwan & Rolstad, 2003)
- Paralinguistic semiotic resources (gestures, graphical representations, other visual designs) recognized in many disciplines as being associated with high-level conceptual engagement (Lang, 2022; van Lier & Walqui, 2012)

Teachers can build on these resources as students expand their repertoires to also include more "standard" forms of expression in English used for different audiences and purposes (Bunch, 2014; Valdés et al., 2005).

Numerous possibilities arise, therefore, when we shift the lens away from perceived deficits in multilingual learners' abilities and instead ask questions such as those proposed by Orellana and Gutierrez (2006) a number of years ago: "'What *do* our students know?' 'What *can* they do?' 'What are their skills, contributions, or experiences that can be useful for them or for the world?'" (p. 120, emphasis in original; see also Gutierrez & Rogoff, 2003). As we will discuss throughout the book and especially in Chapter 11, we have found that many teachers find that students classified as English Learners, when given the opportunity and support to do so, can engage productively with complex and challenging texts and ideas in ways that teachers previously would not have thought possible.

Our intention is not to minimize the significant obstacles, linguistic and otherwise, that multilingual learners may face in achieving academic success. Depending on the learners and the context, these may include the effects of poverty, racism, interrupted schooling, frequent migration, limited formal educational attainment among their parents, and unsettled immigration status (Gándara, 2017; National Academies, 2017). But the experiences of multilingual learners and their families navigating these very obstacles are also the source of significant resources that—when understood and acted upon—can be leveraged for precisely the kind of learning needed for the 21st century.

Why Multilingual Learners Matter—for Everyone

The number of students classified as English Learners continues to grow, with over 10% of all students in U.S. schools now classified as English Learners (NCES, 2024). The numbers are much larger in some states: Over 20% of all students in Texas are classified as English Learners, and 19% in California and New Mexico. But students classified as English Learners now represent a significant proportion of the student population throughout the country: over 10% of the student population in 13 states, and between 6% and 10% in an additional 18 states (NCES, 2024). And of course the broader population of multilingual learners, including those formerly classified as English Learners, is much larger.

In California, over half of all K–12 students have at least one foreign-born parent (Sugerman & Geary, 2018), and the largest states will continue to have a disproportionate number and concentration of immigrants and children of immigrants. But the United States as a whole has also experienced an "unprecedented geographic diversification" of immigrants and their families (Callahan & Muller, 2013, p. 15). The Hispanic population in 15 states more than doubled between 2000 and 2012, including Tennessee, Alabama, Kentucky, and North and South Dakota (National Academies, 2017). And while it is true that immigrant students and English Learners are disproportionally enrolled in urban schools, immigrants are increasingly also settling in rural areas, small towns, and suburbs previously unaccustomed to this kind of diversity (Callahan & Muller, 2013; Irwin et al., 2022; NCES, 2024).

How students from immigrant and English-learning backgrounds fare in the coming years will determine to a large extent how the larger U.S. society fares. Immigrants and their children are projected to represent an additional 18 million working-age people nationwide by 2035, easing the expected decline in the U.S. workforce due to retiring Baby Boomers (Moslimani & Passel, 2024). In fact, in light of an aging workforce, children of immigrants are projected to become the primary source of growth among all U.S. workers (Singer & Myers, 2016).

With an enhanced commitment to providing high-quality education for multilingual learners, models for curriculum and instruction to realize this commitment, and support for teachers in implementing them, we see the current demographic trends as hopeful—not alarming—for the future of the United States. Given what we have outlined above about the assets that multilingual learners and immigrant families bring to the table, it becomes obvious that they are not burdens to bear, but rather bearers of remarkable, often untapped, societal resources. In fact, who better than multilingual learners and others from immigrant families to help lead the way in preparing *all* students for 21st-century challenges?

By virtue of their own experiences, such students are already developing real-life expertise as they encounter situations where, returning to the 21st-century competencies shared earlier from Mehta and Fine (2017), they are called upon to "navigate among plural identities, . . . make informed decisions in the face of uncertainty, . . . engage in productive dialogue across ideological divides, . . . decide among imperfect options, . . . [and] tackle open-ended problems in critical, creative, and collaborative ways" (p. 11). In short, multilingual learners bring precisely the kinds of diverse life perspectives and experiences needed for an intellectually, culturally, and socially vibrant 21st-century milieu, as well as for solving the myriad of challenges that we are currently facing nationally and globally. We offer this book as one possible roadmap for the role that teachers and other educators can play to help realize this potential and advocate for these exceptional young learners.

NOTE

1. The Elementary and Secondary Education Act defines *English Learners* as those students speaking languages other than English "whose difficulties in speaking, reading, writing, or understanding the English language may be sufficient to deny the individual (i) the ability to meet the challenging State academic standards; (ii) the ability to successfully achieve in classrooms where the language of instruction is English; or (iii) the opportunity to participate fully in society" (U.S. Department of Education, 2016, p. 43).

REFERENCES

Anyon, J. (1980). Social class and the hidden curriculum of work. *Journal of Education*, *162*(1), 67–92.

Aragón, M. J., Corella, M., & Lang, N. W. (2024). "They're like slash": Multimodality and embodied agency in students' critical engagements with texts. *Reading Research Quarterly*.

Bourdieu, P. (1973). *Cultural reproduction and social reproduction in knowledge, education, and cultural change*. Tavistock.

Bowles, S., & Gintis, H. (1976). *Schooling in capitalist America: Educational reform and the contradictions of economic life*. Basic Books.

Bransford, J., Brown, A., & Cocking, R. (Eds.). (1999). *How people learn: Brain, mind, experience, and school*. National Academies Press.

Brooks, M. D. (2020). *Transforming literacy education for long-term English Learners: Recognizing brilliance in the undervalued*. Routledge.

Bruner, J. (1996). *The culture of education*. Harvard University Press.

Bryk, A. S. (2015). Accelerating how we learn to improve. *Educational Researcher, 44*(9), 467–477.

Bunch, G. C. (2014). The language of ideas and the language of display: Reconceptualizing "academic language" in linguistically diverse classrooms. *International Multilingual Multicultural Research Journal, 8*(1), 70–86.

Bunch, G. C., Kibler, A., & Pimentel, S. (2012, January). Realizing opportunities for English Learners in the Common Core English Language Arts and Disciplinary Literacy Standards. Paper presented at the Understanding Language Conference, Stanford, CA. https://ell.stanford.edu/papers/practice

Bunch, G. C., & Martin, D. (2021). From "academic language" to the "language of ideas": A disciplinary perspective on using language in K–12 settings. *Language and Education, 35*(6), 539–556. https://doi.org/10.1080/09500782.2020.1842443

Bunch, G. C., Walqui, A., & Pearson, D. P. (2014). Complex text and new common standards in the United States: Pedagogical implications for English Learners. *TESOL Quarterly, 48*(3), 533–559. https://doi.org/10.1002/tesq.175

Callahan, R. M., & Gándara, P. C. (Eds.). (2014). *The bilingual advantage: Language, literacy, and the US labor market* (pp. 286–297). Multilingual Matters.

Callahan, R. M., & Muller, C. (2013). *Coming of political age: American schools and the civic development of immigrant youth*. Russell Sage Foundation.

Chow, B. (2017). Foreword. In R. Heller, R. E. Wolfe, & A. Steinberg (Eds.), *Rethinking readiness: Deeper learning for college, work, and life* (pp. v–vii). Harvard Education Press.

Conley, D. T. (2017). Toward systems of assessment for deeper learning. In R. Heller, R. E. Wolfe, & A. Steinberg (Eds.), *Rethinking readiness: Deeper learning for college, work, and life* (pp. 195–219). Harvard Education Press.

Cook, V. (2007). The goals of ELT: Reproducing native speakers or promoting multi-competence among second-language users? In J. Cummins & C. Davison (Eds.), *International handbook of English language teaching, Part I* (pp. 237–248). Springer.

Cumming, A. (2008). Assessing oral and literate abilities. In E. Shohamy & N. Hornberger (Eds.), *Encyclopedia of language and education: Language testing and assessment*. Springer.

Duhaylongsod, L., Snow, C. E., Selman, R. L., & Donovan, M. S. (2015). Toward disciplinary literacy: Dilemmas and challenges in designing history curriculum to support middle school students. *Harvard Educational Review, 85*(4), 584–608.

Fillmore, L. W., & Fillmore, C. (2012, January). *What does text complexity mean for English learners and language minority students?* [Paper presentation]. Understanding Language Conference, Stanford, CA. http://ell.stanford.edu/papers/language

Fought, C. (2003). *Chicano English in context* (pp. 1–10). Palgrave Macmillan.

Gamoran, A. (2017). *Engaging English Learners with rigorous academic content: Insights from research on tracking.* William T. Grant Foundation.

Gándara, P. (2017). Deeper learning for English language learners. In R. Heller, R. E. Wolfe, & A. Steinberg (Eds.). *Rethinking readiness: Deeper learning for college, work, and life* (pp. 123–144). Harvard Education Press.

García, O., & Kleifgen, J. A. (2018). *Educating emergent bilinguals: Policies, programs, and practices for English language learners* (2nd ed.). Teachers College Press.

García, O., & Kleyn, T. (2016). *Translanguaging with multilingual students: Learning from classroom moments.* Routledge.

Grapin, S. E., & Llosa, L. (2024). Thorny issues with academic language: A perspective from scientific practice. *Linguistics and Education 83*, 101334. https://doi.org/10.1016/j.linged.2024.101334

Green, L. (2004). African American English. In E. Finegan & J. R. Rickford (Eds.), *Language in the USA: Themes for the twenty-first century* (pp. 76–91). Cambridge University Press.

Gutiérrez, K. D., & Rogoff, B. (2003). Cultural ways of learning: Individual traits or repertoires of practice. *Educational Researcher, 32*(5), 19–25.

Gutmann, A. (1987). *Democratic education.* Princeton University Press.

Heller, R., Wolfe, R. E., & Steinberg, A. (2017). Introduction. In R. Heller, R. E. Wolfe, & A. Steinberg (Eds.), *Rethinking readiness: Deeper learning for college, work, and life* (pp. 1–8). Harvard Education Press.

Irwin, V., De La Rosa, J., Wang, K., Hein, S., Zhang, J., Burr, R., Roberts, A., Barmer, A., Bullock Mann, F., Dilig, R., & Parker, S. (2022). *Report on the condition of education 2022* (NCES 2022–144). U.S. Department of Education. National Center for Education Statistics. https://nces.ed.gov/pubsearch/pubsinfo.asp?pubid=2022144

Kanno, Y. (2021). *English Learners' access to postsecondary education: Neither college nor career ready.* Multilingual Matters.

Kanno, Y., Rios-Aguilar, C., & Bunch, G. C. (2024). English learners? Emergent bilinguals? Multilingual learners?: Goals, contexts, and consequences in labeling students. *TESOL Journal, 15*(3), e797. https://onlinelibrary.wiley.com/doi/10.1002/tesj.797

Kibler, A. K., & Valdés, G. (2016). Conceptualizing language learners: Socioinstitutional mechanisms and their consequences. *The Modern Language Journal 100*, 96–116.

Kibler, A. K., Valdés, G., & Walqui, A. (2021). *Reconceptualizing the role of critical dialogue in American classrooms: Promoting equity through dialogic education.* Routledge.

Ladson-Billings, G. (2006). From the achievement gap to the education debt: Understanding achievement in U.S. schools. *Educational Researcher, 35*(7), 3–12.

Lampert, M. (2017). Ambitious teaching: A deep dive. In R. Heller, R. E. Wolfe, & A. Steinberg (Eds.), *Rethinking readiness: Deeper learning for college, work, and life* (pp. 147–173). Harvard Education Press.

Lang, N. W. (2022). Pooling semiotic resources among recently arrived immigrant students in a high school biology class. In M. A. Christison, J. Crandall, & D. Christian (Eds.) *Research on integrating language and content in diverse contexts* (pp. 92–109). Routledge.

Lau v. Nichols, 414 U.S. 563 (1974).

Lee, C. D., Melzoff, A. N., & Kuhl, P. K. (2020). The braid of human learning and development: Neuro-psychological processes and participation in cultural practices. In N. Suad Nasir, C. D. Lee, R. Pea, & M. M. de Royston, *Handbook of the cultural foundations of learning*. Routledge.

Lee, C. D., White, G., & Dong, D. (Eds.). (2021). *Educating for civic reasoning and discourse*. National Academy of Education.

Lee, O., Quinn, H., & Valdés, G. (2013). Science and language for English language learners in relation to Next Generation Science Standards and with implications for Common Core State Standards for English language arts and mathematics. *Educational Researcher, 42*, 234–249.

Lortie, D. C. (1975). *Schoolteacher: A sociological study*. University of Chicago Press.

MacSwan, J., & Rolstad, K. (2003). Linguistic diversity, schooling, and social class: Rethinking our conception of language proficiency in language minority education. In C. B. Paulston & G. R. Tucker (Eds.), *Sociolinguistics: The essential readings* (pp. 329–340). Blackwell.

Mehta, J. (2014, June 20). Deeper learning has a race problem. *Education Week*. https://www.edweek.org/leadership/opinion-deeper-learning-has-a-race-problem/2014/06

Mehta, J., & Fine, S. (2017). How we got here: The imperative for deeper learning. In R. Heller, R. E. Wolfe, & A. Steinberg (Eds.), *Rethinking readiness: Deeper learning for college, work, and life* (pp. 11–35). Harvard Education Press.

Mercer, N., Wegerif, R., & Major, L. (Eds.). (2020). *The Routledge international handbook of research on dialogic education*. Routledge.

Mirra, N., & Garcia, A. (2017). Civic participation reimagined: Youth interrogation and innovation in the multimodal public sphere. *Review of Research in Education, 41*, 136–158.

Moschkovich, J. (2012, January). *Mathematics, the Common Core, and language: Recommendations for mathematics instruction for ELs aligned with the Common Core*. [Paper presentation]. Understanding Language Conference, Stanford, CA. http://ell.stanford.edu/papers/practice

Moslimani, M., & Passel, J. S. (2024, September 27). *What the data says about immigrants and the U.S.* Pew Research Center. https://www.pewresearch.org/short-reads/2024/09/27/key-findings-about-us-immigrants/

Nasir, N. S., de Royston, M. M., Barron, B., Bell, P., Pea, R., Stevens, R., & Goldman, S. (2020). Learning pathways: How learning is culturally organized. In

N. Suad Nasir, C. D. Lee, R. Pea, & M. M. de Royston, *Handbook of the cultural foundations of learning* (pp. 195–211). Routledge.

National Academies of Sciences, Engineering, and Medicine. (2017). *Promoting the educational success of children and youth learning English: Promising futures.* National Academies Press. doi:10.17226/24677

National Academies of Sciences, Engineering, and Medicine. (2018a). *English Learners in STEM subjects: Transforming classrooms, schools, and lives.* The National Academies Press. https://doi.org/10.17226/25182

National Academies of Sciences, Engineering, and Medicine. (2018b). *How people learn II: Learners, contexts, and cultures.* The National Academies Press. doi:10.17226/24783

National Center for Education Statistics [NCES]. (2024). English Learners in public schools. *Condition of Education.* U.S. Department of Education, Institute of Education Sciences. https://nces.ed.gov/programs/coe/indicator/cgf

Noddings, N. (2013). *Education and democracy in the 21st century.* Teachers College Press.

Noguera, P., Darling-Hammond, L., & Friedlaender, D. (2017). Equal opportunity for deeper learning. In R. Heller, R. E. Wolfe, & A. Steinberg (Eds.), *Rethinking readiness: Deeper learning for college, work, and life* (pp. 81–104). Harvard Education Press.

Oakes, J. (1985). *Keeping track: How schools structure inequality.* Yale University Press.

O'Day, J. A., & Smith, M. S. (2016). Quality and equality in American education: Systemic problems, systemic solutions. In I. Kirsch and H. Braun (Eds.), *The dynamics of opportunity in America: Evidence and perspectives* (pp. 297–358). Springer Open and Educational Testing Service. https://link.springer.com/chapter/10.1007/978-3-319-25991-8_9

Office of English Language Acquisition. (2020). *Benefits of multilingualism.* U.S. Department of Education. https://ncela.ed.gov/resources/infographic-benefits-of-multilingualism-english-august-2020

Office of English Language Acquisition. (2023). *The biennial report to Congress on the implementation of the Title III state formula grant program: School Years 2018–2020.* U.S. Department of Education.

Orellana, M. F. (2009). *Translating childhoods: Immigrant youth, language and culture.* Rutgers University Press.

Orellana, M. F., & Gutierrez, K. D. (2006). What's the problem? Constructing *different* genres for the study of English Learners. *Research in the Teaching of English*, *41*(1), 118–123.

Pellegrino, J. W., & Hilton, M. (2012). *Education for life and work: Developing transferable knowledge and skills in the 21st Century.* National Academies Press.

Poza, L. E., & Brooks, M. D. (2024). "A special case of bias": Racialized bilinguals, testing, and the allocation of opportunity. In A. K. Kibler, A. Walqui, G. C. Bunch, & C. Faltis (Eds.), *Equity in multilingual schools and communities: Celebrating the contributions of Guadalupe Valdés* (pp. 206–218). Multilingual Matters.

Plyler v. Doe, 457 U.S. 202 (1982).

REL West [Regional Educational Laboratory West], Institute of Education Sciences. (n.d.). *An asset-based approach to multilingual learner terminology*. U.S. Department of Education. https://ies.ed.gov/ncee/rel/regions/west/pdf/2.1.2.2.1_MultilingualLearners_Infographic01_Approved_508c.pdf

Resnick, L. B., Asterhan, C. S. C., & Clark, S. N. (2015). Introduction: Talk, learning, and teaching. In L. B. Resnick, C. S. C. Asterhan, & S. N. Clarke (Eds.), *Socializing intelligence through academic talk and dialogue* (pp. 1–12). American Educational Research Association.

Rolstad, K., & MacSwan, J. (2024). Bilingual language assessment: A persistent case of bias. In A. K. Kibler, A. Walqui, G. C. Bunch, & C. Faltis (Eds.), *Equity in multilingual schools and communities: Celebrating the contributions of Guadalupe Valdés* (pp. 206–218). Multilingual Matters.

Ruiz, R. (1984). Orientations in language planning. *NABE Journal, 8*(2), 15–34.

Seedhouse, P., & Walsh, S. (2010). Learning a second language through classroom interaction. In P. Seedhouse, S. Walsh, & C. Jenks (Eds.), *Conceptualizing "learning" in applied linguistics* (pp. 127–146). Palgrave Macmillan.

Singer, A., & Myers, D. (2016, September). *Labor force growth increasingly depends on immigrants and their children*. Urban Institute. https://www.urban.org/urban-wire/labor-force-growth-increasingly-depends-immigrants-and-their-children

Sugerman, J., & Geary, C. (2018, August). *English Learners in California: Demographics, outcomes, and state accountability policies*. Migration Policy Institute. https://www.migrationpolicy.org/research/english-learners-demographics-outcomes-state-accountability-policies

Tyack, D., & Cuban, L. (1995). *Tinkering toward utopia: A century of public school reform*. Harvard University Press.

Umansky, I. M., Hopkins, M., & Dabach, D. B. (2020). Ideals and realities: An examination of the factors shaping newcomer programming in six U.S. school districts. *Leadership and Policy in Schools, 19*(1), 36–59.

Umansky, I. M., Shin, N., Thompson, K. D., Avelar, J., & Bovee, J. (in press). Beyond English instruction: A multistate analysis of *Lau's* unfulfilled promise of access to core content. *Bilingual Research Journal*.

U.S. Department of Education. (2016). *Non-regulatory guidance: English Learners and Title III of the Elementary and Secondary Education Act (ESEA), as amended by the Every Student Succeeds Act (ESSA)*. https://www2.ed.gov/policy/elsec/leg/essa/essatitleiiiguidenglishlearners92016.pdf

Valdés, G. (2003). *Expanding definitions of giftedness: The case of young interpreters from immigrant communities*. Lawrence Erlbaum.

Valdés, G., Bunch, G. C., Snow, C. E., & Lee, C. (2005). Enhancing the development of students' language(s). In L. Darling-Hammond, J. Bransford, P. LePage, K. Hammerness, & H. Duffy (Eds.), *Preparing teachers for a changing world: What teachers should learn and be able to do* (pp. 126–168). Jossey-Bass.

Valdés, G., Capitelli, S., & Alvarez, L. (2011). Realistic expectations: English language learners and the acquisition of "academic" English. In *Latino children learning English: Steps in the journey* (pp. 15–42). Teachers College Press.

Valdés, G., Kibler, A., & Walqui, A. (2014). *Changes in the expertise of ESL professionals: Knowledge and action in an era of new standards*. TESOL International

Association. https://www.tesol.org/media/vh1pnlsi/professional-paper-26-march-2014.pdf

Valdés, G., Poza, L., & Brooks, M. (2014). Educating students who do not speak the societal language: The social construction of language learner categories. *Profession*. https://profession.mla.hcommons.org/2014/10/09/educating-students-who-do-not-speak-the-societal-language/

van Lier, L. (2004). *The ecology and semiotics of language learning: A sociocultural perspective*. Kluwer Academic.

van Lier, L., & Walqui, A. (2012, January). Language and the Common Core State Standards [Paper presentation]. Understanding Language Conference, Stanford, CA. http://ell.stanford.edu/papers/language

VanPatten, B. (2003). Some givens about second language acquisition. In *From input to output: A teacher's guide to second language acquisition* (pp. 9–24). McGraw-Hill.

Vygotsky, L. (1962). *Thought and language*. MIT Press.

Vygotsky, L. (1978). *Mind in society*. Harvard University Press.

Walqui, A. (2024). *Equitable and quality education for English Learners and all other students: The role of oracy*. National Research and Development Center to Improve Education for English Learners. WestEd. https://www.elrdcenter.wested.org/_files/ugd/5784a1_b1e932fe560d42bb9b3773e239694c8d.pdf

Walqui, A., & van Lier, L. (2010). *Scaffolding the academic success of adolescent English language learners: A pedagogy of promise*. WestEd.

Wang, S., Lang, N., Bunch, G. C., Basch, S., McHugh, S. R., Huitzilopochtli, S., Calahan, M. (2021). Dismantling persistent deficit narratives about the language and literacy of culturally and linguistically minoritized children and youth: Counter-possibilities. *Frontiers in Education*, 6, 260. https://doi.org/10.3389/feduc.2021.641796

Westheimer, J. (2024). *What kind of citizen? Educating our children for the common good* (2nd edition). Teachers College Press.

Yosso, T. (2005). Whose culture has capital? A critical race theory discussion of community cultural wealth. *Race Ethnicity, and Education*, *8*, 69–91.

CHAPTER 2

What Is Quality Learning for Multilingual Learners?

Aída Walqui and George C. Bunch

How can teachers design and enact stimulating, demanding, well-supported lessons to transform what is currently offered to many multilingual learners, which too often consists of simplified, discrete, individual, and superficial work, as well as teacher-dominated patterns of instruction and unenticing materials? In this chapter, we provide classroom examples to anchor discussions of the significant changes in thinking that teachers and schools need to undertake to *amplify* the curriculum and instruction available to multilingual learners and to address the competencies required by the increasingly complex world discussed in Chapter 1. When these changes are enacted, they result in offering multilingual learners powerful learning opportunities that realize their full potential and develop the knowledge, dispositions, and skills they need to live productive and socially responsible lives. This chapter also presents the theoretical framework for designing quality learning opportunities that we will unpack in Chapter 3 and illustrate in the remaining chapters of the book. While the chapter—as well as the book as a whole—focuses on multilingual learners' opportunities to engage in substantive and generative subject-matter learning in English, the ideas presented here also apply to classes being taught in students' home languages, as is illustrated in Chapter 5, which focuses on Spanish.

QUALITY LEARNING FOR MULTILINGUAL LEARNERS

To realize multilingual learners' immense potential, we promote an ambitious, amplified, high-challenge, high-support pedagogy. This approach offers a way of bringing together congruent ideas from several overlapping orientations to illuminate a process through which students learn under optimal circumstances. More specifically, our pedagogical stance builds from the coherent weaving of several perspectives emanating from second language acquisition (Larsen-Freeman, 2018; Valdés et al., 2017), sociocultural theory (Kozulin et al., 2003; Derewianka & Jones, 2023; van Lier, 2001; Vygotsky, 1962, 1976, 1978), educational sociolinguistics (Gibbons, 2009; Hammond, 2014), the ecology of learning and the concept of affordances (Larsen-Freeman, 2013, 2014; van Lier, 2000, 2004), and general education theory and research (Lee, 2020; Shulman, 1996; Suad Nasir et al., 2020, among others).

Central to this process is the design and enactment of lessons that have students build on what they know and are interested in so that they can work at the edge of their ability (Bruner, 1996), *beyond* their level of comfort. Such lessons provide opportunities for students to participate in activities that offer them support and that eventually enable them to appropriate important intellectual tools they will be able to use independently in other relevant contexts in the future. This proposal also assumes that students who are learning via the medium of home or additional languages bring valuable resources to the educational encounter and that—if provided the right invitations and support—they will willingly engage and learn. It also assumes that the role of educators is *proleptic*, meaning that teachers anticipate in advance the realization of students' potential and treat students accordingly. To use Leont'ev's phrase, education helps learners "become who they are not yet" (as quoted in Bronfenbrenner, 1979). This stance contrasts sharply with orientations toward teaching and learning that assume that students classified as English Learners should not engage in difficult tasks until they are linguistically, developmentally, or academically "ready" to do so.

In this ambitious pedagogy, teachers are pivotal in several ways:

1. In ***selecting*** texts and themes that are relevant to students' lives and studies, and that help them construct deep understandings and generative skills;
2. In ***designing*** environments and opportunities for students to engage in activity that develops learners' autonomy, agency, and voice within democratic, participatory contexts;
3. In ***enacting*** these plans while at the same time observing how students take the invitations, interpreting evidence from their students as learning takes place;
4. In ***reflecting on*** what is working, what is no longer needed, and what assistance must be provided next to keep students growing in intended (and unexpected) ways; and
5. In ***creating*** equitable environments in their classes and school, environments that support students' backgrounds, value their contributions, and build on them to advance students' multilingualism, interculturalism, and participation in society.

We elaborate on four of these aspects in this chapter: *text choice, lesson design*, *enactment*, and *reflection*, including the process of observation and assessment in which teachers continuously engage to redesign and enact instruction to ensure learners meet the goals.

Multilingual learners, like all students, apprentice attitudes and abilities in classrooms through meaningful participation that provides opportunities to appropriate ideas and skills. Thus, making concepts, practices, and language their own will make it possible for students individually to recreate them in future opportunities and use them in powerful, responsive, and creative ways. Students' appropriations, their ownership and personal use of newly developed practices, and their future performances will manifest their growing *autonomy*—that is, their ability to stand on their own two feet while continuing to learn in school and beyond. The sense of feeling in control as they participate in novel applications of knowledge and practice builds students' *agency*. As students exercise their agency and growing autonomy, they develop unique, personal ways of engaging in the practices of the community with whom they are interacting and the right to be heard; that is, they grow their *voice*. Participation, engagement, a sense of belonging, gradual development of competencies, joy, the building of stamina and perseverance—all these feelings and actions characterize classes where quality learning is alive.

KEY TENETS

What, then, defines quality learning for multilingual learners? In the remainder of this chapter, we discuss key tenets that inform the construction and enactment of quality learning opportunities and provide classroom examples that illustrate them.

Tenet 1. Development Emerges in Social Interaction and Is a Consequence of, Not a Prerequisite for, Learning.

The notion of "readiness" is deeply ingrained in American education. It assumes that learning proceeds linearly, in predetermined sequences, each of which is required before the next one is attended to. Applied to learning in a second language, that process is considered as lockstep, one in which students grow linguistically in predetermined fashion, with learning mostly being constructed in the "black box" of the student's head. Talk and interaction are perceived as mere demonstrations that learning is taking place. If learners do not develop as the sequence intends them to, this view concludes that something must be at fault with the students. In those cases, three solutions are offered: courses are repeated, students are "remediated" via alternative arrangements (for example during pull-out sessions), or the intellectual expectations of classes are reduced. Then, to complicate the situation, if "remedial" instruction is chosen, it tends to be similar to that which did not render positive results in the first place. In this sequential and deterministic view, knowledge and teaching are fixed, and teachers impart it in stages, not necessarily in interconnected ways. This learning leads to superficial, inert knowledge.

Our position on learning builds on Vygotsky's idea of the Zone of Proximal Development (ZPD) (Vygotsky, 1978) and on the work of many others who based their work on notions proposed by the influential Russian psychologist in the early part of the 20th century, especially Leo van Lier (2004). Vygotsky asserted that learning always takes place ahead of development; in fact, the development results from the social activity and talk that are part of the learning process. He proposed that all higher mental functions occur in two planes, first interpersonally, and then intrapersonally. Consistent with this view, our first tenet proposes that all learners' development in school unfolds because students are offered opportunities to participate in carefully designed interactions that place them beyond their current ability to respond on their own and that support their engagement with practices, with each other, and with the teacher. This proleptic approach emphasizes ripening students' potential and building their futures, rather than lamenting their pasts or being constrained by their current abilities. It also requires deliberate attention to the construction of social engagements that will support and push their conceptual, analytic, and language development.

In our view, classroom talk is much more than the simple manifestation of learning; it *is* learning. Human beings are meaning-makers, and meaning is created through communication. In communication, human beings not only interpret isolated linguistic elements, such as words and phrases, but they also perceive and use paralinguistic (intonation, stress, rhythm) and extralinguistic features (gesture, distance, pictures, graphics, etc.). Together, these features constitute the affordances—the sensory opportunities for meaning-making—offered by the learning context, a concept we elaborate later on in the chapter. As students listen to others and perceive their surroundings, they respond in ways that have been modeled for them directly or indirectly in the process of communication. That is, learners approximate ways of thinking and acting in specific contexts that their community models for them. In the process, they find and refine conceptual understandings, practice ways of using them, and enhance their use of ideas, phrases, words, texts—all to engage in action. Teachers' and classmates' responses to learners' participation in oral activity encourage—or discourage—students' further learning and sense of belonging. From their first words, and through schooling and life, multilingual learners, and all other students, keep making sense of the world, building knowledge, and evaluating the importance of participating through the use of language and interaction. As they do so, if they are welcomed and supported, they gradually become full-fledged members of specific communities of practice.

Consequently, working with carefully designed supports, as well as with peers and their teachers, all learners grow and gradually become experienced with the concepts and processes intended as the goal for learning. As Vygotsky (1978) wrote, "an essential feature of learning is that it creates the zone of proximal development, that is, learning that is placed beyond students' ability to act on their own, awaken[ing] a variety of developmental processes that are able to operate only when the child is interacting with people in his environment and in collaboration with his peers" (p. 90).

Importantly, and counter to many American educators' understanding of the term, the zone of proximal development in pedagogical settings is not a fixed attribute of the individual learner, but rather a dynamic, interactive space created to afford a group of learners the opportunity to construct needed understandings together. Teachers consider where their students are—in their multiple developmental places—and place learning opportunities ahead of all of them. Some students will be faced with immense challenge, while for others the challenge may be closer to their developed ability. However, interacting with each other, learners will support each other's understanding and will grow in tandem, although they will not all develop in exactly the same way. In this view, "mastery" is neither a possible nor desired outcome; rather, the goal is gradual approximations to the ideal knowledge and performance envisioned.

Scaffolding provides students the needed support for engaging in interactive semiotic (meaning-making) activities that begin to realize their potential. The learner in this view is not construed as a passive recipient of knowledge, but as an active "negotiator of meanings, of pathways, of stances, and of identities" (Kramsch, 2003). Education, in this sense, is no longer about *teaching* (as transmission), but about promoting and supporting students' *learning* as it unfolds.

To be able to grow and begin to appropriate disciplinary practices, including the language required to express them, students need purposeful, dynamic, semiotically negotiated supports. These supports include those that focus on the linguistic structures of a language, such as text purpose, organization, grammar, and vocabulary, as well as a focus on paralinguistic and extralinguistic tools that mediate communication. Elaborating on Gibson's (1979) notion of affordances, van Lier (2004) proposed that what learners are exposed to is not "input," a fixed language construct, but "affordances" from which they perceive and select those that best fit their experience and the activity in which they are engaged. Affordances present learners with possibilities for meaning and action that yield opportunities for them to stimulate intersubjectivity (the tacit agreement between interlocutors to make every effort to understand each other and build from each other's ideas), joint attention, and various kinds of linguistic commentary. Affordances do not *cause* development; rather, they provide learners with *opportunities* for development as they perceive, act, interpret, and eventually appropriate ideas, as we will see in action in an activity we describe later in the chapter.

In van Lier's words:

> The environment is full of meaning potential, especially if it has a rich semiotic budget, which may not be true of all classrooms, textbooks, or pedagogical interactions. The . . . learner . . . has certain abilities, aptitudes, effectiveness, fitness. . . . Affordances are those relationships that provide a "match" between something in the environment (whether it's a chair or an utterance) and the learner. The affordance fuels perception and activity, and brings about meanings—further affordances and signs, and further higher-level activity as well as more differentiated perception. (van Lier, 2004, p. 96)

To design quality opportunities and lessons for multilingual learners, teachers place their focus on the potential for growth that students carry with them, on the experiences and linguistic repertoires (including their family languages) students bring with them to school, and on the intentional provision of supports and affordances that will make specific growth possible.

Tenet 2. Quality Learning Is Deliberately and Contingently Scaffolded

As already discussed, multilingual learners develop discipline-specific practices as a consequence of participating in learning experiences. If these experiences are stimulating and expertly designed and implemented, they provide students with multiple points of entry, action, and growth. Some of the tasks students are offered will be more routine in structure, although novel in content, while others may be more novel in structure and specifically designed to deepen learners' understanding of key concepts and interrelationships. Whichever the case, tasks provide the temporary supports needed by learners to engage in substantive activity and develop autonomy.

The concept of scaffolding derives from Jerome Bruner's readings of Vygotsky's work. Bruner (1976) proposed the scaffolding metaphor to indicate the pedagogical support offered to assist learners in performing beyond their current development, enabling them in the process to develop further. Scaffolding is temporary assistance grounded on a clear sense of where learning needs to be headed and what efforts and supports need to be invested to get there. Scaffolding *amplifies* the opportunities students have to negotiate meaning and action. It works proleptically, always looking ahead, constructing what students will be able to do on their own in the future.

Scaffolding is both planned and responsive (Walqui & van Lier, 2010). It is deliberately constructed in lessons as tasks that offer students support to participate successfully in a given activity to accomplish a specific purpose. It is planned insofar as it is the pedagogical design that supports students' exploration beyond what they know and are able to do. It is also unplanned, offered the moment an unanticipated need arises. Finally, it is responsive because scaffolding is also the contingent support offered after observing how learners engage in the planned scaffolding, determining what is developing well and what requires further assistance to mature.

The design of rigorous and enticing lessons that include the right kind of scaffolding is a complex professional endeavor, one that can be an enriching professional enterprise for teachers. It also presents educators with challenges. One such challenge is the mandate in some schools or districts that teachers move their instruction along "pacing guides" or follow other sorts of predetermined curricular progressions. Since the provision of learning opportunities for students must respond to their specific needs, mandated pacing is nonsensical.

Successful scaffolding ultimately renders itself unnecessary as learners grow and develop their autonomy. When specific scaffolds are no longer needed, however, other scaffolds will be necessary to support further learner development. Thus, scaffolding always requires that teachers engage in close observation of their students' actions to ascertain how it is working, and whether it is still needed as it stands or needs to be modified to respond to emerging needs and ongoing development.

Although the concept of scaffolding was first proposed in the late 1970s and has been widely used in education since that time, it is still a construct that invites misunderstandings. Scaffolds are often construed as a way of reducing or simplifying the complexity of the task at hand. For example, in some curricular approaches, scaffolding is interpreted in closed, mechanistic ways such as asking students to practice a linguistic form by filling in blanks in sentences that require the specified target form. The same repeated fill-in-the-blanks activity takes place across multiple, disconnected sentences, thus promoting atomistic, superficial, inert learning. This is neither the process nor goal of scaffolding.

Other misunderstandings of the concept have resulted in conceptual and linguistic simplifications or in the offering of exercises that have students repeatedly apply discrete linguistic forms singled out for attention, without engaging their agency or creativity. In this sense, scaffolding has been wrongly interpreted to mean *any* assistance, including teacher-driven "steps" to get students from point A to point B without fostering students' autonomy.

In contrast, scaffolding is best conceived as the support that assists students in gaining increasingly deeper and more complex understandings, simultaneously promoting their agency, the sense of knowing what to do in specific academic situations. Agency develops as a result of inviting students to apply practices in meaningful, collaborative environments. Through this engagement, students gain awareness of the (subject-specific) practices that constitute the goal of the lesson, the way they work, and their purposes. The goal is for students to eventually gain conscious control of practices and to finally appropriate them and apply them independently to novel, relevant situations (Walqui & van Lier, 2010).

Practical demonstrations throughout this book will highlight two aspects of scaffolding that are important to teachers' work: structure and process.

Scaffolding Structures. These structures—which propose the way in which students will interact—invite students to build their understanding as they work with each other and offer opportunities for all students in a class to actively participate. Structures create predictability since they entail students' participation in routine moves. Structures translate into tasks, the specific routines used for a purpose that are offered students to actively participate, and thus develop. For example, the task we call the Oral Development Jigsaw, described next, has as its goals the development of students' ability to understand the difference between two distinct genres (descriptions and narratives) and the generation of two different types of text. The task ensures that all students develop awareness of work entailed in understanding and crafting the two genres, and that all students begin to gain familiarity with each.

To understand the work of planned scaffolding, let us analyze the structure of the Oral Development Jigsaw, a learning task designed by Aída for use in her language and content courses when she was a high school teacher. The structure can be used in multiple disciplines, including science and social studies. As described here, it involves students' working with four pictures depicting characters involved in action (shown in Figure 2.1).

The Jigsaw (Figure 2.2) starts with students seated in groups of four called Base Groups. In our example, which comes from a combination English as a Second Language (ESL)/English Language Arts (ELA) class, the following steps are enacted:

Figure 2.1. Pictures for the Oral Development Jigsaw

1. With the whole class, the teacher explains the *purpose* of descriptions (e.g., to paint pictures with words so that someone who has not seen a scene can imagine it); describes the way descriptions are organized (setting, the order in which the author chooses to present details, where the scene takes place, who is present, what characters look like, what they are doing, other interesting relevant features); and offers *formulaic expressions* that are typically used in descriptions (*The picture we have shows . . . The scene takes place in . . . In this picture we can observe . . .*).
2. To practice using these guidelines in their descriptions, new groups of four students are formed by sending each member of the Base Groups to new groups, known as Expert Groups. Four different pictures (such as those in Figure 2.1) will be simultaneously described by Expert Groups, each of which is assigned only one picture. Students within Expert Groups work together to come up with a description of their scene. While students negotiate the description collaboratively, each student will be responsible for describing their picture when they go back to their Base Group. This step simulates real-life descriptions, in which interlocutors usually have not seen what is being described to them. To prepare students for this task, the teacher collects the pictures and invites them to rehearse the descriptions before moving back to their Base Groups to ascertain whether they are ready or need extra support from peers or the teacher.
3. Back in their original Base Groups, students describe their pictures to their teammates using words and body language to enhance their descriptions.
4. To explore the four descriptions further, students are invited to ask each other questions as they mentally connect ideas and ask for elaborations. Note that up to this point, each student will have been engaged in practicing descriptions minimally three times: as they constructed them, during rehearsal, and when they communicated their description to their Base Group that had not seen their picture.
5. Next, to move into narratives, the teacher and students discuss the *purposes* for narratives (stories, myths), how they are *usually organized* in English, and *typical phrases* that signal an event transition in a story (once upon a time, then, after that, meanwhile, finally, etc.).
6. To practice their new understanding of narrative texts, students are now asked to construct a story in their Base Groups, working with the same pictures. As they link scenes and add details to construct their narrative, students have to be creative, understanding that

their story has to be interesting and coherent, and that it must make sense.

7. So far, the activity has been oral, but once the story is completed, all students write their Base Group's full narrative. Their stories created by each Base Group are then read to their classmates—taking turns—so that the whole class can appreciate the varied stories that emerged from the same set of pictures.

This Oral Development Jigsaw (Figure 2.2) structures the activity so that all students participate, having clear rules that move them from simpler (static descriptions) to increasingly more complex practices (dynamic descriptions and abstract construction of stories).

Scaffolding Process. The second critical aspect of scaffolding is what it makes possible: dynamic interactions that, while more or less predictable, are unique. What any student may suggest, and what the group may agree to accept, is not to be dictated by the teacher nor by one student alone. Affordances—pictures, suggestions to use their hands, gestures that accompany utterances—are built into the environment for students to perceive, act on, participate, and learn. However, what causes learning is neither scaffolding nor affordances, but *the active engagement of students*. As a team decides how to construct their description, and later on their narrative, each student advances from where they were before, developing more robust conceptual, analytic, and language practices as a result of their collaborative work with peers and their environment. This example illustrates the essence

Figure 2.2. Oral Development Jigsaw Structure

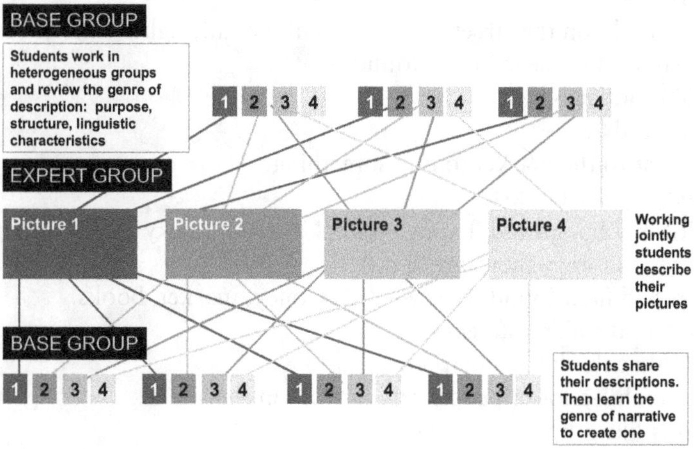

of scaffolding: The predictable support is there to enable the unpredictable appropriation and creativity of students working together to support each other.

Observe the following interaction as a team of four in the ESL/ELA class puts together a story based on the four pictures depicted in Figure 2.1. The transcript comes from Ms. Ng's class at MS 131 in Chinatown, New York City. Reading the transcript, it will be evident that a student called Chen talks the most, while Hue talks the least. However, when they write their story and practice presenting it, Hue will get at least two more opportunities to practice the newly gained ability to construct narratives, and by the end of the 45-minute class she, and all her classmates, will have grown:

Chen: Yeah, he looks sad, right? Walking on the street, hands in his pocket. Found ten-dollar bill, then go to market. And he, they buy books—

Xi: Yeah, buy some—

Chen: Buy cartoon books—

Xi: No, I think, I think this is the first one (signaling to partner who was responsible for describing a different picture), the one on the street, and he saw ten dollar bill, and then he went to market and—

Chen: How about sad first, sad first—

Ben: No, not really—

Chen: Sad first—

Ben: Not really—

Chen: Walking on the street—

Xi: Yeah—

Chen: Yeah, on the street, right? He sad, he sad, right? And he on the street. On the street he found—

Xi: Ten-dollar bill.

Chen: And . . .

Xi: Went to the market to buy something.

Chen: Buy the books!

Xi: To buy books and, happy ending! There, "Lucky Boy" (the name for the story they agreed on).

Chen: Sad first, found money—sad, money, market, books.

Ben: No, it's like a street—

Xi: I don't think it's a market.

Hue: Yeah—a lot of people selling stuff on the street.

Xi: It is like a bookstore, isn't it?

Chen: Uh, book market—
Hue: No, they sell different kinds of stuff.
Chen: Okay. Book market.
Ben: No! No, it's not book market!
Chen: What's it then? That's where you're selling a book.
Ben: It's bigger than selling books, many things are selling. It's not book market.

Students' interactions as they try to organize their stories are made possible because the structure of the task supports their work. It assists them in understanding the features of two different genres and crafting them collaboratively. Without the structure, such a rich process would not have been possible. As we will see below, this structure also makes possible their ability to construct a narrative.

Another essential aspect of scaffolding is that it promotes the emergence of novelty. Students use what they learned in new contexts. In our example, the stories emerging from class are unique and rich in diverse details, although they are based on the same four pictures. This makes the task exciting for students, and as they listen to their peers' stories, they learn new details they may incorporate in future narratives. We include one story as read by the students whose earlier discussion was excerpted above:

Ben: The title of our story is "Lucky Boy." The setting is on the street, in the neighborhood. The characters are Danny and Bobby. One summer day, Danny go out to buy a gift for his brother named Bobby. They are twins; today is their birthday.
Xi: Bobby stayed at home. Meanwhile, Danny is walking on a street. He saw a ten-dollar bill, and he was so surprised.
Chen: He's thinking about how to use the money to buy a birthday gift for his brother. He goes to the outdoor market to look for a gift.
Hue: Then he buy a book, he buy a comic book, and bring the book to his brother. And then, he shared the book, and they are very happy to have these books.

As illustrated in Figure 2.1, pictures required for the Oral Development Jigsaw must each present the same character, while the setting, activity, and other characters depicted have to vary.

The examples above evidence that multilingual learners learn and develop along different trajectories; thus, teachers need to adjust scaffolding contingently based on a continuous stream of specific and timely evidence gathered through observation and interaction during instruction (Walqui &

Heritage, 2012). As students' emerging understandings and misconceptions are revealed, this awareness of their current performance relative to the lesson goal guides the teacher's next actions and supports.

Tenet 3. During Learning, Multilingual Learners Simultaneously Develop Conceptual, Analytic, and Language Practices

The traditional separation of language and content, which offers simplified content to multilingual learners who have not yet "mastered" English, has not proved productive for them. Nor has it promoted quality learning opportunities that focus on important ideas in a subject area, unpack how these ideas interconnect, and introduce students to practices engaged in by disciplinary experts.

We propose that conceptual understandings, analytic skills, and the language required to express them develop simultaneously, as a result of apprenticeship into disciplinary practices, which entails participation in activity (Valdés et al., 2014; see Figure 2.3). In the Oral Development Jigsaw described earlier, *conceptually* students needed to understand first the nature of descriptive texts and then that of narrative texts. They also needed to become aware of how both genres differ in terms of purpose, organization, and preferred language use. In terms of purpose, a description has an interlocutor painting pictures with words to illustrate for someone else what they saw. Thus, it was important to convey the setting of the picture first (the landscape against which characters and actions will be depicted). *Analytically,* students needed to know how these two different types of texts are organized. In the description, for example, following the establishment of the setting, characters needed to be introduced, as well as their characteristics and activities. The sequence in which these elements are announced makes a difference in terms of the interlocutor's ability to imagine the picture. Thus, having a sense of audience is essential for the analytical practice of description. Finally, specific *language* was routinely used to convey the different scenes, the organization of events, and the marking of the sequence of events by—as seen in the examples—using connectors of time.

In their final story lines, we see the emerging proficiency of the students. Throughout human history, the purpose of narratives has been both to entertain and to teach lessons. Stories are typically organized sequentially: a setting and a character are introduced, the character is portrayed as possessing certain characteristics, something happens to the character, and the resolution to the situation changes the character. Typical expressions that move the action include terms such as *one day, because, suddenly,* and *then.* We see this process unfolding in the following story constructed by a second group in Ms. Ng's class:

Jade: The title of our story is "The Lucky Day." The setting is out on the street. The character is Alex and Mike.

Alex: One day Alex went walking alone in the street. He look sad, bored, because he saw, he saw a comic book and he couldn't buy it because he used his allowance, and all his money, in clothes. He wants to buy comic books but don't save one cent to use the money and buy unnecessary things.

Roger: Suddenly a ten-dollar bill popped into Alex's sight. It's like a wick in the darkness. His face full of happiness, he pick it up and put the bill inside his pocket. But he didn't put away his money completely—the half ten-dollar bill stuck out his pocket. Then he walked out of crowded market and into the bookstore.

Mike: He can't wait to tell his best friend Mike what happened to him today. He shared the comic book with him when he gets back home. The happiness, the big smile hanging in their face all day long.

As seen in this excerpt, conceptual, analytic, and language development function as sociocultural formations, resulting from the interactions of students with each other, with teachers, with constructs, with a budget of environmental affordances, and with the positive culture that is constantly established in the class. Learning takes place in the space between students' current and planned development, and it is made possible by teachers who deliberately build opportunities that assist learners in approximating the set destination: the acquisition of conceptual, analytic, and language practices. In the transcript above, the four students involved are at different places in their development, but in their collaborative interactions they support

Figure 2.3. Disciplinary Practices

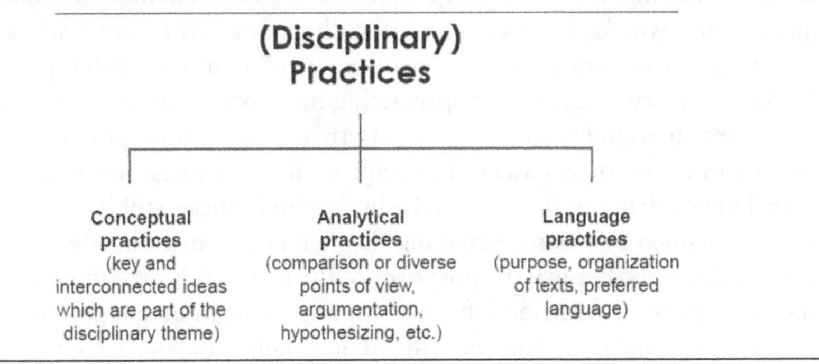

Source: Valdés, Kibler, & Walqui, 2014.

each others' growth in terms of understanding the concepts of description and narrative, analytical practices such as the organization of events, and language such as the expressions that will convey events and transitions. Furthermore, since they each have kept a full script of the narrative, and they can rehearse their presentation before the performance, students get the chance to gradually appropriate language that they initially did not know, such as "it's like a wick in the darkness."

Figure 2.3 illustrates the relationship among the conceptual, analytic, and language practices we have been discussing. It highlights how disciplinary experts share conceptual understandings that are key in their field, process ideas through distinct mental operations, and tend to use language in a specialized way. Building on conceptions of "communities of practice" originally proposed by Lave and Wenger (1991), apprenticeship into disciplinary communities entails a context in which:

(1) learners are gradually introduced into the disciplinary community of practice, one that shares understandings, norms, beliefs, actions, artifacts, and specific ways of expressing itself;
(2) apprentices are considered capable, and they are supported and validated by masters and peers as they approximate their full engagement in communities of practice;
(3) apprentices—while approximating masters—have full view of what the community considers accomplished performance of the discipline; and
(4) apprentices are not expected to develop in exactly the same way nor at the same time, and they are offered multiple contingent opportunities to keep enhancing their new practices.

While students' growing sense of autonomy is the goal, "autonomy in an ecological approach does not mean independence or individualism. . . . It means having the authorship of one's actions, having the voice that speaks one's words, and being emotionally connected to one's actions and speech . . . within one's community of practice" (van Lier, 2004, p. 8).

Users of new languages, apprenticing into specific practices in that language, are surrounded by a community that models those practices and invites them to use their nascent language with an emphasis on participation in exchanges that aim for them to be increasingly successful. Success, in this sense, is defined by meaning-making through engagement in effective action (i.e., students accomplish the purposes of the task), although their responses may be expressed with some formal imperfections in language production. Paralinguistic and extralinguistic affordances help students perceive, convey, understand, and eventually appropriate ideas. During this performance by learners, it is important to value what students can do, and it is equally important—both for learners and for teachers—to develop a clear understanding of what remains to be worked on. If interlocutors value multilingual learners' meaningful communication, their responses confer legitimacy on students (i.e., they belong in the encounter, they have the right to participate and the right to speak—errors and all). In the process, students' agency is fostered, as we saw in the transcript from Ms. Ng's ESL class.

Viewing disciplinary practices as encompassing conceptual understandings, analytic tasks, and the language required to develop them and engage successfully in academic activity does not eliminate the possibility of focusing on one of the subcomponents when needed, in very situated, contingent ways. An explicit focus on conceptual understandings and how to compare, analyze, and the like is essential, as is a focus on language features. However, such a focus must occur together with, and in the service of, subject-matter learning (Kelley et al., 2010).

Tenet 4. Quality School Learning Focuses on Substantive, Generative Disciplinary Practices

Realizing the potential that multilingual learners take to school requires that teachers see their students both for who they are at the moment, full of resources and immense potential, and for who they will be at the end of a unit of teaching, at the end of a course, at the end of their school studies, and in productive and responsible life in their communities and the world (Walqui & van Lier, 2010). Successful growth in classes with multilingual learners entails reciprocal responsibility. Students do their best in terms of rigorous participation and, understanding the goal of their learning, keep working to meet their goals. Teachers, on the other hand, have the responsibility of providing students with supportive and safe environments where the fear of failure is mitigated by the sense that with errors come new opportunities to learn. This tacit agreement also requires that as teachers teach, they increase their own depth of subject-matter knowledge, disciplinary understanding, and the ability to translate them into pedagogical action that builds students' conceptual, analytical, and linguistic strengths while fostering their agency and autonomy (van Lier, 2008). Resnick and colleagues (2015) have called these reciprocal relationships "a pedagogy of effort," and the overall educational endeavor "the socialization of intelligence."

In our model, the teacher's job is to "teach" less (i.e., lecturing from the front of the room) and instead to create more opportunities for students to engage in carefully crafted activity with classmates and thus learn—while the teacher formatively assesses how learning is unfolding to prepare new learning opportunities that will support new growth.

We propose that a rigorous lesson focuses on the understanding of key concepts, texts, problems, and phenomena related to an important theme in the discipline being studied. As students engage with pivotal concepts and their interconnections that build the discipline, anchor concepts become clearer to them, enabling them to deepen and expand their knowledge in an organized, productive manner.

As the examples throughout the book illustrate, teachers' depth of disciplinary understanding becomes essential as they select what to teach, what to emphasize, and how to structure learning opportunities for students. Not everything in the curriculum can be taught, nor should it be, when what teachers are after is quality learning opportunities for multilingual learners (and other students). To move beyond what has been characterized by many as curriculum that is "a mile wide and an inch deep," teachers need to focus on the key constructs and relationships in the theme studied.

If multilingual learners' learning has to focus on key conceptual understandings as well as analytic and language practices, then accomplishing deeper, increasingly interconnected knowledge and the ability to use it creatively requires a spiraling, rather than a linear, curricular organization. With this model, key ideas are introduced with the expectation that they will not be understood fully by every student in class. However, because these ideas are so important in the discipline, they will reoccur time and time again, with each reoccurrence affording students the opportunity to revisit and expand these ideas and practices through different contexts, solidifying and deepening their understandings. Examples of spiraling curriculum are presented and explored throughout this book.

Tenet 5. When It Comes to the Development of Language Practices, Quality Learning Opportunities for Multilingual Learners Selectively Focus on Form in Contextual, Contingent, and Supportive Ways

As the most important tool for learning, language mediates the development of valued practices in a subject-matter area and, as such, it needs to be attended to purposefully. This attention, however, cannot be at the center of learning opportunities, since language is *the vehicle* for learning concepts, and using those concepts through analytic tasks constitutes the central goal of these efforts. However, when language, the tool that mediates work and builds disciplinary and conceptual understandings and practices, stands in the way of expression, a focus on its specific, contextually relevant use is essential. In other words, the redirection needs to focus on the concrete expression that impedes understanding, or on suggestions of alternative wording that might clarify or enhance meaning, and not be an excuse for a lesson on decontextualized, prescriptive language forms.

Three decades ago, Michael Long (1996) drew a useful distinction between approaches to learning English as a second language: they either focused on *forms* or they focused on *form*. Applying the distinction to our situation, a focus on *forms* results when the goal of education for English Learners is to learn how language works in general with a focus on the production of well-formed sentences. As a result, language forms are taught for their own sake, and the emphasis and organization of a course—and of teachers' actions—prioritize grammatical, lexical, or morphological structures. In contrast, a focus on *form* occurs when the emphasis is placed on specific meaningful social activity. In this case, the focus on specific language structures is limited to work on a problematic form that impedes understanding. In these situations, which are part of a larger effort at meaning-making, "the formal knowledge remains connected and can bear fruit in terms of further learning" (van Lier, 2001, p. 259).

An example of a nonproductive focus on forms occurs in the common practice of "frontloading" vocabulary at the beginning of a lesson that dedicates prime time to "teach" a list of isolated words before conceptual understandings are addressed. This focus on lexis—or on grammatical structures—runs the risk of producing superficial knowledge that remains inert, or, even worse, the shoehorning of content lessons to produce artificial opportunities for students to practice the vocabulary (Bruna et al., 2007).

Another example of a common practice derived from curricula focused on forms is the explicit "teaching" (i.e., explanation) of when to use a specific verb tense, followed by applications of the rule that ask students to fill in the blanks with the correct form of the verb in a list of 8 or 10 sentences that are unrelated. In this case, students spend time quietly doing busy work that is superficial, nongenerative, and lacking context or meaning.

This tenet highlights the need for shifting conceptions of language teaching and learning more generally. Starting in the 1950s and influenced by structural linguistics, ESL classes were designed around a sequential development of syntactic and lexical aspects of English, an orientation that still dominates some ESL and world language instruction, both at the K–12 and post-secondary level. The underlying assumption was that there were simpler syntactic forms (the present simple, for example) and more complex ones (present and past perfect) and that this "natural" order suggested the organization of curricula from easier to more complex structures (Mackey, 1967). Having selected the grammatical forms, curriculum developers and the teachers who worked with these materials looked for examples of texts that used them or created those texts. More recently, Valdés (2018) has called this tendency to organize language classes around the grammatical features of language the "curricularization" of language.

Instead, as explored through the Oral Development Jigsaw, students need to get a sense of general aspects of the "text" (whether written or oral discourse), including the purpose that guided its creation, the way different types of texts (stories, speeches, instructions) tend to be organized (what typically comes first, next, and how these texts tend to end), and the usual language used to present and link ideas. To use a common expression, they need to know they are in a forest first to then start making sense of and analyzing the trees. This sense of going from the broader understanding of a text to the specific is not a new idea. It is just one that has not taken much hold in schools.

Multilingual learners learn to use their new language investing all the resources they have at their disposal to make sense of what is said and to express themselves. For them, language is *action* (Walqui & van Lier, 2010), which involves the use of affordances. Furthermore, their ability to express themselves and understand others is always evolving; thus, the term sometimes used for this process is *languaging* (Tocalli-Beller & Swain, 2007). As we will see when we discuss planning and responsive implementation of plans in the subject-matter areas, students' products are never static; they are always in the process of becoming increasingly more accomplished. Languaging is an accurate verb to describe their efforts to increasingly approximate the norm and surpass it.

The most important concept we are trying to convey is that language is a semiotic tool that enables human beings to develop higher mental processes (Vygotsky, 1978). While cognitive theory emphasized the role of the individual and activity in the "black box" of the mind, sociocultural theorists following Vygotsky (1978) placed learning squarely in interactional activity:

> Human development is the product of a broader system than just the system of a person's individual functions, specifically, systems of social connections and relations, of collective forms of behavior and social cooperation. (p. 41)

Examples of how teachers can provide students with an explicit focus on form that is integrated into meaning-making and is not atomistic are provided in the following chapters as we and our colleagues demonstrate and explain how to amplify the curriculum in subject-matter areas.

SHIFTS NECESSARY FOR TEACHERS AND CLASSROOMS

To articulate the implications of the tenets presented in this chapter for teaching multilingual learners, and to preview the multiple curricular examples throughout the book, we conclude this chapter by listing several shifts that are required in the orientation and practice of educators to offer their multilingual, and all other learners, quality and equitable opportunities to learn.

Reorientations Related to Teachers' Perceptions of Students and Their Role in Promoting Students' Learning

- FROM teaching from the front of the classroom in a transmission-oriented mode . . . TO creating opportunities for students to learn by interacting with each other and the teacher.
- FROM believing that there are prerequisites for engaging in certain types of academic activity and uses of language . . . TO believing that development is caused by offering students opportunities to engage in activity that goes beyond their level of independent functioning.

Reorientations About Students and the Process of Learning via the Medium of an Additional Language

- FROM believing that students should arrive to class already motivated to learn . . . TO assuming that motivation is the role of teachers who must ensure that texts, tasks, and lessons are interesting and relevant.
- FROM seeing language learning as a process of acquiring language structures and/or functions . . . TO understanding language as action, a way of getting things accomplished.

Reorientations Connected to Text Selection and Lesson Design

- FROM using simplistic texts . . . TO using rich, complex materials that speak to students' identities and concerns, affirming and expanding their interests and inviting them to critically consider social themes (interthinking).
- FROM designing transmission-oriented classes where lecturing and the teacher asking isolated questions of some students is the trend . . . TO classes that are designed and enacted to engage every single student in the classroom in sustained exchanges that over time help them coconstruct knowledge and practices.
- FROM seeing language acquisition as linear and progressive aimed at the development of accuracy in language production . . . TO understanding that development occurs in nonlinear and complex

ways, ideally promoted by spiraling opportunities for meaning making and language use.

- FROM focusing on the accuracy of individual students' linguistic productions . . . TO valuing students' joint, comprehensive action first.
- FROM delivering lessons structured around isolated ideas or texts that are not interconnected . . . TO the development of lessons that focus on powerful central themes and unpack main interconnections across several texts or concepts/ideas.
- FROM teachers asking questions to which students respond in predictable ways . . . TO teachers inviting students to consider issues and respond critically in novel ways that signal their appropriation of criticality.

The work of teachers—planning units, lessons, and instructional activities, thoughtfully enacting them given myriad and ever-changing contextual challenges, and reflectively planning again—is in itself immensely complex. We acknowledge that adding into that work the consideration of these tenets and shifts may seem overwhelming, especially for teachers in settings where there may be few examples of these practices to learn from. The next chapter (Chapter 3) will propose a concrete framework for planning that can guide teachers and those supporting them in these efforts. The remaining chapters in this book provide concrete examples of the proposed pedagogy, evidence for the promise of this approach from teachers and students involved in its implementation, considerations for preparing teachers, and suggestions for addressing remaining challenges.

REFERENCES

Bronfenbrenner, U. (1979). *The ecology of human development: Experiments by nature and design.* Harvard University Press.

Bruna, K., Vann, R., & Escudero, M. (2007). What's language got to do with it? A case study of academic language instruction in a high school "English Learner Science" class. *Journal of English for Academic Purposes, 6*(1), 36–54.

Bruner, J. (1976). Prelinguistic prerequisites of speech. In R. Campbell & P. Smith (Eds.), *Recent advances in the psychology of language*, 4a, 199–214. Plenum Press.

Bruner, J. (1996). *The culture of education.* Harvard University Press.

Derewianka, B., & Jones, P. (2023). *Teaching language in context.* Oxford.

Gibbons, P. (2009). *English Learners, academic literacy and thinking: Learning in the challenge zone.* Heinemann.

Gibson, J. J. (1979). *The ecological approach to visual perception.* Erlbaum.

Hammond, J. (2014). *The transition of refugee students from intensive English centres to mainstream high schools: Current practices and future possibilities.* Sydney, New South Wales, Department of Education and Communities.

Kelley, J., Lesaux, N., Kieffer, M., & Faller, S. (2010). Effective academic vocabulary instruction in the urban middle school. *Reading Teacher, 64*(1), 5–14.

Kozulin, A., Gindis, B., Ageyev, V., & Miller, S. (Eds.). (2003). *Vygotsky's educational theory in cultural context.* Cambridge University Press.

Kramsch, C. (Ed.). (2003). *Language acquisition and language socialization: Ecological perspectives.* Bloomsbury Academic.

Larsen-Freeman, D. (2013). Complex, dynamic systems and technemes. In J. A. Morgan & T. Murphey (Eds.), *Meaningful action: Earl Stevick's influence on language teaching.* Cambridge University Press.

Larsen-Freeman, D. (2014, April). Saying what we mean: Making the case for second language acquisition to become second language development. *Language Teaching*/FirstView Article, 1–15.

Larsen-Freeman, D. (2018). Looking ahead: Future directions in, and future research into, second language acquisition. *Foreign Language Annals,* 51, 1, ACTFL.

Lave, J., & Wenger, E. (1991). *Situated learning: Legitimate peripheral participation.* Cambridge University Press.

Lee, C. (2020). The braid of human learning and development: Neuro-psychological processes and participation in cultural practices. In N. Suad Nasir, C. D. Lee, R. Pea, & M. M. de Royston (Eds.), *Handbook of the cultural foundations of learning.* Routledge.

Long, M. (1996). The role of the linguistic environment in second language acquisition. In W. C. Ritchie & T. K. Bhatia (Eds.), *Handbook of second language acquisition* (pp. 413–468). Academic Press.

Mackey, W. (1967). *Language teaching analysis.* Longman.

Resnick, L. B., Asterhan, C. S. C., & Clarke, S. N. (2015). *Socializing intelligence through academic talk and dialogue.* American Educational Research Association.

Shulman, L. S. (1996). Paradigms and research programs in the study of teaching: A contemporary perspective. In M. C. Wittrock (Ed.), *Handbook of research on teaching* (3rd ed., pp. 3–36). Macmillan.

Suad Nasir, N., Lee, C. D., Pea, R., & de Royston, M. M. (2020). Introduction: Reconceptualizing learning: A critical task for knowledge building and teaching. In N. Suad Nasir, C. D. Lee, R. Pea, & M. M. de Royston (Eds.), *Handbook of the cultural foundations of learning.* Routledge.

Tocalli-Beller, A., & Swain, M. (2007). Riddles and puns in the ESL classroom: Adults talk to learn. In A. Mackey (Ed.), *Conversational interaction in second language acquisition* (pp. 143–167). Oxford University Press.

Valdés, G. (2018). Analyzing the curricularization of language in two-way immersion education: Restating two cautionary notes. *Bilingual Research Journal, 41*(4), 388–412.

Valdés, G., Kibler, A., & Walqui, A. (2014, March). *Changes in the expertise of ESL professionals: Knowledge and action in an era of new standards.* TESOL International Association.

Valdés, G., Poza, L., & Brooks, M. (2017). Language acquisition in bilingual education. In W. Wright, S. Boun, & O. García (Eds.), *The handbook of bilingual and multilingual education*. Wiley Blackwell.

van Lier, L. (2000). From input to affordance: Social-interactive learning from an ecological perspective. In J. P. Lantolf (Ed.), *Sociocultural theory and second language learning* (pp. 155–177). Oxford University Press.

van Lier, L. (2001). The role of form in language learning. In M. Bax & J. Zwart (Eds.), *Reflections on language and language learning*. John Benjamins Publishing.

van Lier, L. (2004). *The ecology and semiotics of language learning: A sociocultural perspective*. Kluwer Academic.

van Lier, L. (2008). Agency in the classroom. In J. P. Lantolf & M. E. Poehner (Eds.), *Sociocultural theory and the teaching of second languages* (pp. 136–186). Equinox.

Vygotsky, L. S. (1962). *Thought and language*. MIT Press.

Vygotsky, L. S. (1976). Play and its role in the mental development of the child. In J. Bruner, A. Jolly, & K. Sylva (Eds.), *Play: Its role in development and evolution* (pp. 537–554). Penguin Books Ltd.

Vygotsky, L. (1978). *Mind in society*. Harvard University Press.

Walqui, A., & Heritage, M. (2012, January). *Instruction for diverse groups of English language learners* [Paper presentation]. Understanding Language Conference, Stanford, CA.

Walqui, A., & van Lier, L. (2010). *Scaffolding the academic success of English language learners: A pedagogy of promise*. WestEd.

CHAPTER 3

Designing the Amplified Lesson

Aída Walqui

How can teachers design powerful invitations for multilingual learners—and all of their students—that engage the entire class in activity? How can they promote their students' apprenticeship into becoming good practitioners of disciplinary activity, civic engagement, and language use in and out of schools? How can they be mindful of research on the development of both teacher expertise and student autonomy? How can they set in motion during their instructional planning and enactment the conceptual and practical shifts discussed in Chapter 2?

In this chapter we elaborate on how to construct lessons that make possible the attainment of the vision of quality learning proposed in Chapter 2. We provide a framework for lesson design—ideally carried out in collaboration with peers—and discuss the ways in which it can come to life in classes while building learner autonomy. We explain how to determine and use appropriate texts, select and arrange tasks, and assess students' moves toward autonomy as learners. In addition to providing frameworks for planning and implementing quality instruction that embed the necessary shifts, we offer examples of critical dialogic interaction in a classroom and the role it plays in the development of student voice and agency in the search for equitable environments in school and society (Glick & Walqui, 2021.

GETTING STARTED: CONSIDERATIONS AND GUIDELINES

In the same way that architects design buildings and use blueprints to achieve their design goals, teachers plan lessons to support the interests, educational needs, and personal, intellectual, and civic growth of their students. Buildings, as culturally symbolic constructed artifacts, are determined through blueprints based on the purpose for the building, the desires of the future owner, the shape and function of the different rooms to be built, how light and landscape will be used, and other contextual elements. A lesson plan, also a culturally symbolic constructed artifact, identifies what students will learn based on the nature of the disciplinary practices to be developed, curricula and standards, the support students will need to apprentice into the selected goals for the lesson, the time available, and other contextual factors.

Teachers make decisions as to how to use what is available, what else will be needed, and how to organize resources and activities so that their deliberately designed lessons render expected results. Furthermore, in the same way in which architectural blueprints for buildings start with consideration of the characteristics of the land where the building will be constructed, a lesson plan must account first for who the learners are and what they bring to the learning activity. These considerations are taken into account to plan dialogic activity that will develop new practices and meet curriculum goals. The lesson constitutes the space between—that is, the road that will lead students from where they are to their destination, the lesson's established goals, often in unpredictable and even surprising ways.

Our use of the construct "lesson" merits elaboration here. As used in this book, a lesson focuses on developing a small set of interrelated key disciplinary practices through deliberately designed tasks that scaffold students' growth through interaction. As discussed in Chapter 2, such practices encompass conceptual, analytic, and language dimensions. As an example, we will describe a lesson in which the conceptual goals are for students to understand the role of power, the possible rewards and consequences of taking a stand or not when faced with unjust situations, and the notion that protest can bring about societal change. Analytic practices developed in the same lesson center on the critical reading and analysis of multimedia texts and the use of metacognition during reading. Students thereby learn to track their own evolving understanding of texts, solve reading difficulties, self-assess what they understand and don't understand about a text, and learn about what they can do to solve gaps in understanding. The language practices to be developed include the understanding and formulation of ideas and processes involved.

We propose that teachers never design accomplished lessons in the abstract. Lessons are uniquely and specifically situated to satisfy particular goals with specific students, under specific situations in a class, school, and time. A teacher deliberately considers the shifts in thinking that were identified in the prior chapter and selects (1) the substantive focus of the lesson, (2) the interactive process the teacher will invite students to engage in, and (3) the complex disciplinary goals of a lesson. Naturally, what remains constant in planning for offering students quality opportunities to learn is (1) setting highly challenging but inviting goals for learning as represented in the selection of generative texts/key concepts in a discipline; (2) creating high support activities for learning that are grounded in interactions and use of language in context; and (3) supporting all students' eventual autonomy in specific disciplinary conceptual, analytic, and language practices that are embedded in the lesson or unit.

Characteristics of an Effective Lesson

Given the magnitude of the goals that have to be accomplished, a single lesson cannot be synonymous with a class period. It is not likely that students, and multilingual learners in particular, will develop deep, substantive, and generative practices in the short time usually allotted to one class. A lesson's sustained and spiraled revisiting of key themes through analytic, interactive activities invites students to apply the practices time and time again through novel contexts over the course of several days. This sustained engagement makes it possible for students to gradually gain a stronger and clearer grasp of the ideas and their interconnections, as well as to increasingly appropriate higher-order thinking and more precise and eloquent language.

Our comments about the situated nature of lessons so far beg the question of the role of published curricula in creating quality learning opportunities for multilingual learners and other students. We expand on this theme in Chapter 11. Here we will just mention that in the United States, published educational materials, and, more recently, open-access curricula available online, often constitute the tools teachers work with in class. We take the stance that even the best preexisting curriculum needs to be adapted by teachers to meet the needs of the particular students in their classes. Even if the architecture of the materials and the development of lessons are optimal, one or two tasks will need to be changed to meet the interests, maturational levels, and budding development of students.

If the existing lessons leave much to be desired, then it will take as much or more work to modify them for the kinds of ambitious and supportive goals we are arguing for than the time it would take to start a new design (Walqui, 2024). Nevertheless, the teacher's responsibility is to craft good lessons and units that follow an inviting, robust, and flexible design to facilitate multiple adaptations and successful situated enactments. We recognize that teachers in the United States are typically given textbooks and sometimes other curricular material to use in their classes; however, we propose that the hallmark of an accomplished educator is creating and adapting quality curricula. Lesson design is an immensely sophisticated and rewarding professional activity, one that we believe teachers can embrace and grow into if they are provided guidelines and support. At the same time, we believe that much of what this book presents can be used by teachers immediately, including in their efforts to modify—perhaps in small ways at first—the existing and sometimes mandated curriculum they are expected to teach. We discuss these ideas more fully in Chapters 11 and 12.

Choosing Texts

Sometimes lesson design starts with a text we encounter and that calls forth our immediate attention. When we read or observe it, we find it rich and appealing. A text may be an essay, a short story, a photograph, a video clip, or any signifier that connects to themes that are part of the courses we teach. Many teachers are constantly looking for such materials for their lessons, to complement or enhance what they have in their everyday materials. When I was a teacher, my husband used to tease me that I saw everything around me as a potential text for my social studies, English Language Arts, or English as a Second Language (the term we used back in the 1980s) classes. Powerful texts to which we gravitate have the potential to link to other texts, to address learning standards and concepts in our lessons, and also to stimulate students' interests. It is important to remind ourselves, once again, that student motivation is not a prerequisite for participation in a class. A good part of teachers' work consists of ensuring that what they invite students to do in class will be stimulating. Once texts are chosen, we can then decide how to use them, either as the base for building powerful lessons or for connecting to the key ideas we explore in class.

All good lessons are situated in the particular. If a teacher notices that a class loves to hear and read anecdotes about the historical context of a text they are reading, she brings additional brief texts that could be read in a jigsaw format. Spending 20 minutes on this activity renders increased engagement and student productivity. In other classes, this may not be necessary. Those of us who have taught in K–12 classrooms and were given the same course to teach two or three times a day, for example an introductory world history class, know that it is impossible to teach the same lesson in exactly the same way, with the same tasks, and at the same pace to different cohorts of students. Each group of students presents unique characteristics and displays idiosyncrasies that need to be met if we want the lesson to be successful. A concept may have already been clarified in one class because either the idea emerged spontaneously or a question was asked, while in another class the concept needs to be introduced for the first time. In one first-period class, the pace of activity can be faster and students accomplish more, not requiring the revisiting of practices from new perspectives. In the same class, in the fifth period, right after lunch, while students may be engaged and attentive, activities may take longer and more invitations are required for them to make ideas and practices their own. It is, in fact, these accommodations that make lessons successful, and this responsiveness renders students who are motivated, engaged, and willing to remain invested. They know lessons were created for them specifically and appreciate this fact.

Before discussing the complexities of lesson design, our proposed architecture, and construct for units and lessons, let us focus on some general guidelines for that design—addressing their advantages for multilingual learners as well as for other students. A lesson is an invitation teachers issue students to embark on a discovery and knowledge-building journey. There are several requirements for making this journey successful.

Desirable and Motivating Learning Goals and Activities

Students need to understand the goal of the lesson—the destination—and find it desirable. Multilingual learners are motivated as a result of being offered invitations to engage in activities that they find interesting and authentic, that present a challenging problem or significant idea, and that include propositions or questions that in themselves serve as magnets to their interaction and engagement. Valuable, challenging activity that provides the needed support motivates students. Student motivation is not a prerequisite for learning, but rather a consequence of being offered valuable learning opportunities. Motivating students becomes easier to accomplish when prior learning experiences have taught students how stimulating learning can be, even when it entails hard work.

A good lesson surrounds students with possibilities for meaning-making and growth. These opportunities do not constitute "input," that is, segments of a ready-made, fixed language code provided by the teacher to the students—which then students will "output" in more or less mechanical ways, a perspective that was prevalent in the education of multilingual learners for many years and that is still evident in some classrooms. Rather, what facilitates learning is the offering of rich *affordances*—particular properties designed into the environment from which students perceive and select those that best fit in their experience and the activity in which they are engaged (van Lier, 2000, 2004). As introduced in Chapter 2, affordances provide learners the opportunity to notice, engage, and thus develop important understandings and skills they find to be worthwhile, for example video clips, photographs, notes, and texts. Affordances do not cause learning in and of themselves. Thus, an important part of a teacher's role is to surround students with a rich semiotic (meaning-making) budget and to "structure the learners' activities and participation so that access is available and engagement encouraged" (van Lier, 2000, p. 253).

Over half a century ago, Jerome Bruner (1960) wrote that interest in the material to be learned, rather than external goals such as grades or later competitive advantage, is the best stimulus for learning: "In an age of increasing spectatorship, motives for learning must be kept from going passive . . . they must be based as much as possible upon the arousal of interest in what there is to be learned, and they must be kept broad and diverse in expression" (p. 14).

Coherence Across Activities, Lessons, and Units

Goals for learning operate at three levels: *macro objectives* (to be reached at the end of a unit of study lasting a few weeks and composed of several lessons centered on a generative theme); *meso objectives* (to be reached at the end of a lesson taking several class periods, a component of the generative theme addressed in the unit but which stands on its own); and *micro objectives* (to be addressed by the specific tasks that constitute the fluid and organic steps in a lesson and that support students' activity). A task, a lesson, and a unit are interrelated and move the students from simpler understandings of a theme to increasingly more complex, interrelated, deeper ones. Once again, Bruner (1960) provides important insight into this concept: "If earlier learning is to render later learning easier, it must do so by providing a general picture in terms of which the relations between things encountered earlier and later are made as clear as possible" (p. 12).

Tasks as Purposeful Steps Toward a Learning Goal

In the same way that steps in a journey help travelers move forward toward reaching their destination, the role of *tasks* is to help students move toward the goals of a lesson. Tasks are concrete instantiations of individual support manifested through interactions that engage students in critical, thoughtful, and sustained structured participation. Tasks unpack, a bit at a time, the concepts, skills, and language that are in the process of being apprenticed, while linking them and building on prior encounters with such disciplinary practices. Throughout the book, we present multiple examples of tasks (which we also sometimes refer to as "activities"), their purposes, structure, and place, and how they should—in any good design—follow each other seamlessly, each one representing a step forward in the accomplishment of predetermined objectives.

Dynamic Self- and Peer-Assessment as Part of Learning

A final point to note before we unpack the architecture of a lesson is that a lesson needs to invite students to be actively engaged in their own self-assessment and in the assessment of peers. The more aware students are of what counts as quality performance of a task and whether they have reached goals, the clearer it will be to them whether results are being accomplished, in what measure, and what to do about improving their performance. This self- and other-assessment needs to be constant, thus our use of the term dynamic assessment. Using clear examples of prior student work, rubrics, and self-reflection charts, students can own the work of assessing themselves and as a result increase their autonomy.

PEDAGOGICAL DESIGN

With the above considerations in mind, we present a framework for this pedagogy that supports learners' simultaneous conceptual, analytic, and linguistic development. We focus here on the architecture of units and lessons in which tasks are embedded and stress once again the importance of coherence, purpose, and progression at micro (task), meso (lesson), and macro (unit) levels of development.

Unit Design

A unit consists of three to five lessons intended to unpack one large, powerful theme. For example, the unit we will partially discuss in this chapter to illustrate the design choices teachers engage in is called *Power, Protest, and*

Figure 3.1. Spiraled Unit on *Power, Protest, and Change*

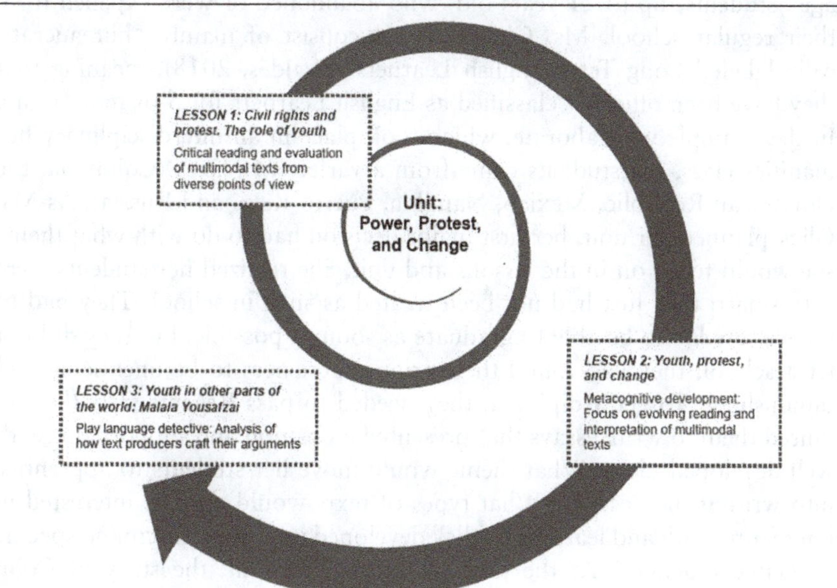

Change. This specific unit, designed for about 4 weeks of work, in its original version is comprised of three lessons (see Figure 3.1). The first lesson centers around the role children played in social protest, and the theme and texts come from the period of the American school desegregation movement in the South. The second lesson, which we will consider in some detail, focuses on the role of protest during current popular sport activities in the United States and abroad. The final lesson considers the role of children in international protests and includes several texts around Malala Yousafzai (a biography, her speech to other adolescents, and a speech Yousafzai gave to the United Nations General Assembly). Throughout the unit, students move from a vague to a more precise understanding of concepts such as power, control, status quo, the significant role youth can play in change as upstanders, the nature of heroic acts, and their consequences. They learn to read and analyze the author's perspective and to analyze language for tone and positionality. They also simultaneously become increasingly more comfortable and precise with their language use on these topics while developing their critical stances.

Lesson Design

To explore the features of our proposed lesson design, we use the example of Lesson 2, "Youth, Protest, and Change," from the unit outlined in Figure 3.1, written by Yael Glick (a teacher at Voyages Academy in New York City), with support from Aída Walqui. Ms. Glick's school is for "overage" students (up to 21 years old) who abandoned or were expelled from their regular school. Ms. Glick's classes consist of mainly "bureaucratically labeled Long Term English Learners" (Valdés, 2018), meaning that they have been officially classified as English Learners for 5 or more years. In the example we elaborate, which took place in an interdisciplinary humanities class, the students came from a variety of places (Colombia, the Dominican Republic, Mexico, Namibia, Puerto Rico, and Russia). As Ms. Glick planned her unit, her first major decision had to do with what theme she would focus on in the lessons and unit. She realized her students were very smart; they just had not been treated as such in school. They had to recover credits to be able to graduate as soon as possible, but they did not trust school; they had found their prior experiences to be unenticing and diminishing. To get a diploma, they needed to pass Regents tests that required them to write essays that presented a position and supported it with well-developed ideas. What theme would move her students to apprentice into writing such essays? What types of texts would they be interested in interacting with and learning as they developed important discipline-specific academic practices? At the time of writing her unit, the story of Colin Kaepernick—the San Francisco 49ers football player who knelt in silent protest as the national anthem played during games to signal his solidarity with the Black Lives Matter movement—had just taken place. Ms. Glick had heard her students refer to Kaepernick's protest, expressing many different opinions. She had also noticed that in school and in the neighborhood, in the same way in which some White people had negative stereotypes about minoritized groups, many Black and Latino students also believed negative overgeneralizations made about White people. She knew that in the broader context there were strong feelings for and against Kaepernick's protest representing a variety of interpretations. That gave her a thematic link for her lesson, which addresses controversial issues that are not only central to the operation of a democratic society but are also very close to the contexts and concerns within which immigrant students live: How diverse groups in society perceive each other, how they interpret each others' actions, and how to engage in debate with others without prejudging them.

Having chosen a theme that would be relevant and compelling for her students, Ms. Glick's next big decision was to find the right texts for her lesson. She wondered how she may surround her students with multimodal texts that, focused on their interests, would help them perceive, engage, and grow. She recalled having read an article online written by James Montague (2012) about an event at the 1968 Olympics that had a profound impact on her. Furthermore, she had at the time looked for videos of the event, the 200-meter race, and been impressed by the joint power of the article and the video. She decided to make Montague's piece the center text of her lesson and to provide other visual texts as resources for her students.

THREE MOMENTS IN A LESSON

We propose that lessons be designed along three key Moments named after what students accomplish with concepts or texts: Preparing Learners, Interacting with Text (or Concept), and Extending Understanding (see Figure 3.2). A lesson may unfold over five or six periods in a middle or high school class and consists of a coherent set of tasks that support students' deepening understanding and appropriation of central—and interrelated—concepts or texts interconnected to the theme of the unit.

Preparing Learners

First, students need to be readied to undertake sustained productive academic work by focusing their attention on the broad theme to be discussed, activating their prior knowledge that is relevant to the lesson at hand, and increasing their familiarity with a few new terms needed in context.

Figure 3.2. The Architecture of a Lesson

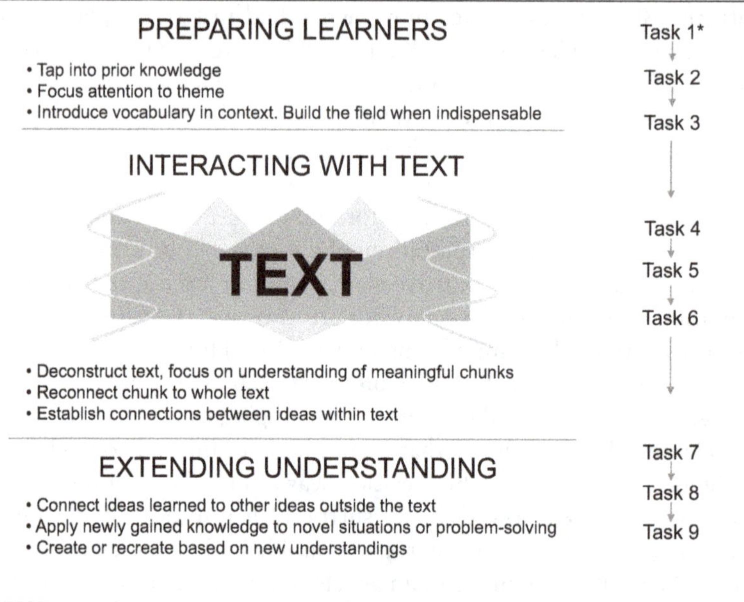

* The number of tasks in a lesson is contingent. It is based on teacher's dynamic observation of students' understanding and the support they need at the moment.

Focusing. A million things happen between one class period and another, and not all students are ready to start anew, picking up where the last class left off. To start the exploration of ideas when everybody is in a different mental space requires that teachers engage them all in an activity that focuses them in the same direction.

Activating Prior Knowledge or Building the Field. Learning in school entails building meaningful interconnections between what students know and that which will be explored in the new lesson. In addition, if students do not have relevant contextual knowledge where new ideas and processes may be anchored, then "building the field" becomes necessary to create the basic contextual understandings for students to make sense of novel ideas. For example, Chapter 6 outlines some building the field tasks that are needed for multilingual learners to read Langston Hughes's poem, "Theme for English B," with understanding. For this lesson, however, given the salience of protest in sports at the time, it was not necessary to Build the Field.

Focusing students' attention, activating their prior relevant knowledge, building the field, and introducing key terms in context are carried out through the implementation of interactive tasks intended to build students' potential beyond their current level of independent ability, in their zone of proximal development.

We will now discuss the tasks Ms. Glick designed and enacted to prepare her students to read Montague's "The Third Man: The Forgotten Black Power Hero."

Because the issues to be addressed in the article had to do with athletes taking a stand against injustice, Ms. Glick decided to begin her lesson with a topic that was polemic and present in her students' minds. She wanted her students to have the time to express their thoughts and feelings unencumbered by having to present them orally. She also knew that some students bureaucratically classified as Long-Term English Learners initially do not like to talk in class. To accomplish this first step, she chose an activity she calls Silent Graffiti. The task invited students, working in groups of four or five, to spend 2 minutes, each with a different color marker, silently and simultaneously writing down their reactions and questions on a big piece of paper, which at the center has Colin Kaepernick's picture. After studying the picture, all students in the team recorded their reactions, writing them down at the same time, and then proceeded to sign their reactions with their color marker. Then, Ms. Glick invited students to move around the table and, still silently, read their partners' thoughts and add their reactions and questions to the comments for the next 2 minutes. Because students had been asked to use the same color markers throughout the activity, it was easy to see what their initial thoughts were as well as their reactions to others' ideas. Students engaged in the task with high interest, as they read and responded to their classmates' reactions. Photo 3.1 shows students working through the activity and Photo 3.2 shows a product that emerged from these highly productive 4 minutes.

As a result of participating in Silent Graffiti, the class manifested their perspectives and focused on the themes that would be further unpacked during the lesson.

Ms. Glick focused on a second goal of Preparing Learners and decided to continue directing students' attention to developing meaningful connections. After students had a short time to discuss orally their similar or different reactions to the picture of Kaepernick, they were then invited to view another photograph engaging in a different task: Guided Reading of a Picture, which would get them closer to the Montague text at the center of the lesson. Students were directed to notice particular details in the iconic sports photograph (Photo 3.3) taken during the 1968 Olympic Games and showing three athletes at the podium: two African American runners and a White runner, who won second place.

Ms. Glick knew that the photograph would probably not be familiar to her students, since none of them had been alive at the time. But she intended for students to study the picture, notice details in it, and record

Photo 3.1. Students in Ms. Glick's Class Work on Silent Graffiti

Photo 3.2. Silent Graffiti Comments

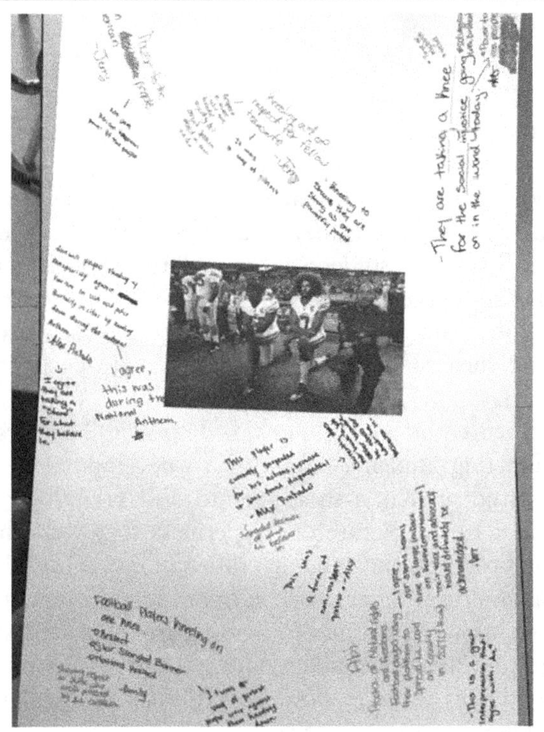

Photo 3.3. Olympic Award Ceremony

Table 3.1. An Iconic Photograph Notetaker

Take a couple of minutes to examine this photograph. Then jot down answers to the questions in the chart.	
What do you observe in the picture?	What do you know about this picture?
Personal questions: What questions do you have as you look at this picture?	
Other interesting questions my teammates asked:	

their responses to the first three questions posed: what they knew about the picture, what they noticed, and questions that the picture suggested to them. They then shared their answers orally in a Round Robin (a task that gives each student the floor to express the ideas they jotted down without being interrupted). When one student is done, the next one continues, acknowledging ideas already expressed and adding ideas they had not thought of to their Iconic Photograph Notetaker charts (Table 3.1).

A third goal of Preparing Learners has to do with the selective introduction of new terms that will be indispensable to understand to begin to make sense of a text or a concept. If this is necessary, the terms should be minimal in number (4 to 6) and introduced in meaningful contexts. Anticipatory Guides begin to focus students' attention to the theme at the heart of the lesson, without directly addressing the specific content of the text. In Ms. Glick's class, students were directed to watch a brief video showing the race (https://www.youtube.com/watch?v=bWI9raEM1-4) and to notice terms they may not have been familiar with. The terms and phrases that students tended to notice were *overshadow, gesture, raise their fists, symbolize, black socks represent Black poverty,* and *human rights*. As an added support, the video has English subtitles, which can be helpful for students among a variety of other meaning-making supports.

Together, the activities described here from the "Youth, Protest, and Change" lesson activate students' prior knowledge and build new knowledge, preparing them to critically read the article at the center of the lesson.

It is important to note, however, that the Preparing Learners tasks do not "pre-teach" ideas. These tasks are not mini-lessons that preview the content of the central lesson. In fact, students are directed to notice and form opinions. Affordances are offered learners to perceive, interpret, and use in further learning. Following important shifts in pedagogical orientation outlined in Chapter 2, Ms. Glick does not correct what her students notice, or their opinions, but she does dynamically track what interpretations or misconceptions come up in order to use that information to design ways of exploring these issues further throughout the lesson. Students themselves will then be invited to check their original understandings and whether, after having explored the lesson in its totality, they still agree with them or have changed their mind, indicating the reasons for their responses. Illustrating this point, the following exchange was recorded during a rich dialogue in Ms. Glick's class during the Round Robin:

Abi: This is not something I know, this is something I am inferring, there's still inequality because even though the guy in the middle is in a higher position, he's still behind the White guy, and the White guy is in third place. If the White guy is in third place, he should be standing behind the second Black guy, but regardless, he's still in first place, because he's the only White man there.

Amity: I agree with that. [nodding] Yeah, I see where you're coming from.

Eric: I agree with Abi that, it's also what I get from this picture is there's still going to be inequality, but as a unit, we'll still be able to take huge steps and achieve many things; this was one of the first ones that we took.

It is evident that the students at this point thought that in spite of coming in second in the race (there is confusion here because Abi mistakenly thought that he came in third), he stands in a more prominent place. All these confusions will be resolved by students themselves as they read the article at the center of this lesson. Throughout, they expand their understanding of the sacrifices social protest usually entails (which they had started working on in Lesson 1 of this unit, focused on the role of children in protest during the Civil Rights Movement and school desegregation in the 1960s).

Interacting With a Text, Concept, Problem, or Phenomenon

During this second Moment of the lesson, students are guided to (1) examine individual components (episodes) of a text to make sense of them; (2) reconnect them, linking them in meaningful clusters of understanding; and (3) develop critical and metacognitive stances as students. Tasks focus on students' gradually going through a text, exploring its meaning components, noticing—guided by teachers' invitations to engage in specific activity—aspects of text and content that are important to understand in terms of the destination of the lesson, and skipping others that may not be essential for the lesson objectives. Once again, proposed shifts in the nature of the work students are invited to carry out are evident. As students explore key pieces through sustained, critical, dialogic interaction, they establish conceptual interconnections, practice analytical thinking, and simultaneously, through constant dialogue with their peers, develop the English required to express their ongoing work. This work entails the learning of structure (triggered by teacher design and moves), rather than simply the limited mastery of discrete facts or techniques. As Bruner (1996) reminded us, to build new practices it is necessary that new learning be placed against a general picture already discussed and that students be invited to interweave connections between earlier and later understandings.

Earlier in this chapter we also discussed that pivotal to the success of a lesson is the careful and deliberate choice of a text or concept. Quality of texts matters; only a strong text can support a complex pedagogical architecture intended to engage both a wide variety of multilingual learners and more proficient speakers of English. Ms. Glick's chosen article tracks three athletes through acts of solidarity, punishment, and lasting friendship. Because Montague's text is rich, robust, and complex, the teacher has "engineered" it. She does not want to water it down, but she has divided the text into meaningful chunks and introduced a brief subtitle to each section that will alert students broadly, not specifically, to what they will be reading (see Figure 3.3).

Back in Ms. Glick's class, students were now invited to start reading the engineered article called "The Third Man: The Forgotten Black Power Hero" (Montague, 2012). To make sense of how the article portrays the three athletes a bit at a time, Ms. Glick asked her students to track what they were learning about the two American runners, Tommie Smith and John Carlos, and their Australian counterpart, Peter Norman, using a task called the Double-Entry Journal (Table 3.2). In groups of four, two students focus on the American runners, Smith and Carlos. The other two, as they read, track information about Peter Norman, the Australian runner who, to the American runners' surprise, won second place. This was not the first time the teacher had worked with Double-Entry Journals with her students, so she asked them to spend 5 minutes individually, reading the first two pages of the article, taking notes from the perspective of their assigned runner. After 5 minutes, dyads who read from the same perspective shared their notes, agreed on important information. Then, armed with their notes, groups of four students shared their information with each other. At the end of the interaction, they had all strengthened their understanding of the actions of the three athletes.

The Double-Entry Journal asks students to generalize characteristics of the men assigned in the left-hand side of the organizer (e.g., bold, self-assured, fast runner) and then to identify evidence that supported their generalizations. As students infer information that is not explicitly stated in the text, they share notes and reasoning, determining whether their conclusions are warranted. Each student in the group of four actively proposes ideas and ascertains whether the evidence offered supports their generalization or not. While each group of four students is actively engaged in dialogic sustained interaction, all students in the class are simultaneously active. In this class the teacher is not "teaching" from the front of the class, but she has provided students with opportunities to engage simultaneously, using emerging ideas, intellectual practices, and English to explore consequential issues together.

Once students were immersed in the reading of the article, the teacher asked them to read the next two sections working silently, adding anything of relevance to their Double-Entry Journals. After 5 minutes of busy silence, Ms. Glick conducted a brief discussion with the entire class on the ideas students were finding. Dyadic interaction restarted with the reading of the next section

Figure 3.3. Excerpt From Engineered Text—Adaptation of "The Third Man: The Forgotten Black Power Hero"

a raft of **prejudicial** laws against its **indigenous** aboriginal population, including a policy of taking Aboriginal children from their birth parents and handing them to white couples for adoption, a practice that continued until the 1970s.

Unexpected threat

Although Norman was a **staunch** anti-racism advocate, no one expected him to take a stand in Mexico. The Australian Olympic Committee had laid out just three rules for him to follow. The first was to repeat his qualification time before the Games.

"Rule number two: don't finish last in any round," Norman recalled.

"Third, and under no circumstances, don't get beaten by a Pom (a British runner)."

Norman had previously been ignored by the U.S. team, who had assumed they'd win a clean sweep of medals in the 200 meters, but he burst on to their radar when he broke the Olympic record in one of the early heats.

"When I first saw Peter, I said, 'Who's this little white guy?'" Carlos told CNN.

He would soon regret the oversight. When the 200 meters final arrived, all eyes were on the U.S. duo. Smith was expected to win easily ("You wouldn't be able to catch him on a motorbike," was Norman's assessment) but the speculation centered on what political gesture the American athletes might make on the podium.

The starting pistol was fired and Smith powered to gold. But out of nowhere Norman stormed down the last 50 meters, taking the line before a shocked Carlos. Norman's time of 20 seconds flat would have won gold four years later at the Munich Olympics and at the Sydney Games in 2000.

A fateful decision

Smith and Carlos had already decided to make a statement on the podium. They were to wear black gloves. But Carlos left his at the Olympic village. It was Norman who suggested they should wear one each on alternate hands. Yet Norman had no means of making a protest of his own. So he asked a member of the U.S. rowing team for his "Olympic Project for Human Rights" badge, so that he could show solidarity.

"He came up to me and said, 'Have you got one of those buttons, mate,'" said U.S. rower Paul Hoffman. "If a white Australian is going to ask me for an Olympic Project for Human

notes

prejudicial: Showing an unfair feeling of dislike for a person or group because of race, sex, religion

indigenous: The original people born to a particular place, native

staunch: Very devoted to a cause

Source: Montague, 2012.

Table 3.2. Double-Entry Journal

What do you learn about Tommie Smith and John Carlos from what you read in the next pages?	Supporting quotes from the text
What do you learn about Peter Norman from what you read in the next pages?	**Supporting quotes from the text**

she had labeled through her chunking of the text, A Fateful Decision. Ms. Glick had determined that this was going to be a difficult section to understand because it refers to what happened to the Australian runner, Peter Norman, when he was unexpectedly flown back to Australia. To assist students in their work through the text, she invited them to use the Clarifying Bookmark.

The Clarifying Bookmark, a metacognitive activity, provides students with six strategies they may use as they work on making sense of complex written text (see Table 3.3). It assumes that multilingual learners are bound to have questions and not understand specific terms, and it helps them express those difficulties. As the Clarifying Bookmark is used in a course, students are introduced to two of these strategies at a time. Later on, two more are added as students appropriate the ones that they have practiced several times, until all strategies are used. In this class, Ms. Glick practiced for the second time the use of all six strategies at once. Working in dyads and taking turns, her students each read a paragraph at a time, pausing to consider which one of the strategies may be more appropriate for them to explore sections of the paragraph they just read aloud (and others already read) that they needed to clarify. The student announces which strategy they are going to use and then explores the passage. On the right-hand side of the bookmark there are three formulaic expressions from which students can choose, if needed, to initiate their discussion of text. Dyads engage in the activity working together for the next four paragraphs.

Table 3.3. Clarifying Bookmark

Clarifying Bookmark 1	
What you can do	**What you can say**
Think about what the selected text may mean.	*I'm not sure what this is about, but I think it may mean . . .*
	This part is tricky, but I think it may mean . . .
	After rereading this part, I think it may mean . . .
Summarize your understanding every so often.	*What I understand about this reading so far is . . .*
	I can summarize this part by saying . . .
	The main points of this section are . . .
Clarifying Bookmark 2	
What you can do	**What you can say**
Use your prior knowledge to help you understand.	*I know something about this from . . .*
	I have read or heard about this when . . .
	I don't understand the section, but I do recognize . . .
Apply related concepts and/or readings.	*One reading/idea I have encountered before that relates to this is . . .*
	We learned about this idea/concept when we studied . . .
	This concept/idea is related to . . .
Clarifying Bookmark 3	
What you can do	**What you can say**
Ask questions about ideas and phrases you don't understand.	*Two questions I have about this section are . . .*
	I understand this part, but I have a question about . . .
	I have a question about . . .
Use related text, pictures, tables, and graphs to help you understand unclear ideas.	*If we look at this graphic, it shows . . .*
	The table gives me more information about . . .
	When I scanned the earlier part of the chapter, I found . . .

Source: Walqui, 2008.

Formulaic expressions are different from sentence frames, which are basically fill-in-the-blanks activities. Formulaic expressions are phrases that are typically used time and time again in academic engagements and mark beginnings or transitions between ideas; thus, they are immensely useful for multilingual learners as well as for English-only students (Walqui & Heritage, 2018). Ellis (2005) discusses formulaic expressions as generative phrases that introduce a type of relationship or comment. They are learned by students as unanalyzed chunks, almost as one word, and only later on, as the students learn more English, they begin to realize it is formed by several words.

We include a transcript of one of several interactions students engaged in during the "Youth, Protest, and Change" lesson (Photo 3.4):

Carmen: [Reading text under A Fateful Decision; Looking at the Clarifying Bookmark] What I can do, I'm going to apply related concepts. One idea I have a concept for that relates to this is the photo where it shows that it's obvious that Smith and Carlos are wearing black gloves for Black power. I also can now answer one of my questions from yesterday: Why is one guy raising his right arm and the other one the left arm?

Maria: I agree with that. Also in the previous lesson when we looked at the photo, and it didn't really show that—it wasn't obvious that Norman was part of the act. Okay. [Reading text] So [looking at the Clarifying Bookmark], what I can do is I can summarize my understanding. My understanding of this is that during this time period when the Olympics took place, segregation still had its toll and people were still agreeing with it. So when people made this movement, they weren't really supportive of it, and they were probably more surprised than anything, that's why they were quiet.

Photo 3.4. Using the Clarifying Bookmark

Carmen: I agree with what you're saying because segregation was at its highest at that time, because why is it when someone decides to speak out and fight for what they think is right, no one else has anything to say and stand up with them. Like, leaving them out on their own.

Ms. Glick carefully listened to see how students themselves were gradually changing their original opinions. She took notes to remind herself of what she needed to keep in mind to provide students with further opportunities to arrive at their own understanding about protest, the individual costs of taking a stance, and human solidarity, all of them immensely important themes for their current and future lives as immigrant students in the United States.

The examples also indicate that no ideas are discussed in isolation. In Ms. Glick's class, as should be the case in any class with English Learners, chunks of text are discussed to then be interwoven into larger networks of understanding.

Extending Understanding

The third Moment, Extending Understanding, is the part of the lesson where students, having completed the examination of a text or sets of texts, connect their new understandings to ideas beyond the lesson to form increasingly complex and generative understandings and reach the preset objective for the lesson. It invites students to apply their knowledge—both longstanding (sometimes corrected) and new—and involves them in participating in new tasks that enhance newly developed practices. For example, they produce new texts (which may be written or multimodal), conduct research on the topic that has become enticing to them, engage in debates where teachers assign what position to take and prepare for, and in general expand their understanding of ideas, processes, and language learned in the lesson to another context. Inequality, power, protest, and the need to engage in change will always be themes that ignite students' interests and are thus especially appropriate for multilingual learners.

When students complete their reading of the central article in Lesson 2, Ms. Glick's lesson is not done. She wants her students to make connections. She has designed tasks that ask students to draw on one page a Compare/Contrast organizer (Table 3.4) that now links the first text in the lesson, Kaepernick's photograph, to what they learned through the reading of "The Third Man: The Forgotten Black Power Hero." Students' focus is directed to key dimensions of the two athletes that they will have to address in their writing.

Ms. Glick tells her students, "In preparation to write a short essay, I want you to compare the two athletes at the center of our lesson. Although

Table 3.4. Compare/Contrast Organizer

	Peter Norman	Colin Kaepernick
Who are they?		
What did they do? Why?		
What were the consequences of their actions?		
Comments		

Norman's and Kaepernick's protest happened decades apart, there are some similarities and differences in their behavior. Outlining your ideas in the chart will be immensely useful when you write your essay."

Then, before students are invited to connect their newly developed understandings to other lessons, using other texts, they are directed to first discuss and then write about acts of heroism. Building on the readings and discussions carried out in class, groups of students come up with definitions of what makes an act heroic and when a person merits the label "hero." Students are then invited to write about someone they know about who engaged in a heroic act or merits being called a hero. At the request of one student in Ms. Glick's class, the writing included another option, presenting the case of someone who has been called a hero but does not deserve the name. Finally, for this lesson, students are invited to assess orally the development of their own understanding, taking turns in their groups of four. The following reflection comes from Abi, a young woman from Eritrea in Ms. Glick's class:

> Originally when I saw this picture, I thought that, um, that Carlos and Smith originally were on one team and they were working together and knew how they were going to do and, um, Norman was just there because he was receiving his award. I also originally thought that he had something against them because he didn't look, and from my thinking I just didn't think he didn't look happy to be there supporting them. I also thought he was repping team USA like I really didn't get into detail with the picture, I didn't think they were on one team together.

> After reading the article I realized that Norman was actually working with Smith and Carlos, not only supported them, but actually gave them ideas and had repercussions for the rest of his life, all represented in this simple picture.

Figure 3.2 outlines our discussion of the Three Moments Architecture of a lesson and the purposes each Moment accomplishes. An important note that needs to be made here is that each Moment does not necessarily contain three tasks, nor should each Moment take the same amount of time. In fact, a rule of thumb we offer teachers when we work with them is that a good proportion for Moments in a lesson is that about 20% of the time be spent in Preparing Learners, 50% Interacting with Text, and 30% in Extending Understanding (homework counts here, as in continuing the writing of an essay initiated in class). This is just a guideline, one that can be overruled by the need to respond to student needs as they emerge.

FOCUS ON LANGUAGE

The unit comprising the lesson discussed above embodies a very important shift, that of understanding language as an entity that needs to be decomposed into its parts (grammar, lexis, etc.), to viewing language as a tool that enables human beings to act in the world, as action. Our lesson design includes opportunities to focus on language use as students are reading or listening to text. This focus centers students' attention on the larger elements of language: the types of ideas discussed in a text, the specific terminology used to create diverse impressions in readers or listeners, and the claims and counterclaims presented in a text. The following three tasks designed by Ms. Glick take us to Lesson 3 of the *Power, Protest, and Change* unit. This lesson invites students to learn about young people around the world who have taken a stand to protest injustices that surround them. One of these youngsters is Nobel Peace prize winner Malala Yousafzai. First, students are asked to read a speech Yousafzai gave to a youth group convened by the United Nations. As students read the text, working in dyads or in groups of four, they discuss the ideas presented and fill out the chart shown in Table 3.5. The activity invites students to reread the text with a purpose, not to look for words in isolation, but to make sense of key ideas in the speech and how they are presented and elaborated throughout.

The next task is designed so that students focus their attention on key aspects of language as they construct meaning from the text. Called Becoming a Language Detective (Table 3.6), this task invites multilingual

Table 3.5. Idea Hunt Matrix

Find three rights that Malala believes all people should have.
Find three challenges Malala and other young people have had to face.
Find three requests Malala makes in her speech.

learners to determine what in the text is essential and how clues construct an explanation. Just as not all clues are of equal importance for a detective, not all words are essential for a reader. This activity guides them to what constitutes the core of the text.

A third activity from the same lesson invites students, this time as they read the speech that Malala gave to the United Nations General Assembly—symbolically wearing the shawl Benazir Bhutto was wearing when she was assassinated—to focus on the claims and counterclaims that she identifies to strengthen her position (see Table 3.7).

Ms. Glick decided that her students were now ready to build their own essay because they had worked through the language of these two remarkable speeches written by a teenager. In three consecutive lessons lasting 3 weeks, they had also explored children's participation in the desegregation of schools in the South of the United States, examined the White "Black" hero's story with contemporary relevance, and studied youth protest in other parts of the world.

THE SPIRALED UNIT

Complexity, as we discussed earlier, emerges when increasing connections are drawn across components of a larger idea. That connecting activity provides students with depth of understanding and generativity, the possibility of extending those meaningful links and uses throughout their lives.

Table 3.6. Becoming a Language Detective

Determining Authors' Tone

Authors who support the topic of their writing choose language that has positive connotations, meaning the words suggest approval. Authors who are upset about the topic of their writing choose language that has negative connotations, meaning the words suggest disapproval or even outrage. When most of the language suggests approval, we say the tone is positive. When most of the language suggests disapproval, we say the tone is negative.

Directions

Read each of the sentences below and identify how words convey either a positive or negative tone. Write those words in the corresponding columns, and provide an explanation for your choice. Then complete the bottom portion of the chart, deciding whether the overall tone of the text is positive or negative. Provide evidence for your choice.

Language from Malala Yousafzai's Speech at the Youth Takeover of the United Nations	Examples of Language Used to Suggest a Positive Tone	Examples of Language Used to Suggest a Negative Tone	Explanation for Choice
1. I raise up my voice—not so that I can shout, but so that those without a voice can be heard.			
2. Today is the day of every woman, every boy and girl who have raised their voice for their rights.			
3. One child, one teacher, one pen, and one book can change the world.			
4. We call upon the world leaders that all the peace deals must protect women's rights. A deal that goes against the dignity of women and their rights is unacceptable.			
Decide whether the overall tone is positive or negative and provide an explanation. Overall the tone of the text is ________________ because			

Table 3.7. Claims and Counterclaims

One claim Malala makes in speech:	One counterclaim she identifies in speech (What do her enemies think or believe?):
Three pieces of evidence from speech she uses to support her claim:	One way Malala refutes the counterclaim ("But . . ."). If she doesn't refute it, write something she could have said to refute the counterclaim:
Evidence 1:	Rebuttal (How does Malala respond to the beliefs of her enemies?):
Evidence 2:	
Evidence 3:	

The lesson described in this chapter is the second in a larger unit (Figure 3.1) that Yael Glick designed to invite her students to explore the power of youth protest in creating change and the costs of protest. (We also discussed some tasks that focus on language in Lesson 3.)

The first lesson has the goal of engaging students in the exploration of the role children played in the desegregation of schools in the South. Many varied and compelling texts (oral, visual, written, and multimodal) are used by students to make issues of segregation relevant and compelling. While these written texts are not easy to read, students are provided with a wide variety of tools to work effectively through them. By the time they have to write an essay at the end of the second lesson, Ms. Glick's students write about the bravery of children who were willing to sacrifice their security in service of a larger ideal as they attended schools that did not want them. The third lesson has students explore similar issues in other parts of the world. When Ms. Glick's students read about Malala Yousafzai, they already have deep understandings about injustice and the power of being upstanders instead of bystanders (terms they have used time and time again in Lesson 1).

In a spiraled unit, when is the time to focus on isolated ideas and the words that represent them? That comes after students have made sense of larger ideas, how they played out in history and are still relevant today. Only then should the teacher check that all students are clear about the meaning of pivotal words that have appeared throughout the lesson, and after students have used new terms time and time again with increasing understanding.

Before proceeding, it is important to note that good units are never "finished." For example, the second time Ms. Glick taught the lesson, students were interested in finding out about the situation in Australia that Peter Norman, the runner in the Olympic games that is at the center of Montague's essay, was reacting to. A fourth lesson was designed to explore the situation of minoritized Bushmen in Australia. This enabled the exploration of cross-cutting themes, such as the search for societal change, forms of oppression, and resistance through four interrelated lessons.

In this chapter, we have discussed how, with the destination in mind, well-designed lessons take students by the hand to lead them along a road where they increasingly take the responsibility for their journey. We have also illustrated how a classroom full of affordances provides students with opportunities to learn, revise their learning, extend it, amend it, and, in the end, own it. We close the chapter by acknowledging some of the challenges that teachers may face in designing such learning opportunities, and how these challenges can be addressed.

CHALLENGES OF DESIGNING POWERFUL LESSONS

Multiple challenges face teachers engaging in the design or redesign of well-crafted lessons. For example, sometimes teachers say they lack subject-matter knowledge to be able to locate good texts, or to decide what is more important and what is less so. Subject-matter knowledge is deepened in the process of searching for materials, in listening to our own internal voices react to the reading of certain texts: "Do I find it compelling? Use it then! Do I find it boring? Then don't use it. The text is very complex? Engineer it! That is, chunk it into its meaningful components, introducing subheadings that alert students but do not tell them what they are going to read. The text is too long? Chunk it and focus the lesson only on the most important parts." Each of these design dilemmas has a design answer, and teachers can, with guidance and over time, become more confident in their own assessment of the intellectual merit and potential challenges associated with focal texts, ideas, and problems.

A second and related concern is teachers' lack of knowledge about language, which in teachers' minds impedes their ability to design lessons for multilingual learners. Galguera (2011) introduced the concept Pedagogical Language Knowledge, which means that teachers need to be aware of the language they use to carry out disciplinary work (see also Bunch, 2013). We call this domain of teacher understanding Pedagogical Disciplinary

Language Knowledge, to emphasize the situated nature of language use (e.g., the way in which mathematicians talk about problems is not the same way in which historians express them). Teachers do not need to be linguists, nor do they need to know how to describe verb conjugations, nominalization, and so on. Rather, they need to know how to use English to carry out activities in their discipline, and they need to gain awareness of what they say as they engage in the doing of their discipline. Once they are conscious of the way language is used in their disciplines, they can give their students options, using, for example, formulaic expressions, alerting them to the relationships connectors introduce, or working on how different types of texts are organized.

A third concern teachers express is the unavailability of time for designing lessons and collaborating in school. Ideally, school leaders understand the immense value of providing teachers who teach the same course with time to work together crafting lessons they will teach and then refine. This investment of time pays huge benefits if the time is indeed used for planning and discussing results to decide where to go next. If this is the case, the returns are high, both in terms of student engagement and learning, and in terms of strengthening and advancing teacher expertise, as well as everybody's civic participation. Even if the value of this investment is not acknowledged in a school, then teachers' personal investment of time to collaborate with peers will still render great results. Once a lesson or unit has been designed and then refined after implementation, it will be a good tool to use for many years.

A fourth and more intractable challenge includes the existence of mandated curricula in schools or districts where no adaptations are allowed by the administration. Similarly, mandated pacing guides that cannot be altered become prisons for students, with devastating consequences for student learning and the quality of schooling multilingual learners receive.

We believe that the answer lies in convincing educators that amplified, not simplified, lessons will engage all students, multilingual learners, and native speakers of English. Amplified lessons entail what we have discussed throughout the chapter: offering students rich semiotic budgets, multiple tools, and opportunities to notice and use for the benefit of their own learning. Not all students will use the opportunities afforded in the same way, but they will all advance, learn, and reach in different ways the goals of a well-crafted lesson. The following chapters in this book illustrate, in more detail, how to design amplified curricula in specific disciplinary areas. Then, in Chapter 11, we will explore the voices of teachers and students from classrooms that featured amplified learning designs for multilingual learners to unpack challenges, successes, and to reaffirm their potential.

REFERENCES

Bruner, J. (1960). *The process of education.* Harvard University Press.

Bruner, J. (1996). *The culture of education.* Harvard University Press.

Bunch, G. C. (2013). Pedagogical language knowledge: Preparing mainstream teachers for English learners in the new standards era. *Review of Research in Education, 37*, 298–341.

Ellis, R. (2005). *Instructed second language acquisition. A literature review.* New Zealand Ministry of Education.

Galguera, T. (2011). Participant structures as professional learning tasks and the development of pedagogical language knowledge among preservice teachers. *Teacher Education Quarterly, 38*(1), 85–106.

Glick, Y., & Walqui, A. (2021). Affordances in the development of student voice and agency: The case of bureaucratically labeled long-term English Learners. In A. Kibler, G. Valdés, & A. Walqui (Eds.), *Reconceptualizing the role of critical dialogue in American classrooms* (pp. 23–51). Routledge.

Montague, J. (2012, April 25). The third man: The forgotten Black Power hero. *CNN.* https://www.cnn.com/2012/04/24/sport/olympics-norman-black-power/index.html

Valdés, G. (2018, March). *What's in a name?* [Paper presentation]. 2018 annual meeting of the American Association for Applied Linguistics, Chicago, IL.

van Lier, L. (2000). From input to affordance: Social-interactive learning from an ecological perspective. In J. P. Lantolf (Ed.), *Sociocultural theory and second language learning* (pp. 155–177). Oxford University Press.

van Lier, L. (2004). *The ecology and semiotics of language learning: A sociocultural perspective.* Kluwer Academic.

Walqui, A. (2008). *Brain injury lesson.* WestEd.

Walqui, A. (2024). The role of curriculum in the development of teacher expertise to enact critical dialogic education. In F. J. Karam & A. K. Kibler (Eds.), *Critical dialogic TESOL teacher education: Preparing future advocates and supporters of multilingual learners* (pp. 23–44). Bloomsbury Academic.

Walqui, A., & Heritage, M. (2018, Fall). *Meaningful classroom talk: Supporting English Learners' oral language development.* American Educator.

Part II

PORTRAITS OF AMPLIFICATION ACROSS THE CURRICULUM

CHAPTER 4

Walking With Vanessa

Designing Quality Learning for Elementary Multilingual Learners

Lyn Westergard

Envision a 1st-grade classroom where young learners are absorbed in a language arts lesson, collaboratively working in groups, and critically discussing the motives and actions of a story character. Students are sharing their ideas, listening to one another, and working together to create an image. They are working on a task that requires them to create a novel scene that was not in the story, where the main characters solve new problems. This classroom is a space where dialogue is encouraged and every voice is heard. Students are eagerly talking, drawing, and coconstructing meaning. As a group, they represent many different linguistic backgrounds and various states of language development, and they are effectively navigating through language and literacy tasks that are intentionally scaffolded to support each student as they engage with rigorous key concepts that are connected to their lived experiences.

This type of interaction is not only possible, even at the earliest grades, but it is also an essential part of effective pedagogy for elementary-aged multilingual learners. Through structured activities that are intentionally designed to build on students' prior knowledge, engage them in critical thinking, and extend their understanding, students' confidence, joy, and content knowledge are all strengthened, along with their autonomy as learners. This approach is facilitated by the Lesson in Three Moments Architecture that, as described in Chapter 3, provides a coherent and dynamic structure for each Moment of the lesson.

In this chapter, I focus on how quality learning experiences can be designed for elementary multilingual learners by prioritizing meaning, enhancing oracy development, and fostering learner autonomy. The chapter discusses essential literacy practices for elementary-aged students and then dives into an exemplar lesson that illustrates these practices. This exemplar lesson is designed for first grade students, but the tasks of the lesson can be adapted for any elementary grade, and I offer ways to modify the tasks for various ages and grade levels. The lesson is centered around a wordless book. Wordless books that contain rich and complex themes offer opportunities for young students, who are still developing the ability to read and write, to engage in meaningful literacy and oracy practices. Wordless books are beneficial for literacy development because they offer opportunities for students to bring their lived experiences to the forefront, create their own meaning, and engage in creativity and critical thinking. These texts invite students to interpret illustrations, fostering visual literacy and inferential thinking, which are key in literacy development. To highlight these key ideas, I designed this lesson in collaboration with some QTEL colleagues to offer elementary educators a vision for quality literacy practices for multilingual learners. This lesson serves as an exemplar lesson to highlight the many ways young learners can independently engage in meaningful literacy practices.

THREE ESSENTIAL SHIFTS FOR ELEMENTARY MULTILINGUAL LEARNERS

Elementary teachers are increasingly recognizing and valuing the community cultural wealth that multilingual learners bring into the classroom (Yosso, 2005). As described in Chapter 1, this wealth encompasses the rich linguistic diversity and cultural practices that students gain from their homes and communities, and which constitute vital contributions to their educational experience. Recognizing that young learners already possess a great deal of community cultural wealth, often underestimated in early education, is pivotal for contemporary teaching practices. Elementary-aged students bring these cultural and linguistic assets from their homes and communities, assets that are not merely in stages of development but that are already fully formed and influential. By understanding and integrating this existing wealth within the elementary classroom, educators can not only enrich the learning environment but also foster an inclusive educational setting where the diverse backgrounds of young learners are acknowledged as immediate and foundational for their educational journey. This approach necessitates three key pedagogical shifts:

1. The need to *prioritize meaning* in lessons, stepping away from rote, skill-based tasks and moving toward engaging students in learning that is meaningful and contextually rich.
2. The need to *enhance oracy*, recognizing its vital role in the conceptual development of content area knowledge, as well as in social action and critical dialogical education.

3. The need to *foster autonomy* among learners, through scaffolding and modeling tasks and activities that enable them to explore and understand new texts and new ideas.

These shifts are not merely a trend but also an essential response to the complexities and strengths multilingual learners bring to their educational experiences; when instruction is responsive, students' learning is deepened and their contributions magnified. The first shift emphasizes the transition from isolated, skill-based instruction toward a learning environment in which meaning and purpose are at the heart of educational activities. This approach recognizes that when students find relevance and their learning is contextualized, they are more engaged and better able to appropriate and apply new knowledge. The second shift underscores oracy's significant role in developing critical thinking and understanding. Through critical dialogic education, students engage in conversations that both develop and deepen their content knowledge and allow them to explore complex ideas, fostering their ability to grasp profound concepts. The third shift focuses on providing students with opportunities to engage in complex tasks that are scaffolded in ways that encourage them to question, problem solve, and think critically. This is crucial for nurturing resilient and adaptable learners who are capable of approaching new texts and new learning with academic confidence. All of these shifts are made possible through the use of the Three Moment Architecture. Each Moment of a lesson provides opportunities where these shifts can be enacted, thereby creating a lesson that is amplified, rather than simplified, in the elementary classroom.

Prioritizing Meaning: Expanding Lessons Beyond Skill-Based Learning

In the elementary classroom, especially in the early grades, there is currently an increasing focus on "foundational" literacy skills, including concepts of print, phonological awareness, phonics, and word recognition. These skills are often thought of as being essential building blocks for developing literacy, providing the groundwork for more advanced literacy skills. In fact, while their communicative skills are emerging, young learners can engage with peers and navigate the challenges of a diverse and interconnected world. Indeed, if young learners are provided with learning experiences that scaffold their conceptual development, literacy, and language, they are capable of meaningful interaction with their environment and can contribute to complex discussions.

While traditional literacy skills are undeniably important, it may be more accurate to view them not as foundational in the conventional sense of being required before anything else can develop, but rather as parallel to other vital competencies such as critical thinking and content comprehension. These abilities are often minimized in early education, but they are equally crucial for holistic educational development. It may be more fitting to refer to these "foundational" skills collectively as "early literacy skills" to reflect their broad scope and impact. Early literacy skills and conceptual development of critical thinking complement and enhance one another, contributing to a more robust learning experience. Quality instruction for multilingual learners occurs when early literacy skills are interwoven with a meaningful and relevant context. This larger context entails the inclusion of rich themes that draw on the human experience. Skills such as phonemic awareness, phonics, fluency, decoding, encoding, vocabulary development, just to name a few, are most effectively taught when integrated within meaningful literacy experiences, rather than in isolation, enabling students to see their immediate relevance and application.

While early literacy skills can be situated in a larger context, the same is true for basic comprehension skills. A focus on comprehension is essential in the elementary classroom and can serve as a bridge to the centrality of meaning. While comprehension involves *understanding* the content that is read or heard, meaning transcends comprehension by *connecting* the content to broader human experiences and providing an application of learning. It is through engaging with the deeper meaning that learners can make connections and build new ideas. Meaning allows for the integration of personal experiences, fostering a richer learning experience. Comprehension is an essential component to this process, but the focus on meaning ensures learning is not just about grasping facts or retelling a text, but about understanding their significance and relevance in a wider context.

For example, in an early literacy lesson, there may be a focus on the comprehension of the story: identifying the characters, the setting, the main events of a story. In addition to this comprehension focus, there can also be a focus on meaning, where students extend their comprehension by making personal connections to the larger themes in the story. Ultimately, finding the meaning of the story involves interweaving conceptual development and analytical practices with the readers' own experiences and unique perspectives.

Understanding the meaning of a story and its broader themes is essential for all learners, and it is important to note that the approach to achieving this understanding can differ between monolingual and multilingual students. The connection between meaning, comprehension, and metalinguistic awareness (the ability to analyze, think about, and manipulate language) has been well documented (Zipke, 2021). This awareness is particularly crucial for multilingual learners, who are navigating meaning across multiple languages. The traditional "one size fits all" approach to literacy development found in most curricula fails to account for the unique conceptual and linguistic capabilities of multilingual students, particularly in the realm of metalinguistic awareness. Metalinguistic awareness plays a pivotal role in literacy development. Take phonemic awareness, for example: For multilingual learners, phonemic awareness is not just about hearing and manipulating sounds, but also about *transferring* phonemic knowledge from their home language to a new language. This transfer can significantly enhance their learning process, as prior knowledge of phonemic structures can facilitate the acquisition of similar structures in the second language (Pollard-Durodola & Simmons, 2009). However, for this transfer to be effective, instruction must be explicitly designed to help students make connections between the languages. This type of targeted instruction is unnecessary for monolingual students, who typically develop phonemic awareness with a focus solely on their primary language, but it is crucial for young multilingual learners who are navigating two or more languages.

Fostering metalinguistic awareness not only aids in literacy development but also deepens students' engagement with textual meaning, allowing them to draw richer connections between their linguistic knowledge and the content they encounter. This integrative approach is effectively supported by the Three Moments Architecture of a lesson, which structures lessons to build on prior knowledge, engage in critical thinking, and extend understanding. By embedding metalinguistic practices within this approach, educators can create dynamic and meaningful literacy experiences that enhance comprehension and meaning-making for all learners.

Enhancing Language in Action: Capitalizing on Oracy's Role in Conceptual Development

In the elementary classroom, oracy plays a crucial role in developing students' conceptual understandings, analytical thinking, and language practices, thereby integrating speaking and listening skills with disciplinary practices. Oracy, which emphasizes the development of speaking and listening skills (Wilkinson, 1965), is distinct from oral language, which can include any form of spoken communication, as oracy implies an intentionality in speaking and listening for content-specific purposes. In the context of elementary education, the development of oracy is crucial. It allows young learners to articulate their thoughts, engage with complex ideas, and enhance their cognitive capabilities (Mercer & Littleton, 2007). Mercer and Littleton (2007) emphasize the role of talk in the coconstruction of knowledge, suggesting that through oracy, students negotiate meaning and build understanding collaboratively.

Oracy is also fundamental to critical dialogic education, a pedagogy that invites students to coconstruct meaning and engage with multiple perspectives, including opportunities to explore and challenge power dynamics. In the elementary classroom this may involve encouraging students to explore the "whys" and reflect on the reasons behind events and actions, as well as to participate in discussions that involve topics such as fairness, justice, and kindness. The focal lesson in this chapter, "Walking With Vanessa," provides an example of a lesson that invites elementary-aged students to engage in the type of critical dialogical education mentioned in Chapter 1. That dialogue encourages students to question and discuss the social structures around them and explore the systems of power and privilege in which they are situated. The lesson focuses on a story that shares the experiences of a young girl who sees a classmate being treated unfairly and decides to take action. This is a topic that every young learner can relate to in some way.

The principles of critical dialogic education suggest that oracy should be fostered in a manner that encourages critical thinking and reflection. This aligns with Philipson and Wegerif's (2017) perspective that dialogic education is not simply about talking more in the classroom; it is about talking better and learning how to engage in dialogue to increase conceptual understanding. Engaging in meaningful dialogue requires students to coconstruct meaning, responding to authentic and relevant questions, while at the same time having active and agentic roles (Lefstein & Snell, 2013). In elementary classrooms, incorporating critical dialogic education means creating an environment where students' oracy skills are developed in the service of exploring and understanding the world. This includes learning to use language to question, to reason, and to persuade. Kibler et al. (2021) argue for the importance of dialogue in learning processes and suggest that dialogue is not merely about the exchange of information but is also essential in the formation of students' identities and cognitive growth. As such, the focus on oracy in the elementary classroom should be twofold: (1) advancing students' linguistic ability to engage in discourse and (2) fostering the critical and reflective use of language to deepen their conceptual understanding. The development of oracy supports not only language growth but also the broader educational goals of critical thinking and understanding, laying the foundation for students to become effective communicators, thoughtful learners, and productive global citizens.

Utilizing the lesson in Three Moments Architecture cultivates a classroom environment that prioritizes critical dialogue and reflection within each Moment in the lesson. To actualize a focus on critical pedagogy, we must perceive all students as capable of deep understanding and recognize that their awareness of ideas such as justice and fairness can be channeled into powerful educational experiences. Through this proleptic lens, teaching becomes a practice of freedom, empowering young students to participate in their education as active agents from the very beginning. This approach not only respects the inherent potential within each child but also plants the seeds for a lifelong commitment to equity and social justice.

Fostering Autonomy: Developing Independent Learners

Fostering autonomy in elementary-aged students is crucial for their development as independent, self-motivated learners who can navigate and contribute to an ever-changing world. Students can gain autonomy when the teacher draws on students' inner motivation and resources and provides learning opportunities where students are actively engaged in their own learning (Reeve, 2006). The act of scaffolding supports evolving student autonomy, as it involves providing supportive structures to guide students toward greater independence (van Lier, 1996). Scaffolding is intended to be temporary; as students' competencies increase, the supports are gradually removed, fostering their ability to learn autonomously. Walqui (2006) emphasizes that effective scaffolding requires a keen understanding of each learner's current abilities and challenges, ensuring that the support provided in a lesson aligns with their immediate developmental needs. It is through this teacher observation where in-the-moment adjustments are made, thus facilitating the development of students' autonomy.

In the context of the Three Moments Architecture, it is crucial to integrate opportunities for students to become autonomous learners within the lesson framework. This approach not only scaffolds learning but also contingently removes supports when they are no longer needed and encourages independence. For elementary-aged students, this involves creating an environment where students can make choices about their learning paths and engage in decision-making processes that impact them. When students are encouraged to make choices and take an active role in their learning, they become more motivated and invested in the process, which reinforces their sense of independence and self-efficacy. By embedding opportunities for autonomy within the focal lesson using the Three Moments Architecture, we recognize and leverage the capacity of young learners to contribute to their own development in meaningful ways.

LESSON DESIGN EXEMPLIFYING HIGH-QUALITY INSTRUCTION FOR MULTILINGUAL LEARNERS IN ELEMENTARY GRADES

This section illustrates how these three pedagogical shifts can be enacted in a 1st-grade classroom using the focal lesson "Walking With Vanessa." This

Table 4.1. Disciplinary Practices of the Lesson "Walking With Vanessa"

Conceptual Understandings	Analytic Practices	Language Practices
• Recognize that story elements work together to create a complete story for the reader. • Understand that authors have a reason or purpose for creating a story, and that their message can be uncovered by the reader. • Understand the concepts of allyship and friendship, and explore ways of responding to unfair situations.	• Analyze illustrations to describe the characters, settings, and events. • Identify cause and effect by determining how characters' actions influence events in a story.	• Use the language of retell and recount when putting story images in order. • Practice taking turns during discussions by building on the ideas of others, working to create multiple exchanges with a partner. • Use sequential language when describing the events of a story.

lesson uses the wordless picture book *I Walk With Vanessa* by Kerascoët to explore social justice–related themes including allyship, fairness, and friendship. This lesson is part of a 1st grade integrated social studies and English Language Arts unit *Building a Caring Community*. It is the initial lesson in a three-part series focused on recognizing and responding to unfair situations, practicing kindness, and taking collective action to create and build a supportive community.

In this story, a new girl arrives at school and is immediately bullied by a classmate. Another girl notices the bullying and decides to take action. She decides to walk to school with the new girl, gathering new friends along the way. By the time they arrive at school, they have a large group of students walking together in an act of solidarity, leaving the bully isolated. This lesson explores key themes about fairness and kindness while simultaneously developing disciplinary practices. Table 4.1 shows the disciplinary practices of the lesson.

The lesson "Walking With Vanessa" uses the Three Moments Architecture to invite students to engage in a series of collaborative tasks to deepen their literacy skills, all within the context of the story and the rich social justice themes it presents. Aligned with the lesson in Three Moments Architecture introduced in Chapter 3, Table 4.2 outlines the sequence of tasks that have been intentionally designed to build on one another to provide purposeful opportunities for students to deeply engage with the key

Table 4.2. Three Moments Lesson Architecture of "Walking With Vanessa"

Task	Purpose	Process
Preparing Learners		
Anticipatory Guide	Activate relevant prior knowledge and contextualize key language of the unit.	Students are presented with statements they must agree or disagree with; they then discuss their viewpoints with other students (one who agrees and another who disagrees with their choice).
Reaching Consensus	Provide opportunities for students to interact with the key themes of fairness, kindness, and friendship that will be further explored in the lesson.	Students are given a scene from an unfamiliar text and reach consensus on the dilemma depicted in the scene, as well as how it might be resolved.
Interacting with the Text		
Wordless Read Aloud	Provide an opportunity for students to listen to a story for enjoyment and extract the main idea.	Students listen to and look at the scenes from the story, as the teacher does "think alouds" to unpack key scenes.
Oral Caption	Scaffold students' use of sequential language and word-awareness skills.	Students work in groups to create an "oral caption" for an assigned scene from the story, using manipulatives to represent the individual words of their caption.
Double-Entry Journal	Provide opportunities for students to identify story elements and make connections to their lived experiences.	Students talk with a partner and then draw pictures representing their personal connections to elements from the story.
Think–Pair–Share	Support students' understanding of the text by exploring the author's purpose.	Students analyze scenes from the story and discuss with a partner why they think the author wrote the story. Students then participate in a whole-group discussion about author's purpose.
Extending Understanding		
Role Play Replay	Provide students with authentic and creative opportunities to use disciplinary language.	Students are provided cut-out images from the story on craft sticks. They reenact key scenes and create novel scenes for their character to reenact.

concepts in the lesson. Key tasks from the lesson are described in this section. The lesson and task progression described in Table 4.2 is based on a 1st-grade classroom (and can also be readily used at the kindergarten level); in addition, the detailed descriptions that follow in the text include recommendations for adjustments for the later elementary grades for each task.

Preparing Learners

The Preparing Learners tasks of this lesson are designed to activate relevant prior knowledge on the themes of fairness and friendship. This introductory Moment in the lesson gets students thinking about and discussing what they already know about the topic at hand, drawing on the innate sense of fairness and justice that all young learners possess.

Anticipatory Guide. The first task of the lesson is the Anticipatory Guide, a dynamic and democratic activity where dual statements are orally presented to students. Students are asked to choose which statement they agree with more, making a decision based on their thinking and feelings at the current moment. This task starts the lesson by giving students an opportunity to draw upon their cultural and linguistic experiential knowledge. This task also gives the teacher the opportunity to hear from students and gain understanding of the language students are currently using, as well as to hear from students themselves about their vision of the world. The rich conversations students have with each other and the whole-class discussion that follows serve to preview the themes and topics that will emerge in the story they are about to read. To facilitate this task, the teacher presents the dual statements to the students as presented in Table 4.3.

The teacher invites students to line up on one side of the room if they agree with the first statement or on the other side of the room if they agree with the alternative statement. Students then talk with a partner who is on the same side of the room about why they are in agreement with the statement they chose. Next, students find a partner from the opposing viewpoint and engage in thoughtful dialogical exchanges, allowing them to consider alternative perspectives. The teacher then presents the second statement and

Table 4.3. Anticipatory Guide Dual Statements

1. Most of the time people are nice.	vs.	Most of the time people are not nice.
2. Most of the time school is fun.	vs.	Most of the time school is not fun.
3. You should always help people who are sad.	vs.	You don't always need to help people who are sad.

its alternative for students to follow the same process, followed by the same process for the third statement and its alternative. This task is done at a brisk pace—taking no more than 10 minutes. Throughout this task, the teacher carefully observes the language that students are using to talk about the topic, in order to tailor subsequent instruction that builds on their current understanding and that guides them toward deeper conceptual understanding and language development.

For students in later grades, Anticipatory Guides are a way to connect new learning with previous learning, for students to explore their own ideas and experiences about a topic, and for students to be introduced to key vocabulary within a specific context. Instead of presenting options orally, teachers in the upper grades can provide open-ended statements for students to read independently. Instead of lining up or giving a thumbs-up to show their agreement, students read the statements and write about whether they agree or disagree and why. They can then discuss their ideas with a peer.

Reaching Consensus. The next task, Reaching Consensus, further deepens students' engagement with themes and ideas that will soon be explored when reading the text. In this task, groups are presented with a scene from the story that depicts Vanessa, the girl who is new to the school, feeling sad and left out. Figure 4.1 shows the girl sitting by herself in the gym while the rest of the kids are playing and having fun, Figure 4.2 shows the girl looking sad in the classroom, and Figure 4.3 shows the girl being bullied. Each image requires students to work with their partner to analyze the scene collaboratively to determine the character's dilemma (which may not be obvious at first glance), and students are then guided to reach a consensus as to the recommendation they are making to solve the dilemma.

Figure 4.1. Reaching Consensus Scene: New Girl in Gym Class

Illustration from *I Walk With Vanessa* by Kerascoët (2018). Used with permission from Penguin Random House LLC.

Figure 4.2. Reaching Consensus Scene: New Girl in the Classroom

Illustration from *I Walk With Vanessa* by Kerascoët (2018). Used with permission from Penguin Random House LLC.

Figure 4.3. Reaching Consensus Scene: New Girl Being Bullied

Illustration from *I Walk With Vanessa* by Kerascoët (2018). Used with permission from Penguin Random House LLC.

The teacher introduces the task and each of the scenes that the groups will explore. Students are asked to discuss what they see happening in the picture, specifically analyzing the picture in terms of the setting, the characters' thoughts and feelings, and why the characters are thinking and feeling this way. The language supports "In the picture I see . . ." and "I think she is feeling . . . because . . ." are provided to support the conversation.

Students are then invited to name the dilemma in the scene, and then share with their partner what they think should happen next in the scene for the dilemma to be solved. For example, one partner might recommend that the sad girl in the picture take action herself, and the other partner might recommend that one of her classmates be the one to take action.

Table 4.4. Formulaic Expressions for Reaching Consensus

Partner A can say . . .	Partner B can respond . . .
My idea is . . .	Can you tell me more about that?
The solution here is to . . .	I agree because . . .
What if . . .	Maybe we could . . .

Finally, partners are asked to reach a consensus on their final recommendation about how the dilemma should be solved. They might choose to combine both of their ideas for their final recommendation or go with one partner's idea. In this portion of the task, students are encouraged to listen closely to one another and build on each other's ideas in order to create multiple exchanges of conversation. Table 4.4 provides an example of the formulaic expressions provided to students, which are modeled several times before students use them on their own. The expressions will be presented orally as well as in writing, and the language modeling provides the support students need to use them with peer and teacher support.

In this task, students engage in dialogue to coconstruct meaning, using their current level of English, with the support of formulaic expressions and other language scaffolds. Students have the opportunity to use examples from their lived experiences to find a solution. Later, when they hear the book being read, they will have deeper connections because they already will have previewed the major themes and made connections as to how those themes connect to their lives. They will also have the opportunity to compare their solutions to how the author chose to solve the central dilemma of the story.

Teachers who teach upper elementary grades can use the same task but increase the complexity of the images and the formulaic expressions. Upper grades may also choose to use written scenarios and vignettes rather than images. The core of the task remains the same—discussing a complex situation where there are multiple possible resolutions, not one single right answer, and coming to agreement on a recommended solution. Such preparatory activities are not mere precursors to learning; they are the scaffolding upon which students construct new disciplinary and linguistic knowledge, anchored firmly in their own experiences.

Interacting With Complex Themes and Texts

The Interacting Moment of the lesson is when students spend the majority of their time engaging in tasks that are scaffolded for them to deepen their understanding of story elements, the author's purpose, and the central themes of the text. Throughout this Moment, students participate in a reading of the wordless text, *I Walk With Vanessa,* which includes a picture analysis. Students then engage in the tasks, Wordless Read Aloud, Oral Caption, Double-Entry Journal, and Think–Pair–Share, described below. The tasks that are part of the Interacting Moment of the lesson, as described in Chapter 3, require students to deconstruct and reconstruct a text, explore key ideas and build their conceptual understandings.

Wordless Read Aloud. In the Wordless Text Read Aloud task, the teacher guides students through a narrative story without written words, solely using images and the spoken words of the teacher. While this is indeed a challenge, it is also an opportunity to enhance students' visual literacy skills and to encourage imaginative and interpretive skills. The purpose of this task is for students to hear and see the story unfold through images, listen for enjoyment, and extract the main ideas of the text. To accomplish this, the teacher uses a guided viewing technique and begins by giving an overview of the text, explaining that this is a book that tells a story through pictures and that this book is about a girl who moves to a new school, where there is a boy who is mean to her, and there is a girl who notices this and decides to take action to stop the unfair situation. For selected pages, the teacher pauses and provides an in-depth analysis by describing the characters and setting, doing a think-aloud of the process of inferring actions and emotions, and inviting predictions, saying something like, "On this page, I see Vanessa sitting off to the side in gym class. She is frowning and she looks sad. I think she is sad because she is watching all of the other kids play and have fun in the gym. I wonder what will happen next." For other pages, the teacher seeks student input as to what they see and think, asking "How do you think this character feels?" and "What is happening here?" The teacher encourages silent reflection and also provides opportunities for students to verbalize and share their thinking. As students will have many opportunities to read and hear the book over the coming week, the focus is the overall meaning of the story, and it is not essential that students understand every detail.

Oral Caption. The next task, Oral Caption, blends the disciplinary practices of using sequential language to retell a story with the early literacy skill of word awareness. In this task, students are organized into small groups and each group is given a key scene from the story. The teacher preselects the scenes based on the number of groups in the class, making sure that at least one scene from the beginning, middle, and end is represented. Groups are given one scene and invited to create an oral caption (a short sentence or phrase) that captures the key idea from the scene. The group is given manipulatives (e.g., cubes, sticks, pom poms) and invited to use the manipulatives to represent each word in their chosen caption, which reinforces word awareness, a key early literacy skill of determining the individual words that make up a sentence, a skill that can be especially tricky for those learning a new language. For example, if a group is given the scene where Vanessa is sad, sitting by herself in the gym watching everyone else play (Figure 4.1), the group might choose the oral caption "Vanessa is sad." Students would then place three manipulatives down—one for each word of the sentence. This skill is often taught out of context and devoid of meaning, and this task provides a meaningful context for early learners to develop key literacy skills.

Once all group members have taken turns learning their team's oral caption and can identify each word in the sentence, the teacher organizes a whole-group retelling of the story, using the oral captions. The group that had the first scene from the book goes first and chorally reads their caption. Then the entire class repeats the caption. The second group then shares their oral caption, and the entire class again repeats their caption. The process repeats until all captions have been presented and the entire class has practiced retelling the story.

In the upper grades, students participate in the same task but may no longer need the support of manipulatives. Their oral captions are scaffolded with language supports and use increasingly sophisticated language to capture the themes depicted in the image. For example, the frame "Vanessa feels . . . because . . ." might be used in a 3rd-grade classroom, and "The boy . . . ; as a result, Vanessa feels . . ." might be used in a 5th-grade classroom. Instead of an oral caption, upper grades might also present their captions in writing.

Double-Entry Journal. The next task in this Moment of the lesson is a Double-Entry Journal. In this task, students deconstruct the text by identifying key story elements while making connections to their lived experiences. The task begins with the teacher creating the Double-Entry Journal by taking a large piece of butcher paper or poster paper and dividing it into two columns. The first column will be a story element (character, setting, problem, solution) from the story. The next column will be students' personal connections. Once the Double-Entry Journal is created, the teacher begins with the first story element (character) and elicits from the class one of the main characters, or simply tells the class one of the characters. A picture of that character is placed in the first column, and the text "character" is added below. The teacher then invites students to make a connection to that character. For example, if the character is Vanessa (the new girl at school who was bullied and felt sad), students might make a connection to a time they were sad, or a time they were new. Students share their connection with a partner and then draw a picture of their connection, labeling their picture with words or writing sentences connected to their drawing. These pictures are done on small pieces of paper (approximately a quarter-sheet of paper, or possibly a sticky note). Students are then invited to attach their drawing to the second column of the Double-Entry Journal.

This process repeats with other elements from the story—first adding a story element to the first column and attaching pictures with words or sentences to the second column. This task will unfold over several days. Upon the completion of a task, the Double-Entry Journal can be displayed in the classroom and referenced throughout the rest of the unit.

Students in the upper grades can create their Double-Entry Journals in small groups or individually. They will use increasingly sophisticated story elements corresponding to their grade levels, such as point of view, theme, figurative language, rising action, climax, and so forth. In the second column of the Double-Entry Journal, upper elementary students can cite text evidence, rather than provide a personal connection.

Think-Pair-Share. The final task in the Interacting Moment is Think–Pair–Share. In this task, students are asked to think about the author's purpose for writing the story. Students are asked to look at scenes from the Oral Caption task and the Double-Entry Journal of story elements and to think about what the author might have wanted to teach the reader. A teacher might say,

> Look at all of these scenes. The author put these pictures together in this order, because they wanted to tell a story about a new girl at school. Think about all of the elements the author included in the story. What do you think the message in this story could be? Why did the author write this story?

Then, students discuss their ideas with a partner, using the following formulaic expressions:

- *My idea is . . . OR I think . . .*
- *What do you think? OR Tell me your thoughts about . . .*
- *I agree/disagree with you because . . . OR I agree a little, but I also think . . .*
- *Another idea is . . OR Another perspective could be . . .*

The teacher then asks students to share what their partners said. This leads into a class discussion about the potential message in the text. It is not the intention of this task for 1st graders to accurately identify the theme of the story with supporting evidence, but rather to be exposed to the idea that there is often a message or a lesson that can be attributed to many narrative stories. In this story, there are many potential messages of varying complexity that can be inferred from the story, including:

- Bullying is bad.
- Being a new student in class is hard.
- It takes courage to stand up against unfairness.
- Being an ally means standing up against something that is unfair, even when the unfairness is not happening to you, or even one of your friends.

Encourage all types of responses that are related to themes of kindness, friendship, bullying, and allyship, keeping in mind there is no single correct answer.

Extending Understanding of Complex Themes

In the final Moment of the lesson, students extend their understanding of the themes of allyship, kindness, and friendship presented in the book by engaging in a Role Play Replay task. In this task students reenact key moments in the story and act out novel scenarios provided by the teacher that are not in the story, as well as create their own unique scenarios that are centered on the key themes of the text. Throughout this task students are working on the disciplinary practices of identifying story elements, deepening understanding of the theme of fairness, and creating multiple oral exchanges in conversation (and dialogue).

Role Play Replay. Students work in small groups of two or three. Each group is heterogeneous, with students of mixed ability and language backgrounds. In the first round of the task, groups are given cut-out images of the characters in the scene, which can optionally be glued on a craft stick (see Figure 4.4), and are also provided a scene from the story that prominently features dialogue. Groups are invited to choose one of the characters and reenact the scene, creating original dialogue that realistically reflects that scene.

In the next round, students choose a different character to role play with. In this round the teacher provides a scene, selecting it contingently based on the conversations that have occurred throughout the lesson, and intentionally including story elements such as characters and setting. For example, the teacher may choose a scene that involves an unfair situation where bystanders are not required to act, such as when a child is hurt on the playground and there are already several adults and children who are aware of and helping with the situation.

Figure 4.4. Role Play Replay Task: Students Use Characters From the Book to Reenact Scenes From the Book

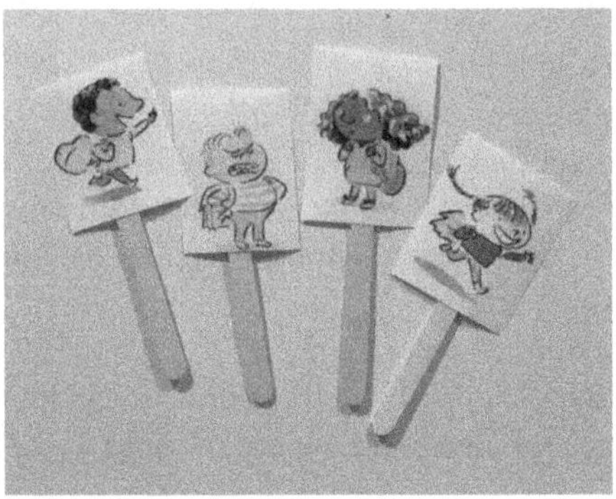

Illustration from *I Walk With Vanessa* by Kerascoët (2018). Used with permission from Penguin Random House LLC.

In subsequent rounds, students themselves are invited to choose their scenarios that are centered on allyship, friendship, and kindness and include specific story elements. This task is especially beneficial for multilingual learners as it allows them to express their understanding and creativity in a supportive environment, enhancing and practicing their language skills through authentic, meaningful use of English in a variety of contexts. These scenarios all invite students to think creatively, use authentic language, and deepen their understandings of story elements, plot, and the themes of unfairness and kindness.

Collaborative Dialogue. Students in the upper grades can engage in a similar task called Collaborative Dialogue, an activity that invites students to construct dialogues that go along with the scenes presented in the text and replace it. Instead of acting out the scene, students work together in small groups to write original dialogue for their scene. First, students discuss their ideas and reach a consensus on the direction of their dialogue. Then, each group member writes out the agreed-upon dialogue, ensuring consistency across the group. They later present their dialogue to the entire class and listen to the original dialogues of the other groups.

PUTTING IT ALL TOGETHER: TRANSFORMATIVE AND GENERATIVE LEARNING

This section presents an analysis of how the lesson "Walking With Vanessa" unfolds within an elementary classroom, illustrating the practical application of the Three Moments Architecture of a lesson. Implementing lessons using this approach works well in any grade level and subject area, though it requires intentionality and purposeful planning. The Three Moments Architecture emphasizes meaning-making as central to learning, oracy as the key to critical thinking, and the potential for even the youngest of students to become autonomous learners. In addition, the lesson design engages students with the disciplinary practices, including conceptual understandings, analytical practices, and language practices. In this way, students develop their literacy skills through learning that is deeply connected to their lived experiences. With this in mind, two key "teacher moves" facilitate this process:

1. *Curriculum Redesign*: The Three Moments Architecture of a lesson allows educators to examine their given curriculum and strategically layer in additional tasks, if needed, at key Moments—Preparing Learners, Interacting with the Text/Concept, and Extending Understanding.
2. *Dynamic Assessment:* The task design provides opportunities for in-the-moment scaffolding, providing real-time insights based on the teacher's observations that guide immediate and future pedagogical decisions.

Curriculum Redesign and the Lesson in Three Moments Architecture

Educators at the elementary level are typically provided with curricular resources to support them in teaching the standards, competencies, and content for their grade level. These resources come in varying degrees of quality. Some materials are high quality, while others can be less comprehensive, requiring additional enhancement or amplification by the teacher to fully meet the needs of students. Teachers need to be critical consumers of the materials they are given in order to make informed decisions about how to amplify their effectiveness and address any gaps or limitations. This is especially true for teachers of multilingual learners, where curriculum development often lags behind current pedagogical best practices.

The Three Moments Architecture of a lesson can be used to determine where to supplement, amplify, and adjust lessons. For example, a teacher might have a curriculum that immediately jumps into the lesson at the Interacting Moment, without any tasks designed to prepare the students to engage in the rigorous tasks of the lesson. In this case, a teacher might choose to amplify the curriculum by adding a task or two in the Preparing Learners Moment, such as an Anticipatory Guide, to activate relevant prior knowledge and set the stage for quality learning. Likewise, if during the Interacting with Text Moment, the curricular resource is insufficient in meeting the needs of multilingual learners, the teacher might opt to add several additional tasks where students collaboratively take apart and put back together the text as a way to focus on key concepts of the lesson. It is rare that one single curricular resource can meet the diverse needs of all learners in a classroom. Quality curriculum must incorporate students' lived experiences and the context in which they live (Walqui & van Lier, 2010). Teachers, therefore, must become adept at tailoring their curricular resources, a task that is as demanding as it is crucial. Using the Three Moments of a Lesson Architecture provides a structured method for educators to enhance and amplify the curriculum.

Dynamic Assessment: The Role of Task Design and Scaffolding

Each task within a lesson provides the opportunity for dynamic assessment, offering invaluable insights to the teacher. Careful observation of student responses and their engagement levels during these tasks provides real-time feedback, allowing for immediate adjustments. This ongoing assessment is instrumental in customizing instruction to better align with learners' needs. It transforms the classroom into a responsive learning environment where tasks evolve based on student interaction with the material, each other, and the key ideas. Additionally, these observations have a profound impact on the planning of future lessons, ensuring that instruction is not simply reactive but also proactive in addressing students' learning trajectories. This approach ensures that instruction is a fluid process, continuously shaped and reshaped by the lived experiences of the students as well as their linguistic abilities. It is through this process that students gradually increase their own understanding of the criteria and expectations for engaging successfully in communicative and classroom practices. Students will then eventually come to their own understanding as to what counts as legitimate communication or participation and gain the ability to self-assess. This is possible for students at every grade level, and it requires the teacher to dynamically assess current participation and scaffold deeper levels of participation throughout the school year.

The lesson "Walking With Vanessa" illustrates how meaning-making is central to learning, oracy is the foundation of building skills and generative knowledge, and even the earliest of students can be autonomous learners with voice and choice in their learning experiences. This can all be accomplished through use of the Three Moments Architecture of a lesson in addition to curriculum redesign, dynamic assessments, and supportive scaffolding. This process of reframing and transforming the elementary classroom is essential for all students, but especially for multilingual learners, who are eager and ready to make sense of the world around them and engage in learning that has meaning at its core.

REFERENCES

Kibler, A., Valdés, G., & Walqui, A. (Eds.). (2021). *Reconceptualizing the role of critical dialogue in American classrooms: Promoting equity through dialogic education.* Routledge.

Lefstein, A., & Snell, J. (2013). *Better than best practice: Developing teaching and learning through dialogue.* Routledge. https://doi.org/10.4324/9781315884516

Mercer, N., & Littleton, K. (2007). *Dialogue and the development of children's thinking: A sociocultural approach.* Routledge.

Philipson, N., & Wegerif, R. (2017). *Dialogic education: Mastering core concepts through thinking together.* Routledge. https://doi.org/10.4324/9781315621869

Pollard-Durodola, S. D., & Simmons, D. C. (2009). The role of explicit instruction and instructional design in promoting phonemic awareness development and transfer from Spanish to English. *Reading & Writing Quarterly, 25*(2–3), 139–161.

Reeve, J. (2006). Teachers as facilitators: What autonomy-supportive teachers do and why their students benefit. *The Elementary School Journal, 106*(3), 225–236.

van Lier, L. (1996). *Interaction in the language curriculum: Awareness, autonomy, and authenticity.* Routledge. https://doi.org/10.4324/9781315843223

Walqui, A. (2006). Scaffolding instruction for English language learners: A conceptual framework. *International Journal of Bilingual Education and Bilingualism, 9*(2), 159–180.

Walqui, A., & van Lier, L. (2010) *Scaffolding the academic success of adolescent English language learners.* WestEd.

Wilkinson, A. (1965). The concept of oracy. *Educational Review, 17*(3), 65–76.

Yosso, T. J. (2005). Whose culture has capital? A critical race theory discussion of community cultural wealth. *Race Ethnicity and Education, 8*(1), 69–91.

Zipke, M. (2021). *Playing with language: Improving elementary reading through metalinguistic awareness.* Teachers College Press.

¡Por supuesto que sí se puede!

Una pedagogía dialógica, crítica, y de calidad para los estudiantes latinos.

Aída Walqui y Viviana Galdames

Chapter 5, cowritten by two colleagues who have collaborated over the last 3 decades in intercultural bilingual education programs in Latin America, uses the pedagogical framework proposed in the book to demonstrate its validity for heritage language classes in the United States. The two lessons presented, one geared at upper elementary classes, and the other intended for middle or high school students, follow the Three Moment Architecture of a lesson proposed in Chapter 3, as well as its "high-challenge/high-support" scaffolding. Texts and tasks invite and support students to dialogically and metacognitively develop multiliteracies as well as their reasoned voice, agency, and autonomy.

Using socially relevant topics, one story, written by Chilean author Antonio Skármeta, addresses the impact of political oppression on children; the other, by the American writer Martha Salinas, is set in a rural community and presents a case of discrimination, happily resolved, in a middle school. Both lessons, which have been successfully implemented many times, foster students' critical stances and civic participation.

En este capítulo presentamos una propuesta con fundamentos pedagógicos para la enseñanza del español en escuelas norteamericanas, dentro de un enmarque ecológico/sociocultural. Nuestra propuesta está basada en la firme convicción de que debemos redistribuir profundamente las oportunidades que les ofrecemos a los estudiantes que hablan español en los Estados Unidos. Actualmente, todavía se enseña el español como una actividad filológica, enfatizando las formas lingüísticas: conjugaciones, tipos de palabras, vocabulario, y pronunciación que eran típicas en la enseñanza de idiomas extranjeros. A los estudiantes que se comunican bien en español, porque es su idioma familiar, se les hace estudiar aspectos lingüísticos formales que no les son intrínsicamente interesantes. Por lo mismo reciben notas bajas en estos cursos y su rendimiento contribuye más aun a que sean inferiorizados, porque erróneamente se piensa que 'ni español saben hablar' (Chávez-Moreno, 2025). Sin embargo, antes de llegar a la escuela estos niños, niñas[1] y adolescentes han tenido experiencias muy ricas que deben servir como base para el desarrollo de su potencial. Más importante aún, el desarrollo de este talento es la responsabilidad de la escuela, y debe ser anclado en el tratamiento de temas relevantes que sean parte de su existir cotidiano.

Para plantear una formulación específica de cómo lograrlo, retomamos los principios expuestos en el capítulo 2, enfatizando la necesidad de reorientar actitudes, conocimientos, prácticas docentes y características del contexto que son indispensables para que lenguas socialmente estigmatizadas, como el español en nuestro contexto, sean utilizadas en aulas, escuelas y comunidades, revalorando el potencial que presentan a los estudiantes personal, intelectual y socialmente. Luego, presentamos dos lecciones, una más elaborada que la otra, para después discutir cómo diseñar la enseñanza de calidad que merecen los jóvenes latinos. Ellas se centran en temas sociales de gran relevancia, con los cuales los alumnos tienen muchas experiencias que merecen ser procesadas para lograr que desarrollen una voz crítica, razonada, y competente. Ya es hora de que cambiemos de manera profunda el currículum y la enseñanza en español para así profundizar y acelerar los logros de estos alumnos tanto en español como en inglés.

¿QUIÉNES HABLAN ESPAÑOL EN LOS ESTADOS UNIDOS?

El país cuenta con la segunda población más numerosa de hablantes de español en el mundo, siguiendo a México, y seguidos a su vez por España. El número total de hispanohablantes en los Estados Unidos de Norteamérica supera los 62 millones de personas, sin agregar los 3 millones de habitantes de Puerto Rico (González, 2022). Sin embargo, a pesar de su cuantiosa presencia, y de las contribuciones económicas ($3.2 trillones de dólares anuales, Universidad de Arizona, 2023) y culturales que le ofrecen a este país, la situación de los estudiantes que hablan español como primera lengua en las escuelas norteamericanas es muy diferente social, económica y sociolingüísticamente de la que gozan los alumnos hispanohablantes en España o México. En los Estados Unidos, el español es una lengua minorizada y su utilización -a pesar de algunos cambios positivos en las últimas décadas- todavía conlleva discriminación. Esto sucede, sobre todo, cuando el manejo del español es circunstancial, como resultado de dinámicas familiares y sociales, y no por haber sido aprendido en la escuela como lengua extranjera, como curso electivo (Valdés & Figueroa, 1994; Wiley, 2024). Por estas razones, y porque en el país todavía se consideran a otros idiomas como problemas, y no como recursos (Ruiz, 1984) en contextos escolares norteamericanos, los estudiantes hispanoamericanos no son considerados como alumnos talentosos y su educación escolar tiende a ser disminuida. Creemos firmemente que esta situación debe cambiar, y que gran parte del cambio se puede lograr a través de una reorientación pedagógica crítica en las escuelas.

PRINCIPIOS QUE SUSTENTAN EL APRENDIZAJE DE LA LENGUA ESPAÑOLA CON CALIDAD Y EQUIDAD.

En esta primera sección de nuestro capítulo, sintetizamos los principios que sostienen la visión de excelencia y equidad que proponemos para la educación de los estudiantes latinos en el capítulo 2. Estos principios se basan en una lectura crítica del desarrollo de multiliteracidades en lengua materna, teorías socioculturales del aprendizaje y desarrollos en la ecología del aprendizaje.

1. El ser humano se desarrolla a través de la interacción social. El desarrollo es consecuencia de -y no un prerrequisito para- el aprendizaje

En una sociedad estratificada, como la norteamericana, donde algunos creen que los beneficios que gozan unos pocos son merecidos (Markowits, 2019), la inferencia equivocada que muchos hacen, es que los estudiantes latinos que no saben utilizar el inglés fluidamente, carecen también de desarrollo conceptual, académico y lingüístico en español. Esta actitud monoglósica, es decir que acepta una sola forma discursiva como aceptable (Bakhtin, 1989), acusa peyorativamente a los estudiantes de ser semilingües (Cummins, 1979), personas que no han desarrollado proficiencia lingüística en ninguna lengua. En estas actitudes confluyen conceptos raciales y lingüísticos como si estos estuvieran íntimamente relacionados (Flores y Garcia, 2017; Rosa, 2019). Como ya hemos discutido, esta falsa apreciación ignora el hecho de que los niños y jóvenes latinos llegan a la escuela con vivencias muy ricas y muchos de ellos como niños han experimentado y tenido que tomar decisiones de vida sumamente complejas. A través de estas y otras experiencias, ellos han desarrollado habilidades de análisis crítico y se han cuestionado las responsabilidades mutuas que existen en la vida en comunidad y en una sociedad que promete el ejercicio de una falsa democracia.

Basándonos en postulados teóricos elaborados inicialmente por Vygotsky (1962; 1976; 1978) y ampliados por muchos investigadores educativos (i.e. Alexander, 2020; Mercer, 2019; van Lier, 1996; 2000; 2004); sabemos que para desarrollar nuevas habilidades, los estudiantes necesitan interactuar practicando nuevas ideas y destrezas con guías, y sintiéndose valorados por otros, con legitimidad. Vygotsky enfatizó la primacía de la mediación lingüística en el desarrollo de procesos mentales más complejos, arguyendo que el lenguaje es el vehículo principal del pensamiento y que todo uso del lenguaje es dialógico, es decir, está basado en la interacción social.

El famoso dictum Vygotskiano "lo que el niño puede hacer con asistencia hoy lo podrá hacer individualmente mañana" sintetiza esta idea (Vygotsky, 1976). Este proceso de *apprenticeship* (Lave & Wenger, 1991), la socialización de novicios académicos en una cultura intelectualmente más compleja de pensamiento y participación, requiere precisamente de ello, de la participación. Así como los niños aprenden a caminar por primera vez caminando, los estudiantes desarrollan sus conocimientos utilizando nuevas ideas y operaciones. Si bien su participación no será perfecta inicialmente, el proceso de constante aproximación -apoyado por modelos auténticos, contingentes, y significativos, manifestado a través de invitaciones que sean atractivas, logrará que ellos desarrollen competencias que luego les servirán en otros contextos (Vygotsky, 1976).

Muchas veces pensamos que algunas personas se comunican bien porque nacieron con el talento de la expresión oral. Dentro de una perspectiva sociolingüística, sin embargo, sabemos que las habilidades que tenemos, son inicialmente adquiridas y desarrolladas en actividades comunitarias, por procesos de *aprendizaje*. Así como la inteligencia es socializada (Resnick et al, 2015), una persona que se comunica oralmente de manera competente, es el resultado de procesos de socialización: ha sido invitada a expresar sus ideas, se ha prestado atención a sus contribuciones, y nuevas interacciones han surgido de las ideas aportadas. La realización de su potencial ha sido lograda gracias a la práctica con otros. Por eso decimos que la teoría sociocultural constituye una "pedagogía de promesa" (Walqui y van Lier, 2010), porque es proléptica, apunta hacia el futuro y se plantea lograr que los estudiantes lleguen a ser quienes todavía no son. (Leontiev, en Bronfenbrenner, 1979).

2. Los andamiajes pedagógicos son diseñados tanto de manera deliberada (planeada) como contingentemente.

¿Cómo, entonces, se promueve el desarrollo de los estudiantes? Invitándolos a que participen en actividades que están más allá de su campo de competencia y autónomía. Vygotsky propuso el concepto de la Zona del Desarrollo Próximo (ZDP) para señalar el espacio más allá de la competencia individual en donde se localiza la acción educativa. Pero 'más allá' no está pensado como una progresión de desarrollo paso a paso, sino más bien lo que necesitamos hacer ahora, definido por las circunstancias del contexto. Se invita a los niños a que conversen sobre temas importantes, a que participen en actividades que empujan su competencia. Para lograr este avance, se le ofrecen andamiajes.

Un andamio constituye el apoyo temporal que se ofrece a los estudiantes, para que a través de su utilización desarrollen su eventual autonomía. La premisa del andamio es que une lo que el estudiante puede hacer por sí mismo con lo que solo puede hacer con apoyo, y en colaboración. Este andamio se desmantela a medida que el aprendiz muestra iniciativa. Esta responsabilización llega en diversos momentos para alumnos individuales, no todos aprenden lo mismo al mismo tiempo. Por ejemplo, ¿aprenden todos los niños a montar bicicleta de la misma manera invariable y tomando precisamente el mismo tiempo? De hecho, no. Algunos niños requieren que el padre o la madre tome de la mano el asiento y se movilice con ellos tratando de mantener su equilibrio. Otros niños están contentos con tener ruedas temporales extra que como triciclo le den mayor estabilidad. Algunos querrán tanto ruedas de entrenamiento como al adulto sujetando la silla. Y habrá los más aventurados que se resistan a cualquier tipo de apoyo y que prefieren aprender con un par de caídas. El andamio tanto en la mano del padre, o las ruedas extra, le permiten al niño aprender a montar una bicicleta, pero una vez que sabe hacerlo, las ruedas o el apoyo personal se vuelven innecesarios.

Los andamiajes tienen dos aspectos: estructura y proceso. La estructura es el ritual predecible que le presta apoyo a los estudiantes. El proceso es lo que los alumnos logran hacer gracias al apoyo ofrecido. Los maestros tienen que estar vigilantes para poder determinar en qué momento disminuir el apoyo, retirarlo totalmente, o prestar otro andamiaje para que los estudiantes desarrollen.

Igualmente, algunos andamios son elaborados en la planificación de la clase, respondiendo a preguntas tales como ¿Qué tipo de apoyo necesitan mis estudiantes para poder participar en esta actividad? ¿Cuál ha sido mi experiencia con esta lección en el pasado? ¿Qué sé respecto a mis alumnos que me permita plantearles ciertas actividades y no otras? Estos andamios son planificados por los maestros y las maestras en anticipación de la actividad. Otros andamios son contingentes, es decir, se vuelven necesarios después de observar con cuidado de qué manera están participando los estudiantes. Es posible que los alumnos hayan malinterpretado parte del proceso, en cuyo caso, una explicación inmediata sirve para aclarar la duda. Sin embargo, los maestros deben ejercitar su juicio para determinar qué acciones de los alumnos merecen su intervención. Un error gramatical cometido por un estudiante en su participación durante una conversación profunda, no merece una intervención del maestro. En cambio, una malinterpretación de un pasaje de un texto leído, puede generar el que la maestra pida a los alumnos que reconsideren lo que están diciendo, guiándolos a que repasen los párrafos relevantes en el texto.

El ofrecerle a un grupo de estudiantes los andamios adecuados para su participación no es fácil. A medida que una maestra gana experiencia y reflexiona, aprende para futuras instancias de enseñanza, y gana experticia. Por eso recomendamos que los maestros trabajen en equipo, porque así pueden servir como espejos reflexivos los unos de los otros.

3. Las invitaciones que se les ofrecen a los alumnos para que aprendan, deben enfocarse en prácticas y temas que son centrales en la materia, y que por lo mismo, son generativos.

Lo que estudian los alumnos en la escuela, debe servirles para desarrollar ideas y destrezas que le sean útiles en la vida. Todo tema o texto tiene una idea central e ideas secundarias que se articulan alrededor de este tema, expandiéndolo y dándole sentido. Los estudiantes deben poder comprender cuál es esa idea principal en un texto, y luego relacionar esta idea con otras que lo sustentan y le dan vida. No tiene sentido el que una maestra se enfoque en todos los detalles contenidos en el texto, porque no toda idea tiene la misma importancia. El docente debe priorizar las ideas centrales y las destrezas esenciales primero. Luego, en otra lección, podrá tomar otros géneros discursivos con temática similar para solidificar y extender las conexiones a ese tema central. De esta manera contribuye a que los estudiantes creen redes de conocimientos que tendrán a su disposición para el resto de sus vidas. En este capítulo ofrecemos dos ejemplos de temas centrales en la vida de los estudiantes latinos que pueden servir para reforzar conocimientos y destrezas críticas para una vida intercultural y multilingüe.

4. En la enseñanza del español como idioma de herencia se desarrollan simultáneamente ideas, así como prácticas analíticas y la manera de expresarlas lingüísticamente.

Los conceptos esenciales, su análisis, y cómo comunicarlos de manera oral, escrita, o utilizando multimedios constituyen el quehacer del aprendizaje escolar. La lectura, por ejemplo, no se desarrolla solo prestando atención a los fonemas. El significado y los procesos a través de los cuales se discuten esos conceptos: comparación, interpretación, análisis de si las ideas están bien fundamentadas, si las inferencias están bien justificadas, etc. son esenciales. Igualmente es importante, y de manera simultánea, el desarrollar la habilidad de expresar todo este quehacer de manera clara, fluida, y potente. Claro está que esto es una meta. Los alumnos son invitados a aprender a través del tiempo. No se trata de que un profesor enseñe algo y los alumnos lo aprendan de inmediato. El aprendizaje, incremento, y refinamiento de prácticas es una actividad que toma toda la vida. La escuela señala las bases integradas para esta construcción (Valdés, 2017).

5. La enseñanza de aspectos formales de la lengua debe ser contextualizada y contingente.

Si bien es verdad que el manejo preciso, correcto, e impactante de la lengua es uno de los objetivos de la educación, no se puede empezar con la corrección. Primordialmente queremos que nuestros estudiantes se entusiasmen con ideas, que las encuentren relevantes para su vida, que puedan desarrollar criterios para evaluarlas, y compartirlas con otros efectivamente. Luego, en segundo lugar, uno se preocupa de que puedan pulir su manejo de los aspectos más formales de la expresión para convertirse cada vez en comunicadores más efectivos y correctos.

En la enseñanza del español como lengua materna, por ejemplo, hay una gran preocupación por el uso de tildes. Si la fuerza de voz va en la sílaba correcta durante participaciones orales, eso es lo esencial. Luego, se puede tratar de tipos de palabras que se clasifican según donde cae la fuerza de voz, y de acuerdo con eso, aprender las reglas para la acentuación. Ofrecemos en la discusión de la lección de primaria una actividad lúdica, el Rompecabezas de Vocabulario, que permite que los estudiantes después de haber tratado el tema del texto leído se enfoquen en la problemática de la acentuación del español de manera individual y grupal.

6. La selección de temas y de textos para las lecciones es esencial.

Los alumnos deben ser tratados como los intelectuales y ciudadanos responsables que llegarán a ser (Westheimer, 2024), ofreciéndoles para su estudio temas relevantes para sus vidas presentes y futuras. Sobre todo, si queremos poner en ejercicio e incrementar la capacidad crítica que propone este capítulo, es necesario ofrecer a los estudiantes oportunidades de reflexionar críticamente sobre situaciones de justicia e injusticias en variados contextos, con el fin de desarrollar en ellos valores ciudadanos (Cassany y Castella, 2010) y la manera de expresarlos. La literatura es una excelente fuente de contextos donde ocurren hechos, que tal vez los estudiantes no tendrán oportunidad de experimentar en sus vidas cotidianas. Sin embargo, una lectura crítica y reflexiva les permitirá vivirlas de manera vicaria, como si fueran ventanas a un mundo amplio y diverso; al mismo tiempo, a modo de espejos, a través de su lectura ellos podrán conectar esos contenidos con su propia realidad y reflexionar sobre maneras de enfrentar las situaciones de injusticia que a veces caracteriza a la sociedad. Por eso mismo, los estudiantes, al leer un texto deben identificar de dónde procede el texto, la ideología que lo promueve, los valores o interpretaciones que el autor destaca. Igualmente deben ser invitados a que construyan un punto de vista personal bien razonado frente a estos elementos. De ese modo, estaremos preparando futuros ciudadanos responsables de transformar su mundo para hacerlo cada vez más justo y democrático.

ARQUITECTURA DE UNA LECCIÓN

En esta sección de nuestro capítulo elaboramos conceptos pedagógicos que subyacen el diseño de una lección de calidad. En concordancia con los otros capítulos, planteamos una arquitectura en tres momentos, cada uno de ellos con una secuencia de actividades que acercan cada vez mas a los estudiantes a la meta de la lección, con logros conceptuales y de práctica, y con avances en el manejo de la lengua. Lo importante tanto en los momentos como en las actividades, es su razón de ser, el propósito con el que se utilizan.

1. Primer Momento: Preparémonos para Leer.

Este primer momento tiene como principales objetivos, desarrollar en los estudiantes la capacidad de activar conocimientos y experiencias previas relacionados con los contenidos del texto que se va a leer, formular hipótesis y predicciones. La posibilidad de desarrollar la capacidad de ser lectores críticos, depende a menudo del tipo de actividades que propongamos a los estudiantes, y las orientaciones que desarrollen antes de leerlo. En general, las actividades que corresponden a este primer momento incluyen múltiples y variadas situaciones de comunicación oral (oracidad), propias del enfoque dialógico (Aguilar, 2012; Iturrioz, 2019; Freire, 2017; Jurado y Lomas, 2021, Walqui, 2024) que contribuyen a enfocar la atención de los estudiantes hacia el tema que se va a desarrollar.

2. Segundo Momento: Leamos Interactivamente.

Este momento tiene como principal propósito, lograr que los estudiantes realicen una lectura caracterizada por su comprensión profunda del texto. Se enfatizan los niveles de lectura inferencial y crítico, basados en sus experiencias y conocimientos del mundo, en las conexiones con otros textos y en los diálogos establecidos con sus compañeros. Las actividades diseñadas favorecen la capacidad de enfocarse en los aspectos significativos del texto para poder comprender lo que se lee. Es también el momento para el desarrollo de diferentes destrezas metalingüísticas referidas a la gramática, el vocabulario, ortografía, etc (Galdames y Walqui, 2008).

Un objetivo esencial del desarrollo de lectores competentes considera varios grados de comprensión de los textos leídos. Cassany (2009) propone los siguientes:

Recomendaciones para la lectura interactiva

- Leer las líneas: comprensión literal. Implica localizar información explícita, es poco desafiante, pero necesaria.
- Leer entre líneas: comprensión inferencial. Implica un alto desafío, es un nivel lector interesante
- Leer tras las líneas: comprensión crítica. Implica un posicionamiento personal, un punto de vista, una interpretación que identifique la ideología y valores que promueven los textos, para luego construir una postura que los respalde o los rechace, basados en su cultura, en sus experiencias y en otras lecturas. (Cassany, 2010)
- Leer en línea, refiere a la comprensión desde la multimodalidad (Martos y Martos, 2014). En el siglo XXI es indispensable incluir variadas modalidades comunicativas, especialmente las que ofrecen las nuevas tecnologías, muy cercanas a las experiencias de los estudiantes.

3. Tercer Momento: Profundicemos Nuestra Comprensión.

Son actividades que apuntan a profundizar lo que los alumnos han comprendido, aplicando las nuevas ideas y prácticas desarrolladas a otros temas y contextos. El enfoque sociocultural y ecológico entiende la lectura, la escritura y la oralidad como prácticas sociales, en las que las personas utilizan los textos, situados dentro de contextos particulares, para desarrollar funciones concretas; para ello se proponen actividades con variados géneros discursivos (Bronckart, 2007) a través de los cuales se estimula el diálogo, la creatividad y la participación activa de los estudiantes en situaciones desafiantes y con andamiajes robustos, los que se van retirando gradualmente para generar autonomía y apropiación (Walqui, 2022).

DOS LECCIONES, A MANERA DE EJEMPLOS

Dos lecciones, una para estudiantes de los grados 3–6 de primaria, y otra para niveles intermedio o secundario, grados 7–9 ilustran los postulados que hemos presentado para desarrollar las capacidades de lectura crítica y de dialogicidad. Hemos escogido como tema central en ambos, una lectura de la realidad (Freire y Shor, 2014), que permite exploraciones acerca de la *justicia e injusticia* que a veces experimentan los niños y los jóvenes en sus contextos cotidianos. Las lecciones incluyen también varios géneros discursivos, de acuerdo con lo señalado en los principios pedagógicos en el capítulo 2.

El siguiente cuadro panorámico (Cuadro 5.1) lista las actividades propuestas, a manera de ilustración, para las dos lecciones. Estas se basan, respectivamente, en el cuento La Composición del chileno Antonio Skármeta y en el cuento El Premio, de la escritora californiana de origen mexicano, Martha Salinas. Como podremos apreciar, en ambos casos la arquitectura de la lección sigue la misma estructura de tres momentos: Preparémonos para leer, Leamos interactivamente, y Profundicemos nuestra comprensión. Más adelante, exploramos algunas de las actividades para poder discutirlas en términos de sus objetivos y procesos, incluyendo algunas sugerencias para la evaluación formativa.

Cuando observamos de manera rápida las actividades que proponemos para ambos cuentos, vemos inicialmente la invitación que se ofrece a todos los alumnos a que se comprometan en actividades variadas y de lectura crítica. Los estudiantes tienen oportunidades de proponer ideas oralmente, prestar atención a lo que sus compañeros dicen, y responder a las ideas ofrecidas, creando nuevas interpretaciones que han sido elaboradas en conjunto. Igualmente, es esencial el que entablen conversaciones en torno a los temas relacionados a lo que es justo e injusto en los contextos presentados en los dos cuentos, para luego poder analizar mejor los puntos de vista propios.

El tratamiento pedagógico en ambas lecciones contiene muchas similitudes, la diferencia está basada en la edad relativa de los estudiantes a quienes van dirigidas. Por ejemplo, en el momento de la preparación para la lectura hay coincidencia en una actividad: la Guía de Anticipación. Sin embargo, el contenido de las aseveraciones es diferente. Si bien a los niños más pequeños se les pide que decidan si están de acuerdo o no con la afirmación "a los niños desde pequeños se les debe insistir que nunca mientan", tema que está más relacionado a su campo de conocimiento, a los adolescentes se les pide que decidan si "La raza o el grupo étnico al que pertenece un estudiante no influye para nada en la asignación de premios en la escuela". Esta segunda aseveración solo puede ser contestada por alumnos que, ya, después de 6 o 7 años en la escuela, han tenido u observado experiencias de discriminación (Chávez-Moreno, 2025).

Cuadro 5.1. Panorama de las dos lecciones: Momentos y actividades

DOS LECCIONES		
	"LA COMPOSICION" Grados 3–6	"EL PREMIO" Grados 7–9
	ACTIVIDADES	
PREPARÉMONOS PARA LEER	Guía de anticipación	Guía de anticipación
	Rompecabezas de desarrollo oral	Piensa, anota y comparte
	Cuadro de anticipación a partir de una foto (Parte 1)	
LEAMOS INTERACTIVAMENTE	Lectura de un cuento	Lectura con enfoque
	Cuatro tipos de preguntas	Guía metacognitiva
	Mapa del personaje	
	Rompecabezas de vocabulario	
	Lectura de una noticia	
	Completar cuadro de anticipación a partis de una foto (Parte 2) Lectura a Cuatro Voces de un relato	
PROFUNDICEMOS NUESTRA COMPRENSIÓN	Cuadro de dos Columnas	Espejo de mente abierta
	Espejo de mente abierta	Diálogos colaborativos
	"Lo que a mí me tocó el corazón"	Escritura de un ensayo

EXPLORANDO LA LECCIÓN 1: A PARTIR DEL CUENTO "LA COMPOSICIÓN" (GRADOS 3-6)

1. Primer momento: Preparémonos para leer.

En este primer momento previo a la lectura del texto, un cuento, se enfatiza: (1) la importancia de activar en los estudiantes su capacidad de análisis crítico frente a una serie de planteamientos controversiales relacionados con el contenido del texto, (2) la capacidad de tomar una postura y fundamentarla con argumentos que permitan eventualmente llegar a un consenso dentro de un grupo, y (3) una preparación para la lectura crítica a través de diálogos entre compañeros sugeridos por ilustraciones. Las actividades "Guía de Anticipación" y "Cuadro de Anticipación" apuntan a ese desarrollo. Por otra parte, la actividad "Rompecabezas de Desarrollo Oral" enfatiza el desarrollo de varias habilidades: (1) la descripción de una lámina en sus aspectos más relevantes, (2) la construcción de un relato coherente y creativo basado en las descripciones, (3) la capacidad de dialogar de manera empática y respetuosa ante las diferencias de opinión (Flecha y Torrego, 2012) y (4) la presentación oral de su creación frente al curso. Estos cuatro aspectos son esenciales en el desarrollo de la oracidad.

a. Guía de Anticipación

Esta actividad favorece la lectura crítica al invitar a los estudiantes a leer un conjunto de planteamientos controversiales relacionados con el contenido del texto que leerán después. Los estudiantes comparten sus puntos de vista en un diálogo respetuoso de las diferentes opiniones y en una escucha empática de los argumentos que las respaldan. La actividad tiene el doble propósito de explorar actitudes, y no establecer si las afirmaciones son verdaderas o falsas, aceptables o rechazables. Igualmente, la actividad dirige la atención del estudiante hacia un tema que luego será explorado en direcciones novedosas.

En parejas, los estudiantes leen las siguientes afirmaciones (Cuadro 5.2), reflexionan sobre ellas y deciden si están de acuerdo o en desacuerdo, fundamentando su respuesta.

Cuadro 5.2. Aseveraciones para la Guía Anticipatoria.

AFIRMACIONES	De acuerdo	En desacuerdo
1. Desde pequeños los niños deben aprender que nunca deben mentir.		
2. Los prisioneros en las cárceles llegan ahí por haber cometido graves delitos contra la sociedad.		
3. Los padres no deben hablar de sus preferencias políticas frente a los niños pequeños.		
4. Los únicos responsables de lo que se enseña en sus aulas son los maestros.		

El trabajar la guía en conjunto, les permite a los estudiantes empezar a enfocarse desde un punto de vista personal en temas similares que luego analizarán desde la perspectiva del texto. La lección continúa con una actividad que enfoca el desarrollo de la oracidad de los estudiantes.

b. Rompecabezas de Desarrollo Oral

Las actividades que permiten que los estudiantes colaborativamente desarrollen la habilidad de comunicar ideas específicas, para luego ser compartidas individualmente con un nuevo grupo, son ideales para una clase heterogénea y se llaman rompecabezas. A continuación, presentaremos un tipo de rompecabezas, el de Desarrollo oral.

Descripción

Grupo Base: Formados en grupo de cuatro, los estudiantes repasan, guiados por la maestra, cómo se elabora una descripción y luego deciden quién va a ir a cada grupo de 4 expertos.

Grupo Experto: Colaborativamente, los estudiantes describen la escena que se les ha asignado siguiendo los lineamientos discutidos en el grupo base. Se les aclara que deben describir lo que ven, no sugerir lo que podría ser el caso. Su labor es la de describir la escena con palabras muy precisas, para que así, aquellos que no hayan visto la imagen se la puedan imaginar con detalle. Con este objetivo, cada grupo experto recibe una lámina diferente, habiendo 4 láminas en total.

Como es importante que los estudiantes construyan descripciones que "pinten escenas con palabras", incluimos algunas preguntas apropiadas para una descripción -y que guían la producción del texto oral- para aproximarlo a una descripción de calidad (Cuadro 5.2). Sugerimos que los estudiantes pasen 15 minutos aproximadamente en este componente para evitar el peligro de alargar desproporcionadamente la actividad, tema que se discute en el capítulo 11.

Cuadro 5.3. Guías para la descripción

- ¿Dónde se desarrolla la escena? (Enseñar que el primer paso de una buena descripción es presentar el escenario donde ocurre la situación de la lámina).
- ¿Quién es el personaje central en el dibujo? (Los estudiantes aprenden que es importante describir el o los personajes que aparecen en la lámina)
- ¿Cómo es esta persona (¿hombre? ¿mujer? ¿niño? ¿niña? ¿joven? (edad aproximada, altura, cara, cabello, vestimenta, etc.)
- ¿Qué está(n) haciendo esta(s) persona(s)?
- ¿Alguna otra información de interés?

Ilustración 5.1. Dibujos para el rompecabezas

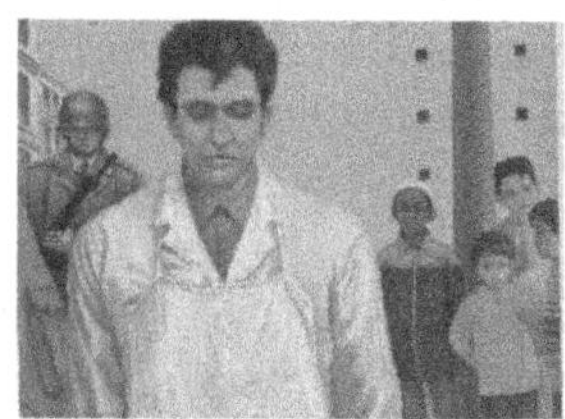

Durante el proceso de descripción, es necesario que la maestra observe el trabajo de los estudiantes para determinar dónde los alumnos podrían necesitar andamiajes adicionales apropiados. Una vez que todos los alumnos, trabajando colaborativamente, han producido descripciones, ya están listos para el trabajo en sus grupos base. Entonces son recogidas las tarjetas y los estudiantes regresan a sus grupos originales.

Grupo Base: Turnándose, los estudiantes comparten las cuatro descripciones que prepararon, esta vez sin tener las láminas visibles. Una vez que todas las descripciones han terminado, los miembros del grupo pueden hacerse preguntas descriptivas acerca de sus respectivas escenas. (5 minutos aproximadamente).

Narración (aproximadamente 15 minutos)

Recién después de que todos los niños están satisfechos con las descripciones de las láminas que los compañeros han hecho, y luego que la maestra haya proporcionado lineamientos para crear una historia, pueden comenzar a imaginarla y agregar detalles a los dibujos. Los lineamientos consisten en una orientación sobre el lugar donde se va a desarrollar la historia, la introducción de personajes centrales, una alusión a su estado anímico; luego algo inesperado sucede; finalmente la situación se resuelve transformando al personaje central de la historia. El objetivo es que construyan un cuento coherente al agregar elementos creativos que unan y den lógica a las ilustraciones.

No existe un solo cuento correcto, cualquier relato que sea coherente es correcto. Esto demuestra uno de los postulados elaborados a través del libro de que a los estudiantes se les debe ofrecer la oportunidad de tener opciones. Una vez que el cuento ha sido construido, los alumnos preparan su presentación frente a la clase.

La maestra pide que un grupo comparta su cuento, el que es presentado colaborativamente por los cuatro estudiantes, tomando el orden de palabra de acuerdo con la lógica de la narrativa que crearon. Luego, la maestra invita a que otro grupo con una historia diferente comparta su versión. Una vez que se hayan compartido varios cuentos, se discuten las diversas variaciones ofrecidas por alumnos.

Se sugiere tener una pauta de evaluación con criterios que han sido compartidos previamente con los estudiantes, de modo que les sirva como un apoyo para elaborar la mejor presentación posible

c. Cuadro de Anticipación y Reflexión a partir de una foto (Parte 1)

Esta actividad tiene como objetivo desarrollar en los estudiantes la capacidad de analizar una fotografía, describir lo que observan e interpretarla

Cuadro 5.4. Anticipación y reflexión

Lo que percibo y sé	Me gustaría saber	Lo que aprendí

de acuerdo con su conocimiento del mundo, de su imaginación y de los aportes que hacen sus compañeros. Aquí vemos en funcionamiento la idea de *affordances* (p. 103): contextos semióticos que invitan a las estudiantes a observar, percibir, interpretar y actuar.

Para acceder a la foto:
https://www.bbc.com/mundo/noticias/2013/09/130910_galeria_chile_golpe_am; seleccionar la foto que presenta a un grupo de personas que son detenidas por militares mientras salen del palacio de Gobierno.

- Antes de leer el cuento los estudiantes observan la fotografía y en el primer recuadro responden individualmente a las siguientes preguntas ¿Qué observas en esta foto? ¿Qué crees que está ocurriendo? ¿Quiénes son las personas que aparecen? ¿Qué están haciendo? ¿Por qué crees que lo están haciendo? ¿Cómo crees que se sienten esas personas? Anota todo lo que piensas. Escucha las interpretaciones de tus compañeros
- En el segundo recuadro anota todo lo que quieres saber en torno a la información entregada por la fotografía. Es el momento para comunicar lo que te interesa sobre el tema.
- Después de leer el cuento y cuando el maestro lo indique, completarás el último recuadro que se refiere a lo que aprendiste sobre el tema.

2. Segundo Momento: Leamos interactivamente

Este momento corresponde a la lectura del texto central de la lección, combinando lectura en forma silenciosa con lectura en voz alta de manera colaborativa. Su principal objetivo es desarrollar en los estudiantes una comprensión profunda de lo leído, el desarrollo de técnicas de lectura con comprensión a varios niveles de complejidad: localización de información que está explícita en el texto, comprensión de información que está implícita en el texto; de relaciones expresadas o sugeridas que exigen realizar inferencias, y una profundización de lo comprendido a partir de diversas estrategias de carácter metacognitivo y de su ampliación utilizando otros géneros discursivos sobre el mismo tema, entre ellos los multimodales.

a. *Lectura del cuento "La Composición"* de Antonio Skármeta, chileno (*)

Resumen del cuento

El cuento se desarrolla en los tiempos de la dictadura de Pinochet, un período de tremenda opresión del pueblo chileno. Pedro es el hijo único de una modesta familia que secretamente escucha en las noches la radio del extranjero en donde se dan noticias acerca de lo que está pasando en Chile, noticias que la radio y prensa chilenas no publican. Un día, cuando Pedro jugaba futbol con sus amigos,vieron que unos militares llevaban arrastrando y apuntado con metralletas al papá de uno de ellos Para averiguar quiénes son subversivos, un capitán militar visita la clase de Pedro y les pide a los estudiantes que todos escriban una composición contando lo que hacen sus padres después de la cena. La mejor composición ganará un premio.

Al enterarse los padres de que Pedro había escrito una composición narrando lo que los padres hacían en las noches, se alarmaron, pero Pedro entonces les leyó su texto que el capitán les había devuelto ese día. Entre otras frases decía:

> *"Entonces yo salgo a jugar fútbol y me gusta meter goles de cabecita. Después viene mi mamá y me dice ya Pedrito venga a comer y luego nos sentamos a la mesa y yo siempre me como todo menos la sopa que no me gusta. Después, todas las noches mi papá y mi mamá se sientan en el sillón y juegan ajedrez y yo termino la tarea. Y ellos siguen jugando ajedrez hasta que es la hora de irse a dormir".*
>
> Sus padres sonriendo aliviados dijeron que habría que comprar un juego de ajedrez, por si acaso . . .[2]

b. Cuatro tipos de preguntas

El objetivo de esta actividad es desarrollar conciencia de los distintos tipos de relación que se dan entre una pregunta y el tipo de respuesta que requiere. Esta es una actividad metacognitiva ya que invita a los alumnos a que deliberadamente exploren relaciones entre lo que se dice y lo que se logra hacer a través de las preguntas. Es importante que los maestros formulen preguntas variadas, especialmente las que implican inferencias e interpretación crítica del texto. Por ejemplo, en este caso sería interesante preguntar:

¿Por qué Pedro no escribe lo que realmente hacían sus padres? Implica hacer una inferencia.

¿Cómo puede afectar la vida de las personas el vivir bajo un gobierno autoritario? Implica interpretación crítica.

c. Mapa del personaje

El objetivo de esta actividad, es desarrollar la capacidad de inferir los rasgos de personalidad de un personaje de un texto leído, además de mostrar evidencias que respaldan esa caracterización.

En parejas, los estudiantes completan este organizador gráfico siguiendo las instrucciones que este entrega (Cuadro 5.5). Esta actividad puede constituir también una instancia evaluativa del nivel de comprensión de los estudiantes, estableciendo dos o tres indicadores de logro para ello.

d. Rompecabezas de Vocabulario

Esta actividad tiene como objetivo desarrollar en los estudiantes destrezas metalingüística de una manera lúdica y colaborativa. Los estudiantes ampliarán su vocabulario y aprenderán aspectos ortográficos de la lengua.

Para la realización de la actividad Rompecabezas de Vocabulario (Ilustración 5.2), invitar a los estudiantes a tener a mano el texto leído con el fin de releer para identificar las palabras que deben descubrir a partir de este juego lingüístico.

- Los alumnos -sentados en grupos de cuatro- reciben cuatro tarjetas claramente marcadas: Estudiante A, Estudiante B, Estudiante C, Estudiante D.

Cuadro 5.5. Mapa del personaje

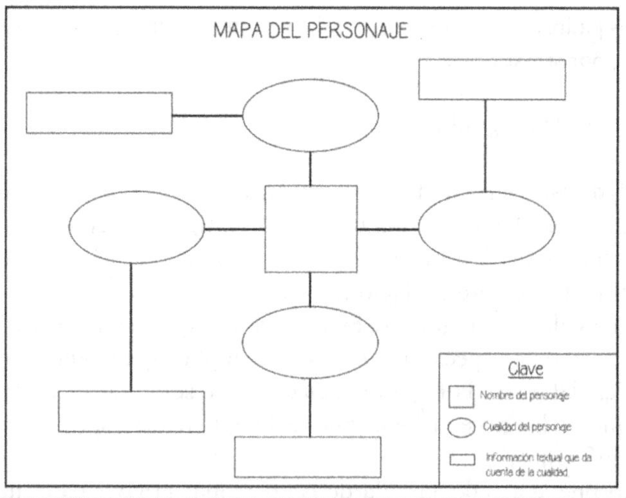

- Cada tarjeta contiene una de las claves para que trabajando colaborativamente ellos puedan adivinar una palabra. Cada tarjeta tiene un título que define el tema que agrupa a las palabras de manera significativa.
- Como preparación para el trabajo, los alumnos tienen papel y lápiz, copian el título, y numeran los reglones de su papel del 1 al 12 o del 1 al 8 (siempre múltiplos de 4).
- Ahora ya están listos para "jugar."

Para facilitar la comprensión de la actividad, se sugiere modelar con un ejemplo en la pizarra con cuatro estudiantes:

El estudiante con la tarjeta A, señala un número del término en el que trabajará el grupo en desorden, y lo anuncia. Los compañeros ponen un círculo alrededor del número señalado, y el alumno con la tarjeta A lee la primera clave:

A: Vamos a empezar con el número 6. Esta palabra comienza con la letra Z.

El estudiante que ha recibido la tarjeta B lee su clave.

B: Esta palabra tiene 3 sílabas. *Todos escriben tres rayas en sus notas para indicar el número de sílabas.*

C lee su clave.

Esta es una palabra grave que no lleva tilde. Ahora los alumnos sobre el espacio de la penúltima sílaba marcan una tilde.

D lee su clave. (Nadie puede responder hasta que la última clave haya sido leída)

Esta palabra significa "algo que se usa en los pies para facilitar la marcha, generalmente de cuero y con una suela"

Quienes tengan una respuesta la ofrecen: Zapato

Los alumnos se ponen de acuerdo y el juego comienza nuevamente. Si hay 8 palabras en este rompecabezas, A toma el liderazgo dos veces. Luego las tarjetas se rotan en una misma dirección. Cada dos palabras vuelven a rotarse. De esta manera todos los alumnos llegan a leer cada tipo de clave dos veces. Algunas sugerencias para crear Rompecabezas de Vocabulario:

- Lo primero es determinar un tema y luego los conceptos que han aprendido en clases o que aparecen en un texto que se ha leído.
- Luego se listan 8 o 12 términos importantes relacionados con el tema seleccionado; en este caso proponemos las siguientes: ajedrez, adivinar, gol, preso, arquero, metralleta, dictadura, susurrantes.

- La tarjeta con la letra A entregará la letra inicial de cada palabra del listado; la tarjeta B entregará el número de sílabas que tiene la palabra; la letra C indicará si es una palabra aguda, grave o esdrújula, y sí tiene tilde. La rotación de cartas cada dos o tres ítems es necesaria para que así cada tipo de clave haya sido practicado por todos los miembros del grupo equitativamente (Walqui et al., 2006).
- La tarjeta más difícil de escribir es la última (D) ya que no se debe proponer una definición de la palabra sacada del diccionario, sino una que funcione para los alumnos y que se refiera a lo estudiado en clase. Esta es la primera tarjeta que se escribe.
- Las otras tarjetas son bastante fáciles de diseñar.

Como se puede apreciar, esta actividad presenta una manera lúdica de repasar algunos aspectos formales del español sin hacer el trabajo tedioso. La práctica de si una palabra es aguda, grave, o esdrújula y si lleva tilde o no se trata como un juego, no como reglas importantes que deben ser el centro de una lección. Es importante recalcar que el tratamiento lingüístico se realiza como juego, y luego de haber explorado lo importante del texto: ideas y prácticas analíticas. De ninguna manera este trabajo formal debe anteceder lo esencial.

Una vez que los estudiantes han terminado de leer el cuento interactivamente, explorándolo desde varios ángulos, llega el momento de aplicar los nuevos conocimientos al análisis y creatividad en otras circunstancias. Sugerimos algunas actividades para lograr esta aplicación.

Illustración 5.2. Ejemplo de Rompecabezas de vocabulario

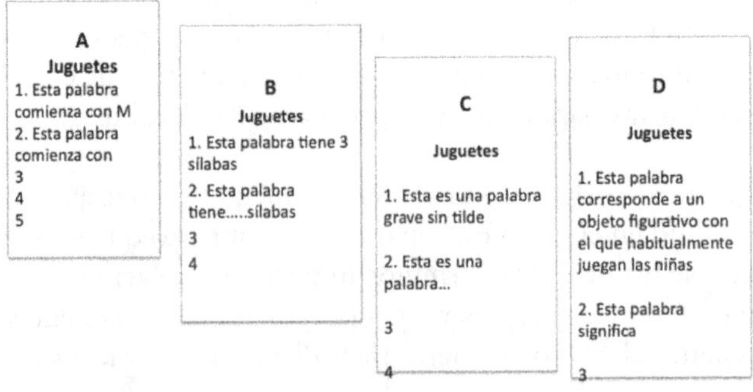

e. Lectura de una noticia

El objetivo de esta actividad es invitar la ampliación de la comprensión del cuento "La Composición" a la lectura de una noticia aparecida en un periódico sobre niños que sufrieron injustamente durante la dictadura; se trata de un género discursivo informativo que presenta hechos reales, no de ficción.

La maestra presenta el texto informativo en power point y solicita a los estudiantes señalar las características de la estructura de una noticia, de acuerdo con lo que han estudiado previamente. Luego inicia la lectura para ceder este rol a otros estudiantes.

La noticia que se propone para esta actividad se titula: "Niños y adolescentes en dictadura: la herida menos visible del Chile militarizado tras 1973" publicada por Los Ángeles Times y se encuentra en:

https://www.latimes.com/espanol/internacional/articulo/2023-09-08/ninos-y-adolescentes-en-dictadura-la-herida-menos-visible-del-chile-militarizado-tras-1973. Cada maestro escogerá algunos párrafos de esta noticia para ser leída a los alumnos.

En síntesis, la noticia expone el caso de varios niños y niñas que estuvieron encarcelados junto a sus madres durante la dictadura de Pinochet en Chile. Se enfoca en el caso de una mujer, hoy de 50 años, que recuerda su experiencia en la cárcel cuando tenía dos años y comparte todo el horror que eso significó para toda su familia

- *Reflexión sobre el contenido de la noticia:* Con el propósito de desarrollar la capacidad de una lectura intertextual, los estudiantes son invitados a señalar los puntos en común que identifican este texto informativo con el cuento "La Composición".

f. Completar el Cuadro de Anticipación (Parte 2)

Los estudiantes retoman el Cuadro de Anticipación que respondieron al comienzo de la lección y escriben en la tercera columna lo que aprendieron. Se trata de un momento metacognitivo, pues requiere que los estudiantes analicen lo que han logrado con la lectura de dos textos.

g. Lectura a Cuatro Voces de un Relato del Uruguay en el pasado

La lectura de este relato permitirá a los estudiantes conocer otra experiencia de una niña uruguaya que sufre por la situación de su padre injustamente en prisión durante una dictadura.

La maestra lee en voz alta el texto y llama la atención de los alumnos sobre la presencia de cuatro modalidades: en negrita, en caracteres normales, en

Illustración 5.3. Lectura a Cuatro Voces de un Relato del Uruguay en el pasado.

Lectura a Cuatro Voces de un relato del Uruguay

Durante la dictadura militar uruguaya, en una cárcel llamada Libertad, *los presos no podían dibujar ni recibir dibujos de mujeres embarazadas, parejas, mariposas, estrellas, ni pájaros.*

Didaskó Pérez, maestro de escuela, torturado y preso por tener ideas políticas, recibió un domingo la visita de su hija Milay, de cinco años. *La hija le trajo un dibujo de pájaros.* Los guardias se lo rompieron a la entrada de la cárcel.

Al domingo siguiente, Milay le trajo un dibujo de árboles. *Como los árboles no estaban prohibidos, el dibujo pasó.* **El padre le elogió la obra y le preguntó por esos circulitos de colores que aparecían en las copas de los árboles, muchos pequeños círculos entre las ramas:**

- ¿Son naranjas? ¿Qué frutas son?

La niña lo hizo callar: -Ssshhhh.

Y en secreto le explicó:

-Bobo. ¿No ves que son ojos? Los ojos de los pájaros, que te traje a escondidas."

Eduardo Galeano (Uruguayo)

itálica y subrayado (Illustración 5.3). Luego separa el curso en cuatro grupos y asigna a cada uno de ellos una modalidad distinta; los grupos leen en voz alta las partes del texto que corresponden a su modalidad. Esta modalidad de lectura en voz alta es muy útil, ya que muestra el andamio invisible que la maestra preparó para que los alumnos le presten atención a los diversos elementos significativos que contribuyen al impacto general del texto. Además, la actividad resultará atractiva para los estudiantes porque ellos la realizarán con todo el curso al mismo tiempo, sintiendo el impacto del texto, sin tener que asumir lecturas en voz alta individuales que no siempre son apreciadas.

Tercer Momento: Profundicemos nuestra comprensión

a. Cuadro de dos columnas

Esta actividad permitirá a los estudiantes profundizar la comprensión del cuento, al recordar con sentido crítico el texto "La Composición", especialmente algunas acciones de sus personajes (Cuadro 5.6).

Los alumnos, trabajando en parejas, completarán este cuadro escribiendo en la columna de izquierda algún hecho o comportamiento de Pedro que les haya llamado la atención; luego, en la columna derecha, escribirán la opinión que ellos tienen de esa acción. Realizarán lo mismo respecto al militar que se presenta en la sala de clases de Pedro.

Cuadro 5.6. Cuadro de Dos Columnas.

Los personajes hicieron lo siguiente . . .	Mi opinión es . . .
Pedro hizo . . .	
El militar hizo . . .	

b. Espejo de Mente Abierta

Esta actividad combina (Ilustración 5.4) expresión artística con profundización del conocimiento sobre las características y preocupaciones centrales de un personaje. La actividad pretende que los estudiantes identifiquen lo que le está sucediendo al personaje, sus emociones, preguntas, preocupaciones, sueños, etc., y que los representen como si se estuviera mirando a un espejo que refleja lo que ocurre en su mente. Además, se incluye la dimensión de lectura crítica al solicitar incluir una opinión sobre el actuar del personaje.

Los requisitos de la actividad son, que los alumnos utilicen citas apropiadas, frases creadas por ellos y que presenten sus opiniones sobre el personaje escogido. Igualmente, se les pide a los equipos que elaboren frases que sinteticen ideas importantes referidas al personaje, dibujos y símbolos. La primera vez que se realice esta actividad será una buena oportunidad para explicar a los niños que un símbolo es algo que representa otra cosa; se puede utilizar la bandera de un país como uno de los símbolos más conocidos a nivel nacional. De igual manera, se podrán utilizar otros símbolos que sean de uso frecuente en la comunidad.

Este tipo de actividad funciona muy bien si el docente la modela, utilizando ejemplos concretos de otros trabajos de cursos anteriores. La primera vez quizás usted pueda utilizar un «Espejo» que usted mismo haya elaborado durante una jornada de capacitación. Es igualmente esencial, que antes de que los niños comiencen a trabajar, tengan una comprensión clara de las características del trabajo que se espera al final. Para eso se les ofrece una rúbrica; de esta manera se comunica a los estudiantes que si siguen los criterios, todos pueden obtener un resultado excelente.

El Espejo de Mente Abierta (Illustración 5.4) es una actividad que puede realizarse en grupos de 4 estudiantes. Primero los miembros del grupo se ponen de acuerdo acerca del diseño y luego comienzan a elaborar simultáneamente el espejo, utilizando cada uno un color diverso, con el cual firmarán el producto final. Para lograr participación equilibrada, se les puede sugerir a los niños que las citas y frases se escriban a cuatro colores. También es importante que los maestros exhiban las diversas producciones. Si no cuenta con demasiado espacio, este tipo de trabajo puede colgarse fácilmente a lo largo de una cuerda y puede ir de pared a pared, agregándole atractivo a su aula. Antes de ser exhibidos, cada grupo se autoevalúa utilizando la rúbrica y mencionando tres razones para la calificación. Mientras los jóvenes trabajan, la maestra se pasea alrededor de los grupos observando cómo está funcionando la actividad para decidir si algún andamiaje contingente es necesario para darle dirección al trabajo grupal. Igualmente, al exponerse los productos de los diversos grupos se hace evidente el que, si bien la invitación a comprometerse en acción grupal fue la misma, los resultados, gracias a la riqueza, creatividad y diferentes perspectivas de los participantes, aunque apuntan en la misma dirección, son diversos y ricos. Para la próxima vez los estudiantes tendrán más ideas respecto a cómo elaborar sus Espejos de Mente Abierta

Forme grupos de cuatro estudiantes, cuidando que sean lo más heterogéneos posible.

1. Pídales que seleccionen uno de los personajes del texto leído y que hagan una lluvia de ideas acerca de todo lo que saben de él. El Mapa del Personaje que elaboraron anteriormente les entregará elementos para esto. Cada alumno mantiene una copia de la lluvia de ideas generada por el grupo.
2. Explique lo que es un Espejo de Mente Abierta. Modele, de ser posible, utilizando algunos Espejos realizados por clases anteriores. No olvide indicar que para que el espejo sea exitoso, debe tener al menos:
    - **Dos citas textuales** (recuérdeles que son oraciones que aparecen textualmente y muéstreles que se escriben entre comillas)
    - **Dos frases creadas** por ellos que presentan la opinión de los estudiantes sobre el actuar del personaje
    - **Una frase original** sobre el personaje con creatividad y humor (puede ser parte de una canción, un refrán, etc.)
    - **Dos dibujos** que comunican ideas relevantes acerca de la situación del personaje.
    - **Dos símbolos** que representan las ideas del personaje.

3. Pídales que distribuyan esos 4 tipos de elementos de manera creativa sobre la hoja, para que el personaje aparezca con sus facciones, su cabello y otras partes del rostro diseñados con las frases y los dibujos. Recuérdeles que deben utilizar colores y lograr un producto creativo. Cada grupo tendrá una hoja con el perfil del personaje y otorgue aproximadamente 25 minutos para realizar la actividad; la rúbrica permitirá a los estudiantes realizar un excelente trabajo.

Illustración 5.4. Espejo de Mente Abierta: Esquema y Ejemplos

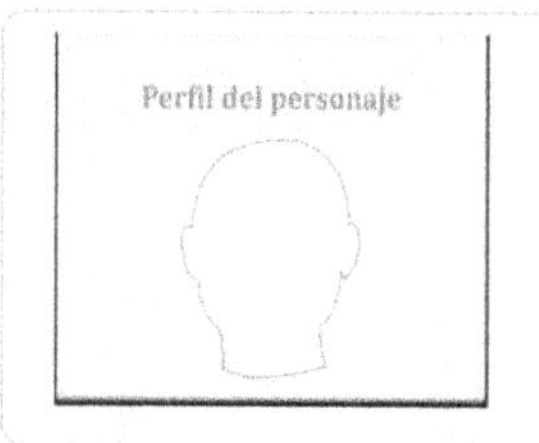

4. Exponga todos los trabajos en el aula y organice un "Paseo por la galería" para que los estudiantes observen y evalúen los espejos de sus compañeros. Si hubiera tiempo, se le puede pedir al grupo que se enfocó en un personaje específico a que presenten su trabajo a la clase. Como hay cuatro requisitos, estos guían la participación colaborativa de todos. De allí en adelante, solo se presentan espejos que sean suficientemente diferentes.
5. Antes de que los alumnos comiencen a planear su espejo, es bueno que entiendan los criterios que determinan el completar con éxito la actividad (Cuadro 5.7). Con este fin se les entrega esta rúbrica la cual además, guiará la evaluación del producto. De esta manera, las alumnas saben claramente hacia qué calidad deben apuntar su trabajo.

c. "Lo que a mí me tocó el corazón"

Esta actividad tiene como objetivo establecer una vinculación emocional del lector con eventos o situaciones que aparecen en el texto leído.

Para realizar la actividad los estudiantes dibujan un corazón -o cualquier otro diseño apropiado- y al interior escriben aquello que los conmovió en esta historia. La pregunta que el maestro puede formular es: -Al leer la historia de Pedro ¿hay algo que te emocionó? ¿Qué fue? Escríbelo dentro de este corazón.

Explorando un ejemplo de lección para adolescentes.

La adolescencia es la edad en la cual las personas desarrollan más activamente su personalidad. Los adolescentes contemplan situaciones en sus contextos y deciden, consciente o inconscientemente, cómo reaccionar. Estos momentos de decisión ocurren en interacción con sus familias, vecinos, compañeros de escuela, maestros, etc. y les ayuda a definirse a sí

Cuadro 5.7. Criterios para la evaluación del Espejo de Mente Abierta.

Espejo de Mente Abierta: Criterios para la Evaluación			
Indicadores de logro	**Muy bien**	**Satisfactorio**	**Necesita Revisión**
Contenido	Incluye: - **Dos o más citas** relevantes del cuento. - **Dos frases creadas** que presentan **opiniones** de los lectores sobre el personaje escogido. - **Una frase original** sobre el personaje, con creatividad y humor (puede ser parte de una canción, de un refrán, etc. - Dos o más dibujos que comunican ideas relevantes acerca de la situación del personaje - Dos o más símbolos que representan las ideas del personaje. En general, el Espejo de mente abierta comunica con efectividad el punto de vista o estado anímico del personaje seleccionado y las opiniones de los lectores sobre su actuar.	Incluye: - Una cita apropiada extraída del cuento. - Frases originales basadas en la lectura del cuento que presentan opiniones de los lectores poco relevantes sobre el personaje escogido. - Una frase original sobre el personaje demasiado obvia, poco original - Uno o dos dibujos que no son centrales para comunicar la situación del personaje escogido. - Uno o mas símbolos que representan ideas no centrales a las circunstancias del personaje escogido. En general, el espejo de mente abierta comunica parcialmente el punto de vista o estado anímico del personaje seleccionado y solo una de las opiniones resulta relevante . . .	Le faltan algunos de los Siguientes elementos: - citas - frases originales - símbolos - dibujos -Las frases y dibujos no se relacionan con el personaje representado. En general, el espejo de mente abierta no comunica el punto de vista o estado anímico del personaje seleccionado, ni las opiniones de los lectores.

(*continued*)

Cuadro 5.7 (*continuación*).

Espejo de Mente AbiertaCriterios para la Evaluación			
Indicadores de logro	**Muy bien**	**Satisfactorio**	**Necesita Revisión**
Presentación	- Cada miembro del grupo contribuye al desarrollo del espejo y a la presentación oral frente a la clase. - El Espejo de mente abierta utiliza un diseño creativo para persuadir al espectador del punto de visto o estado de ánimo del personaje, al igual que las opiniones de los lectores. - Los dibujos, símbolos y textos están utilizados con efectividad y el diagrama está muy bien presentado y limpio.	- Cada miembro del grupo contribuye al desarrollo del espejo y a la presentación oral frente a la clase. - Se utilizan de manera apropiada dibujos, símbolos y palabras en el diagrama. - El Espejo de mente abierta está bien presentado y limpio.	- Uno a más miembros del equipo no contribuye a la elaboración del espejo de mente abietra o a su presentación oral frente a la clase. - No se utilizaron todos los elementos necesarios en el diseño del diagrama. - El Espejo de mente abierta se ve desordenado y/o sucio.

mismos, y en relación con familiares y amigos. Por eso es sumamente importante el que se les ofrezca a los estudiantes oportunidades para explorar críticamente circunstancias comunes para que -en diálogo con compañeros, con maestros, y consigo mismos- puedan reflexionar, considerar opciones, y decidir qué opción tomar y por qué. Esto es lo que constituye un diálogo crítico (Freire, 2005; Kibler, Valdés y Walqui, 2021), la exploración profunda de eventos para determinar el bien común, como lo propone una vida democrática.

Esta lección, destinada a adolescentes en los grados 7 a 9 también gira alrededor de temas relevantes para los estudiantes, y que les permiten explorar y ejercitar, además de sus destrezas de oracidad y literacidad, su sentido de justicia social. "El Premio," un cuento de Marta Salinas,[3] se desarrolla en una escuela rural intermedia en Texas. Marta, la protagonista, es una joven de pocos recursos económicos y muy estudiosa. Su sueño es que para la graduación de la escuela intermedia va a ganar el premio, una chamarra académica muy bonita que se le entrega al mejor estudiante de la escuela desde el grado 1 hasta el 8. Ya anteriormente su hermana mayor había ganado la chamarra, y Marta está segura, dado su rendimiento académico, de que la chaqueta le corresponderá. Sin embargo, hay un problema. Joanne, la hija del dueño de la única tienda en el pueblo, un señor que también es miembro de la junta directiva del distrito, y quien es una adolescente no muy estudiosa, quiere la chamarra. Como su familia es rica y poderosa, el director de la escuela se ve en un gran dilema. El cuento narra la actitud del abuelo de Marta, la disputa entre un maestro y el director, y la resolución final que se basa en la sabiduría del parco pero justo abuelo.

El texto ha sido seleccionado deliberadamente para explorar temas en los cuales los personajes experimentan ambivalencias acerca de cómo reaccionar. El director de la escuela quiere la aprobación de los maestros para darle la chaqueta a Joanne. El señor Schmidt, uno de los maestros, defiende el sentido justo del premio y el hecho de que Marta se lo merece. Cuando Marta le cuenta a su abuelo, un hombre sencillo de pocas palabras, que el director dice que hay una nueva regla para obtener el premio, pagar una suma de dinero, el abuelo le pregunta a Marta ¿qué significa un premio? Aunque la respuesta del abuelo no le satisface, Martha la acepta y a lo largo del tiempo entiende cada vez mejor lo que significa enfrentarse a la injusticia.

1. Preparémonos para leer.

Como podemos observar en el cuadro de la página 7, nuestra propuesta pedagógica empieza con la misma actividad que la ofrecida para "La Composición", con una Guía de Anticipación (Cuadro 5.8) que orienta y permite que los estudiantes exploren su posición frente a ciertos temas (Aguilar, 2012).

a. Guía de Anticipación

Las aseveraciones en el Cuadro 5.8 son discutidas por dos estundiantes, con la clase entera trabajando al mismo tiempo, permiten que un alumno lea una idea y exprese si está de acuerdo o no con ella, dando un ejemplo o argumento que explica la base para su respuesta. El otro compañero ofrece su opinión, su ejemplo, y su justificación. Vemos aquí como se comienzan a discutir temas relevantes al cuento, a las experiencias personales de los estudiantes, y a la vida en general, temas que van a ser revisados constantemente de manera dialógica a través de la lección.

Cuadro 5.8. Guía de Anticipación

AFIRMACIONES	De acuerdo	En desacuerdo
1. En la mayoría de los casos los maestros son justos con sus estudiantes.		
2. La justicia siempre triunfa al final.		
3. Los estudiantes deben siempre respetar las decisiones de los maestros, aunque no estén de acuerdo con ellas.		
4. Uno siempre debe defender sus derechos.		
5. Los estudiantes de bajos recursos económicos generalmente no destacan en sus estudios.		
6. La raza o el grupo étnico al que pertenece un estudiante no influye para nada en la asignación de premios en la escuela.		

b. Piensa, anota y comparte.

Una segunda propuesta para Preparemos Nuestra Lectura es la actividad "Piensa, Anota, y Comparte". Esta es una de las actividades más usadas en clases, que no obstante se ha convertido en "Voltea y Habla" (Turn and talk"). Sin embargo, cuando nos enfrascamos en una conversación con alguien, siempre iniciamos la interacción bien sea con un comentario, o con una pregunta. Joel Westheimer, quien ha escrito acerca de la formación ciudadana en las escuelas (2024) comenta que un buen ciudadano formula preguntas críticas, y que las escuelas deben prepararlos para su deber ciudadano. Eso significa que debemos dar a los estudiantes frecuentes oportunidades de práctica en hacer preguntas. En este caso, se les ofrece un modelo que puede ser variado sin cambiar el significado de lo que se pide:

Piensa en alguna ocasión en la que fuiste tratado injustamente. Comparte tu respuesta con tu compañero.

-¿Qué sucedió? ¿Cómo te sentiste? ¿Cuál fue tu reacción?

Sin revelar el tema concreto del texto a explorarse, estas actividades han preparado a los alumnos a leerlo con comprensión y de manera crítica.

2. Leamos interactivamente.

a. Preguntas de enfoque

El texto se divide en momentos significativos, y antes de leer un componente, se les ofrece a los alumnos preguntas que enfocan su atención en la interpretación de temas centrales en la narrativa y que incluso -basado en los desarrollos hasta el momento- les permite inferir lo que va a suceder. Por ejemplo, en la primera sección del cuento, se ofrece a los alumnos -antes de leer la sección- las siguientes preguntas:

- ¿Qué significado tiene la chaqueta para Marta?
- ¿Cuál es el dilema que enfrenta el director con relación al premio?
- ¿Qué crees que va a pasar?

Estas preguntas requieren que el alumno sintetice e infiera en base al texto, ambas actividades analíticas esenciales.

b. Guía Metacognitiva

El propósito de esta guía es desarrollar en los estudiantes habilidades metacognitivas, como su nombre lo indica. El desarrollo consciente de habilidades lectoras, practicado con la actividad en nivel primario de reconocer tipos de pregunta, a nivel intermedio es ofrecido por la Guía Metacognitiva (Cuadro 5.9). Esta actividad invita a los estudiantes a que, tomando turnos en la lectura de párrafos, le lean el párrafo asignado a su compañero y escojan una estrategia

Cuadro 5.9. Guías Metacognitivas

GUÍA 1	
Cuando no entiendo bien lo que leo . . .	
Puedo hacer lo siguiente:	Por eso puedo decir:
Pensar acerca de lo que este texto podría significar *(hacer predicciones, formular hipótesis)*	No estoy segura de qué se trata esto, pero creo que . . .
	Esta parte es confusa, pero pienso que significa . . .
	Después de releer esta parte, pienso que puede significar . . .
Hacer un resumen de lo que entiendo en cada parte del texto que leo.	Lo que entiendo de este texto hasta el momento es . . .
	Puedo resumir esta parte del texto diciendo . . .
	Los puntos principales de esta parte son . . .

Cuadro 5.9 (*continuación*).

GUÍA 2	
Cuando no entiendo bien lo que leo . . .	
Puedo hacer lo siguiente:	Por eso puedo decir . . .
Usar mis conocimientos previos para tratar de entender	Yo sé algo de esto porque . . .
	Leí u oí algo acerca de esto cuando . . .
	No entiendo esta sección, pero reconozco . . .
Aplicar conceptos y/o lecturas que se relacionen con el texto	Un texto/idea que he encontrado antes que se relaciona con esto es . . .
	Aprendimos sobre esta idea/concepto cuando estudiamos . . .
	Esta idea/concepto se relaciona con . . .

GUÍA 3	
Cuando no entiendo bien lo que leo . . .	
Puedo hacer lo siguiente:	Por eso puedo decir:
Hacer preguntas acerca de las ideas o frases que no entiendo	Tengo dos preguntas sobre esta parte del texto . . .
	Entiendo esta parte, pero tengo una pregunta acerca de . . .
Usar textos, dibujos, tablas, y organizadores gráficos para ayudarme a aclarar mis ideas.	Si miramos este gráfico, podemos ver que . . .
	Esta tabla me da más información sobre . . .
	Cuando revisé la primera parte de este capítulo, encontré que . . .

apropiada de las seis ofrecidas en la columna de la izquierda. Si necesitan apoyo con la formulación inicial de su contribución, pueden utilizar una de las frases fórmula (Ellis, 2016) ofrecidas en la columna de la derecha, pero esto no es necesario, siempre y cuando los alumnos introduzcan su reflexión. La Guía indica seis estrategias que comúnmente utilizan de manera inconsciente los buenos lectores. A través de esta actividad, conscientemente los alumnos practican de manera significativa las estrategias, y por lo tanto comienzan a apropiárselas. La generatividad de la actividad les permite a los estudiantes que en el futuro las usen de manera creativa, en contextos diferentes de aquellos en que las aprendieron. Para que la actividad sea productiva es importante escoger cuatro párrafos continuos que sean ricos en contenido y que puedan crear confusión en el lector, de esta manera, leyendo y discutiendo en conjunto, se exploran estas posibles dificultades.

3. Profundicemos nuestra comprensión.

En el tercer momento de esta lección, se ofrece a los estudiantes oportunidades que le permiten aplicar ideas exploradas en la lección, imaginando y situando las circunstancias en contextos no tomados por la narrativa de manera crítica. Vemos, por ejemplo, que un Espejo de Mente Abierta puede ser propuesto para analizar a protagonistas presentes y no presentes. Por ejemplo, el padre de Joanne, ¿qué desea? ¿cómo va a actuar y por qué?, o la misma Joanne, quien no es una protagonista en el cuento. El abuelo, igualmente podría ser un personaje importante para explorar ya que habla tan poco.

a. Espejo de mente abierta.

Las características de esta estrategia fueron presentadas en el ejemplo con la lectura de "La Composición".

b. Diálogo colaborativo.

Si el espejo ha sido utilizado en las últimas dos semanas en clase, una buena alternativa es el diálogo colaborativo. En este caso, se divide el cuento en sus momentos esenciales, y se les pide a grupos de cuatro alumnos que imaginen los diálogos que se llevaron a cabo durante un momento del cuento. Parte del contenido está dado por el cuento, pero la gran parte debe explorar situaciones lógicas que se le ocurrirían a los personajes. Para esta actividad es muy importante que los alumnos en conjunto creen el diálogo y que cada uno tenga un guion completo. De esta manera pueden -después de 15 minutos- pararse -guiones en mano- y leer dramáticamente, y en secuencia, compartir sus contribuciones.

En este caso, los diálogos pueden surgir en las siguientes situaciones:

- Marta conversa con una compañera acerca de sus expectativas de recibir la chamarra.
- Camino al gimnasio, Marta escucha que dos maestros comentan lo que quiere hacer el director de la escuela con la chamarra.

- Marta habla con el director por primera vez.
- Marta habla con su abuelo.
- Marta habla con el director por segunda vez.
- Martha habla con su abuelo por segunda vez, cuando se ha solucionado el dilema.

c. Escribir un ensayo.

El propósito de esta actividad es el de ampliar la comprensión del texto leído a partir de la producción de un texto escrito que corresponde a otro género discursivo: un ensayo. Al escribir en conjunto, los estudiantes exploran un momento del cuento, y las razones, preocupaciones, deseos, frustraciones y largos comentarios sociales. Esto los prepara para luego culminar con una actividad en la cual en un ensayo que primero es discutido en grupos de cuatro, pero eventualmente es escrito de manera individual. En este ensayo se exploran acciones que se podrían tomar en la escuela o la comunidad frente a situaciones de discriminación. Así se le da la agencia para decidir y formular cambios a los protagonistas de la clase, preparándolos para una vida crítica en sociedad.

A MODO DE CONCLUSIÓN

Este capítulo presenta un conjunto de principios pedagógicos que sustentan conceptualmente las dimensiones más importantes que debe tener una propuesta pedagógica de calidad y equidad para los estudiantes latinos. Ellas ilustran los importantes cambios en conceptualización y práctica que deben guiar el desarrollo de currículum y clases para los alumnos latinos. Se enfatiza la relevancia de diseñar actividades desafiantes, que apoyen los procesos de aprendizaje de los estudiantes en la Zona de Desarrollo Próximo con andamiajes robustos, bien diseñados para que todos se comprometan activamente, y contingentes, para responder a situaciones no previstas. Frente a las exigencias que plantea el siglo XXI para la formación de ciudadanos que puedan desenvolverse de manera competente en una sociedad democrática, se otorga gran importancia a la capacidad de convertir a los estudiantes en lectores críticos, capaces de comprender variados tipos de textos con profundidad, identificando la ideología detrás de ellos y elaborando puntos de vista personales y reflexivos. La selección de temas relevantes e interesantes que se relacionen con los desafíos que plantea la sociedad donde se desenvuelven los estudiantes resulta muy importante para lograr ese tipo de lectores.

NOTAS

1. Este capítulo utiliza en una oportunidad "niños y niñas" al igual que "maestros y maestras" pero no a lo largo de todo el texto con el fin de no recargarlo

2. La composición, publicado por Ediciones Ekaré. © 2000 Antonio Skármeta, texto © 2000 Alfonso Ruano, ilustraciones. Para leer el cuento completo: https://amsafe.org.ar/wpcontent/uploads/SkarmeaLacomposicion.pdf

3. "El Premio," traducido por Ruth Barraza y Aída Walqui-van Lier, del original The Scholarship Jacket, se encuentra en: https://apespa.weebly.com/uploads/1/2/5/0/12505802/el_premio-salinas.pdf

REFERENCIAS BIBLIOGRÁFICAS

Aguilar, C. (2012) *La didáctica de la lengua y la literatura y la teoría crítica.* Barcelona. Revista Lenguaje y Textos. Núm. 36, noviembre.

Alexander, R. (2020). *A dialogic teaching companion.* Routledge.

Arizona State University. (2023, October 3). Willian Seidman Reserch Institute. https://news.asu.edu/20231003-discoveries-ldc-us-latino-gdp-report-impact-economy-asu-authors#:~:text=Latinos%20are%20the%20fastest%2Dgrowing,researchers%20from%20Arizona%20State%20University.

Bakhtin, M. (1989) *El problema de los géneros discursivos.*Siglo XXI.

Bronckart, J.P. (2007) Los géneros de textos y su contribución al desarrollo psicológico. In J.-P. Bronckart, *Desarrollo del lenguaje y didáctica de las lenguas.* Miño y Davila.

Bronfenbrenner, U. (1979). *The ecology of human development: Experiments by nature and design.* Harvard University Press.

Cassany, D. (2009). Prácticas letradas contemporáneas. Claves para su Desarrollo. Ministerio de Educación de España.

Cassany, D. y Castella, J. (2010) PERSPECTIVA, Florianópolis, v. 28(2) 353–374

Chávez-Moreno, L. (2025). *How schools make race. Teaching Latinx racialization in America.* Harvard Education Press.

Cummins, J. (1979). Cognitive/academic language proficiency, linguistic interdependence, the optimum age question and other matters. Working papers in bilingualism, No.19, Vol. 19.

Ellis, R., (2016). Instructed second language acquisition. A literatura review. New Zealand Ministry of Education.

Flecha, R. y Torrego, L. (2012) *Aprendizaje dialógico y transformaciones sociales: más allá de los límites.* Barcelona. Revista Lenguaje y Textos. Núm. 36, noviembre.

Flores, N., & García, O. (2017). A critical review of bilingual education in the United States: From basementsnd pride to boutiques and profit. *Annual Review of Applied Linguistics, 37*, pp. 14–19.

Freire, P. y Shor, I. (2014) *Miedo y osadía: la cotidianidad del docente que se arriesga a practicar una pedagogía transformadora.* Siglo Veintiuno Editores.

Freire, P. (2017). *La importancia del acto de leer.* Caracas, Editorial El perro y la rana.

Galdames, V. y Walqui, A. (2008) Enseñanza de la lengua indígena como lengua materna. SEP. México, Mineduc, GIZ Guatemala.

Gonzalez, J. (2022). *Harvest of empire. A history of latinos in America.* Penguin Books.

Iturrioz, P. (2019) La enseñanza de la oralidad en la clase de lengua. Barcelona, Revista Textos: Didáctica de la Lengua y de la Literatura, 83, Año XXV, 23–28

Jurado, F. y Lomas, C. (2021) Lengua del alumnado, lengua de la escuela. Barcelona, Revista Textos, 24, pp 6–10.

Lave, J. y Wenger, E. (1991). *Situated learning: Legitimate peripheral participation.* Cambridge University Press.

Markovits, D. (2020). *The meritocracy trap. How America's foundational myth feeds inequality, dismantles the middle class, and devours the elite.* Penguin Books.

Martos, E. y Martos, A. (2014) Artefactos culturales y alfabetización en la era digital: discusiones conceptuales y praxis educativa. Salamanca, España. Teoría de la Educación. *Revista interuniversitaria, 26*(1), 119–135.

Mercer, N. (2019). *Language and the joint construction of knowledge. The selected Works of Neil Mercer.* Routledge.

Resnick, L., Asterhan, C. S. C., y Clark, S. N. (2015). *Socializing intelligence through academic talk and dialogue.* American Research Association.

Rosa, J. y Flores, N. (2017). Unsettling race and language. Toward a raciolinguistic perspective. *Language in Society. 45*(5), 621–647.

Rosa, J. (2019). *Looking like a language, sounding like a race. Raciolinguistic ideologies and the learning of latinidad.* Oxford University Press.

Ruiz, R. (1984). Orientations to language planning. *NABE Journal, 8*, 15–34.

Valdés, G. y Figueroa, R. (1994). *Bilingualism and testing: A special case of bias.* Ablex.

Valdés, G. (2017). From language maintenance and intergenerational transmission to language survivance: Will 'heritage language' education help or hinder? *International Journal of the Sociology of Language* 2017 (243), 67–95.

van Lier, L. (1996). *Interaction in the language curriculum: Awareness, autonomy, and authenticity.* Longman.

van Lier, L. (2000). From input to affordance. Social interactive learning from an ecological perspective. In J. P. Lantolf (Ed.), *Sociocultural theory and second language learning: Recent advances.* Oxford University Press.

van Lier, L. (2004). *The ecology and semiotics of language learning: A sociocultural perspective.* Kluwer Academic.

Vygotsky, L. (1962). *Thought and language.* Harvard University Press.

Vygotsky, L. (1976). Play and its role in the mental development of the child. In J. Bruner, A. Jolly, & K. Sylva (Eds.), *Play: Its role in development and evolution* (pp. 537–554). UK Penguin.

Vygotsky, L. (1978). *Mind in society.* Harvard Education Press.

Walqui, A. (2024). Equitable and quality education for English Learners and all other students: The role of oracy. National Research and Development Center to Improve Education for English Learners. WestEd.

Walqui, A. y Schmida, M. (2022). Reconceptualización del andamiaje para estudiantes de inglés. En: de Oliveira, L. y Westerlund, R. (Editores). (2022).

Andamiaje para estudiantes multilingües en escuelas primarias y secundarias. Routledge.

Westheimer, J. (2024). *What kind of citizen? Educating our citizens for the common good.* (2nd ed.). Teachers College Press.

Wiley, T. (2024). Heritage and community languages and education: Revisiting Valdes's cautionary concerns. In Kibler et al (Eds.). *Equity in multilingual schools and communities. Celebrating the contributions of Guadalupe Valdés.* Multilingual Matters.

CHAPTER 6

Beyond Vocabulary, Similes, and Metaphors

Making Poetry an Engaging and Accessible Genre for Multilingual Learners

Mary Schmida

In this chapter, I propose that poetry is a powerful genre for multilingual learners. With the kind of supports that our amplified approach and instructional design provide, students will be well positioned to take a critical stance toward the themes and ideas presented in the text, as well as engage in quality learning and deep conversations. Especially within the ELA classroom, poetry affords students opportunities to delve deeply into a text and apprentice into key disciplinary practices that are at the heart of English Language Arts.

I have found through my own teaching, whether it is with middle school students or college freshmen, poetry can provide multilingual learners with a powerful connection to literature, as many poets expound on themes, contexts, and events that mirror students' life experiences. Even poetry from decades or centuries past often contains themes that transcend time and space. Themes of loss, fear, belonging (or lack of belonging), transitions, identity, and the like are themes that many students, especially multilingual learners, have experienced first-hand. Students can then draw on these lived experiences to support their reading, understanding, and interpretation of texts. In addition to relatable themes, the often-predictable language patterns of poetry, such as the repetition of words and phrases, identifiable rhyming pattern and structure, and alliteration make poetry a genre that multilingual learners—and all students—can appreciate and engage with and through which they can deepen and strengthen their understanding of language.

One of the pedagogical shifts mentioned in Chapter 2 is relevant here when choosing and preparing students, especially multilingual learners, to read poetry; namely, the shift from believing that students need to arrive to the classroom already motivated to read and engage with the complex—and often historically placed—themes of poetry to recognizing that motivating students is the job of the teacher. This chapter highlights how teachers can entice students and make them curious about authors and texts they are going to read.

Engaging multilingual learners in the genre of poetry can at times feel daunting for educators. Teachers know that for many students, regardless of language background, it is not an easy genre to access. In part, this is because of the literary features of poetry, such as the use of metaphors and idioms, which are almost always culturally specific. Even commonly used metaphors and idioms may need some unpacking for students who do not share their cultural referent. Frequently used poems in the secondary ELA classroom, such as Emily Dickinson's "Because I Could Not Stop for Death," Robert Frost's "The Road Not Taken," Maya Angelou's "Still I Rise," and Edgar Allan Poe's "The Raven," are filled with rich, figurative language—symbolism, metaphor, idiom, and personification—that make them compelling and powerful texts, but that can also make them confusing. Similarly, poetry is one of the genres in which the frequent use of imagery requires students to read beyond the words themselves to create a picture or an image in their mind's eye.

In addition to sometimes having difficulty with the figurative language found in poetry, many students have had negative experiences with the genre in school, having been taught that the goal of reading poetry is to understand its singular interpretation, rather than to identify shared human experiences or to focus on the richness of language (Curran & Wetherbee, 2014). Thus poetry, especially at the secondary level, is often met by students with "It's so boring!" or even the occasional "I hate poetry!" For this reason, teachers, too, often find poetry difficult to teach.

Whether students are reading a single poem or an anthology of poems, it behooves us to prepare all students adequately for the contexts, themes, and time periods in which the prose takes place. This is even more important for multilingual learners, both because they may be less likely to be familiar with cultural referents and also because such contexts can assist them in comprehending the language of the text, especially if it is in English. In this chapter, I will present a lesson in Three Moments (see Chapter 3) for Langston Hughes's "Theme for English B" and explain the pedagogical choices that went into the writing of this lesson. In particular, this lesson contains a robust Preparing Learners activity that serves to build students' background knowledge, which is necessary for them to engage deeply and meaningfully with the author's message and with the poem itself. First, however, I discuss necessary changes in teachers' orientations toward lesson planning in English Language Arts.

CRITICAL CONSIDERATIONS AND SHIFTS IN PLANNING

Text Choice

When choosing a text for students, especially for multilingual learners, it is important to select texts that have the potential to engage them in meaningful content, as well as texts that explore complex topics. As an author, Langston Hughes is an ideal choice to promote the critical dialogic interactions in which we want students to engage. Through his poetry, novels, and plays, Hughes wrote about the collective and individual experiences of African Americans, highlighting themes of social and political injustice. Writing during the Harlem Renaissance—a time when creative and intellectual life flourished within African American communities—Hughes's poems describe both the triumphs and struggles of working-class African Americans. These themes speak to all students, as his prose captures a wide array of emotions, experiences, and dreams that he considered common to all people (Rampersad & Roessel, 1994). The text selected for this chapter, "A Theme for English B," was chosen specifically for this reason. Writing in the early 1950s and in the first person, Hughes shares his personal account of being one of only a few African American students at Columbia University, but the text more broadly addresses the complexities of identity and one's place in society, a theme to which most, if not all, adolescents today can relate. "A Theme for English B"—though written over 70 years ago—speaks to today's young people and their struggle to define themselves in a sometimes unkind and unjust world.

This chapter illustrates how one lesson was developed to highlight the powerful elements of poetry as a genre. The text chosen for this chapter highlights the relatable experiences of the author with respect to race, belonging, society, and identity, and has the potential to actively engage multilingual learners and to support their exploration of literary themes, author's purpose, figurative language, imagery, and so on. Additionally, as discussed in Chapter 2, and as presented by Kibler et al. (2021), this chapter also explores how opportunities for critical dialogic interactions can foster students' ability to build upon their own life experiences and their understanding of the world in which they live. Specifically, the lesson was designed so that within each of the Three Moments, students will experience deliberately crafted and frequent opportunities to coconstruct understandings and to engage with multiple perspectives, ideas, and backgrounds.

Where to Begin

One of the challenges faced by students—especially multilingual learners—is that they struggle to make sense of texts that are situated in a particular time period, setting, or culture with which they are not familiar. To account for this, students' comprehension of a text can be facilitated by first building the necessary background knowledge (Bunch et al., 2014). For example, consider the student who is reading Arthur Miller's *The Crucible*: Understanding the historical and political context of the play and its allegorical reference to McCarthysim and the Red Scare of the United States in the 1950s supports that student in understanding the events about which the author writes. Without this knowledge, the student may struggle to grasp why the characters act in particular ways and why they make some of the choices they do. Similarly, a student who is reading Steinbeck's *Of Mice and Men* may benefit greatly from having some background knowledge about migrant farm workers, the Great Depression, and California in the 1930s. Thus, background knowledge plays a dual role. It supports the literal comprehension of a text and also helps the reader understand the potentially unfamiliar cultural interpretations and context of texts. Thus, providing multilingual learners early on in a lesson with at least some of this context is essential.

However, rather than focusing on situating poetry within a particular cultural and historical context to prepare students for reading, often a teacher's tendency might be to front-load vocabulary, believing that if students know all the words in a poem, they will understand the meaning of the text. I recall a conversation I had with a middle school student who was listening to his teacher read aloud Rita Joe's poem, "I Lost My Talk." The opening stanza of the poem references the author's childhood educational experiences in a Native American residential school, where she was forbidden to speak her home language. The author continues to articulate in subsequent stanzas the deep connection between language, culture, and identity and her desire to relearn her home tongue in order to know herself. The poem has the potential of being a powerful piece of literature for all students, especially multilingual learners, who may have had experiences similar to those of the author. The teacher, having identified words that might be unfamiliar to the students, had the day before pretaught *snatched* and *ballad*. The students spent a class period creating what the teacher called "vocabulary maps," where they wrote a definition of each vocabulary word, a synonym, and an antonym, and also drew a picture. She also explained to students that *Shubenacadie* was the name of a boarding school the author attended as a child.

I LOST MY TALK
Rita Joe

I lost my talk
The talk you took away.

When I was a little girl
At Shubenacadie school.

You snatched it away:
I speak like you
I think like you
I create like you
The scrambled ballad, about my word.

Two ways I talk
Both ways I say,
Your way is more powerful.

So gently I offer my hand and ask,
Let me find my talk
So I can teach you about me.

When the teacher finished reading aloud, I asked a student what he thought of the poem, expecting to hear something, perhaps, about the power dynamics of learning the language of school, or the pain of losing a language, or the relationship between language and identity. Instead, however, the student replied, "Well, I understood all the words, but not what [the teacher] is saying!" This is unfortunately typical of many poetry lessons students encounter in school. The teacher had spent time at the word level, and the student here understood every word; indeed, he had engaged in a vocabulary-building activity the day before to ensure that this was the case. But knowing every word did not help him understand the essence of the poem or the powerful and painful message of its author. Rather, to make sense of such a complex text, students need the necessary background information with respect to context, author, and time period. Lacking this information, poetry can be a frustrating and "boring" genre to read (and teach!).

In contrast, using the Three Moments Architecture for a lesson described in Chapter 3, the lesson described in this Chapter was developed to include in the Preparing Learners Moment a robust activity that serves to Build the Field for students. Table 6.1 provides the lesson architecture for "Theme for English B" and describes each task within each Moment. While this lesson was created specifically for this poem, it is easy to see how the lesson architecture and sequence of tasks in Table 6.1 can be applied to a wide range of texts that may require a building the field activity to support student engagement and deep understanding.

Table 6.1. Lesson Architecture

	Purpose	Description
Preparing Learners		
Jigsaw Project	Build the field of knowledge that prepares students to read and engage with the text in meaningful ways.	Students read different background texts on Langston Hughes, the Harlem Renaissance, Jim Crow Laws, and whom Hughes influenced and was influenced by. Students discuss, summarize, and share with others what they have learned.
Quick Write	Activate students' background knowledge about their relationships with teachers.	Students respond to a prompt about what they want teachers to know about them, their lives, their hopes, and their dreams.
Round Robin	Build and deepen understanding of who students are and who they want to become.	In their small groups, students take turns sharing one idea from their Quick Write.
Interacting with Text		
Silent reading with a Focus	Scaffold the reading of a text by providing focus questions.	Students silently read the poem, using the focus questions to guide their reading.
Reading in Four Voices	Chunk a text for meaning to make key ideas more transparent.	Working in their groups of 4, students are assigned one of four typefaces and together read their parts aloud.
Triple-Entry Journal	Scaffold students' reading by providing specific foci and a structure for them to document their findings.	Students read and log their findings in a Triple-Entry Journal.
Partner Share and Class Share Out	Share and deepen understanding of reading, based on the foci.	Students share with a partner and hear their partner's ideas; they then share out as a class and at each step have an opportunity to add to their notetaker.
Extending Understanding		
Collaborative Poster	Synthesize understanding of a text through visual and textual representation.	Students respond to specific criteria to collaboratively summarize their understanding of the poem.

A LESSON IN THREE MOMENTS

Preparing Learners

As has been described in previous chapters, the Preparing Learners Moment of a lesson is the initial part of a lesson that supports students in undertaking sustained productive academic work. This first Moment provides that support by focusing students' attention on themes or concepts that they will be engaging with, activating prior knowledge that is relevant to the lesson, and increasing their familiarity with a few new terms needed in context. Within this Moment of the lesson it may also be necessary to provide essential background information and contextual understandings in order for students to construct new understandings. We call this Building the Field.

Building the Field. As mentioned earlier in this chapter, when presenting multilingual learners with complex texts that contain themes and contexts that are beyond their lived experiences, it is necessary to include as part of the lesson the opportunity for students to create a foundation on which new learning will take place. Derewianka and Jones (2016) describe this initial phase of learning as "[b]uilding knowledge of the field," and they offer that when dealing with unfamiliar subject matter, the initial moment in a lesson should focus on engaging students in learning *about* the topic of the text (not preteaching the text itself), both by activating prior knowledge and by supporting students in building a shared understanding about the context, people, and circumstances. Thus, if students are to engage meaningfully with a text that is from a particular era, or a text that makes cultural, political, or historical references with which students are unaware, they must first build their understanding of those contexts, as well as of the genre or purpose of the particular text.

In designing the Preparing Learners Moment of a lesson connected to a literary text, teachers can begin by asking themselves two questions: (1) Are the themes and contexts ones that my multilingual learners can relate to from their prior experience and, if so, how can tasks help to activate that knowledge? and (2) Where my multilingual learners have little or no prior experience that enables them to relate to the themes, context, setting, or purpose of the text, how can tasks help to build the field of knowledge that will make it possible for them to connect more fully with the meaning of the text? Since few, if any, will have the background knowledge they need to fully understand the social commentary Langston Hughes makes in his prose, it is necessary to first engage students in an activity that serves to build that knowledge, on which they will construct new understandings.

In this Jigsaw Project, four Expert Group texts serve to build background knowledge before students begin reading the poem "A Theme for

Figure 6.1. Designing a Jigsaw Project

Designing a Jigsaw Project

Many teachers implement Jigsaws in their classroom, though because there are many different types, it is important to describe here the specific type of Jigsaw in this lesson. This Jigsaw is one that Ellis (2003) describes as having an "information gap." That is, each student or group has information that the others do not. Working together, students solve a problem or reach a conclusion that requires everyone's information and critical thinking.

Step 1: Students sit in their Base Groups

- We advocate for heterogenous Base Groups, based on language ability
- In their Base Groups, students are assigned number 1, 2, 3, or 4

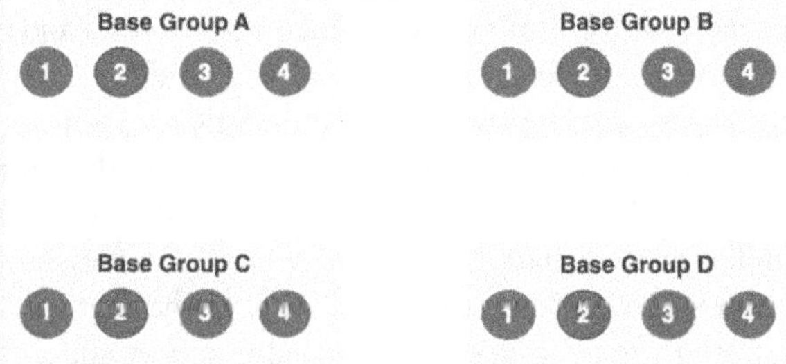

Step 2: Students move to their Expert Group, based on their assigned number

- Students read and become experts on one of four texts, working together to discuss, analyze, and question the text.
- If needed, Expert Groups can be differentiated or homogeneous. Thus, one or more expert groups can be assigned a specific, highly scaffolded text while others receive a less scaffolded text.
- The more scaffolded texts include images or pictures, headings, subheadings, guiding questions, or other amplifications to support students' reading and discussion of the text. Teachers may provide additional support as needed to specific Expert Groups.
- Students who need the least support may be assigned to read a text that is longer, has fewer pictures, no headings, and so on.
- Note: While the individual texts can be differentiated, the cognitive task of each group remains the same, with each group focusing on the central ideas of the text they are assigned.

(*continued*)

Figure 6.1. (*continued*)

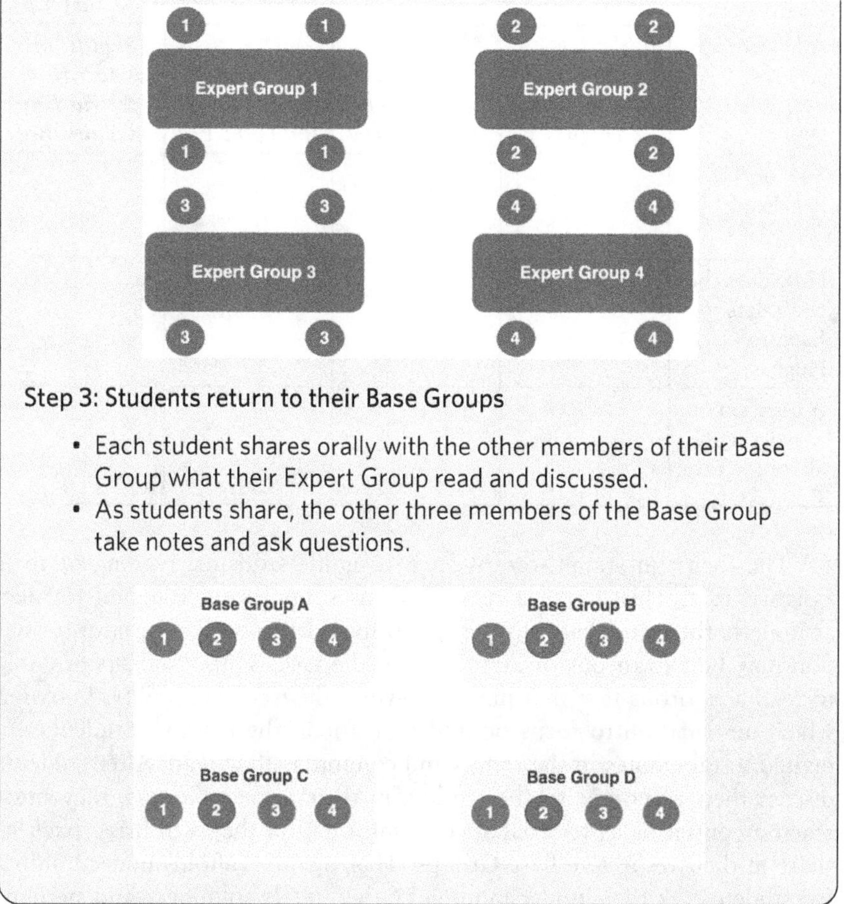

English B." Students who are assigned to Expert Group 1 read a text entitled *A Biography of Langston Hughes*; students assigned to Expert Group 2 read a text called *The Harlem Renaissance*; students in Expert Group 3 read *The Jim Crow Era*; students in Expert Group 4 read *Significant Artists from the Harlem Renaissance*. For each background reading in the Jigsaw, students focus on the following three questions:

(1) What are two or three key ideas presented in the text?
(2) How does the text relate to Langston Hughes?
(3) What is a question or wondering you have about what you have read?

Table 6.2. Notetaker

	Text 1	Text 2	Text 3	Text 4
	A Biography of Langston Hughes	*The Harlem Renaissance*	*Jim Crow Era*	*Significant Artists from the Harlem Renaissance*
Two or three key details				
How does the text relate to Langston Hughes?				
A question or wondering about the text				

The focus questions were written to guide students' reading of their assigned text. This use of a reading focus supports multilingual learners as it alerts them to what information to focus on as well as what information may be extraneous or additional to the task. Thus, students are able to read a rigorous text that may be beyond their current ability, knowing which information to focus on and look for in the reading. Students are invited to take notes in the right-hand column as they read. After students discuss their responses to the reading in their Expert Groups, they must reach a consensus as to what specific information they will bring back to share in their respective Base Groups. This, again, scaffolds understanding for students, as their understanding of the text is solidified, and perhaps deepened, as they share and listen to the ideas of others. Only after reaching a consensus may students write down their responses in the column of the Notetaker (Table 6.2) that corresponds with their reading. When ready, students return to their Base Groups and share their findings. As each student shares, others in the group fill out the Notetaker, jotting down important or pertinent information, as shared by the "Expert" in the group.

Whether students are reading a single text (in this case, a poem by Langston Hughes), a series of texts, or a longer length text, such as a novel, building students' background knowledge enables them to engage more deeply in what they are reading and learning. The Notetaker that students use serves to guide their reading and support their discussion in their Expert Group as well as support the subsequent sharing and listening to others' summaries of their reading in their Base Group.

A Note About Expert Groups. In a Jigsaw Project, as described above, students move from a heterogeneous Base Group to an Expert Group. It is important to recognize the potential that the Expert Group affords learners who may be less confident or hesitant to speak in a group setting. It is the job of the Expert Group to share, discuss, and reach a consensus as to the information they will bring back to their respective Base Groups. This structure gives students who may need more support the opportunity to participate in what Lave and Wenger (1991) described as "situated learning," and to be apprenticed into a community of practice. Further, the purpose of the Expert Group discussion is not for students to display knowledge, a practice Clarke (2015) suggests may silence students who think they do not have the right answer. Rather, the Expert Group discussion is to coconstruct understanding as members of the classroom community (Chapter 2). Benefitting from the Expert Group discussion, students are positioned to be able to return to their Base Group and to take ownership over their newly developed expertise by sharing what they learned with others.

Quick Write. While the Jigsaw Project was included to build the field for students, providing a foundation on which they will construct new understandings, the Quick Write prompt was designed to activate students' prior knowledge. The prompt in this task—"What would you like your teacher to know about you?"—calls upon students to write silently and jot down their thoughts. This prompt mirrors how the narrator in "A Theme for English B" tackles his writing assignment, by writing a sort of inventory of who he is and what his passions are. When students read what the author wants his teacher to know about him, they will have already considered such a prompt and how they might respond, thus preparing them both thematically as well as personally for the text they will be reading.

Round Robin. A Round Robin was developed for students to share orally one idea from their Quick Write in their small group. Here, each student speaks without interruption; once every student has shared, they are free to have a discussion regarding the prompt. By being invited to share only one idea from their Quick Writes, students are able to select something they are comfortable sharing with their small group and are also less likely to read aloud verbatim what they wrote. In this way, as they are only sharing one idea, students are more likely to look at the people they are speaking to, make eye contact, and remember what others have shared. Additionally, the other students in the group are likely to be able to add something that has not already been said.

The tasks presented in this lesson thus far were designed to prepare students for interacting with the central text, in this case, a Langston Hughes poem. Students have now had an opportunity to build a field of knowledge that will support their understanding of the context of the poem, and they have also tapped into their own prior knowledge to reflect on one of the main themes of the text they are going to read.

Interacting With Text

The second Moment of an ELA lesson, also following the architecture described in Chapter 3, was designed to support student engagement in the exploration and analysis of a text, understanding of its key themes, and development of the language needed to discuss their ideas and analyses. For this lesson, students have multiple opportunities to read and deepen their understanding of the poem and the two characters they meet as they read the text.

Reading With a Focus. Poetry is a unique genre—not unlike speeches—in that when read aloud, often the pauses, cadence, and inflection help to communicate the meaning or message of the text. Thus, the first time students read Hughes's text silently on their own, they may not understand it entirely or pick up on some of the nuances the author uses to distinguish and compare himself to his teacher. It is important to tell students that though the text might seem confusing at first, they will have multiple opportunities to engage with the text and with the author's message. For this first reading, students are invited to think about two focus questions:

(1) Why does the author describe himself? What does he want his teacher to know?
(2) In what ways is the teacher similar to and different from Hughes?

These questions are crafted to alert students to what Hughes is doing in the poem—taking an almost stream-of-consciousness inventory of his life in order to communicate the roles of racial difference and power in establishing identity—and to prepare them for delving more deeply into the poem in the subsequent tasks. This particular task was intended to have minimal scaffolding; that is, while the focus questions scaffold students' reading of a text, students read silently on their own. A more heavily scaffolded example of this same task is described in the chapter that discusses how to scaffold the reading of complex texts with Newcomers (Chapter 10).

Reading in Four Voices. This lesson was designed to allow students to read the poem one more time, in four voices before students share their ideas with each other. The Reading in Four Voices task gives students a chance to hear the poem read aloud. For this task, prior to class, the teacher divides the text

Figure 6.2. Reading in Four Voices

"Theme for English B"

The instructor said,

Go home and write
a page tonight.
And let that page come out of you—
Then, it will be true.

I wonder if it's that simple?
I am twenty-two, **colored**, *born in Winston-Salem.*
I went to school there, **then Durham**, then here
to this college on the hill above Harlem.
I am the only colored student in my class.
The steps from the hill lead down into Harlem,
through a park, then I cross St. Nicholas,
Eighth Avenue, Seventh, **and I come to the Y**,
the Harlem Branch Y, where I take the elevator
up to my room, **sit down**, *and write this page*:

It's not easy to know what is true for you **or me**
at twenty-two, *my age*. But I guess I'm what
I feel and see and hear, **Harlem, I hear you**:
hear you, hear me—we two—you, **me**, talk on this page.
(*I hear New York, too.*) **Me—who?**
Well, I like to eat, *sleep*, drink, **and be in love**.
I like to work, read, *learn*, **and understand life**.
I like a pipe for a Christmas present,
or records—Bessie, bop, **or Bach**.
I guess being colored doesn't make me not like
the same things other folks like who are other races.
So will my page be colored that I write?

Being me, it will not be white.
But it will be
a part of you, instructor.
You are white—
yet a part of me, as I am a part of you.
That's American.
Sometimes *perhaps* **you don't want to be a part of me**.
Nor do I often want to be a part of you.
But we are, **that's true!**
As I learn from you,
I guess you learn from me—
although you're older—**and white**—
and somewhat more free.

This is my page for English B.

into meaningful chunks. A teacher does this by changing the physical typeface of the text into four different type faces: **bold**, *italics*, underlined, and regular type (Figure 6.2). Working in groups of four, each student selects and then reads a different text type. As they read the text together aloud, students can hear more clearly how the two people in the poem are described and what the descriptions may mean or suggest. Thus, this chunking of the text allows students to hear the poem read aloud with important ideas, musings, thoughts, and messages of the author made more transparent and clear.

Triple-Entry Journal. Now that students have read the poem twice—once silently on their own and again aloud in four voices—they will read and complete the first row of the Triple-Entry Journal (Table 6.3). The Triple-Entry Journal is scaffolded to support students' own interpretation of the poem, and then their understanding is deepened by sharing with and hearing the ideas of their partner. The questions in each column go deeper than the original reading focus questions, requiring students to go beyond the words uttered by the narrator to his intention and purpose. Here, students have an opportunity to ask each other questions, explain their interpretations, and build on each other's ideas. In this way, the talk is dialogic, as it affords students the opportunity to work together in coconstructing understanding in intellectually purposeful and respectful ways (Kibler et al., 2021).

The final row of the matrix offers a last step for the teacher to ask different dyads to share out their ideas with the class. Students can jot down any new ideas or extensions of ideas they may already have as they hear their classmates' ideas and responses to the questions in the matrix.

Table 6.3. Triple-Entry Journal

	Why does the author make an inventory of himself? What does he want the professor to know?	**What are the differences between the narrator and the teacher? What do they share?**	**What does the narrator mean when he writes, "That's American"? What is "American"?**
Step 1: My ideas			
Step 2: My partner's ideas			
Step 3: Ideas from my classmates			

Extending Understanding

As described in Chapter 3, this last Moment of the lesson was designed to give students the opportunity to synthesize their understanding and apply that understanding in new ways or to new contexts. Many ELA lessons end with a writing assignment, which can certainly be incorporated into this lesson as well. However, before students are asked to write, it is vital that they first have an opportunity to grapple with what they have learned and to present that information in new ways.

Collaborative Poster. In the previous set of tasks that students engaged in during the Interacting with Text Moment of the lesson, they had multiple opportunities to read the poem and, supported by guiding questions and peer interactions, have analyzed what the author is trying to convey, and why. Now students turn their attention to solidifying their understanding and presenting those understandings in a Collaborative Poster.

In the Collaborative Poster activity, the class first reviews a rubric provided by the teacher to establish a clear understanding of the goals of the task and how to self-assess the products each small group creates. Next, students work in their small groups of four to synthesize their understandings of the text. For this task, each member of the group selects a colored marker and must only use that color during the duration of the task. It is the responsibility of the group to make sure there is an equal distribution of colors used in the poster; thus, students must support, encourage, and even apprentice their peers as they create a visual representation of their understanding. Each poster must include:

- Two quotes from the text that show the narrator's frame of mind;
- Two original phrases that paraphrase or explain the author's position, point of view, or message; and
- One drawing that shows how the author is feeling and what he wants his teacher to know.

The task engages students in textual analysis as they discuss which texts to select, how to write the original phrases based on their understanding of the poem, and their individual ideas and final consensus about the author's feeling and intent. Only after this discussion do students move forward to produce an artistic summary of the message in the text.

Thus, using information they gathered during the building the field portion of the lesson, coupled with their reading of the poem, students discuss what they have learned about the author and his reality to coconstruct a Collaborative Poster. If a writing task follows, the Collaborative Poster becomes a powerful resource for student writing, as they may turn to their own poster, as well as the posters of their classmates, to construct thesis statements (building on the original phrases, textual evidence, and symbols or imagery taken from the drawings). They may also draw upon their posters to extend the themes presented in "A Theme for English B" to writing about society today and their own experiences with identity, power, and so on.

CONCLUSION

This chapter has taken the reader through the process of designing a lesson using a Three Moments instructional design that supports multilingual learners' engagement with a complex literary text in interactive and collaborative ways. Through intentional design features, the lesson was structured to give students an opportunity to first build the field of new knowledge that they will need to comprehend unfamiliar text genres and contexts. By creating a foundation on which students will construct new understandings, they are better prepared for the subsequent activities that ask them to engage deeply with complex texts, especially poetry, speeches, and novels for which understanding the context is indispensable. Having worked together, collaborated with their classmates, and held deep conversations throughout the lesson, students are then able to extend that understanding into new contexts within their communities and the larger society.

REFERENCES

Bunch, G. C., Walqui, A., & Pearson, P. D. (2014). Complex text and new common standards in the United States: Pedagogical implications for English learners. *TESOL Quarterly*, *48*(3), 533–559.

Clarke, S. (2015). The right to speak. In L. B. Resnick, C. S. C. Asterhan, & S. N. Clarke (Eds.), *Socializing intelligence through academic talk and dialogue* (pp. 167–180). American Educational Research Association. https://doi.org/10.3102/978-0-935302-43-1_13

Curran, B., & Wetherbee, N. (2014). *Engaged, connected, empowered: Teaching and learning in the 21st century*. Routledge.

Derewianka, B., & Jones, P. (2016). *Teaching language in context*. Oxford University Press.

Ellis, R. (2003). *Task-based language learning and teaching*. Oxford University Press.

Kibler, A., Valdés, G., & Walqui, A. (2021). *Reconceptualizing the role of critical dialogue in American classrooms*. Routledge Research in Education.

Lave, J., & Wenger, E. (1991). *Situated learning: Legitimate peripheral participation*. Cambridge University Press.

Rampersad, A., & Roessel, D. (Eds.). (1994). *The collected poems of Langston Hughes*. Vintage Classics.

CHAPTER 7

Developing a Conceptual Understanding of Mean as Point of Balance With Multilingual Learners

Designing Mathematical Learning With Rich Interactions

Leslie Hamburger and Haiwen Chu

Imagine a middle school statistics classroom buzzing as diverse groups of students with different language backgrounds talk in small groups about different graphs. The students are focusing on dot plots, a data display in which each point of data on a number line is shown with a dot. They are tasked with sorting these dot plots into categories (see Figure 7.1). The groups of four students reflect the language diversity of students in the United States, including Chinese speakers who arrived in the late elementary grades, speakers of Spanish who have been recently reclassified as English language proficient, speakers of various languages other than English who were born in the United States, and students who have never been classified as English Learners. Put together, these students in all their diversity are multilingual learners.

Members of each group are talking about, describing, and then sorting a series of line plots according to criteria that they observe as relevant to distinguish one line plot from another. As designed, the task allows multiple points of entry, as students can look at the overall range of values, the geometrical distribution, or notions of balance. They discuss their ideas and reach a consensus to make categories, for which they create labels on sticky notes.

As they work together, each student talks, listens, and asks questions. Each student takes a turn as the describer, and all students contribute for the group to succeed. As students talk with each other, they build shared understandings of key mathematical representations and relationships related to data distributions and balance. As they develop labels that they can

Figure 7.1. Students Sorting Dot Plots

compare with other groups, they explore different groupings of the plots and alternative ways to label the "same" groups.

This kind of student activity illustrates opportunities that help all students learn mathematics conceptually and that are especially critical for multilingual learners. If teachers offer abundant opportunities for multilingual learners to connect their own experiences to new ideas, to participate in activities with their peers, and to engage in sustained talk that develops mathematical ideas, all students will benefit. Structured, quality interactions with peers support the development of conceptual, analytic, and language practices. Such interactions help balance the high challenge of rigorous mathematics with the high support multilingual learners need to enter and derive benefit from the activities.

Unfortunately, typical mathematics instruction for multilingual learners does not yet consistently feature all these characteristics (de Araujo & Smith, 2022). For multilingual learners to meet the ambitious demands of educational and civic life in a 21st-century information society, where students need to grapple with complex ideas, engage in critical dialogue and problem solving, access multimodal information critically, and engage productively as an informed citizen, their teachers will need to shift instruction. Specifically, shifts in practice are needed to ensure that students have greater access to complex mathematical ideas and enhanced opportunities to participate in dialogic and disciplinary practices to advance learning and development. This kind of deep, conceptual understanding is required by the advanced quantitative literacies (including understanding data distributions) required in 21st-century life. The shifts required of educators connect three key areas: cross-cutting concepts, participation by design, and purposeful opportunities to develop and use dialogic language practices. In this chapter, we explore how shifts in these three areas provide explicit guidance for the design of learning opportunities in mathematics that benefit all learners, particularly multilingual learners.

As former secondary mathematics teachers who together have more than four decades of experience designing and enacting professional development for teachers of multilingual learners, we share in this chapter a lesson on *mean* as the point of balance in a data set. Besides being a core concept in the K–12 mathematics curriculum, understanding the mean of a data set is critical to understand how we represent information about the world, engage in critical reflection and discourse about data, and participate thoughtfully to distinguish information from misinformation. We provide this example to illustrate three key characteristics of effective instructional design: cross-cutting concepts, a variety of opportunities to participate, and a focus on language that enables multilingual learners to connect ideas and engage in disciplinary practices.

These three characteristics of instructional design are related to three shifts that extend the progress already made by reform-oriented approaches to mathematics education, but with an explicit focus on challenging and supporting multilingual learners:

- Moving away from traditional math teaching focused on procedures without connections, we instead focus on cross-cutting concepts to drive learning.
- Instead of prevailing patterns where teachers dominate discourse, we offer multilingual learners opportunities to participate in carefully designed and structured peer dialogue.
- Instead of reductive sentence frames meant to script students' responses in the moment, multilingual learners need formulaic expressions to help generate current and future expression of their ideas.

Enacting these shifts requires transforming how teachers design and implement lessons. In this chapter, we illustrate how to enact these shifts by examining an exemplar lesson on the concept of mean, a central idea of statistics. The focal lesson's conception of mean extends beyond the formulaic and algorithmic understandings usually featured in mathematics classrooms (Pollatsek et al., 1981). Instead of focusing on implementing an algorithm like adding all data and dividing by the number of data points to arrive at a calculation for mean, the lesson develops students' understanding of mean as a point of balance among the data. This understanding is built through well-structured and well-supported interactions and opportunities to explore and use language, without which multilingual learners may be excluded from this type of conceptually oriented understanding of mean.

SHIFTS IN MATHEMATICS INSTRUCTION FOR MULTILINGUAL LEARNERS

From Procedures Without Connections to Cross-Cutting Concepts

Mathematics instruction in the United States has typically centered on teachers modeling procedures without providing mathematical or practical explanation for what those procedures mean and why they work (Stigler & Hiebert, 1999). This teaching of procedures without connections to meaning results in limited understanding and leaves students unable to independently select and apply mathematical procedures in novel situations (Stein et al., 2009). In contrast, solving rich, contextualized problems enables students to understand multiple solution approaches and develop important mathematical ideas (Wilson & Smith, 2022). To enable this development, teachers need to orchestrate whole-class discussions that support students as they compare and connect solution methods, rather than just engage in "show and tell" (e.g., Stein et al., 2008). We acknowledge the promise of the problem-centered approach as we further claim that multilingual learners will benefit from mathematics lessons with designs that focus on developing procedures explicitly from open explorations. That is, sometimes a real-world situation can provide the basis for developing a mathematical idea (Chu & Rubel, 2013).

We have seen how multilingual learners benefit by focusing on cross-cutting concepts, such as equivalence and transformation (Chu & Hamburger, 2022; Lampert, 2017). Cross-cutting concepts allow students to see mathematics ideas as connected, to see the relationships that undergird key concepts, and to recognize that they have prior knowledge and understandings to make sense of and engage with complex new ideas and concepts. For example, in geometry, two shapes are congruent if they can be transformed into one another by rigid motions. In algebra, two equations are equivalent if they can be transformed into each other with arithmetic operations. In this chapter, we will describe how students explore the notion of mean or *average* as point of balance, with certain data sets equivalent up to a set of transformations. That is, students work collaboratively to transform data sets to make the "point of balance" easier to see by inspection.

From Interactions Led by Teachers to Rich Participatory Opportunities For Students

Teachers have traditionally controlled the discourse in mathematics classes, such as with the Initiation-Response-Feedback pattern in which a teacher asks a question, a student responds, and the teacher provides feedback about whether the student is right or wrong (Herbel-Eisenmann & Breyfogle, 2005). As the teacher dominates interactions with students, key mathematical ideas often fade into the background (Stigler & Hiebert, 1999). Alternatives to teacher domination have been centered primarily on teacher facilitation moves for students' sharing or presenting ideas to the whole class (Stein et al., 2008).

These approaches rely on students' presenting their finished solution methods, rather than expressing their negotiation of meaning as it develops. From a sociocultural perspective, we agree with Vygotsky (2012) that thinking can be achieved *through* speech, as students develop ideas and negotiate understandings together. These quality interactions characterized by sustained talk and reciprocal interactions are central for students to develop ideas and disciplinary practices together (Walqui & Heritage, 2018). A dialogic education is key to developing the types of knowledge and skills for success in our current educational and societal contexts.

From Memorizing Words to Using Language for Developing and Connecting Ideas

Although it is widely agreed that language is central to conceptual development and student participation, in math, attention to language has typically focused on multilingual learners' acquiring vocabulary (Moschkovich, 2002). Often, definitions are introduced well before students need them (Chu et al., 2022), an approach that is less productive than definitions that formalize a concept that students have already been exploring. We propose instead that a working definition is more inviting and provides greater access to the central idea of a lesson. A working definition captures the idea behind a concept in a way that is immediately accessible and that then leads to a more formal definition.

For example, we explained in an earlier edition of this book (Hamburger & Chu, 2019) how to think of the slope as a unit rate of change, which is to say that as x increases by 1, how y changes is the rate of change, a more generative approach that links many different ideas. Therefore, if x increases by 2, y decreases by 3 would correspond to a slope of -1.5, because when x increases by 1, y decreases by 1½ or 3/2 or 1.5. Initially understanding the slope as the unit rate of change allows students to work toward the more generative approaches and arrive at a more formal definition.

Other language opportunities for multilingual learners in mathematics instruction frequently involve closed activities in which students fill in the blanks in writing or complete oral scripts (such as, "The square root of 25 is . . ."). Such sentence starters, while intended to be supportive, place attention primarily on bits and pieces of language, grammatical correctness, and the substitution of specific words in isolated contexts.

In contrast, we propose a focus on understanding the purposes for language broader than teaching individual words in isolation. To develop deep conceptual understanding, multilingual learners need ample opportunities to connect personal experiences, mathematical ideas, representations, and procedures. They need opportunities to engage in sustained dialogue to coconstruct ideas, to critically explore arguments, and to justify their reasoning. This grappling with ideas is only achieved with language, so participating in mathematical practices includes the development of conceptual understandings and simultaneous engagement in mathematical and language practices (Heritage et al., 2015). Rich opportunities to use language develop deeper analogies and can offer multilingual learners access to important mathematical concepts (Chu & Rubel, 2013).

DEVELOPING CONCEPTUAL UNDERSTANDING OF MEAN

One of the key generative understandings in statistics is how to describe and analyze numerical data sets in terms of their characteristics. Two ideas are that of center and spread of a set of data. What makes statistics conceptually rich is how it employs both representations and representatives. Whereas a representation seeks to show the actual data faithfully (e.g., a dot plot that shows each value of the data), a representative seeks to summarize many different numbers with a single value—and the mean is such as a representative. The notions of representative and representation are ideally closely connected, and indeed, the lesson described offers students a way to explore how the representative can emerge directly from the representation (Roberts et al., 2021).

Mean as a Central and Generative Idea of Statistics

Our approach to teaching about the mean includes the usual procedure but begins with the broader idea of finding the point on which a set of data, graphed as a dot plot, would balance. Focusing on the idea of balance rather than the procedure of "adding up the numbers and dividing by the number of numbers" to calculate the mean gives the average more meaning. Indeed, the mean serves as a "representative" of the whole set of data—a single number that "sums up" all of the other points to understand the data set as a whole. The power of this lesson is that it helps students explicitly connect the standard formula for the mean of a set of data with that set's representation as a dot plot, through the notion of "balance point."

Mean as Anchor for an Instructional Unit

While this chapter focuses on the mean lesson, we do so understanding that it must connect to broader ideas and practices. The lesson called "What is the Point of Balance?" is in a larger unit about measures of center, entitled *Moving Measures of Center.* In this unit, students explore representations and concepts about different measures of center. They begin with the "Many Ways to Midway" lesson, as students explore how to find the *median,* or the number in the middle position of a set of data. These procedures compare the familiar school algorithm of crossing off numbers from both ends of the data set with using the overall sample size to identify the position that the median would occupy. From there, students explore in the lesson "A Higher Frequency" the idea that a single data value can occur multiple times (as with the ages of students in a classroom), and the *mode* is the data value that occurs with the greatest frequency. In the present lesson, students explore the mean as a point of balance. Finally, in the culminating lesson, "The More Things Change," they analyze how changes to the data affect the mean, median, and mode, all without recomputing. We present the overall spiral trajectory of this unit in Figure 7.2.

These lessons illustrate not only how to make strategic choices about when to contextualize—maintaining an explicit focus on real-world contexts to draw upon prior knowledge or apply to new situations—but also when to decontextualize, focusing on the relations and connections between representations such as dot plots. These practices are instances of how students are asked to "reason abstractly and quantitatively" in the Common Core Standards. Indeed, decontextualizing (i.e., not attending to real-world units) can facilitate other practices, such as "look for and make use of structure" in reasoning directly about representations such as dot plots or other graphs.

Mean as Developed in the Lesson

The third lesson in this unit, "What is the Point of Balance?," consists of Three Moments (see Chapter 3) comprised of six tasks that provide explicit

Figure 7.2. Design and Trajectory of a Unit on Measures of Center

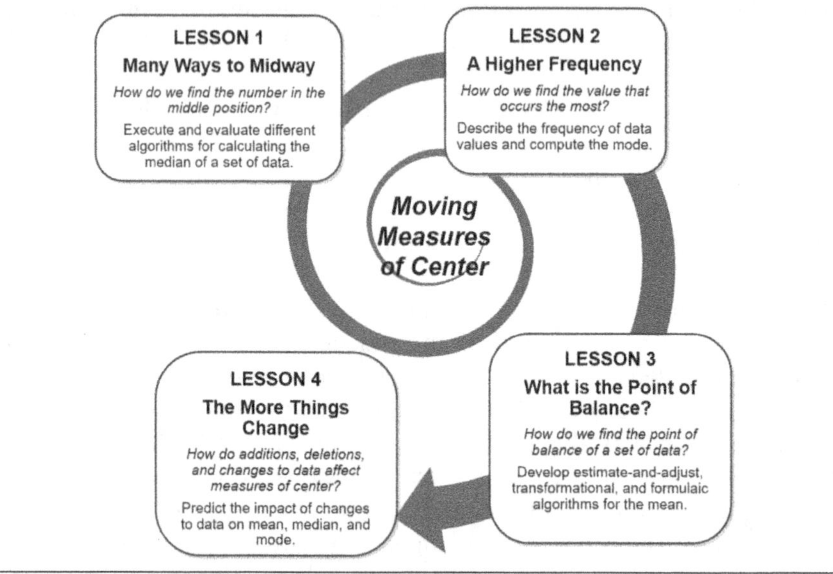

Figure 7.3. The "Story" of the Mean as Point of Balance

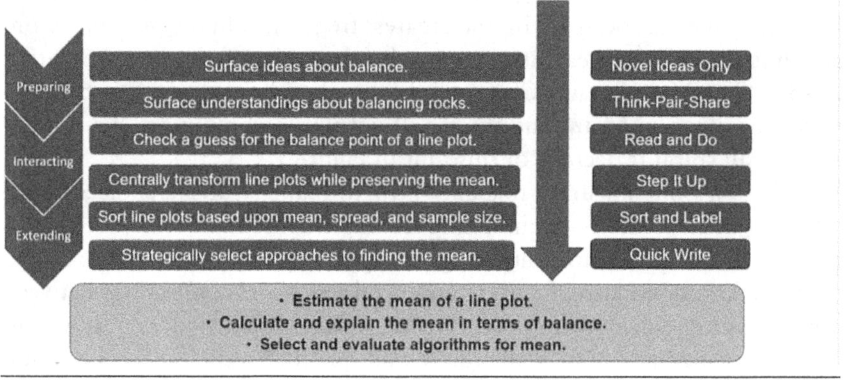

structures for students to interact with one another in the exploration of mathematical ideas. These tasks are represented in Figure 7.3, with the conceptual objective of each task displayed on the left and specific type of scaffolding task names on the right. This diagram shows the "story" of the lesson, a scheme for making public both the conceptual trajectory of the lesson (the "what") and the specific pedagogical structures (the "how") that teachers will use to assist students in achieving those objectives in ways that purposefully attend to language and discourse. The focus of this overview is on the conceptual trajectory of the lesson; in later sections we will unpack the peer interactions that the scaffolding tasks enable and the language supports that further facilitate these interactions. These tasks follow the Three Moments Architecture (see Chapter 3).

Preparing Multilingual Learners to Engage With Ideas of Balance. To maximize multilingual learners' access to the ideas underlying the mean and to tap into the resources they bring to the learning experience, the lesson solicits students' prior, but not prerequisite, knowledge through two interactive discussion tasks. The first draws upon students' brainstorming about the word "balance," inviting and allowing them to share all sorts of experiences that highlight how two "sides" are balanced, beyond physical experiences of seesaws toward broader ideas about balanced diets and bank balances.

Pairs of students then examine images of rocks that may or may not be balanced and engage in a Think–Pair–Share (see Figure 7.4). The structure of the task has students think individually before they talk with a partner with whom they are paired. If called upon by their teacher, they share not what they said, but rather what their partner said. The teacher's role is to

Figure 7.4. Think-Pair-Share Images and Prompt

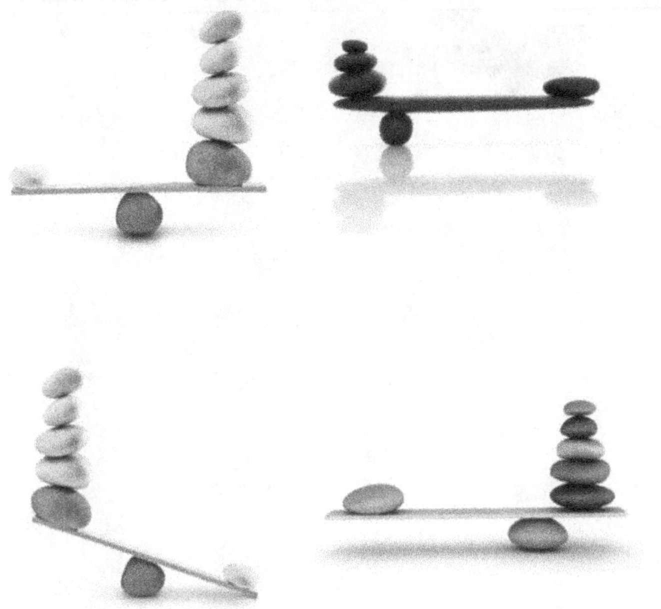

highlight the key variables, including the number of rocks, their position, their presumed weight or density, and the position of the "point of balance."

Interacting With Mathematical Representations. The Interacting Moment of the mean lesson is centered on two tasks that are focused on two different approaches to finding the point of balance: systematically checking the distances of an estimate on both sides and transforming the data set to make the point of balance easier to see, all without changing where the point of balance would be. This approach to transforming the data, and constructing a chain of equivalent dot plots, better develops students' explicit understanding of equivalence as related to transformation.

The teacher then engages the whole class in discussion to compare different dot plots that are transformed progressively until the point of balance is easier to determine through visual inspection. Figure 7.5 shows pairs of students working progressively through equivalent dot plots to arrive at a clearer mean. The teacher leads a whole-class analysis of how the total of the data values and sample size does not change within the sequence of plots that partners generate, such as those shown in Figure 7.5—leading to the idea of developing the traditional formula of "adding up the numbers" and dividing evenly by the number of data points.

Figure 7.5. Students Transforming Dot Plots to See the Mean in the Data

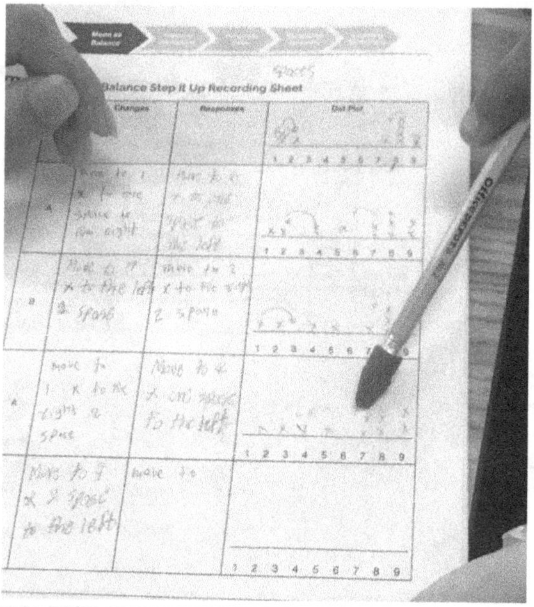

Extending Understanding of Mean to Novel Situations. Students extend their understanding of mean as the lesson concludes with a sorting task, where they must group and create labels for a number of different dot plots. This task extends their understanding because they analyze across a wide variety of dot plots, rather than trying to preserve the equivalence of a family of dot plots. Finally, students engage in an individual reflection by writing about how their different groups connect with the three different algorithms: 1) estimating and adjusting the point of balance; 2) systematically transforming the data set; and 3) using the standard formula. We find that individual writing leads to good small-group discussions.

SHIFTS IN ACTION

In this section, we unpack how the mean lesson puts each of the three shifts described earlier into action. Quality learning opportunities for multilingual learners support students' engagement in rigorous disciplinary practices (Walqui & van Lier, 2010; Chu & Hamburger, 2022). This kind of instruction includes conceptual understandings along with the analytic and language practices valued by the mathematics community and required for "doing mathematics." In well-constructed instructional experiences, these practices are woven together seamlessly, but for the purpose of understanding the design of such instruction and to unpack how lesson plans can be amplified for multilingual learners, we will attend to different design elements one at a time. We introduce each redesign action with some generative questions that we have found useful for thinking through lesson design.

Center Lessons on Concepts Driving Lesson Activities

For teachers to ensure that lessons are centered on concepts, the following three actions are helpful.

Develop A Clear Conceptual Focus. "What Is the Point of Balance?" demonstrates a lesson design in which the concept is placed at the center of the lesson. At first, the concept uses real-world contexts to serve as an analogical basis for understanding the central idea. Then, the lesson activities offer students opportunities to explore more decontextualized representations and relationships. We can retrace the design choices that went into the lesson on the mean from the middle out. That is, the starting point for the design of a lesson is anticipating the kinds of transformations that students will need to visualize and execute in manipulating the representation of dot plots so that there is representational fluency with those objects. To make certain that students can read these graphs, we worked backwards to focus their attention on the idea of balance and provide more structured language for them to divide the work of focusing on the left and right sides from the point of balance.

Tap Into Students' Experiences and Knowledge. Because we decided that students would benefit from thinking of the mean as a point of balance, we created the brainstorming task to invite students to explore a variety of ideas around balance. When we view the lesson as a whole, we see how the sequence of activities narrows from broad notions of balance, the balancing of rocks to the abstraction of the dot plot. While students bring up many ideas, we make transparent some of the assumptions—such as equal weights for the data points—that dot plots and more mathematical representations make, and we focus their attention on where the lesson is going in terms of finding the point of balance of a data set initially represented by the rocks, then by data plots and eventually by sets of numbers.

Enrich Connection Potential. Once multilingual learners have moved from the real-world scenarios involving balance to a more abstract and decontextualized mathematical representation, we still offer them rich opportunities to think analogically through the grounding context of balanced rocks. The focus of the Extending Moment of the lesson is for students to connect representations and determine which is the most appropriate, given the three algorithms that they develop. One notable feature of this approach is how it uses real-world contexts to analogically support conceptual development, rather than as the setting of a problem (Chu & Rubel, 2013).

The central Read and Do and Step It Up tasks, however, are actually decontextualized, as small groups focus on dot plots, but ideas about rock and balance remain as a supportive "fallback" context for thinking about what they are doing with the plots. Providing this real-world anchor promotes students' flexibility in thinking about and with concepts, as it is an additional resource they can choose to exercise: it is an optional heuristic, not a compulsory algorithm.

Foster Quality Peer Interactions That Coconstruct Understanding

This design consideration attends to a key tenet of sociocultural theory: the centrality of oral interaction in learning (Walqui & Heritage, 2018; Walqui & van Lier, 2010). Oracy is critical to the development of understanding and the construction of meaning. Students develop mathematical understandings through sustained oral interactions with peers and with the teacher as they question, explore, test hypotheses, articulate ideas, and clarify their thoughts. Given the centrality of oral interactions to learning, lessons must maximize students' opportunities to engage in sustained, rigorous interactions about disciplinary concepts. These opportunities are especially critical for multilingual learners who need abundant practice and support as they construct and articulate nascent understandings in a language they are simultaneously learning.

Given these considerations, we offer four actions to consider in redesigning the interactions offered multilingual learners in a math lesson.

Structure Activities to Maximize Participation. The scaffolding tasks within the mean lesson illustrate multiple types of interactions among peers, which provide a range of opportunities for multilingual learners to engage in sustained and reciprocal talk through which they coconstruct mathematical ideas and collaboratively engage in mathematical practices (Chu, 2013). These interactions include brainstorming connected ideas, providing arguments for whether images are balanced, and negotiating meaning together. This section highlights three tasks that span these different purposes and formats of interactions.

The mean lesson opens with Novel Ideas Only, in which students engage in multiple interactions. First, they brainstorm responses to the prompt, "When I hear the word 'balance,' I think of . . ." in small groups. As one student uses the prompt (to frame their idea as connected to the central notion of balance) and offers an idea, another student echoes that idea (repeats it verbatim). Then, all students write the idea down so that all members of the group have an identical list. This coordination is critical for the next part of the sharing, in which groups share out only ideas that have not been said yet. Specifically, all students stand up and each group takes a turn to share out only the ideas that have not already been said. After a group has shared, they sit down to signal that they are taking on a different role—still listening to other groups' ideas, all of which should be novel, while jotting down one or two additional ideas that they like.

Every student will have participated in oral interactions during this time and would have had to listen attentively, speak, and possibly paraphrase or summarize what they heard their partners say.

Offer Different Roles in Interactions. The Read and Do task is set up to model for students the two sides that they need to attend to in determining whether a dot plot is balanced on a particular estimate for the mean. Specifically, one partner focuses on the number and distances from the point of balance for the points on the left side, while their partner is working on the points on the right. Because these two roles are parallel, students each attend to the total distance, taking into account frequencies of data points, on either side of the distribution. This is an information gap task, in which each partner holds the information for their side of the line plot and must relay this information orally to determine if the two sides are balanced, which makes the contributions of each member indispensable for the success of the group. Once they decide whether or not the plot is indeed balanced at that point, they collectively decide which way to adjust their estimate. Students switch roles after each turn to adjust their focus and attend to the distances and frequencies in search of the point of balance. This approach to estimate-and-adjust is more generative than guess-and-check that may not offer students more strategic knowledge of related quantities, as it focuses on the two sides of the line plot and draws students' attention to the key elements (distances and frequency) that are key to finding the point of balance.

Support Coconstructing Mathematics. How do these roles support the coconstruction of mathematical knowledge? The Step It Up task again has students work in pairs, but now they are more actively coconstructing ideas in ways that require them to respond to one another as they iteratively transform the dot plots. We find that this kind of structured, back-and-forth approach more evenly distributes the work as they negotiate. A sample interaction between two students as they explore how to find the point of balance in a dot plot follows. Notice how students engage in sustained dialogue that explores what to do, what it means, and how to correct their misunderstandings to arrive at a better approach to the mean.

Student 1: I think the point of balance is at 3 or maybe 2. (marking the estimate for the center and dividing the line plot into two sides)
Student 1: You need to write here. Move one x to the left.
Student 2: Move 7 to 5. Move 7 two spaces to the left to 5.
Student 1: Move two spaces to the right (points to the other side of the line plot)
Student 2: Move to 6, 8 two spaces to the right
Student 1: Is that the right? Are we closer to the center?
Student 2: So move to the left?
Student 1: No, that move is not getting closer to the center, that is not OK.
Student 2: Umm, so move from here, move 1 to the right 2 spaces to 3.
Student 1: Yes! That gets closer to the center.

Ensure Participation Changes Over Time. Looking back at the mean lesson, Table 7.1 summarizes the different structured opportunities that students have to interact with their peers. These opportunities allow for participation to change over time as students become more knowledgeable about the concept of mean.

Table 7.1. Types of Peer Interactions in the Lesson

Moment	Scaffolding Task	Conceptual Objective	Structured Interactions
Preparing	Novel Ideas Only	Brainstorm ideas about "balance."	In small groups, students brainstorm ideas. In whole class, students share only new ideas.
	Think–Pair–Share	Surface ideas about what contributes to balance.	In pairs, students develop arguments for balance or not.
Interacting	Read and Do	Check an estimate for the point of balance, and make changes as necessary.	In pairs, students compare distances on the left and right from a point of balance.
	Step It Up	Transform graphs to make the point of balance easier to see changes.	In pairs, students transform dot plots without changing the point of balance.
Extending	Sort and Label	Apply the concept of *mean* to a wide variety of data distributions.	In groups of four, students sort through different dot plots and construct labels.
	Quick Write	Connect algorithms for the *mean* to different distributions.	Individually, students connect different algorithms to different plots.

The two tasks in the Preparing Moment lesson have been carefully structured to require students to engage in discussions with their peers that converge in different ways. In the Novel Ideas Only task, small groups brainstorm and reach a common list that they then share with the whole class, with attention to novelty. In the Think–Pair–Share, they may generate different ideas, either selecting different images or focusing on different key variables, yet their thinking converges on a single context for balance—balancing rocks that becomes an analogical basis for thinking through the more abstract representation of dot plots.

As students move into the Interacting Moment, however, activities are structured to engage them in close exploration of ideas related to the concept of mean through the reading and discussion of graphical representations of data. Students jointly clarify ideas and elaborate on the meaning of those representations as they collaborate with a partner in the reading of several texts. The Read and Do task presents a parallel task where partners must share and compare the two sides of a dot plot (Chu & Hamburger, 2019). Here, through the structure of the task, one party works alongside their partner, and the communication works back and forth, stressing the key ideas of distance, frequency and balance.

Through the Interacting Moment and into the Extending Moment, students' interaction with peers supports participation in key mathematical practices. As they "look for and make use of structure" in dot plots, they also "attend to precision" and elaborate on similarities and differences. By the end of the lesson, students have negotiated a new genre of explanatory writing.

Offer Language Supports to Connect Ideas and Engage in Disciplinary Practices

To engage in doing mathematics, students must use language to develop conceptual and procedural understandings, reason abstractly, construct arguments, justify their solutions, solve problems, and critique the reasoning of others. All these mathematical practices require sophisticated uses of language that go far beyond learning key vocabulary terms. To amplify the curriculum for multilingual learners and provide them with the supports necessary to carry out these practices, teachers must consider how they will need to use language and what supports must be designed into the lesson to allow them such sophisticated participation.

We offer the following actions for teachers to consider as they redesign a lesson to better serve multilingual learners.

Structure a Variety of Language Use Opportunities. The language opportunities offered in "What is the Point of Balance?" are designed into the materials as well as embedded in the structures and processes of tasks. These include brainstorming, offering reasons, describing differences, and balancing transformations. These invitations include opportunities both to potentially diverge (in stating opinions) as well as to converge in getting closer to a central point of balance in the Step It Up activity.

Offer Language Supports for Disciplinary Practices. The mean lesson further provides models and supports for multilingual learners as they engage in disciplinary practices and explore diverse purposes for using language, including:

- *describing* relationships, distances, and overall distributions;
- *comparing* dot plots in terms of key attributes or relationships;

- *identifying* parts related to wholes, instances of types, and salient features; and
- *characterizing* how transformations relate to one another.

To engage in these language practices, the mean lesson models explicit formulaic expressions that students can use as they engage in the tasks and accomplish the conceptual goals for the lesson. These formulaic expressions serve as generative language structures that students can use to enter into and navigate through the tasks. The expressions highlight key conceptual points students must attend to as they develop understanding of the relationship between balance, distance, and frequency. Some formulaic expressions provided for different tasks include:

- The estimate for the point of balance is . . .
- One of the points is . . . units to the left of the estimate.
- The frequency of points at this distance is . . .
- The total distance of the points on the left is . . .
- A better estimate for the point of balance would be . . .

Invite Students to Develop Greater Autonomy in Using Language Over Time. The language invited in the mean lesson is open and broad in the Preparing and Extending Moments that introduce and conclude the lesson, while narrower and more focused in the Interacting Moment in between. That is, students are relatively free in the Preparing Moment to use their own language resources to express their experiences and initial understandings. During the Interacting Moment, students are offered carefully selected phrases from which they can choose, as well as an elaborate formulaic expression carefully tailored to the conceptual goal of having students notice and discuss distances and transformations. Over time, students are given more choice over how they will use language to achieve their goals. This growing freedom is demonstrated in the Extending Moment tasks in which, while the content and substance of the Quick Write are specified, the choices of language are left entirely up to students (see Table 7.2).

Design for Growth in Language Practices. The language that students are invited and supported to use moves across multiple continua over the course of the lesson. Rather than rely on the misleading dichotomy thought to exist between "everyday" and "academic" language (Walqui & van Lier, 2010), we may consider instead how students over the course of the lesson develop more authority in using more technical language to develop more products that involve writing.

Table 7.2. Progressions of Language Across Mean Tasks

Task	Language Practices	Formulaic Expressions		Key Words
		Supplied by Students	Offered as Explicit Models	
Novel Ideas Only	Brainstorming ideas and examples of balance		"When I hear the word 'balance,' I think of . . ."	"gymnastics" "diet"
Think–Pair–Share	Sharing and comparing reasons and arguments for why rock images may or may not be balanced	". . . is / is not balanced because . . ."		"rocks" "side" "stick" "heavy" "more"
Read and Do	Describing distances and frequencies from an estimated point of balance		"The estimate for the point of balance is . . ." "There are . . . points on the left/right . . ." "The distance is . . .	"estimate" "point" "left" "right" "distance"
Step It Up			"This won't change the Mean because . . ." "This balances with your move because . . ."	"won't change"
Sort and Label		"It's a number line with boxes on . . ." "I think these are all the same because . . ."	"I think these plots go together because . . ." "These plots are different because . . ." "We need a new group of plots because . . ."	"stacked" "balanced" "symmetrical"
Quick Write			None offered	

The mean lesson begins with dialogic interactions among classmates who are sharing opinions and information to coconstruct understandings and mathematical representations. By the end of the lesson, they are creating written products that require synthesis, editing, and integration of multimodal elements. Students develop more authority about the subject of mean. They begin on an equal footing as they discuss experiences and express initial ideas about the balancing rock images. As the lesson culminates in students' becoming experts about plots and procedures, they write with greater authority to a more distant, imagined audience.

Students' language also develops as they use more "technical" terms to concisely and precisely refer to ideas. "Academic" terminology is just one category of technical language, because the specialized, technical terminology used to describe football, cricket, or motorcycle maintenance may be just as opaque to outsiders as mathematical terms, at least initially. In the mean lesson, the language moves from everyday contexts such as gymnastics and diet, to more specific contexts such as rocks and plots. Later, Interacting tasks provide explicit models for the kinds of language that could be used to describe plots, transformations, and relationships between data more typical of language used by communities engaged in mathematics.

SO WHAT ARE MATHEMATICS EDUCATORS TO DO?

This mean lesson is just one instantiation of how instruction can be transformed through the three key shifts and redesign actions to better support multilingual learners as they engage in rigorous mathematics learning. To fully enact this vision, multiple groups of educators will need to contribute in concerted ways because educators not only work in different settings but also may be required to implement instructional materials that they did not design.

At the lesson level, classroom-based educators can ask themselves critical questions about the lessons they are designing and the instructional materials they are using. Based on these answers, they can potentially take the steps shown in Table 7.3.

For educators who support classroom-based teachers or create instructional materials and lessons meant to be enacted broadly, a long-term agenda is necessary. This work will need to subsume the work on lessons and include the strategic planning and redesign of units and courses. Educators will need to reframe the design of their curricula to meet the needs of multilingual learners. Putting the shifts into practice will benefit all learners and will provide the equitable opportunities that are particularly critical for multilingual learners both to gain initial entry and to subsequently participate in increasingly sophisticated ways.

Table 7.3. Questions to Consider and Potential Steps to Take

	Questions to Consider	Potential Steps to Take
Conceptual Focus	• How clearly is the conceptual focus defined? • How does the conceptual approach tap into students' experiences or funds of knowledge? • How rich is the connection potential of the ideas, representations, and procedures in a lesson?	• Anticipate students' prior experiences and provide opportunities to make explicit connections. • Identify the minimal "working definition" students need to get in various lesson activities. • Select metaphors or analogies to frame the conceptual ideas in ways students can recognize.
Quality Interactions	• How are activities structured to ensure maximum participation by all learners? • How are students offered different roles in interacting with each other? • How do these roles support the coconstruction of mathematical knowledge? • How do opportunities to participate change across time?	• Employ different structures for participation to ensure all learners are engaged in sustained oral interactions about disciplinary ideas. • Create opportunities for students to offer opinions and information, but also to converge and reach consensus. Aim for coconstruction. • Employ a variety of scaffolding tasks to ensure that students have different ways to contribute.
Language Focus	• How are language opportunities structured throughout the lesson? • What language supports will students need to be offered to engage in disciplinary practices? • How do language practices grow over the course of the lesson? • To what extent do students have greater autonomy in making language choices over time?	• Provide structured opportunities for disciplinary language practice to develop conceptual understanding. • Map language progressions and identify when to introduce key terms in rich, multimodal texts. • Provide formulaic expressions when necessary and attend to degrees of freedom. • Solicit and highlight explicit features of language performances in mathematical practices, but give students substantial latitude.

REFERENCES

Chu, H. (2013). Scaffolding tasks for the professional development of mathematics teachers of English language learners. In C. Margolinas (Ed.), *Task design in mathematics education* (pp. 559–567). International Commission on Mathematics Instruction.

Chu, H., & Hamburger, L. (2019). Designing mathematical interactions for English Learners. *Mathematics Teaching in the Middle School, 24*(4), 218–225. https://doi.org/10.5951/mathteacmiddscho.24.4.0218

Chu, H., & Hamburger, L. (2022). Educative curriculum materials for English Learners: Varying the intensity of scaffolding. In L. de Oliveira & R. Westerlund (Eds.), *Scaffolding for multilingual learners in elementary and secondary schools* (pp. 181–196). Routledge.

Chu, H., & Rubel, L. H. (2013). When the world is not the problem: Real-world contexts in analogies. In M. Berger, K. Brodie, V. Frith, & K. le Roux (Eds.), *Proceedings of the Seventh International Mathematics Education and Society Conference* (pp. 262–271). Mathematics Education and Society.

Chu, H., Tran, T., & Hamburger, L. (2022). *Redefining approaches for engaging English Learners with mathematical ideas.* National Research and Development Center to Improve Education for Secondary English Learners at WestEd.

de Araujo, Z., & Smith, E. (2022). Examining English Language Learners' needs through the lens of algebra curriculum materials. *Educational Studies in Mathematics, 109,* 65–87.

Hamburger, L., & Chu, H. (2019). Making slope a less slippery concept for English Learners: Redesigning mathematics instruction with rich interactions. In A. Walqui & G. Bunch (Eds.), *Amplifying the curriculum: Designing quality learning opportunities for English Learners* (pp. 115–137). Teachers College Press.

Herbel-Eisenmann, B., & Breyfogle, L. (2005). Questioning our patterns of questioning. *Mathematics Teaching in the Middle School, 10*(9), 484–489.

Heritage, M., Walqui, A., & Linquanti, R. (2015). *English Language Learners and the new standards. Developing language, content knowledge and analytical practices in the classroom.* Harvard Education Press.

Lampert, M. (2017). Ambitious teaching: A deep dive. In R. Heller, R.E. Wolfe, & A. Steinberg (Eds.), *Rethinking readiness: Deeper learning for college, work, and life* (pp. 147–173). Harvard Education Press.

Moschkovich, J. (2002). A situated and sociocultural perspective on bilingual mathematics learners. *Mathematical Thinking and Learning, 4,* 189–212.

Pollatsek, A., Lima, S., & Well, A. (1981). Concept or computation: Students' understanding of the mean. *Educational Studies in Mathematics, 12*(2), 191–204.

Roberts, S., de Araujo, Z., Willey, C., & Zahner, W., (2021). Three ways to enhance tasks for multilingual learners. *Mathematics Teacher: Learning and Teaching PK–12, 115,* 458–467.

Stein, M. K., Engle, R. A., Smith, M. S., & Hughes, E. K. (2008). Orchestrating productive mathematical discussions: Five practices for helping teachers move beyond show and tell. *Mathematical Thinking and Learning, 10*(4), 313–340. https://doi.org/10.1080/10986060802229675

Stein, M., Smith, M., Henningsen, M., & Silver, E. (2009). *Implementing standards-based mathematics instruction: A casebook for professional development* (2nd edition). Teachers College Press.

Stigler, J., & Hiebert, J. (1999). *The teaching gap*. Free Press.

Vygotsky, L. (2012). *Thought and language*. MIT Press.

Walqui, A., & Heritage, M. (2018). Meaningful classroom talk: Supporting English Learners' oral language development. *American Educator*, *42*(3), 18–23, 35.

Walqui, A., & van Lier, L. (2010). *Scaffolding the academic success of adolescent English Language Learners: A pedagogy of promise*. WestEd.

Wilson, J., & Smith, E. (2022). Increasing multilingual learners' access in mathematics. *Mathematics Teacher: Learning and Teaching PK–12, 115*, 104–112.

CHAPTER 8

Amplifying Texts for Multilingual Learners

Selecting, Preparing, and Using Multiple Sources in the History Classroom

Daisy Martin and George C. Bunch

"What's going on? The textbook says most Mexican workers left willingly, so why does this interview say that everyone is crying?" Sophie can't wait to blurt out the contradiction that she has found between her textbook's account of Mexican deportation in the 1930s and the excerpt from Lucas Lucio, a man who experienced the deportation. Sophie and her peers are learning about 1930s America in this hypothetical 11th-grade U.S. history class. Ms. Jones, Sophie's teacher, has asked them to read two different historical sources to investigate the question *What was the 1930s deportation of Mexican Americans?* Another student, Jorge, raises his hand and asks, "Wait, I've never heard of this deportation before—is it really a thing?"

Ms. Jones, a teacher we have invented for this chapter based on teachers we have worked with in the past, has deliberately chosen two short accounts that contradict one another for her students to read. The accounts are working as she intended: to provoke students' questions, even confusions. Notably, Sophie has read carefully and noticed that the sources contradict each other. Ms. Jones could not have taken for granted that students would notice these discrepancies, but she paved the way for such observations, in part through asking students to use different accounts to investigate the reading question stated above. The reading question invites students to notice the contradictions as they read with purpose, even without any hint from Ms. Jones that they can expect contradictions.

The teacher, however, is not the only one asking questions. Students themselves, both in partner work and in whole-class discussion, generate different kinds of questions. The ensuing discussion prompts Ms. Jones to chime in with more questions of her own: What do you know about who wrote and produced each account? What might you expect from a textbook account? From an interview with a participant? How, if at all, do the accounts agree? How do they differ? What specific information or quotes can you point to that show that comparison? What additional questions do you have about these events or sources? In short, the two texts become a springboard for both students and teachers to propose new questions, creating ripe opportunities for further inquiry.

In this chapter, we illustrate how teachers like Ms. Jones can design challenging and engaging learning opportunities for multilingual learners to read and think like historians. We draw on scholarship in history education and language and literacy education, our own expertise as teachers and teacher educators, and our experiences working with teachers in the design of amplified history curricula for multilingual learners. We begin by arguing that studying history necessarily relies on engaging with texts, and that teachers play the key role in selecting the historical texts that will be at the heart of historical inquiry lessons. We then argue that multilingual learners should have opportunities to access the same kinds of texts that are recommended for other students, and that there are a number of ways that texts can be amplified to make them accessible for multilingual learners to read like historians. We share a range of activities, based on the frameworks and models presented earlier in this book, that can coalesce in an amplified lesson for multilingual learners and their classmates.

STUDYING HISTORY RELIES ON ENGAGING WITH TEXTS

As is clear from the above description, students in Ms. Jones's classroom are invited to question and puzzle over textual sources as they try to make sense of multiple accounts. Reading in this classroom looks very different from reading in many traditional history classrooms, where students too often merely engage with identifying the main names, dates, and places mentioned in a single account. Ms. Jones structures as many lessons and units as she can around a historical problem or question. In the discussion above, she has chosen contradictory texts to help introduce this lesson, which will eventually have students considering the historical significance of these deportations in the 1930s.

Ms. Jones knows many students think history is the textbook, and that it is a single story that they are meant to remember and regurgitate. But memorization and recitation are not the disciplinary practices that matter most to Ms. Jones, nor are they what is valued in her state's framework or the broader historical discipline. Additionally, they are not what is needed for students to engage in the civic life of their community or in a multiracial democracy. She has deliberately chosen these texts to represent history as an investigation into the past that requires reading multiple sources and perspectives, which are often contradictory and incomplete. Ms. Jones's lesson about the deportations will also include students learning facts and background information, but that is not the agenda for today.

Teachers' Role in Selecting Texts

Ms. Jones knows that engaging students in doing history is what may get left behind as curricular resources, pacing guides, and textbooks all hurry students through a seemingly interminable list of disconnected historical facts. Carefully choosing the texts and sources that students will read, analyze, cross-check, and synthesize during specific lessons is an essential part of ensuring that she is engaging students in doing history.

And Ms. Jones knows that to plan the kinds of lessons that will engage both teachers and students, it is important that teachers themselves are the ones selecting the texts, ideally but not necessarily working collaboratively with other teachers. While a plethora of resources exists from which to find relevant and engaging texts (some of which we will share in this chapter), we argue that the teacher is the most important agent in selecting these texts.

Doing history means Ms. Jones's students will learn that history is an inquiry into the past as well as learning ways of thinking, reading, and writing essential to that inquiry. Driven by specific questions and curiosities, historians search for, collect, and interrogate multiple sources that tell multiple stories and represent multiple perspectives. They craft answers to their questions (even while the questions may have changed as they learn more from the voices of the past and others who have studied them) and write historical arguments. These arguments must be warranted by evidence, which can take many forms; they also require historians to test their assertions by asking counterfactuals and submitting their work to knowledgeable others for review and critique. While neither Ms. Jones nor her state's history education framework intend for her students to become professional historians, she does want them to learn specific disciplinary practices embedded in this sophisticated endeavor.

This means that over the months that Ms. Jones works with her students, they will read a number of primary and secondary sources of varied types and formats. Primary sources, or any source created during the time under study, might be excerpts from government reports, newspaper articles, political speeches, oral histories, novels, personal diaries or letters, and so on. And while all of those examples include text, primary sources would also include photographs, film and video, political cartoons, memes, objects, and more. Secondary sources interpret, retell, or analyze primary sources and events and are created after the time under study. Textbooks and historians' monographs are secondary sources, as are modern-day historical documentaries. Secondary sources make arguments about historical events and times, sometimes outright, sometimes hidden. In the opening scenario, the textbook is a secondary source, and one hidden argument that it makes is about what is historically significant, given its inclusion and elaboration (or not) of particular historical information. But a single source is not necessarily always primary or always secondary, as it depends on what is being investigated. In short, reading multiple types of sources is a cornerstone of Ms. Jones's class, and she thinks in terms of text or source sets rather than a single source when studying a particular topic.

But What About Multilingual Learners?

At this point in our discussion, teachers may be asking the obvious question: Given the language and literacy challenges that many students face, including home speakers of English, when encountering the kinds of texts and discussions described above, what special considerations need to be made when choosing texts and designing learning activities to ensure that these texts are accessible for multilingual learners?

The first answer to this question is that the same disciplinary principles and approaches discussed above apply! That is, the most important thing for teachers to remember when considering how to support multilingual learners is not to abandon the core ideas discussed above simply because students are at different points in learning English. Using the tenets and architecture for amplifying the curriculum described in Chapters 2 and 3 of this book, multilingual learners can engage with the same inquiry questions, big ideas, and types of texts as other students do. It is true that, depending on students' English language proficiency and reading background, some additional considerations need to be made when selecting and preparing texts and scaffolding activities for multilingual learners. But it is essential that the disciplinary goals outlined above remain intact for multilingual learners—not only to ensure that this population has equitable opportunities to develop the kinds of civic discourse and reasoning that will be essential for our communities, nation, and the world (Lee et al., 2021), but also because this kind of history education provides exceptional opportunities for developing language and literacy. Further, as discussed in Chapter 1, multilingual learners bring an incredible array of perspectives, knowledge, and experience to these conversations (Gándara, 2017; Yosso, 2005).

So the real question becomes: Given the importance of opportunities to read and grapple with challenging historical texts, how do teachers or other curriculum developers ensure that the texts and learning activities they choose are made accessible for students from a wide range of language and literacy backgrounds, and especially for students currently classified as English Learners? It might seem that the best first step would be to choose different texts at different reading levels for different students in the class, based on their language proficiency or reading background. However, we argue that attempting to select only texts predetermined to be at an "appropriate" reading level often represents a severe miscalculation of students' true potential. That is, choosing "simpler" texts for multilingual learners denies students opportunities to engage with higher-level texts that they may well be capable of accessing when provided with collaborative and supportive learning activities such as those described in this book. It is also the case that attempting to revise texts by simplifying their language may actually make some texts *more* difficult to comprehend, because contextual clues essential for reading comprehension are often lost in the simplification process. Simultaneously, choosing only simple texts, or simplifying existing ones, carries the danger of foreclosing access to opportunities for the kinds of disciplinary thinking addressed at the beginning of this chapter, as well as constricting opportunities for language and literacy development.

Text Complexity, Text Difficulty, and Text Accessibility

To understand why building curriculum around simple or simplified texts is problematic for multilingual learners in history classrooms, it is helpful to distinguish between text *complexity* and text *difficulty* (Bunch et al., 2014). It turns out that the question "What is the appropriate reading level?" might be the wrong question to be asking in the first place. The better questions might be "How can we find a range of texts for the inquiry at hand?" and "How can we engage and support multilingual learners in accessing and engaging with those texts?" We will illustrate several tools to help do this later in this chapter.

Text Complexity. Most attempts to determine a text's reading level begin with some measure of the *complexity* of the text itself, regardless of who might be reading it, for what purposes, or the circumstances under which it might be read. A common practice in school reading instruction is to use quantitative analyses of the proportion of uncommon or long words a text contains, sentence length, grammatical complexity, and other features to assign each text a "reading level" and then to modify a single text by manipulating these features into different reading levels. Students with different "reading proficiency levels," based on how students do on standardized texts of these manipulated texts, are then often assigned texts that purportedly match those reading levels (National Governors Association,

2010, p. 7). Text complexity can also be measured qualitatively by analyzing how closely a text follows the structure of a particular genre, the extent to which the text presents conventional vs. unconventional uses of language (e.g., literal and unambiguous vs. ironic, archaic, or purposefully misleading), and how many different levels of meaning are signaled simultaneously by the author (National Governors Association, 2010, p. 5).

Text Difficulty. The problem with focusing so sharply on measures of text complexity as the guide for matching students with texts is that the measures provide no information about a range of important *student-related* factors known to play a large role in reading comprehension. These variables include students' interest in the topic at hand, their background knowledge of the content, their own perception of the purpose of reading the assigned text, and the cognitive and metacognitive strategies that readers have developed over time. Nor do measures of text complexity tell us anything about what readers are being asked to *do* with the text or what kind of support they may have access to as they read (Bunch et al., 2014; Greenleaf et al., 2023; RAND Reading Study Group, 2002). All of these variables contribute significantly to the *difficulty* of texts for particular students in particular contexts, and they provide clues for how to support students in accessing them.

As teachers may recognize from their own reading practices, it is often more difficult to understand a less complex text about a topic we do not know or care very much about, especially when trying to read it in an unsupportive or hostile environment, than it is to understand a complex text about a topic we are knowledgeable about, care deeply about, are highly motivated to read, and are reading in a friendly and supportive environment. Further, simplifying texts actually may make them *more* difficult to read. For example, phrases or clauses that are often removed in the simplification process actually serve as important contextual clues. Meanwhile, a text may become more difficult to read for multilingual learners when longer words that may be cognates with students' home languages are replaced with shorter words that may have no relationship to their home language (e.g., for Spanish speakers, replacing the word *evaluate*, which is similar to *evaluar* in Spanish and has the same meaning, with a shorter word such as *test* that would not be recognizable for Spanish speakers unless they had already learned that word in English).

For multilingual learners, there is evidence that it is even *more* important to consider the reader and task dimensions of reading comprehension than it is for readers of texts in their home language. That is because the less language proficiency the reader has in the language of the text, the more important other factors become in determining their ability to comprehend the text: their reading skills and strategies in their home language; their background knowledge of the subject of the text; their interest and motivation in reading it; the nature of what they are being asked to do with the text; and the supports available for them to read it (Bernhardt, 2011; Bunch et al., 2014).

Text Accessibility. In short, a number of variables impact readers' ability to engage with and comprehend text, many of them beyond the features of the text itself. Ensuring that texts are "accessible" for multilingual learners, therefore, involves *amplifying* opportunities that students have to engage meaningfully with complex and difficult texts, as well as providing scaffolding as they do so—rather than *simplifying* the texts they are asked to read.

Before concluding this section, we want to offer two brief notes of clarification. First, we are not arguing that teachers and others developing learning activities, lessons, and units for multilingual learners should ignore their students' language proficiency and reading background when selecting texts. There may well be some texts, especially some historical primary sources, whose complexity makes them unproductive for multilingual learners (and likely other students) even with significant scaffolding, especially for students at the beginning stages of English language development and those who may have little experience reading similar disciplinary texts. It is reasonable for teachers to have an "eye" for texts that meet their disciplinary goals that may be more or less suitable for their students. But often teachers and other curriculum developers are too quick to conclude that multilingual learners won't be able to handle particular texts, often assuming that students have to read them alone and without support, and that "reading" a text means starting at the beginning, reading every word until the end, and gaining a holistic comprehension of the entire text. As will become clear in our examples in this chapter, there are multiple meaningful, intellectually challenging, disciplinarily robust, and well-supported ways that teachers can amplify—rather than simplify—complex historical texts, both primary and secondary.

Second, we want to clarify that, for multilingual learners, the historical texts that we ask students to read and discuss don't necessarily have to be in English. Depending on the topic and available texts, some of the sources could be in the home language of the students. There will be different ways of integrating these texts based on whether the teacher or classroom peers also speak this language, the range of languages spoken by students in the class, and whether the class is designed to be taught in English or in the students' home languages (see Chapter 5). As a word of caution, it is important to keep in mind that all of our discussion above about text complexity, difficulty, and accessibility also applies to texts we ask students to read in their home languages. That is, home-language texts will exhibit the same range of complexity as texts in English, and the difficulty of the text will be relative to the same kinds of student and contextual factors discussed above. In other words, assigning multilingual learners a text in their home language does not automatically result in accessibility, and a range of supports may be necessary for students' to meaningfully access these texts.

Reading Like a Historian

In discussing text complexity, difficulty, and accessibility, we have focused on comprehension and engagement with texts without specifying the *disciplinary* nature of reading, discussing, and writing about texts, as expressed in the goals of Ms. Jones and the history education profession articulated at the beginning of this chapter. Reading comprehension is necessary but not sufficient for historical inquiry and understanding, and amplifying the curriculum for multilingual learners implies focusing on the latter as well as the former.

Doing history means students not only comprehend multiple texts, attempting to understand what each text says, but also *interrogate* those texts in disciplinary ways. That is, they "read like historians" (Wineburg, 1991; Wineburg et al., 2012). This means that texts are not merely banks of information from which the reader can faithfully pull details and quotes, but voices from the past—sources that have been created by humans. As such, these "voices," or texts, can include hidden agendas and motivations, connect to the events and times in which they were created, and ultimately, cannot be taken at face value. Researchers and educators have developed a framework for this interrogation that reflects how historians read, which includes sourcing, contextualizing, and corroborating texts. Thus, reading like a historian means asking and addressing questions such as the following: Who created this text? When and where? What was its purpose? What was happening when this text was created? What do other sources say? Where do they agree and disagree? Rather than categorizing texts as unbiased or biased, informational or fictional, all texts become worthy of interrogation. In short, reading like a historian means not only reading to see what a text *says*, it also means reading to see what a text *does*.

Similarly, doing history requires learning how historical argumentation works. This includes planning, writing, and critiquing evidence-based arguments; learning that claims must be warranted by evidence and also must acknowledge conflicting evidence; and understanding that not all arguments are considered legitimate, as some include cherry-picked, misinterpreted or decontextualized evidence or outright lies. When students learn disciplinary practices in history, history becomes an ongoing argument that requires students to enact approaches and skills that help them seek out the most truthful, complete pictures of the past that are currently available. They learn that historians routinely argue about how to explain specific historical events and processes and that understanding those events and processes helps illuminate why and how current events and circumstances exist. These reading and argumentative practices are undergirded by important historical thinking concepts. These concepts, framed by different professional organizations, include historical significance, evidence, continuity and change, context, causation, perspectives, and the ethical dimensions of history (National Council for the Social Studies [NCSS], 2013; The Historical Thinking Project, n.d.).

AMPLIFYING THE CURRICULUM FOR MULTILINGUAL LEARNERS IN THE HISTORY CLASSROOM

In the remainder of this chapter, we share guidelines and examples for how teachers like Ms. Jones might approach selecting texts, preparing those texts for students in linguistically diverse classrooms, and designing scaffolded learning activities that promote both the accessibility of texts and opportunities for students to read like historians.

Selecting Texts

Where might teachers start in selecting texts to help their students study a particular historical topic while also learning and enacting particular historical reading, writing, and thinking practices? Using the topic that Ms. Jones and her colleagues had chosen (the deportation of Mexicans and Mexican Americans in the 1930s) as an example, we begin by elucidating some of the thinking and questioning that are essential for teachers to do when looking for texts that will help create such learning opportunities for students.

Because history is an argument, Ms. Jones and her colleagues teaching the same topic began their planning by asking a number of questions, including *What have historians and other scholars argued about, now or in the past, regarding these deportations*? They consulted secondary literature that addressed U.S. history writ large, where they found that some books and their stories of the 1930s didn't even mention these deportations. But they found others that did, like Paul Ortiz's *An African American and Latinx History of the United States* (2018) and Ronald Takaki's *A Different Mirror* (1993). In fact, such uneven treatment of this topic in secondary sources was a clue to help them connect this topic to the core concept of historical significance: Whose stories get told in history books? What past events, people, phenomena are depicted as historically significant?

Ms. Jones and colleagues then explored and read further, bolstering their knowledge of these events. They were reminded that the onset of the Great Depression led to increased scapegoating of immigrants who were blamed for "stealing" jobs from "real" Americans. They learned that, in the Southwest, Mexicans faced the brunt of the scapegoating and in places like Los Angeles, a concerted effort of fearmongering reached its zenith in 1931. Local newspapers announced upcoming immigration raids in an effort to scare Mexican residents, and on February 26, 1931, members of the Los Angeles Police Department and U.S. immigration agents raided La Placita Olvera in downtown Los Angeles, a central hub for Mexican migrants looking for housing and employment (Sanchez, 1993, p. 135). Officials held hundreds for questioning before ultimately arresting 17 people: 1 Japanese man, 5 Chinese immigrants and 11 Mexicans, including 1 legal U.S. resident. The tactics local officials employed in Los Angeles were replicated across the United States from 1929 to 1939. Ms. Jones and her colleagues found that historian Adam Goodman argued that it is impossible to know exactly how many people left the United States during the time period but the collective efforts of local, state, and federal officials contributed to the repatriation of as many as half a million people (Goodman, 2020, pp. 43–46).

The teachers noticed that different sources give different explanations of *why* these deportations happened. Among other factors, Ortiz (2018) writes of President Hoover's cabinet whipping up anti-Mexican sentiments to distract from the federal government's failure in addressing the economic crises of the time (p. 131) and about labor historian Carey McWilliams' idea of "terror campaigns" that worked against farm labor organizing (p. 132). Takaki (1993) asserts that Mexican workers were "blamed for white unemployment" (p. 333) while George Sanchez argues some "county officials and local businessmen . . . believed the hard times made it imperative that the scarce jobs and resources be reserved for American citizens" (p. 210). These sources provide clues toward a possible inquiry question: *What factors led to the deportations?* Explaining why something happened is a core endeavor of historical inquiry and requires constructing an evidence-based argument about cause, which always includes a consideration of the idea of *multiple* causation—another core historical concept.

These two possibilities—an inquiry focusing on historical significance and one that focuses on an argument explaining the deportations—emerged as Ms. Jones and her colleagues learned and read more about the deportations. Either of these concepts could become an inquiry question, but neither would work to engage students in reading like a historian unless accompanied by sources for students to read that allowed them to see different possible legitimate answers.

In other words, developing inquiry questions and selecting texts happens simultaneously and symbiotically in an iterative process. Here, we have identified two possible inquiries, but the availability, format, and content of sources that align with the possible inquiries are not clear yet. *What factors explain the deportations of Mexicans and Mexican Americans in the 1930s?* or *What is the historical significance of these deportations?* are both possible questions with multiple correct answers. (If it's an inquiry, it should not have only one possible answer!) The key next question is what sources could students explore, read, and talk about together to help them construct a possible answer for either of these questions? A question that requires the *teacher* to show students the answer, as opposed to a question that *students* can answer using the sources, does not allow students to learn how to read historically.

For example, if students are to investigate and explain why deportations in the 1930s happened, the sources that teachers might choose for them to read would include texts that reference different reasons. These might include a chronology of earlier events and policies restricting immigration, a source that highlights the economic disaster that was the Depression, excerpts that show anti-immigrant and anti-Mexican rhetoric from news organizations and legislators, excerpts from deportees or Mexican consuls addressing why they think these deportations are happening, and so on. These would allow students to identify and assess multiple causes. But the historical record here is grim. Historians talk about political and media rhetoric and scapegoating as being key to explaining these deportations, and it is no accident that, in 2005, the California legislature passed the "Apology Act for the 1930s Mexican Repatriation Program" (2005).

That Apology Act was, in part, accomplished by the efforts of one California state senator, Joseph Dunn. Dunn credited Francisco E. Balderrama and Raymond Rodríguez's book-length treatment of this event, *Decade of Betrayal: Mexican Repatriation in the 1930s* (2006), for educating him and spurring his actions to ensure that public officials addressed and tried to correct what he named as illegal, unjust, and unconstitutional

TEXTBOX 8.1. SOURCING: ANALYZING TITLES FOR ARGUMENT AND STORY

Decade of Betrayal: Mexican Repatriation in the 1930s, by Francisco E. Balderrama and Raymond Rodríguez, published in 1995. Second edition published in 2006.

"Apology Act for the 1930s Mexican Repatriation Program." This California Senate Bill 670 was made into law in 2005.

deportations. Indeed, these two complete titles are ripe for students, including multilingual learners, to analyze: *Decade of Betrayal* and the Apology Act. In each, a clear argument is signaled in just a few words. Ms. Jones and her colleagues decided that a text for an inquiry focusing on significance could be this source information itself (see Textbox 8.1).

Additionally, two paragraphs in the Introduction to Balderrama and Rodríguez's book include an overarching argument about how these deportations happened and how barrio residents resisted. Students can read these paragraphs to consider historical significance. (See an excerpt of the paragraphs in the Textbox 8.2.)

But if students are to read multiple sources, Ms. Jones also needed to consider their relationship to one another and how the entire set of sources would help students answer the inquiry question. How does a particular source interact with the other sources students will read? Does it support, extend or contest other sources' content and perspectives? (Bain,

Textbox 8.2. Excerpt for Discussing Historical Significance

Headnote: The book *Decade of Betrayal* documented the history of Mexican deportations in the 1930s with a detailed story and many primary sources. California state senator J. Dunn gave this book credit when he pushed California to apologize for these deportations. In 2006, a new edition of the book was published, including more information about California's apology. Below are two paragraphs where the authors lay out their overarching argument.

* * *

Americans, reeling from the economic disorientation of the depression, sought a convenient scapegoat. They found it in the Mexican community. In a frenzy of anti-Mexican hysteria, wholesale punitive measures were proposed and undertaken by government officials at the federal, state, and local levels. . . .

Although the Mexican community was especially hard hit by the depression and endured incredible suffering, discrimination, and maltreatment, barrio residents did not lose hope. With unwavering determination, they withstood the onslaught unleashed against them. In their efforts to survive, a cadre of grassroots organizations developed. . . .

Source: Excerpt from *Decade of Betrayal: Mexican Repatriation in the 1930s*, by Francisco E. Balderrama and Raymond Rodríguez, published in 1995. Second edition published in 2006 (pp. 1–2).

2005). How does a particular source help students answer an overarching question about historical significance and how do the sources as a group help students answer that same inquiry question? Here, a transcript of a 5-minute *Washington Post* podcast, "The time the United States illegally deported 1 million Mexican Americans" (Bernard, 2018) might be partnered with the excerpt from Balderrama and Rodríguez (2006). This podcast is written for readers who know nothing about these deportations and includes multiple details and facts about the events, references Balderrama and Rodríguez and Dunn, and brings the story up to the present day.

In considering text selection for investigating deportation in the 1930s, we, and Ms. Jones's teaching team, are in some ways treading new ground. While this topic is now in the California State Framework (partly as a result of the Apology Act), it is not a topic that is commonly taught or included in any detail in secondary history textbooks and published curricula. Jorge's question in the opening scenario indicated that he was unfamiliar with this topic and events and implied an additional question—Why don't I know about this? These kinds of confusions and unfamiliarities become a frame for deepening students' inquiry. What should the textbook say about this? Are these events, these deportations, historically significant? What criteria for historical significance are we using to judge? We argue that teachers themselves should have the agency and support to pursue such understudied topics as inquiry opportunities for their students, especially when the topic is likely to have salience in students' lives and communities.

Other factors that can drive text selection include potential student interest and what the topic, content, and easily available sources allow one to teach and learn. In California, where we do our work, these deportations and the Apology Act are relevant to our local and state histories, and may be part of a student's family or community histories. An excerpt of the Apology Act brings the deportations into more modern day, but also addresses a larger question of how we address past historical wrongs. While not necessarily a historical question, it is a valuable course-long question that allows students to understand and even participate in some of the contemporary reparations discourse and policy. Likewise, present-day rhetoric and politics regarding immigrants, Mexican Americans, and agricultural and industrial labor echo some of what we see in the 1930s, offering possibilities for students to consider continuities and changes across time.

The entirety of a teacher's course also plays a role in text selection. What course-long questions and themes will students work with? How does any single text, or text set, inform those throughlines? How might these texts complicate or strengthen other specific lessons, texts, and topics tied to those throughlines? Might using a text students have used before, but using it in a different way or in a different lesson, be a good idea?

Amplifying Texts for a Linguistically Diverse Classroom

Once texts have been selected, amplifying them will include careful preparation of each text and designing activities that scaffold student learning in the generative and agentive ways described in Chapters 2 and 3. Below, we identify some specific ways to prepare each source to make it more comprehensible and useful for engaging students, especially multilingual learners. We then share examples of tasks that are particularly useful for promoting reading comprehension and supporting students' abilities to read like a historian.

Concrete ways to prepare historical sources to enhance accessibility include amplifying and adding features that matter for historical reading and inquiry, considering the visual appearance of the sources, and ensuring coherence between the inquiry question and selected sources. Students will need amplified source information, which is information about the origins of a text. See Textbox 8.1, which demonstrates how to offer such information. While these examples include title, authors, and date, this source information might also include audience, place of origin and other factors important to understanding a particular text. It is important to note that "source" here refers to the origins of the text itself, not where a teacher or curriculum designer might have found it. For example, that a text can be found in the Library of Congress's archives is less useful for a reader than knowing it is a photo taken by Dorothea Lange in the 1930s. That Library of Congress information might still serve as a reference and attribution, but it is the information about the text's origins that needs amplifying.

"Headnotes" or brief introductory notes about the source, such as the one shown in Textbox 8.2, can also be added to offer the reader important contextual and background information about the document. This note may tell readers more about the author, the situation of the source's origin, and the specific names and places mentioned in the source. All of this can help readers understand the document.

Amplifying source information and adding a headnote support students' disciplinary reading. But the document can also be amplified to promote more general comprehension. A vocabulary bank or synonyms can be added in brackets to help students with unfamiliar vocabulary, and carefully selected parts of the text can be cut (those not necessary for the historical inquiry at hand), using ellipses to indicate where any words have been deleted from the document (see Textbox 8.2). Excerpting documents can be important when doing source-based historical inquiry. Students need to do the cognitive work of understanding, analyzing, and corroborating each document and also considering how these sources together inform the guiding inquiry question. The cognitive demand of this task is significant, and having shorter excerpts is appropriate when trying to teach these specific historical reading practices. To excerpt, teachers can consider the inquiry question that students are working to answer and how an excerpt does (or does not) answer that question and how the sources work together. Paying attention to maintaining the author's original meanings is also always important. This all sounds like a lot of work, but free expert online curriculum providers have often done this work already and teachers can draw from their well-prepared source sets, e.g., *Read.Inquire.Write* (n.d.), Digital Inquiry Group (DIG [n.d.], formerly known as the Stanford History Education Group, or SHEG), C3 Teachers, and The World History Project (OER Project, n.d.). Lastly, it is worthwhile to consider the look of the text and if it is reader friendly. Is the font big enough? (14 point can be a minimal size.) Is there white space on the page or is it a very crowded page that can intimidate?

All of the above adaptations are designed to amplify rather than simplify the texts. That is, historical context is added in the prefatory descriptions; sourcing is clarified; and key words are glossed, not simplified. The grammatical structure of sentences is not simplified, longer words are not replaced with shorter ones, and historical texts are not reworded.

DESIGNING LEARNING OPPORTUNITIES FOR HISTORICAL TEXTS

Once key historical texts are selected and prepared, what might teachers plan for their students to actually *do* with those texts? In this section, we provide examples consistent with the tenets in Chapter 2. In organizing those activities into a single lesson, which will be a multiday learning sequence, we use a modified version of the lesson architecture presented in Chapter 3, with its Three Moments: Preparing Learners, Interacting With Texts, and Extending Understanding. The modifications we made to the architecture align it with the approaches to history education discussed throughout this chapter (see Figure 8.1). (Please note that a particular lesson would not include all of the bulleted actions within each Moment.)

As we discuss the learning activities Ms. Jones could use in this lesson, it is important to remember that, before this lesson begins, students have already done some work learning about the 1930s and the Great Depression and New Deal in other parts of the course. They have heard of the stock market crash and bank failures, high unemployment rates, and the failure of President Hoover's policies to improve conditions for the everyman. They have seen pictures of the Dust Bowl and migrants and learned of President Roosevelt's flurry of federal policies and agencies to tackle or mitigate the economic crisis. They have also heard of uneven impacts of the economic

Figure 8.1. Three Moments in a History Lesson

PREPARING LEARNERS • Activate student interest • Focus attention on key concepts • Activate and develop relevant background knowledge • Provide historical context • Introduce central inquiry question	Task 1 Task 2 Task 3

INTERACTING WITH TEXT(s)
TEXTS
• Source the text
• Use questions to guide comprehension
• Use questions to read historically
  ○ Contextualize
  ○ Compare accounts
• Make connections to historical concepts/themes
• Marshal evidence to build an argument
	Task 4
	Task 5
	Task 6
	Task 7

EXTENDING UNDERSTANDING • Connect takeaways to other ideas and topics outside the texts • Communicate arguments, conclusions, questions and connections • Apply newly gained knowledge to novel situations or problem-solving • Create or recreate based on new understandings	Task 8 Task 9

Source: Adapted from Walqui et al., this volume, Figure 3.2.

hardships as well as the policies intended to help. This is also not the first time that students have engaged with multiple historical sources or been asked to read historically; Ms. Jones has been teaching the class for some months with a goal of engaging students in doing history.

Preparing Learners

Even with these foundations laid in the weeks and months leading up to this lesson, it is helpful to begin by engaging learners in the kinds of activities designed to prepare learners introduced in Chapter 3 and illustrated in the other chapters in this book before they begin interacting with complex, challenging, and text-heavy historical sources in this lesson. In a history lesson in particular, preparing learners includes activating and developing relevant background knowledge and providing historical context (what is called Building the Field in other chapters in this book). This is a Moment when students can review what they already know and have learned about the time and place they will be studying, as well as draw on what happened in earlier times. This means that preparing learners includes focusing attention on the course-level themes, concepts or questions relevant to this particular lesson. Additionally, preparing learners should activate student interest and introduce a central inquiry question.

Silent Graffiti. First, students engage in a version of the Silent Graffiti activity structure introduced in Chapter 3, in this case focused on a recent news photograph depicting a crowd protesting immigration policies. (Such photographs are easy for teachers to find online.) In this particular Silent Graffiti activity, students initially are not provided with the source of the photo, in order to help them focus on observing carefully and raising questions. Students, seated in small groups around tables with enlargements of the photographs taped to even larger pieces of poster paper, are asked to simultaneously write on the white paper surrounding the image in response to the following prompt: "What do you see? What are your reactions? What questions do you have?" Each student writes with a different colored marker and signs their name or initials, as a mechanism for holding students accountable for their thoughts and avoiding irresponsible, reckless, or damaging comments. Still silently, students walk around their own group's table to observe their classmates' responses.

In the next step of the Silent Graffiti activity, groups hang their posters on the wall and then circulate silently and notice similarities and differences among the commentary on the different posters reflecting on the same images. They then return to tables and—for the first time—discuss orally what they saw, first in their small groups and then in a larger whole-class discussion with the teacher. During the larger discussion, the teacher reveals the source of the photo, which prompts further discussion. Especially useful for controversial topics, Silent Graffiti is a means of discussing a potentially heated issue by writing, reading others' comments, and noting trends—rather than immediately arguing for one's own perspective. For multilingual learners, the activity allows them to access a non-text-heavy (although still complex and historically relevant) source with a means of engagement (writing individual words and short phrases and questions) with which some may feel more comfortable compared to an oral discussion. Further, there are no "right" or "wrong" answers when students write what they see, observe, and think about a visual image. This activity also allows students to remember and access a theme they are working with across curricular units: immigration and borders. Finally, since the group is observing the writing of other groups and gathering and discussing trends, the activity lowers the "temperature" of discussion around a potentially contentious issue.

Round Robin. After Silent Graffiti has activated students' interest and reminded them of one of the course themes, borders and immigration, Ms. Jones turns to an activity targeting background knowledge that will help students access and develop their existing knowledge about the 1930s in the United States and prepare them to engage in more challenging texts later in the lesson. For this purpose, she uses a Round Robin structure to invite students to carefully examine several primary source documents depicting Mexicans and Mexican Americans in the 1930s (such as those in Photo 8.1). Students look closely at photos of Mexican farmworkers in the 1930s, including Dorothea Lange's photos, creating an opportunity to review and activate what students have already studied about the Great Depression in previous lessons. There are several elements of the Round Robin structure that are particularly essential for multilingual learners: One is that all students have the opportunity to think for a few minutes silently and complete

Photo 8.1. Dorothea Lange's Photos Used With Preparing Learners

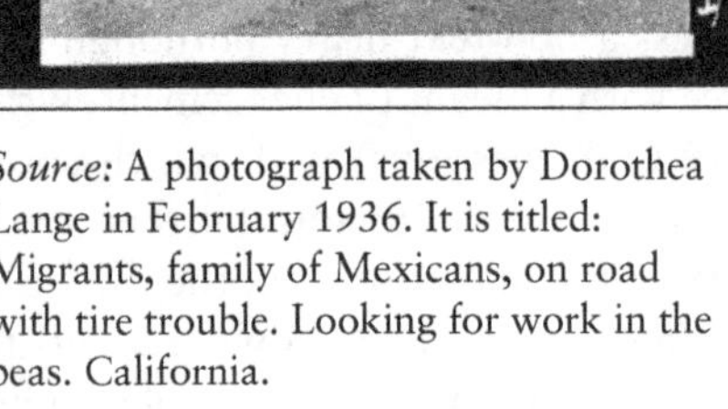

Source: A photograph taken by Dorothea Lange in February 1936. It is titled: Migrants, family of Mexicans, on road with tire trouble. Looking for work in the peas. California.

Source: A photograph taken by Dorothea Lange in June 1935. It is titled: Mexican mother in California. "Sometimes I tell my children that I would like to go to Mexico, but they tell me 'We don't want to go, we belong here.'" (Note on Mexican labor situation in repatriation.)

the following prompt: "I see . . . I think . . . I wonder . . ." The next essential step is that each student in the small group shares one of their responses, thereby increasing the likelihood that everyone can share a novel response. After the first round, students continue to share, one response at a time, until all responses have been shared (or until the allotted time expires).

After sharing individually in the Round Robin, each group is then tasked with collectively discussing what they heard from their groupmates that they hadn't initially noticed, and what new questions they have at this point. Collectively, the group formulates two or three questions related to the photo that they think would be important to spend some time exploring further. As a whole class, the teacher asks each group to share one of the new questions that they have formulated and leads a whole-class discussion. This activity allows students to build and access knowledge (which will help with reading written texts next), grapple with key themes, and build comprehension and inquiry practices or skills.

Only after engaging in these Preparing Learners activities will students read the conflicting accounts mentioned at the beginning of this chapter, making deportation the focus topic they will be studying. Jorge's question indicating that he didn't know about these deportations sets up the lesson's central inquiry question: What is the historical significance of the deportations of Mexicans and Mexican Americans in the 1930s? Not only does the topic under study connect to Ms. Jones's course theme of immigration and borders, this question directly connects to a throughline of Ms. Jones's course: investigating and understanding the idea of historical significance. Over multiple lessons and units, students work on constructing and evaluating shared criteria for historical significance; studying the 1930s deportations serves as another chance for them to construct an argument using and testing those criteria.

Interacting With Texts

In history, interacting with texts can begin by sourcing the texts, and then using questions and activities to both guide reading comprehension and to read historically, contextualizing and comparing accounts. Making connections between text and theme and considering whether and how each text helps the readers answer the central inquiry question is another piece of this interaction. Finally, students use evidence from the texts (and background knowledge as appropriate) to answer the inquiry question and communicate their argument, conclusions, questions, and/or connections. The set of activities and tasks in this Interacting With Texts Moment is contingent on what is being studied and read, and all of these things don't happen in every lesson. What is consistent is that students have a purpose for reading and that is most often communicated by a central inquiry question.

Table 8.1 Sources for Source Sorting Activity

- Image of current-day rally that shows people with signs about immigration.
- Dorothea Lange's photos of the 1930s, including Mexican migrant mother and Mexican travelers.
- Textbook (2019) excerpt.
- Excerpt from Oral History Interview with Lucas Lucio about his experience in the 1930s. Santa Ana, California, March 1976.
- *Mexican Deportation in the 1930s*, by Emma Gomez Martinez, 2012, Longmont, Colorado.
- Source information for *Decade of Betrayal* and Apology Act (see Textbox 8.1).
- Excerpt from Balderrama and Rodriguez's *Decade of Betrayal* (see Textbox 8.2).
- California Apology Act.
- Transcript of a 5-minute *Washington Post* podcast, "The time the United States illegally deported 1 million Mexican Americans" (Bernard, 2018).

In Ms. Jones's lesson, during the Interacting With Texts Moment, students work with several texts including the photographs used in the Preparing Learners Moment, and the other texts referenced earlier in the chapter. (See Table 8.1 for complete list of texts.) Here, we describe several activities that Ms. Jones uses that are particularly helpful for engaging multilingual learners in accessing historical sources that may be too challenging for some to read and understand without support.

Source Sorting. As students move toward engaging with specific written texts, this part of the lesson begins with an activity called Source Sorting, developed by our colleague Jana Peale, a secondary teacher in Santa Cruz, California. The activity provides an opportunity for students to physically handle a set of multiple texts, categorizing them first in whatever way students see fit and later in ways suggested by Ms. Jones (Table 8.1).

After each group is handed a number of sources, there are several rounds of sorting. For example:

Sort 1: Students create their own categories and sort the sources. Even with little background knowledge of the topic and even if not able to read and fully comprehend each source, all students can participate in sorting. Groups might divide the sources into images vs. written texts, positive or negative portrayals of deportation, by time period, or in other ways that the teacher might not have predicted. After the groups have completed their sorting, Ms.

Jones leads a whole-class discussion during which each group discusses how they decided to sort their sources.

Sort 2: Next, Ms. Jones asks students to sort the sources into primary vs. secondary sources. This activity supports the development of the historical thinking skill of "sourcing"—that is, identifying the author, venue, time period, and other contextual details and hypothesizing about the potential perspectives of the author.

Sort 3: Finally, Ms. Jones asks students to sort the sources into those that they find most interesting and/or significant to delve into deeper to understand the deportations.

The Source Sort allows multilingual learners to engage with real historical documents: both primary and secondary, in a way that—while requiring some reading—does not, at least initially, require them to read the entirety of the text. They can focus on titles, authors, images, and headings. Students have agency in terms of how they decide to group their materials, especially in the first round (chronologically, by type of sources, thematically, etc.). Even if they are not able to comprehend or make historical sense of the documents at this stage, when students are later asked to focus in more depth on two or three of the sources, they will recognize them and thus be more interested and aware.

Stop and Source. Ms. Jones asks students to Stop and Source throughout her course. Sourcing activities ask students to consider the source information before reading or closely looking at the content of any particular historical text and source. Stop and Source asks students to pause and consider what they might expect from this source given its origins. This activity can be done with any number of documents. When done with multiple documents, the source information can be pulled out and becomes its own classroom source that students will work with. So, for example, in this Deportation lesson, after source sorting, students will look at the source information for two documents, *Decade of Betrayal* and the Apology Act (Textbox 8.1). They will, in pairs, answer three questions about each of these attributions: What is this source and what can you tell about it from this information? Is there an argument in the title? What can you tell about what that argument is? Then after discussing their answers in a whole group, Ms. Jones will ask, what possible stories might these sources tell?

Sourcing activities like these do two important things, both of particular value for multilingual learners. Sourcing represents an essential part of reading like a historian, both in the activity of pausing and considering source information before reading a document, and in showing that texts are "voices," rather than infallible banks of information. This activity also helps prepare readers to read complex and likely difficult text.

After the sourcing activity, students will read an excerpt from Balderrama and Rodríguez's book, *Decade of Betrayal* (see Textbox 8.2). The excerpt that Ms. Jones has selected and prepared briefly lays out the authors' overarching argument, including the legal and political scapegoating of the Mexican community during the Depression and also the resistance and resilience of that same community. Before reading this passage, Ms. Jones again asks students to stop and source, asking students, "Who are the authors?" In a guided or modelled internet search, the class finds out, at the least, that Balderrama as a Chicano Studies and history professor and Rodríguez as a teacher and university administrator are both credentialled experts. When students then read this excerpt, they will work to answer a central reading question: *What is the author's argument in this passage?* Ms. Jones's next two activities support students in answering this question and, more specifically, in building metacognitive reading strategies (Clarifying Bookmark) and historical reading skills (*Read.Inquire.Write.* Bookmark Tool), while learning more about this historical event.

Clarifying Bookmark. The Clarifying Bookmark is a tool designed to model, support, and develop students' metacognitive reading skills, particularly important for readers grappling with texts in languages other than those they speak at home and essential for students with less experience reading complex texts in any language. As described in Chapter 3, the task involves students working in dyads, with one student reading one sentence, paragraph, or short section of the text aloud, then choosing one of the categories on the Bookmark, and announcing to their partner their selected focus (e.g., "I am going to summarize my understanding so far" or "I am going to use my prior knowledge to help me understand" or "I am going to ask questions about ideas and phrases I don't understand"). That same student (the one who was reading aloud) then responds to the chosen topic, with or without the help of some formulaic expressions included on the Bookmark (e.g., "What I understand about this reading so far is . . ." or "I don't understand this section, but I do recognize . . ." or "I understand this part, but I have a question about . . .").

It is important to note that the *reader* is asking themselves these monitoring and clarifying questions, and choosing which questions to ask themselves, and then sharing this process aloud with their partner. The partner listens actively, offering supporting comments or asking clarifying questions about the first partner's comments. Then, the roles shift, and the second partner reads the next section aloud, using the Clarifying Bookmark to comment while the first partner becomes the active listener. And the process can be repeated for the next several sentences or sections, with the teacher leading a whole-class discussion periodically for students in the class to share their metacognitive process and for the teacher and other students to help clarify understandings of the content of the passage.

Inexperienced readers often do not view reading as the manifestation of a number of active practices that more experienced readers are actively, although often subconsciously, employing (Greenleaf et al., 2023). From the perspective of supporting and developing reading comprehension, the Clarifying Bookmark therefore is part of making the invisible visible (Greenleaf et al., 2023; Martin & Wineburg, 2008). The teacher can begin by modeling their own metacognitive process, using the Clarifying Bookmark with a section or two as an example, demonstrating metacognitive reading strategies that students can then use and notice when working with their partners. These "metacognitive conversations" help to demystify the reading process and allow students to become curious about their own reading practice as well as those of their teachers and classmates (Greenleaf et al, 2023. p. 93).

Read.Inquire.Write. Bookmark Tool. Meanwhile, the *Read.Inquire.Write.* team at the University of Michigan has created a metacognitive bookmark designed to enable students to read *historically*. The *Read.Inquire.Write.* Bookmark Tool: Reading and Analyzing Sources (Figure 8.2) more specifically includes metacognitive questions and methods for annotating text that enable students to enact the historical reading strategies of sourcing, contextualizing, and corroborating. It also includes questions that help students read sources to answer a central inquiry question. Importantly, this student tool and activity, like the Clarifying Bookmark, is intended to be used by students in multiple lessons and over time.

Jigsaws. Finally, Jigsaws of various sorts can scaffold multilingual learners' comprehension and historical reading skills. As described in Chapter 2, in a Jigsaw, the class is assigned into small "base" groups. Each member of the base group then leaves the group to join a new "expert group" assigned to tackle some assignment that is different from all of the other expert groups. The members of each expert group then return to their original base group and share what they have learned, while the other members take notes, usually with the assistance of a graphic organizer. There are a number of options for how Jigsaws can be designed to analyze historical documents. Expert groups could each be working with a different text (perhaps asking the same questions of each text), or they could be analyzing different parts of a single text, or each group could be asking different questions about the same text. In Ms. Jones's deportation lesson, expert groups will analyze

Figure 8.2. The *Read. Write. Inquire.* Bookmark Tool: Reading and Analyzing Sources

Bookmark

Part 1: the **Headnote** and **Attribution**

As you read:

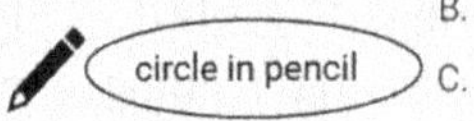

A. What do we know about **who** said, drew, or wrote this?

B. **When** and **where** was it said, drawn, or written?

C. **What type** of source is this?

D. **Why** was it said, drawn, or written? Or, **for whom** was it created?

After you read:

Discuss with your partner.

Make a note.

Which of these details matter and why?

Part 2: the **Source**

As you read:

Use **one** question;

Underline in pencil;

Make a note when you have strong reactions.

A. What people, institutions, ideas, and systems are **actors in the source**? What is the **relationship** between those people, institutions, ideas, and systems?

B. What parts of the source tell you what the author or people in the text **think, want,** or **experience**?

C. Find sentences that begin with transition words or introductory phrases. What key ideas come **after transition words or introductory phrases**?

D. What parts of the source seem **most important for understanding** it? Why?

After you read:

Discuss with your partner.

Make a note.

What do the underlined parts and your reactions help us understand about the source or central question?

(*continued*)

Figure 8.2. *(continued)*

Part 3: **Reasoning** about the Source

Discuss with your partner(s):

What questions does this source lead you to ask?	How reliable is this source for our Central Question? (***See Reasoning Questions below***)	How does this source help us think about our Central Question?

Write down your thoughts.

Box important evidence for responding to the Central Question

*Reasoning Questions

1. **What do we know about the author that shapes our thinking about the CQ ?**
   a. Was the author in a `position to know` about the issues? Who could have been in a better position to know?
   b. What was the author's `point of view`? What do they want or feel?
   c. What does the author want their `audience` to `think` or `feel`?
2. **Does the context of the source make it more/less useful for our CQ?**
   a. Was the source created in the `time/place` of the events?
   b. What was going on then/there, that might have `influenced` the author?
   c. Whose voices or perspectives are `not represented` in the source?
3. **How do we weigh this source in comparison with others?**
   a. How does this source `agree or disagree` with others?
   b. What can this source `tell us`? What `can't we learn` from it?
   c. Do you share any identities, experiences, or perspectives with the author?
4. **What connections between the source and you/your community do you see?**
   a. How is the time/place in the source `similar` to or `different` from yours?
   b. Based on your experience and what you know, is the source `believable`?
   c. What `social systems` or `issues of power` does this source help you think about?

Source: *Read.Inquire.Write.* materials are created by Chauncey Monte-Sano and the *Read.Inquire.Write.* team at the University of Michigan, 2024.

different parts of a single text, the *Washington Post* article that addresses the events of the 1930s: the impact of *Decade of Betrayal* on a California congressman, California's apology, and current politics. This article is split into multiple excerpts and each expert group answers questions about the time their excerpt is addressing, new facts or details in their excerpt, and any information or quotes that help shed light on the historical significance of the deportations. In this scenario, multilingual learners have the support of the other members of their expert group as they prepare to return and report to their base group, yet they also have an agentive role and an authentic need to communicate information that the base group needs. In turn, in their base groups, each student is individually responsible for taking notes on their graphic organizer on what the members of each expert group are sharing, but they also have the other members of the group to support them if they are having trouble comprehending what the reporting member is saying.

Extending Understanding

In the Extending Understanding Moment in history lessons, students deepen their understanding of an existing idea and/or connect it to other historical topics and events. Considering this Moment when initially planning her lesson helped remind Ms. Jones of the importance of having guiding concepts, themes, and/or essential questions that students use and study multiple times over the course of a specific history class. In her lesson on the deportations of Mexicans and Mexican Americans in the 1930s, Ms. Jones decided to return students to the idea of historical significance and criteria for establishing that significance for specific historical events, peoples, and places. Criteria for historical significance can include the changes (or continuities) that these events made or contributed to, the revelatory quality of the events such as illustrating important themes or embedding lessons for today, and more. Students revisited their ongoing list of criteria to see if changes need to be made given the case of the 1930s deportations. To conclude the lesson, Ms. Jones led a discussion that constituted a different kind of Extending Understanding Moment in this lesson, asking students to reflect on an additional essential question that Ms. Jones uses in her history class: *How do we address past historical wrongs?*

CONCLUSION

In this chapter, we have illustrated how teachers might go about selecting and preparing historical texts to center lessons around for multilingual learners (and all students). We have also shared a range of activities that can be particularly helpful for preparing learners for the texts, concepts, and arguments at the heart of history lessons; for inviting them to interact in recursive ways with multiple sources as they learn to read and think like historians; and for extending their understanding as they make connections with the themes of the lesson and other historical (and contemporary) topics and events. We hope that it is clear from the discussion above that the activities are not just randomly drawn from an activity bank, or chosen because they appear to be "fun" or "engaging." Rather, they are carefully chosen in ways that connect questions, topics, ideas, and arguments throughout the lesson—all of which have been refined through the process of selecting the texts themselves. Likewise, the lesson itself is part of a larger set of related historical concepts and analytical processes that are spiraled through larger units and even an entire course.

We concede that readers may think that all of the activities we have shown above as particularly useful for multilingual learners—part of an extended, multiday lesson on deportation in the 1930s—will take much more class time than they typically allot for a particular topic. This is an ongoing dilemma in history education more broadly: breadth vs. depth of the content covered. Teachers should know that they are not alone in feeling this tension—and that it is not about multilingual learners per se. We join many others in arguing that the goal of history education is for students to learn history and historical practices, rather than to atomistically "cover" every topic in the curriculum. This often means slowing down and *un*covering fewer things but in more detail, with *more* preparation, *more* interaction with texts, and *more* extensions of understanding—rather than reducing the depth of focus to superficially cover more topics. And this is where best practices in history education align precisely with the argument for quality education for multilingual learners advanced throughout this book: In both cases, it is about choosing amplification over simplification.

ACKNOWLEDGMENTS

We thank Erik Bernardino, assistant professor of history at Bates College, for his expert content review and suggestions. Any errors are of course our own.

REFERENCES

"Apology Act for the 1930s Mexican Repatriation Program," California Senate Bill 670 (2005). http://www.leginfo.ca.gov/pub/05-06/bill/sen/sb_0651-0700/sb_670_bill_20051007_chaptered.html

Bain, R. B. (2005). "They thought the world was flat?" Applying the principles of how people learn in teaching high school history. In J. Bransford and S. Donovan (Eds.), *How students learn: History, mathematics, and science in the classroom* (pp. 179–214). The National Academies Press.

Balderrama, F. E., & Rodríguez, R. (2006). *Decade of betrayal: Mexican repatriation in the 1930s* (rev. ed). University of New Mexico Press.

Bernard, D. (2018). The time a president deported 1 million Mexican Americans for supposedly stealing US jobs. *The Washington Post, 13*. https://www.washingtonpost.com/news/retropolis/wp/2018/08/13/the-time-a-president-deported-1-million-mexican-americans-for-stealing-u-s-jobs/

Bernhardt, E. B. (2011). *Understanding advanced second-language reading*. Routledge.

Bunch, G. C., Walqui, A., & Pearson, D. P. (2014). Complex text and new common standards in the United States: Pedagogical implications for English Learners. *TESOL Quarterly, 48*(3), 533–559. https://doi.org/10.1002/tesq.175

Digital Inquiry Group [DIG]. (n.d.). Retrieved July 31, 2024, from https://inquirygroup.org

Gándara, P. (2017). Deeper learning for English language learners. In R. Heller, R. E. Wolfe, & A. Steinberg (Eds.), *Rethinking readiness: Deeper learning for college, work, and life* (pp. 123–144). Harvard Education Press.

Greenleaf, C., Schoenbach, R., Friedrich, L., Murphy, L., & Hogan, N. (2023). *Reading for understanding: How reading apprenticeship improves disciplinary learning in secondary and college classrooms* (3rd ed.). Jossey-Bass and WestEd.

Goodman, A. (2020) *The deportation machine: America's long history of expelling immigrants*. Princeton University Press.

The Historical Thinking Project. (n.d.) *Historical thinking concepts*. https://historicalthinking.ca/historical-thinking-concepts

Lange, D. (Photographer). (1936). *Migrants, family of Mexicans, on road with tire trouble. Looking for work in the peas. California*. California, United States, 1936. Feb. [Photograph]. Retrieved from the Library of Congress, https://www.loc.gov/item/2017759829/

Lange, D. (Photographer). (1935). *Mexican mother in California. "Sometimes I tell my children that I would like to go to Mexico, but they tell me, 'We don't want to go, we belong here.'" (Note on Mexican labor situation in repatriation.)* [Photograph]. Library of Congress. https://loc.gov/pictures/resource/fsa.8b26837/

Lee, C. D., White, G., & Dong, D. (Eds.). (2021). *Educating for civic reasoning and discourse*. National Academy of Education.

Martin, D., & Wineburg, S. (2008). Seeing thinking on the web. *The History Teacher*, *41*(3), 305–319.

Martinez, E. G. (n.d.). *Mexican deportation in the 1930's by Emma Gomez Martinez*. Boulder County Latino History. https://teachbocolatinohistory.colorado.edu/primarysource/mexican-deportation-in-the-1930s-by-emma-gomez-martinez/

National Council for the Social Studies (NCSS). (2013). *The college, career, and civic life (C3) framework for social studies state standards: Guidance for enhancing the rigor of K–12 civics, economics, geography, and history*. https://www.socialstudies.org/system/files/2022/c3-framework-for-social-studies-rev0617.2.pdf

National Governors Association and Council of Chief State School Officers (2010). Appendix A: Research supporting key elements of the standards. https://achievethecore.org/page/1192/ccss-ela-literacy-appendix-a-research-supporting-key-elements-of-the-standards-glossary-of-key-terms

OER Project. (n.d.). *World history project.* https://www.oerproject.com/World-History?WT.mc_id=20201201000000_Tfc_WHP-SEM-S3Mg-l1k3&WT.tsrc=WHPSEM&gad_source=1&gclid=CjwKCAjwko21BhAPEiwAwfaQCBklc1R5IHglWFzO8Tcrp3qdyY1qNASVYKV6HdUyIM2-szQuKhKYOxoCZNYQAvD_BwE

Ortiz, P. (2018). *An African American and Latinx history of the United States.* Beacon Press.

RAND Reading Study Group. (2002). *Reading for understanding: Toward an R&D program in reading comprehension.* RAND.

Read.Inquire.Write. (n.d.). *Teaching social studies inquiry and argument writing with sources.* https://readinquirewrite.umich.edu

Sanchez, G. (1993). *Becoming Mexican American: Ethnicity, culture, and identity in Chicano Los Angeles, 1900–1945.* Oxford University Press.

Takaki, R. (1993). *A different mirror: A history of multicultural America.* Little Brown and Company.

Wineburg, S. (1991). Historical problem solving: A study of the cognitive processes used in the evaluation of documentary and pictorial evidence. *Journal of Educational Psychology, 83*(1), 73–87. https://doi.org/10.1037/0022-0663.83.1.73

Wineburg, S., Martin, D., & Monte-Sano, C. (2012). *Reading like a historian: Teaching literacy in middle and high school history classrooms.* Teachers College Press.

Yosso, T. (2005). Whose culture has capital? A critical race theory discussion of community cultural wealth. *Race Ethnicity, and Education*, *8*, 69–91.

CHAPTER 9

Amplifying Opportunities for Meaning-Making in Science for Multilingual Learners

Tanya Warren

Imagine a high school biology class as students are beginning to explore the structure and function of deoxyribonucleic acid (DNA) in cells. Students, many of them multilingual learners, are working in small groups to explore puzzles, make connections to readings and videos about DNA, and construct three-dimensional models with color and paper. They talk with one another as together they advance ideas and connections, including the structure of DNA, the base pairs and their complementary functions, and explorations of how microscopic processes that are not directly visible to human beings can have life-changing consequences. Later in the unit, students will further explore the processes that allow for DNA to copy itself and how it plays a central role in protein synthesis.

Such learning illustrates shifts in science education: toward a focus on cross-cutting concepts instead of facts; toward students actively participating in meaning-making rather than the teacher telling; and toward a focus on language that purposefully supports both conceptual development and meaningful participation in science discourse, rather than a focus on individual words or grammatical correctness.

This was a lesson with no lecture or note-taking activities taught from the front of the class. Instead, students first discussed the ideas and knowledge they brought to the lesson with them and shared their noticings and wonderings about a phenomenon. Next, students exchanged ideas and coconstructed understandings through multiple modes including images, texts, videos, and card sorts. To extend their understanding, students were then asked to sort a set of cards that connected images and text including analogies and examples. The teacher was there throughout the lesson to introduce the tasks, monitor and collect ideas from the group, and provide a connection among the tasks. However, it was students themselves who did the talking and sense-making.

This chapter explores these critical pedagogical shifts in teaching and learning, both in science education and in the education of multilingual students, as well as the teachers' role in creating learning opportunities to achieve these ambitious shifts. To illustrate the purposeful scaffolding in the design of a Lesson in Three Moments, I describe and analyze one specific lesson in a larger unit sequence that I designed and piloted with feedback from biology teachers in a district whose population includes over 40% of students identified as English Learners. I begin by discussing the pedagogical purpose of each moment. Then, I apply the ideas to a lesson showing a series of tasks that build on each other to achieve the purpose of the Moment and provide connections, cohesion, and deepening of the concept. Explaining several of the tasks in detail to highlight the structure of the task, I show how that structure supports students' interactions with each other and the concepts. The chapter concludes with a reflection on how the lesson supports multilingual students in achieving the current shifts in science learning.

SHIFTS IN TEACHING AND LEARNING

Shifts in Science Learning

With the introduction of A Framework for K–12 Science Education (National Research Council [NRC], 2012), science education for the 21st century has been reframed significantly. The Framework posits that science learning is not just learning about science but instead about making meaning. This shift means students must take an active role in learning as they develop scientific sense-making by grappling with science concepts while simultaneously engaging in scientific practices. Such student learning is consistent with a view of science as a discipline in which models are continually developed, refined, and revised in light of new observations, through a process of inquiry (NRC, 2012).

The Next Generation Science Standards (NGSS) emphasize the connections among three dimensions: (1) disciplinary core ideas; (2) science and engineering practices; and (3) cross-cutting concepts that unite ideas across life, physical, and earth sciences (NGSS Lead States, 2013). Students must be at the center of sense-making, so that students' learning process parallels the nature of science itself—as a process of ongoing inquiry—to the greatest extent possible.

This view of learning science challenges the traditional paradigm of the teacher as the holder of knowledge and instruction as the process in which the teacher explains the concepts and transfers that knowledge to the students. This type of instruction, where students are *learning about* science, does not allow students the opportunity to make meaning. In contrast, students who are taught in accordance with the NGSS principles are placed at the center of meaning-making and take an active role as they grapple with concepts, engage in scientific practices where they are not certain of the outcome, develop and compare different models, and formulate their own explanations, all while engaging in multimodal communication. In essence, they are apprenticed—through well-designed activities—into the scientific enterprise constructed to engage them with concepts, practices, and language use that makes it possible for them to hypothesize, generalize, describe, and explain their understandings.

Shifts in Language Learning

These shifts in science education are similar to the shifts happening in second language learning (Grapin et al., 2021). The science education shifts present rich opportunities for *all* students to engage in science, but these opportunities are especially important for English Learners who are learning science and developing greater proficiency in the English language.

All students deserve to engage in deep, meaningful learning or what is referred to in Chapter 2 as "quality learning," and that includes multilingual learners who have not yet "mastered" English. A central tenet of this quality learning is how learning should center on simultaneously developing conceptual, analytic, and language practices (Heritage et al., 2016). It is through interactions of students with each other, with teachers, with concepts, and with the culture that students develop the ideas and practices that build deep, generative understandings. Therefore, instruction should engage students in learning opportunities that occur between the students' current understandings and their future development designed and supported by the teacher for acquiring the conceptual, analytic, and language practices for science.

SCAFFOLDING MEANING-MAKING FOR MULTILINGUAL LEARNERS

These learning opportunities do not happen by chance. As noted in Chapter 2, they must be deliberately planned and contingently adjusted to respond to students and maximize their participation (see also Walqui & Schmida, 2021). The metaphor of scaffolding is meant to evoke temporary support that builds greater autonomy and agency in the student over time. Providing students with a step-by-step procedure to be followed mechanically would not be scaffolding in this sense, as it does not engage students in active meaning-making and appropriation of the ideas and practices.

It is important to consider the structure of tasks to ensure that all students are able to engage in the activity and that the structure supports sustained interactions where students can negotiate meaning together. To achieve this, tasks often have a routine structure so that they quickly become classroom rituals and students are able to focus more on engaging with the ideas and less on the procedure. The structure only exists to enable an interactive process through which students engage in making meaning with others and with the teacher, all in service of exploring ideas and engaging in practices. Once the practice is appropriated by students, it is no longer necessary, and new structures scaffold the continuing development of students (Walqui & van Lier, 2010, pp. 23–24).

DNA AS THE BASIS FOR A UNIT

The following example of a unit, with a close examination of one lesson, will illustrate how amplifying opportunities for meaning-making addresses the shifts in both science and language learning for multilingual learners. The unit incorporates a spiral design that creates multiple opportunities to engage in science concepts and develop scientific practices over the course of several lessons that are sequenced to deepen understandings while apprenticing students into the scientific enterprise over time.

Unit Design

Scientists in all disciplines closely examine the relationship between structure and function in their quest to create scientific explanations for different phenomena. One way scientists are able to examine this relationship is by constructing and examining models. The Unit presented here, *DNA: The Molecule of Heredity* (Figure 9.1), offers multiple opportunities for students to engage with a variety of models to explore the relationship between the functions of DNA and how those functions are related to the unique structure of DNA.

Unit Overview

The unit's first lesson, "Phenomenon: Genetic Disorder," begins by introducing students to a video titled "Why I Am Proud of My Albinism" from the BBC's *Living Differently* series (BBC Three, 2018). It presents the story of a young Black man who was born with albinism, a genetic disorder that

Figure 9.1. Unit Design for *DNA: The Molecule of Heredity*

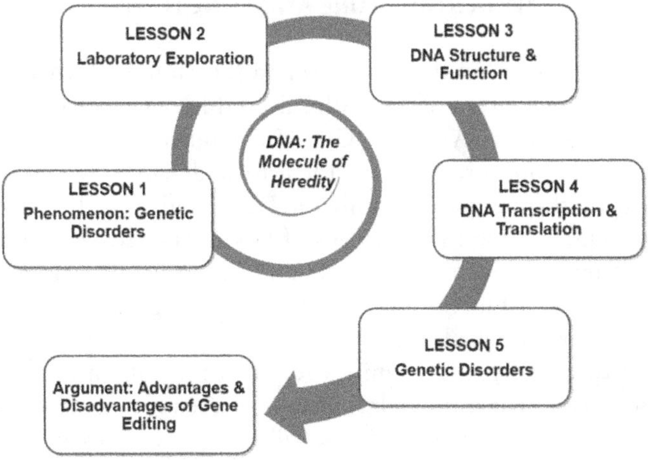

makes him look White. The story explores how living with the disorder has been challenging to his health, his identity, and his place in society. But it also shows how he has embraced this difference and is proud of his uniqueness. As students watch the video, they notice different things and discuss many questions the story raises for them. These ideas are shared with the class and used to connect to a central question about what makes each person unique and what causes disorders that may influence the health and well-being of an individual. These discussions prepare students for the lessons that follow, in which they will be discussing DNA and its role in heredity that makes each of us unique. They will also examine its role in understanding, treating, and possibly eliminating genetic disorders.

In Lesson 2, students participate in a demonstration lab to extract and observe the DNA of strawberries. Once students have a general concept of what DNA is and looks like, they engage in a lesson about how the structure of DNA facilitates the function of DNA. This third lesson, "DNA Structure and Function," which we describe in detail in the remainder of this chapter, is foundational for students to understand not only how DNA functions in designating the characteristics of living things and its role in inheritance, but also how the structure of the DNA molecule facilitates its replication. That process is further explored in Lesson 4, "Transcription and Translation." Lesson 5, "Genetic Disorders," concludes the unit with students researching genetic engineering and gene editing in a Jigsaw project that involves them in examining case studies of several different genetic disorders and developing arguments detailing the possible benefits and consequences of altering the DNA of living things.

FOCUS ON ONE LESSON: "DNA STRUCTURE AND FUNCTION"

While a typical lesson on the structure and function of DNA might focus solely on the composition of the molecule and how the nitrogenous bases always pair together as AT and GC, asking students to simply remember these facts limits opportunities for them to understand the elegance and importance of the unique structure of DNA and how the structure is important in facilitating the functions of DNA. The cross-cutting concept of Structure invites students to understand the complex relationships between structure and function and supports meaning-making across disciplines when they are asked to engage deeply with this concept. This lesson is designed to amplify opportunities for multilingual learners and other students to make sense of the relationship between the structure and functions of the DNA molecule. Students will interact with explanations in a variety of modes and engage with several different models, approximating how scientists use models to both deepen their understandings and communicate their ideas.

Within this lesson, students will not only explore the composition of DNA but also understand how the geometric design of the double-helix structure allows DNA to achieve its function in heredity. This lesson amplifies opportunities for students to engage in meaning-making through rich, multimodal experiences that are essential in understanding the complexity of DNA.

THE LESSON IN THREE MOMENTS

Following the architecture introduced in Chapter 3, the lesson is designed in Three Moments, with tasks that are sequenced to scaffold the apprenticing of multilingual students into the concepts, practices, and language of science. Each Moment achieves a specific purpose in this process. The purpose of the Preparing Moment is to access prior knowledge, to introduce a context or shared experience, and to focus attention on the concept to be explored without preteaching. In the Interacting With the Text or Concept Moment, students engage with different representations of the concept and make connections between and among the representations. In the Extending Understanding Moment, students make connections beyond the concept and relate the ideas to a broader context including other disciplines, social implications, and the scientific enterprise, or to their own experiences (Table 9.1).

Table 9.1. Three Moments of the Lesson: "DNA Structure and Function"

Moment of the Lesson	Task	Purpose	Prompt
Preparing Learners	Novel Ideas Only	Surface ideas about models.	*When I hear the word model, I think about . . .*
	Simulation & Viewing with a Focus	Build background through a shared experience and video: introduce analogies.	*How did you put the puzzle together? What clues did you use?* *How does this simulation connect to models?* *How is the discovery of DNA like the puzzle simulation?*
Interacting With the Concept	Describe & Connect	Describe, compare parts of a diagram, and connect pieces together to see the whole picture.	*My image shows . . .* *My image shows . . . It is similar or different from yours because . . .*
	Viewing With a Focus	View a video to introduce the structure of DNA and how DNA functions; also, to further engage with analogies used to model structure and function of DNA.	*How do the scientists describe and explain the structure of DNA?* *How do the scientists describe and explain the function of DNA?*
	Talk to the Text	Use an engineered text to deepen understanding of DNA through text, talk, pictures, and diagrams.	*What does the text say about the structure of DNA? What does the text say are the functions of DNA?* *How does the structure of DNA enable these functions?*

(*continued*)

Table 9.1. (*continued*)

Moment of the Lesson	Task	Purpose	Prompt
Extending Understanding	Create and Reflect On Models	Create a 3D model of a DNA molecule using understandings of DNA in a different mode; Analyze similarities and differences in models—what each shows and doesn't show.	*What important features of the structure of DNA are present in each model (3D model and diagram)? What features are not present in each model?*
	Collaborative Poster	Explain the structure and function of DNA using analogies, drawings, and explanations.	*Choose an analogy to explain the structure and function of DNA. Analyze what the analogy does and* does not *illustrate about the structure and function of DNA.*

Preparing Learners

In the Preparing Learners Moment of the lesson, the purpose is to activate prior knowledge, create a shared experience, and build background about the scientific enterprise. This part of the lesson includes an introduction to the scientific practice of using models as well as the nature of how science knowledge is produced. By examining different models and learning about the history of the DNA molecule, students have an opportunity to engage in discussions highlighting this enterprise.

The lesson opens by inviting students to look at the shape of their hands and consider how they help them grow and stay alive. Then posing the question, "How might your life be different if you had feet in place of your hands?," students take a few minutes to write their responses then share their ideas with a partner. This prompt invites students to consider the structure and function of their hands and how a different structure might influence different functioning in their everyday lives as well as how it might affect the structure and function of everyday items they use. It is meant to start students thinking about the relationship between how structure might affect the function and how functions might affect the structure.

Novel Ideas Only. Next, students engage in brainstorming ideas about models. Instead of the typical "frontloading" of vocabulary by which students are offered lists of isolated words corresponding to the theme of the lesson to be studied even before exploring the idea, students engage in an activity that builds on ideas and language that they already possess. In this task, students are invited to offer ideas about a word that focuses on a central idea of the lesson and may be familiar to them in many different contexts. They brainstorm ideas generated by the prompt "When I think about models, I think about. . . ." Asking students to choose their own ideas associated with the target word—*models*—allows them to access their prior knowledge about where they have encountered the idea before in their own lives. Ideas could include model cars, fashion models, role models, etc. This task creates a variety of shared ideas that are similar in concept and offer a familiar context on which to build a more technical understanding of the use of models in science. It offers multiple entry points for all students to contribute their ideas from their own lived experiences, validates their ideas, and increases their confidence at the very beginning of the lesson.

After generating a variety of examples, students are then asked to consider how their ideas or examples may be similar as they work together in small groups to negotiate meaning, coconstruct understandings, and reach a consensus about a possible definition for models. Their collective definitions are then compared to the way science uses models as a representation of a phenomenon that is difficult to observe directly. Students will engage with many different models including physical models, visual models, and even mental models as they explore the relationship between the structure of the DNA molecule and its function. This preparing activity clearly shows the dialogic and interactive nature of students' work, which is carried out along the whole lesson as students co-scaffold each others' growing understanding.

Simulation and Viewing With a Focus. Armed with a nascent understanding of models as representations of scientific phenomena, students then engage in a simulation where they explore the concept of structure and function more deeply by completing a puzzle together. First, students work independently to fit their own pieces of the puzzle together. Then, they collaborate with their peers to complete the puzzle. This simulation offers students a sensory context that introduces an analogy for both how scientific knowledge is constructed as well as how models are used to explain scientific concepts. This analogy also serves as a shared anchoring experience that provides a leitmotif that will be spiraled throughout the lesson.

To connect their experiences with the simulation to the more nuanced information they will encounter in a video to be viewed in the next task, students are asked to think about and discuss the processes they used to complete the puzzle and what clues they used to accomplish the work. Responses might include "the edges and corners provided an outline structure," "the colors provided clues," "using trial and error about how the pieces fit together," and "using my prior knowledge of what the picture represented." The class then discusses how the puzzle connects to the ideas of structure and function, and even models—the puzzle is a model of the original artwork.

The puzzle thus provides a context for viewing a video about the discovery of DNA that will begin to support students in applying the concept of models to scientific practices that describe the work of scientists to identify the structure of DNA and how that discovery involved the contributions of many scientists. The purpose for watching the video in this Moment of the lesson is not to gather and report information about the discovery of DNA by listing each scientist who contributed to the discovery of DNA and identifying their specific contribution. Instead, since this viewing occurs in the Preparing the Learner Moment of the lesson, the purpose here is to prompt students to connect the ideas of modeling they engaged in during the puzzle simulation with the discovery of the structure of DNA and the nature of the scientific enterprise. So, the focus question offered students for viewing the video draws attention to the processes of scientific discovery and how they are similar to the processes they used during the puzzle simulation.

After watching the video, students discuss their responses. This interaction allows students to share the information they understood and perhaps complete ideas that were captured by their partner. Students offer ideas such as "The discovery was made by many scientists" and "Watson and Crick used the ideas from many different scientists and put them together to create a model of the DNA molecule" and "They tried many different combinations of how the pieces fit together until they found the one way they could fit . . . like we did with the puzzle" and "We didn't see the whole picture until everyone put their pieces together, just like all of the knowledge from the other scientists had to be pieced together to see how DNA is structured." The class is then introduced to the idea that the puzzle simulation could act as a representation of the process of how scientists work together, or even for the structure of DNA. These representations are called analogies and are a different type of model used in science for explaining and communicating scientific ideas.

Students watch the video a second time; however, in this viewing they are invited to notice the analogies that are used to describe the structure or explain the function of DNA. Students share the analogies with the class and their ideas are listed on a class chart.

Interacting With the Concept

The Preparing Moment of the lesson has introduced the concept of structure and function as well as the use of models in science to examine relationships between the two, including analogies. These threads are more deeply explored and connected as students engage with more complex resources that combine multiple modes including images, text, videos, and diagrams. As students examine these resources, they are offered structured opportunities to engage with these resources and their peers in sustained interactions that support them in asking questions, connecting ideas, exploring relationships, and coconstructing understandings.

Now that students have thought about their own ideas of what models are and have begun to explore how scientists use models to explain their ideas, they are invited to interact more deeply and directly with the structure of DNA by examining a diagram of the DNA molecule. Diagrams are widely used in science to represent structures and processes and can range from simple representations of a few components to more complex processes with multiple steps. Students, especially multilingual learners, benefit from purposefully planned opportunities to explicitly engage in analyzing diagrams. This analysis, however, does not need to consist of explicit instruction, out of context, on how to read a diagram before students engage with the diagram. Designing a task that amplifies opportunities for students to make meaning will invite students to examine the pieces of a diagram and discuss what each piece represents as well as how these different pieces fit together. This offers students ways to notice both the features as well as the content of the diagram and discuss how each piece is connected to the whole.

In the next task, students notice the different components of DNA, the sequence and directionality of the components, and the overall structure of the molecule. The steps of this task are purposefully parallel to the puzzle simulation from the previous Moment as students decide how different parts are connected to create a complete picture of the diagram.

Describe and Connect. This is the students' first encounter with DNA itself within the lesson intended to examine the structure of DNA and for that reason, a representational diagram was chosen for this task (see Figure 9.2). This diagram shows the components of DNA and their positions within the structure as well as the overall structure of the DNA molecule. It also offers students multiple entry points for describing the components including common descriptive language such as colors, shapes, letters, quantities, and

Figure 9.2. Describe and Connect Cards

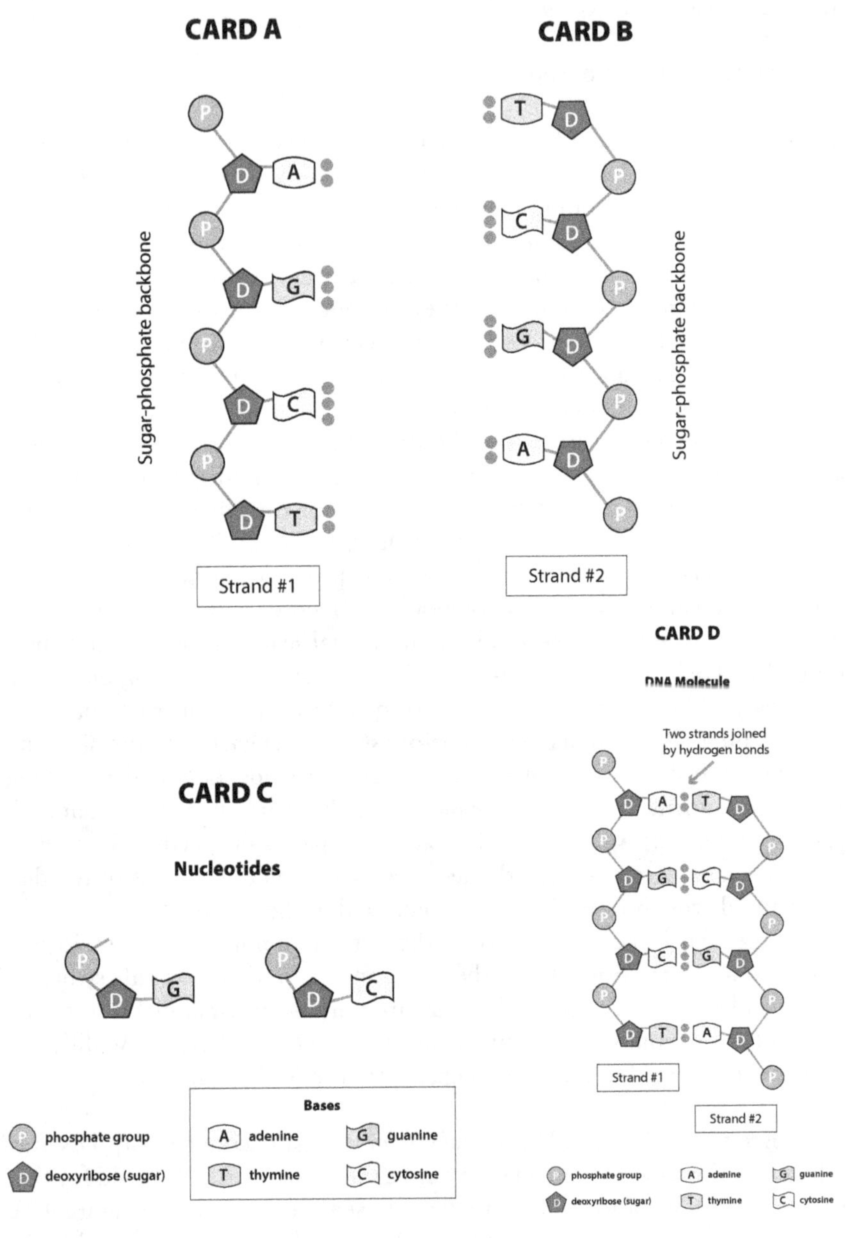

text as well as more complex descriptions that identify their position and directionality within the diagram. Each student in a group of four is given a different part of a diagram of DNA. They cannot see anyone else's cards. One student begins by describing the image on their card as the others listen and look at their cards to find similarities or differences. The next student then describes how their image may be similar or different and provides a description of their image. Since the images are similar, multilingual students are able to listen to others describe their cards and perhaps borrow some language from their peers to describe their own. After all of the cards have been described, students can ask questions and start discussing how the images might be connected. Once everyone agrees on an explanation of how they are connected, students place their cards on the table. Students then discuss the connections and confirm or revise their ideas. Once all diagram pieces are revealed, discussed, and revised, the task culminates with an opportunity to negotiate ideas, coconstruct meaning, and work together to reach a consensus on a caption that describes the diagram.

Viewing with a Focus. So far, students have engaged with multiple modalities including talk, gestures, images, video, text, and manual manipulation of materials as well as two types of models to introduce the components and structure of DNA. Students are now asked to continue engaging with multiple modes to examine how the structure of DNA supports the specific functions of DNA by watching a video. This video consists of narration from expert scientists on which images and text are superimposed. Students are asked to work in dyads, each with a different focus for viewing. One student will focus on how the scientists describe and explain the structure of the DNA molecule, while the other student focuses on information about the function of DNA or what DNA does. After watching the video, each student will share their findings and discuss their ideas to coconstruct understandings of the relationship between the structure and function of the DNA molecule.

Talk to the Text. The understandings that students have developed through interactions with the diagram, videos, and their peers have introduced the structure and function of DNA in a meaningful way. These surfacing understandings will provide context for students as they continue to engage with the concept of DNA by providing many experiences and resources for them to access and deploy as they engage more complex ideas in the reading of a text. The text students will read is a DNA Fact Sheet from the National Human Genome Research Institute that has been amplified by inserting focus questions for each section, adding images and diagrams with captions, and bolding important words to add emphasis. Working with a partner, students will first review the structure of the text (sections, questions, images, and captions), discuss and record what they know about the topic, and record questions they have. Students will then take turns reading paragraphs aloud and pausing at intervals to summarize their understandings and discuss their questions and the focus question for each section.

Extending Understanding

The Extending Understanding Moment designs opportunities for students to apply concepts in a different context, reflect on their learning, and present understandings in a different genre. Students create their own model of DNA, compare it with other models, analyze what it demonstrates and what it does not, and revise the model. The relationship between the structure and function of DNA is further extended by students' creations of collaborative posters, each with an image and text of an analogy explaining the structure and function of DNA. In a gallery walk, students are able to discuss and compare their own analogy poster with those of others. All of these tasks, in combination, amplify opportunities for multilingual students to apply their ideas in interactions with their peers and to demonstrate their understandings in various modalities.

In the first Extending Understanding task, students are prompted to use all the resources from the lesson, including diagrams, text, etc., to construct a three-dimensional model of a DNA molecule (Figure 9.3). Each dyad is given a partially completed plastic model of a DNA molecule, and students work together to complete it using what they have learned about the structure of DNA. Students discuss the sequence of the pieces of the model and reason out which pieces should be matched together to complete the sequence. Once again, the importance of the first Moment of the lesson is reflected in this task as students use the skills they appropriated during the puzzle activity to engage in a similar process with much more complex ideas.

Create and Reflect On Models. Students are then asked to focus on how different models supported their understanding of DNA's composition and structure by comparing the 3D model with the diagram. Students are asked to discuss what their model shows about the structure of DNA, as well as what their model does *not* show. They are invited to add to their model to better illustrate the structure of DNA using any ideas and information they have developed during the lesson. Options could include creating a key for their model or creating labels for the pieces of the model. Students then write a short description of their model. Finally, they are asked to reflect on how engaging with different models (including diagrams, three-dimensional

Figure 9.3. Model of a DNA Molecule for Students to Complete

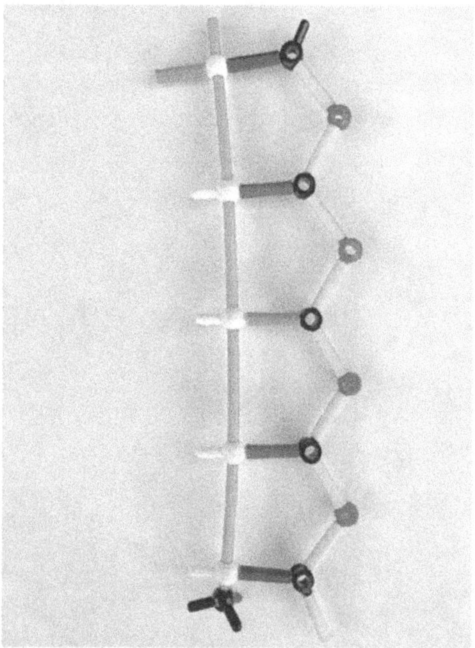

models, and analogies) advanced their understanding of the relationship between the structure of DNA and its function.

As they construct and analyze their three-dimensional models, students discuss and compare the models to each other and connect ideas to previous models they experienced in different modalities. In the end, they reflect on how all the models in all of the different modes supported their understanding of the structure and function of DNA. The purpose of this process goes beyond allowing students to access different modes that appeal to different learners. It is about engaging with and across these multiple modalities to develop deeper understandings. In so doing, students learn and create new meanings in a way that is more than just the sum of its parts. This mirrors the way people in the scientific community use models to represent concepts and communicate their ideas in a variety of modalities.

Collaborative Poster. While the model students create may be a good model for representing the structure of DNA, it may not show how the structure is related to the function. With this purpose in mind, students will need to create another model. So, in their table groups of four, students are invited

Figure 9.4. Collaborative Poster of DNA Analogies

to discuss ideas and reach a consensus about an analogy that they think best explains the function of DNA. It can be an analogy discussed in class or one of their own. Potential analogies might include a jigsaw puzzle with pieces, a blueprint with instructions, a recipe with ingredients and directions, or a library with books containing information. They then collaboratively create a poster that synthesizes all their agreed upon ideas and represents them with an image, an explanation of the analogy, and an analysis of what the analogy does and does not illustrate about the function of DNA.

Once all posters are completed, groups are invited to do a gallery walk of all the other posters. As groups view the posters of other groups, they discuss the image and the benefits and limitations of the analogy. Then, they discuss how the analogy is similar to or different from their own analogy. At the end of the gallery walk, students are asked to discuss in their groups of four how the different analogies showed different aspects of DNA and how all of the analogies together deepened their understanding of the structure and function of DNA.

LESSON REFLECTION: SHIFTS IN ACTION

The lesson design described above is structured and sequenced to explicitly demonstrate how scientific knowledge is constructed and developed. As multilingual students engage in multiple modalities, they are offered many structured opportunities to discuss and reflect on their understandings and develop the language needed to do so. The Preparing Moment of the lesson is an incredibly powerful entry point for students to recognize and value the experiences and resources they bring to lessons. In this lesson, the activity, Novel Ideas Only, is used to surface what students already know about models from their own lived experiences and show that these understandings, their prior knowledge, connects to the scientific understandings they are and will be developing. As students offer ideas and hear the ideas of others, they build rich connections with the concept of models that are important in comparing how the models they know are similar to and different from how scientists conceive, construct, and use models.

Building the field in the design of the Preparing Moment helps develop essential background knowledge connected to the concept and focuses students' attention so that as they interact with the concept, they are ready to engage in meaning-making around it. It is important to underscore that this is not a pre-teaching activity because, while preparing learners, it does not present the content of the lesson. Rather, it offers a rich context and foundation for anchoring and connecting concepts. A similar example of building the field is discussed in Chapter 6, the ELA chapter, where students build the field about the context of the Civil Rights movement before they read a poem by Langston Hughes. In this lesson about the structure and function of DNA, students engage in a puzzle simulation to provide an analogy for examining the context for the process of science discoveries and the structure of DNA. It also provides an entry point and establishes a common experience for exploring how scientists use analogical models by creating a coherent through line, or leitmotif, which is revisited and spiraled throughout the lesson.

In the Interacting With the Concept Moment, students engage with many different models representing the DNA molecule including three-dimensional models, diagrams, and various analogies (e.g., spiral staircase, code, blueprint, recipe, zipper, etc.). In addition, students read a text and watch several videos that incorporate many of these models in their descriptions and explanations. As students move from watching a video to examining and analyzing diagrams, they talk about and connect ideas. As they read the text aloud and discuss their ideas, they are engaging in written texts, images, and oral interactions to analyze, hypothesize, generalize, and make connections both within the text and to previous ideas and representations.

Through the juxtaposition and intertextuality of these different models and modalities, students are able to understand the structure and function of DNA more fully than if they were to examine only one.

In the Extending Understanding Moment, as students construct and analyze their three-dimensional models, they also discuss, compare, and connect to previous models they experienced in different modalities. In the end, they reflect on how all the models in the different modes supported their understanding of the structure and function of DNA. The purpose goes beyond students accessing different modes to appeal to different learners. It is about engaging with and across these multiple modalities to develop deeper understandings (Kress et al., 2001). In so doing, students learn and create new meanings in a way that is more than just the sum of its parts. This mirrors the way people in the scientific community use models and different modes for representing and communicating scientific ideas. This reflection is an important step in students gaining confidence and recognizing their developing agency as learners apprenticing into the scientific community. This process allows students to think metacognitively about the nature of science or how scientific knowledge is built and to recognize their capacity and potential for engaging in the scientific community.

CONCLUSION

By designing opportunities for students to engage in this scientific sensemaking, students are apprenticing into the scientific enterprise. In the lesson described in this chapter, I have demonstrated how multiple visitations to the same sources and practices serve to deepen students' understanding and motivate them by showing them that precisely what they are engaged in are the processes scientists practice. Multilingual learners need to see themselves with viable options for the future, they need to have science demystified for them, and they need to know that in the future they may be able to collaboratively solve enduring problems that society faces. That is what a pedagogy of promise offers (Walqui & van Lier, 2010).

REFERENCES

BBC Three. (2018, January 11). *Why I am proud of my albinism* [Video]. YouTube. https://youtu.be/dpHAXPv4T8Y?si=O-_VUMhkrZl77npb

Grapin, S. E., Llosa, L., Haas, A., & Lee, O. (2021). Rethinking instructional strategies with English learners in the content areas. *TESOL Journal, 12*(2), e557. https://doi.org/10.1002/tesj.557

Heritage, M., Walqui, A., & Linquanti, R. (2016). *English Learners and the New Standards: Developing Language, Content Knowledge, and Analytical Practices in the Classroom.* Harvard University Press.

Kress, G., Jewitt, C., Ogborn, J., & Tsatsarelis, C. (2001). *Multimodal teaching and learning: The rhetorics of the science classroom.* Continuum.

National Research Council. (2012). *A framework for K–12 science education: Practices, crosscutting concepts, and core ideas.* Committee on a Conceptual Framework for New K-12 Science Education Standards. Board on Science Education, Division of Behavioral and Social Sciences and Education. The National Academies Press.

Next Generation Science Standards Lead States. (2013). *Next generation science standards: For states, by states.* The National Academies Press.

Walqui, A. & Schmida, M. (2022). Reconceptualizing scaffolding for English learners: An ecological/sociocultural perspective. In L. de Oliveira & R. Westerlund (Eds.), *Scaffolding for multilingual learners in elementary and secondary schools.* Routledge.

Walqui, A., & van Lier, L. (2010). *Scaffolding the academic success of adolescent English Language Learners: A pedagogy of promise.* http://ci.nii.ac.jp/ncid/BB01743114

CHAPTER 10

What Makes Me Who I Am?

Designing Quality Learning Opportunities for Newcomer Multilingual Learners

Lee Hartman and Elsa Billings

This chapter, unlike most of the chapters in this book, focuses not on a single discipline, but rather on a specific group of learners: beginning-level English Learners, who are also often newcomers to the United States and to U.S. schools. This small, but important, subset of multilingual learners is comprised of immigrants who are enrolled for the first time in U.S. schools and who have attended classes taught in English for fewer than 3 years (Office of English Language Acquisition, 2023).

As discussed in Chapter 1, multiple terms are used for the complex array of students designated by their schools as multilingual learners. Different terms highlight not only students' language proficiency, but also their experience in education and in U.S. schools. The Office of English Language Acquisition at the U.S. Department of Education (2023) uses the term "Newcomers" to describe "any foreign-born students and their families who have recently arrived in the United States" (p. 8). More recently, the term "Recently Arrived Immigrant English Learners" (RAIELs) was coined to include students who have been in U.S. schools for up to 3 academic years and who, upon entry into U.S. schools, were classified as English Learners (Umansky et al., 2018). Other terms refer to ways these students' experiences differ, including the nature of their prior schooling. For example, many schools identify "Students with Interrupted Formal Education" (SIFE) or "Students with Limited or Interrupted Formal Education" (SLIFE). Of course, these acronyms and labels are dangerous in that they treat each group of students as monolithic and classify them by specific characteristics that only change based on their educational experience and level of language development, not taking into account the entirety of their identities. However, for the purposes of this chapter, we use Newcomers, Newcomer students, and beginning English Learners interchangeably to refer to this group of students. While it is important to understand the specific experiences and backgrounds of students that these terms attempt to capture, it is also critical that we recognize and build on students' significant potential—something all multilingual learners bring with them—in order to provide them with the optimal opportunities to achieve academically, participate civically, and engage in productive careers.

Newcomers are often enrolled in courses designed to specifically address their English language development, and the majority of the time they are placed in classes based on state standardized assessments that measure English language proficiency only. Teachers of beginning-level English as a Second Language (ESL) courses, also called English Language Development (ELD), English as a New Language (ENL), or English for Speakers of Other Languages (ESOL), experience a unique set of instructional challenges. They are faced with the task of supporting the rapid English language development, enhancement of analytic thinking, and high-challenge subject-matter learning of diverse groups of students who enter their classrooms with a range of English language exposure and educational histories. As noted in Chapter 1, all multilingual learners, including those who are just beginning the process of learning English, bring with them often unrecognized language abilities, life experiences, problem-solving skills, and knowledge of the world. Therefore, providing beginning English Learners with quality learning experiences that build on their strengths to realize their extraordinary potential, while being significantly challenging for teachers, can also be profoundly rewarding.

DESIGNING A LESSON IN THREE MOMENTS

In this chapter, we describe a lesson designed for the first weeks Newcomers spend in school, demonstrating how Newcomer classrooms can function as spaces where multilingual learners develop conceptual and analytic practices related to English Language Arts while simultaneously developing language. The lesson is envisioned to be appropriate for high school students, but the approach is relevant for instruction at other grade levels as well, ranging from early elementary to 12th grade. As discussed above, the lesson stands in stark contrast to current practices in Newcomer pedagogy and provides an alternative conceptualization of what is possible and what students are capable of doing and learning, even at the early stages of English language development.

The Context

This lesson is part of a larger unit based on the theme of identity that was created by a team of three teachers, one of whom was the first author of this chapter, in a high school that served only Newcomer students, most of whom had been in the United States less than a year. Students ranged in age from 14–20 years, and they brought a considerable variety of years of prior schooling (from a few years to 11 years). However, they were all officially designated as 9th graders, since they arrived in the United States with no official prior credits from their home countries. As in other ESL classrooms, the students brought with them diverse backgrounds in language proficiency and content knowledge. Some had nearly finished high school in their home countries, while others had experienced severe interruptions in their education and were unable to read or write in their first languages.

All the students were in the same classroom and were receiving state credit for English Language Arts I, although the teachers were allowed to create their own curriculum if it matched the standards of the mainstream curriculum. The curriculum objectives thus matched the standards required of their native English-speaking peers, although the level of support given was much higher. In this way, the school, which supported students for only their first year of school in the United States, was able to best prepare them for subsequent years in their neighborhood high schools. There was no time to waste on countless vocabulary drills and fill-in-the-blank grammar worksheets to prepare them for entering a "sheltered" class the following year. Rather, this was a high-challenge Beginning ESL/ELA course with the goal of apprenticing students into becoming accomplished readers and writers who could do well in mainstream classes by the end of the year.

Teachers introduced this unit during the first 6-week grading cycle of the first semester of students' first year of school in the United States, after students had been in classes for 3 weeks. The students were representative of many ESL classes around the nation, which are comprised of students from different countries and linguistic backgrounds, each with varying levels of education in their home countries and family languages. Those first 3 weeks had oriented students to the classroom, the school, schedules, and the discourse protocols and patterns needed for successful participation in U.S. schools. During this introductory period, students had engaged in a series of structured tasks that invited them to begin to use English in sustained interactions with one another from day one. These structures and lessons facilitated the construction of new knowledge, quality interactions, and language development while introducing students to the workings of the educational system. These interactive activities and routine structures would prove invaluable as students then progressed into deep disciplinary practices in English Language Arts.

Once students had begun to grasp how schools operate in the United States, teachers introduced compelling concepts and the analytic practices and related language needed to engage with such content. Since the teachers at this school wanted students, even at this budding level of language learning, to be challenged and to engage authentically with rigorous texts, the same unit theme (Identity) and text from the mainstream English Language Arts curriculum were used, rejecting the simplified text that had been designated as the district's adopted textbook for ESL classes. Lessons were constructed around this more rigorous text, concentrating on linking the text's themes to students' own identities: who they are, including who they are in the context of their respective families and communities.

Rather than creating activities in which students simply talk superficially and in disconnected statements about themselves, their families, and their communities, teachers invited students to use vignettes from Sandra Cisneros's *The House on Mango Street* (1984) as a base for reflecting on their own identities and how these were shaping their own lives. The aims of the discourse went beyond students' producing statements such as "My name is . . ." and "I like to. . . ." The goal in this first unit was to have students express complex ideas and begin to apprentice into becoming accomplished readers and authors in English, acquiring and using new language along the way. Identity was used as a meaningful connector to the exploration of their identities and how they were being transformed in a new setting.

The Unit

While the focus of this chapter is on one lesson, the unit as a whole consists of three lessons, each presenting selections from the main text and revisiting varied aspects of identity. Each lesson was designed to take roughly 2 weeks—10 class periods of about 1 hour each. Figure 10.1 shows how the three lessons spiral around the central theme. The lessons generate from text selections and build upon one another, starting with the concrete and most personal theme of students' views of themselves and moving toward more abstract themes of how students identify as part of a family and of a wider community.

The English Language Arts practices are introduced and engaged in spirally to enable students to appropriate them over time. For example, in each lesson students first engaged in tasks that tapped their prior knowledge and experience and built new fields of understanding and language about the main themes and literary devices, which are always interconnected. Second, students read and discussed the text as needed to invite them to interpret its meaning. Finally, students extended their understanding by applying those ideas and literary structures in their own writing. By the end of the unit, students produced and edited three pieces of original writing in English for assembly in a small book that became part of their classroom library.

Table 10.1. English Language Arts Standards for 9th–10th Grades Addressed in Identity Lesson

- Cite strong and thorough textual evidence to support analysis of what the text says explicitly as well as inferences drawn from the text.
- Analyze how complex characters develop over the course of a text, interact with other characters, and advance the plot or develop the theme.
- Determine the meaning of words and phrases as they are used in the text, including figurative and connotative meanings; analyze the cumulative impact of specific word choices on meaning and tone.

Source: Common Core State Standards Initiative, 2010, p. 38

The teachers developing this unit did not, of course, place a grade-level text in front of Newcomers and expect that they would be able to read and understand every word completely. To engage their students in language, conceptual, and analytic practices in deep and accelerated ways, they knew it was necessary to identify key themes that would be gradually built upon so as to construct high-challenge lessons coupled with high support, building the scaffolding students needed to access the meaning and language of the text. Table 10.1 shows the main Common Core Standards addressed in the lesson.

Text Choice

As explained in Chapters 2 and 3, to reach our objectives and invite students to engage with this deep and thought-provoking theme, we needed a robust text. The ESL textbook was not much help, so the teacher team decided to go outside the classroom textbook and use parts of the text being taught in mainstream English I classes. For this lesson, the vignette "Hairs" by Sandra Cisneros from the book *The House on Mango Street* (1984) was chosen.

We included this text in the lesson not only because it made it possible to reach the objectives set as a destination for the lesson (understanding key ideas and character descriptions), but also because it constituted an example of the kinds of complex texts with which beginning English Learners can interact when supported through careful and strategic lesson design. Furthermore, this text was chosen because it was required reading for mainstream English classes in the district. Trusting the immense potential of these learners, we offered them the original version as opposed to a simplified or "ESL-friendly" text. We amplified the text by elaborating on it (e.g., chunking the text and adding guiding headlines), thereby giving beginning-level English Learners access to literature that might otherwise be beyond their reach—because of its style and use of figurative language.

Figure 10.1. Three Lessons in a Spiraling Unit

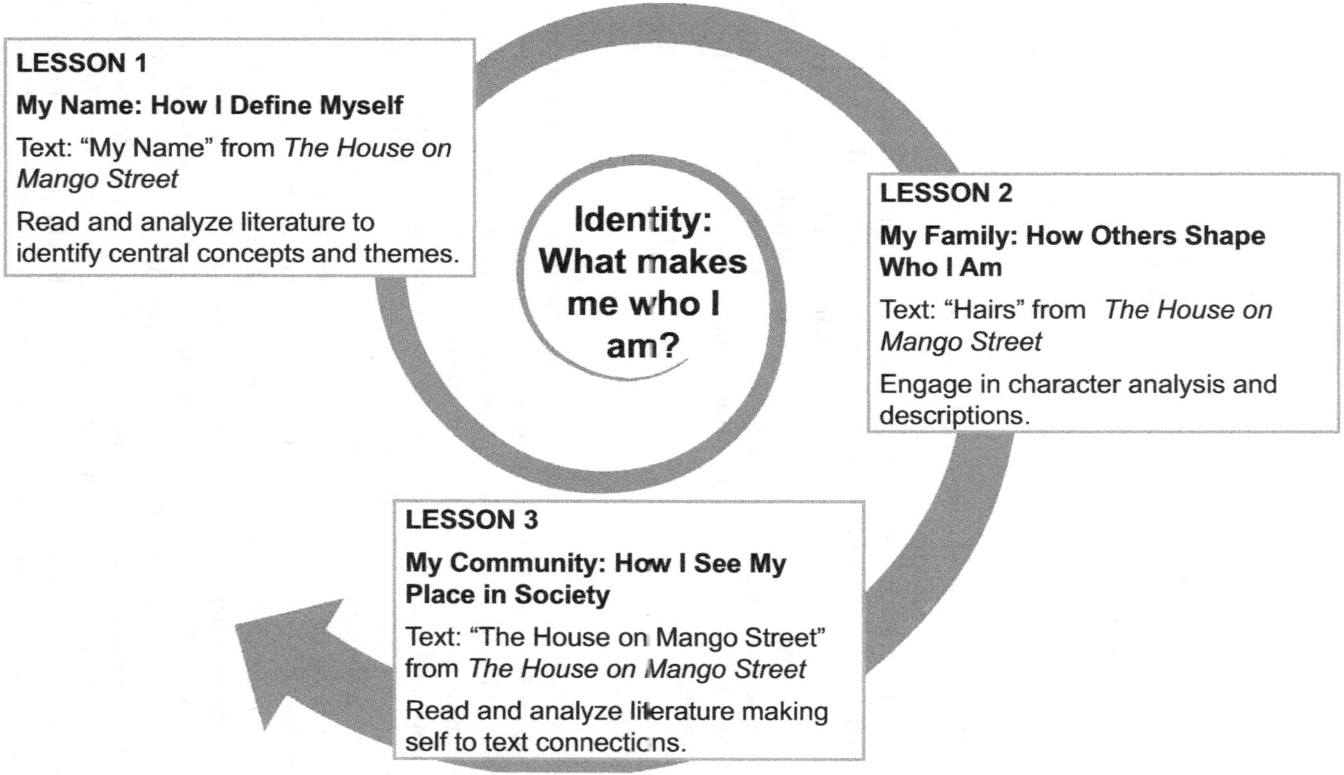

At the same time, we structured tasks in a way that invited students to coconstruct new knowledge through peer interactions, thus equipping them with strategies to access other comparable texts in the future. While the lesson may appear different from what beginning-level English Learners' peers in mainstream English Language Arts classes might encounter, the learning goals for students were the same.

Often the tendency is to find a text that is "at the right level" for students to complete these objectives (Bunch et al., 2014). It is not unheard of for beginning-level adolescent English Learners to be offered books designed for students in the primary grades. Because we, the unit designers, wanted students to be successful in attaining learning objectives, offering them simplified texts would not have conveyed belief in their intellectual ability, nor would it have inspired in them the motivation to grapple with more difficult texts. Our approach turns the notion of simplification on its head and offers students *amplified texts*—those that keep the author's authentic expressions, ideas, and themes intact while providing enhancements helpful for multilingual learners to understand contexts and ideas. Designers divided the text into meaningful segments and added subheadings to each part to focus students' attention on the purposes accomplished by the text segment. As a result, the text may *look* different from what students in other classes encounter. The structure and wording of this portion of the text is the original, but the presentation has been engineered with subtitles to support students' accessing the meaning.

The focus of amplified learning opportunities is on the big ideas, and we do not require that students understand every word in the text. Since we are apprenticing them into the practices that skilled readers use when they encounter complex texts, we want them to be comfortable with not understanding each word and to trust that they will acquire the language as they move from what may be ambiguous now to what is increasingly clear over time.

Designing the Lesson

Designing lessons for Newcomers using the ambitious, sociocultural approach described in this book is not a linear process. Traditionally, teachers have offered their Newcomer students lessons that focus primarily on language and then go in "logical order" with the goal of language acquisition in the form of vocabulary words or grammatical structures. To accomplish the learning objectives of the lesson, we challenge the sequential assumption of this process and instead design quality learning opportunities for Newcomers that focus on key ideas and disciplinary practices using language as the tool for accomplishing the goals (describing, persuading, informing, etc.). This approach is based on the understanding that all learning and development (including language development) happens in spiraling ways. It stands to reason that lesson design is not always a linear process either, as teachers think about where students in particular contexts will need more support or less, in what order students will be introduced to key ideas, and how they will interact with those ideas.

Lesson Goals and Objectives

In designing the lesson described here, we began not with the first task but with the objectives we wanted students to achieve. In short, students would learn how to reflect on who they are as people (identity) and some of the most important people in their world—their families. To do this, they would need to understand and be able to apply key disciplinary practices of Language Arts—in this case, the use of literary devices such as comparison through metaphor or simile and the practice of providing rich descriptions of people that help others understand who they are and what they mean to us. These deep themes and practices are at the heart of the lesson. Of course, as students engage with these complex and rigorous ideas, they need support both in content and language.

Once we identified the objectives of our lesson, we had to make sure that the text we chose was rich enough to allow for such exploration of the themes. In many ELD/ESL classes, the texts used are simplified to the point that they do not allow for quality opportunities to learn. Since they have been stripped of all "complex language" and nonliteral meaning, they do not lend themselves to deep analysis and individual interpretation. So, in our exemplar lesson, we chose the text "Hairs" by Sandra Cisneros both because it is a beautifully written, profound text and because it was what the students in mainstream classes were reading as well. Of course, as lesson designers and the teachers who would implement the lesson, we knew that the text would be challenging for our students and one that would not be accessible to them on their own. However, we were confident in the knowledge that if we supported the students through carefully designed and enacted tasks, they would be able to distill the ideas and themes from the text and engage with them in authentic ways, albeit with imperfect English; and they did just that.

Of course, our lesson in the Newcomer classroom would look very different from what native speaking students would see. The levels of support needed for our students to access such a text in their first semester of English instruction had to be maximized. Newcomer students are no less capable of abstract thought or literary analysis than their native-speaking counterparts, but many times they are not supported in engaging with texts like this one for fear that they will not understand everything. It is therefore even more important that Newcomer teachers understand what the major themes and goals of the lesson are so that they are able to recognize when students have achieved them—even when these themes and goals are obtained using English that is still quite imperfect and borrowed heavily from the teacher.

Just as we would in classes with more linguistically advanced students, we began planning the lesson thinking about where we wanted the students to end up. Using the Three Moment Architecture of lessons, we drew two lines on a piece of paper to divide it into three parts—each representing one of the Moments. At this point, we knew what the goals of the lesson were, and what the text would be in the second Moment (Interacting With Text), so we next considered how students would show that they had reached the ambitious goals we set for them. Since the final Moment of the lesson is the time when students apply what they have learned through reading text and creating something new, we decided to have students use the text as a model to create an original piece of writing in which they express who their family members are and what they mean to them, while going more in depth into one special family member. This way of using the main text of the lesson as a model for writing not only supports students' development of their own writing practices but reinforces that the purpose of language is the communication of ideas—not speaking or writing "correctly." All parts of language work together and reinforce one another for us to communicate (or understand) things that are important in the real world rather than just memorizing random words or phrases to use at some unknown time in the future.

LESSON ARCHITECTURE

Preparing Students to Interact With a Rigorous Text

With the overarching purpose and goals of our lesson in place, we began to construct the tasks students would engage in that would lead them step by step to the goals. As stated in Chapter 3, students need to be prepared for the themes, ideas, and concepts they will encounter in the text of a lesson—especially a text as ambitious as the one we chose. This need for preparation is especially true for Newcomer students. Therefore, in the first Moment of the lesson, Preparing Learners, the design team deliberately crafted nine tasks to accomplish this purpose. While this may seem like a large number, an increased number of tasks is often necessary in lessons designed for students who are new to English. However, it is important to note that when working with Newcomer students, often one task will need to be divided into two or three. In learning anything new and unfamiliar, such as tying your shoes or making your bed, when we first encounter something unknown, we need to break down what we do into manageable tasks. To do this, the lesson designer must always keep in mind what the purpose of each task is and give students just enough support to fulfill that purpose. With more linguistically advanced students, that might mean that just two or three tasks in the Preparing Learners Moment would be sufficient, while with Newcomers there can be many more, as seen in our example.

The Choice of Tasks Based on Purpose. Take, for example, the first six tasks in our lesson. Together, they serve the purpose of having students think about themselves and other people and how they can describe their physical attributes as well as their character and personality. Of course, this understanding of identity is vital in preparing them for the rest of the lesson as this is exactly what they will be expected to identify in their reading and create in their writing. This series of tasks fulfills that goal, and each task in and of itself has a purpose that serves to support students in moving one step closer to the overarching purpose of the Moment.

The tasks ask students to draw themselves (Task 1: Self-Sketch), share their drawings with a peer (Task 2: Dyad Pair-Share), add information to their drawings about personality traits (Task 3: Self-Portrait), ask their peers about how they have represented themselves (Task 4: Interview a Peer), draw their peers based on their interviews (Task 5: Peer Portraits), and present their descriptions of their peers to others (Task 6: Peer Portraits Presentations). As a whole, these tasks build upon each other to fulfill the purpose of the Preparing Learners Moment of the lesson: focus students' attention on key concepts, introduce the themes of the lesson, and introduce vocabulary in context. If the teacher were to ask students, "Describe yourself and then describe one of the friends in the class," students would, of course, struggle to do so in English, and their descriptions might be more cursory and not include details like personality traits or ideas about who their classmates really are. However, by breaking down the activity into smaller tasks that build upon one another, students are able to see how we describe people on many levels while simultaneously using the developing language practices of asking questions, receiving information, agreeing, and the like. They are not in our classes to spend countless hours coloring and drawing but rather to work with meaningful and important ideas. Of course, with more linguistically advanced students, perhaps all of these goals could be accomplished in two or three tasks, but that is exactly the work of the Newcomer teacher—recognizing that our students are just as capable as others in the important

Table 10.2. Lesson Architecture

Lesson Title: My Family: How Others Shape Who I Am	
Analyzing Important Characters in a Text and in My Life	
Moment One: Preparing Learners	
Task	**Description**
Task 1: Self-Sketch	Students sketch themselves, labeling body parts, facial features, and associated colors.
Task 2: Dyad Pair-Share	Dyads share their sketches of themselves.
Task 3: Self-Portrait	Students focus on thoughts and personality traits as they include more information in a self-portrait.
Task 4: Interview a Peer	Students interview one another to find out how each one has described himself/herself.
Task 5: Quick-Write	Students write a quick description of a special family member.
Task 6: Dyad Pair-Share	Students share and listen to their peers' ideas.
Moment Two: Interacting With Text	
Task 7: Read Aloud With a Focus	The teacher models how she reads and finds the gist of a text.
Task 8: Reading Aloud in Four Voices	Students are assigned parts or chunks of the text to read out loud.
Task 9: Character Description Matrix	Using the text as a model, students describe one of the characters.
Moment Three: Extending Understanding	
Task 10: Character Portraits	Students make a character portrait of their own that is similar to the character from the text.
Task 11: Family Member Description Matrix	Students use a similar matrix to that used in the Interacting Moment to describe their own family members
Task 12: Writing	Students use their portraits and matrices to construct a two-paragraph description of their own families, similar to the text they have just read.

work of deep thinking and analysis, while also recognizing that they need higher levels of support that must be designed in logical, thoughtful ways.

The goal of designing lessons in this way is that students engage in a characteristic of scaffolding referred to as "flow" as they move through the lesson (Walqui & van Lier, 2010). When teachers provide students with just the right level of scaffolding they need while simultaneously challenging them, students experience the lesson as a series of activities that are logical and make sense. They do not notice an abrupt change from one task to another. The transitions make sense to them in such a way that they become absorbed in the work. Of course, if Newcomer students are not adequately supported, they cannot achieve flow and therefore become frustrated with work and shut down. Conversely, if students are provided with unnecessary support as they advance, they can feel held back by the activities and become bored. As students develop, the Newcomer teacher must constantly reflect on the level of scaffolding she offers her students and make adjustments based on what students need.

Simultaneously Supporting Students' Social and Emotional Development. What we have described so far is an example of how students can be supported to interact with each other to build understanding of a theme or concept with the goal of apprenticing disciplinary practices. However, we know that many other things are happening in their interactions that go far beyond fostering students' understanding of ELA or ELD standards. As they learn, students are simultaneously developing social and emotional skills that will serve them their entire lives. For example, in a task as apparently simple as the dyad interview, students learn that their classmates have lived very interesting lives, have been influenced by incredible people, and have stories that are worth hearing. Conversely, they also learn that their own stories are worthy of being heard and others can learn from them. They learn to listen to what others say, evaluate its validity, and question, add to, or even disagree with what they hear. As with any other exchange of ideas among two or more different people, students are also sharing their cultures and learning about the cultures of others, even those who come from very similar backgrounds. With this approach to pedagogy, the "curricularization" (Valdés, 2018) of social–emotional learning or cultural competencies is not necessary. Rather, such things are a part of who we are and are therefore unable to be extracted from what we do and say. Furthermore, by creating opportunities for students to make connections between relevant themes and their own experiences, we are engaging in a more authentic form of social–emotional learning. Teaching and creating opportunities for deep learning is complex and sophisticated work, and teachers of Newcomers especially have the obligation and privilege to support students as they develop all of these practices simultaneously while focusing on the pedagogical objectives that will help them to become academically successful.

Supporting Students' Interactions With Rigorous Text

Once students have engaged with the ideas in these tasks of the first Moment of the lesson, they are prepared to encounter them in the text. As mentioned earlier, this text, while not lengthy, is quite rigorous in that it allows us to explore key concepts, such as identity and how our families influence who we are, while engaging in practices that are central to language arts as a discipline: description, comparison, and the use of literary elements. To fully access such deep ideas in a new language, once again we must maximize levels of support for our Newcomer students.

Take for example, the third task in this Interacting With Text Moment of the lesson—Task 9: Character Description Matrix (see Table 10.2: Lesson Architecture). The purpose of this task is to have students identify how the author uses description and comparison to help the reader imagine not only what each character may look like but also to gain insight into what their personalities are like. Students analyze how the author uses simile and metaphor (although they do not yet name these literary devices) to paint a picture both of what the character looks like and who they are. With the added support of the Character Description Matrix (Table 10.3), students are guided to look closely only for this key information. That means that they do not need to understand all the words on the page. In fact, they are not expected to. For example, the author says, "Papa's hair is like a broom." To engage with the text, students need only to understand the words "papa" and "broom." Of course, since quality interactions and coconstruction of knowledge make up the essence of our approach to lesson design, students support one another as they go through the task. The teachers structured the activity in such a way that students need to engage with one another, clarify for those who may need more help, add information when necessary, and ultimately come to a consensus about what the author has done with comparisons. Students are provided with formulaic expressions—model phrases that can be used across many situations to help students start to express or connect ideas and that support their having rich interactions in English (Walqui & Heritage, 2018). (See Table 10.4 for examples.)

Of course, students may not know the word "broom" at this point. A quick search on their phones can give them the word, or the teacher can supply a picture of a broom—just enough support needed to engage in the

Table 10.3. Character Description Matrix

Family Member's Hair	Comparison/Description	Picture
Papa's hair		
Esperanza's (me) hair		
Carlos's hair		
Nenny's hair		
Kiki's hair		
Mother's hair		

Table 10.4. Formulaic Expressions

Student 1: I think the author compares Papa's hair to ________ because . . .
Student 2: I agree with you and can add that . . .
or
I disagree with you because . . .

activity. Again, students do not need to understand every word, so spending time translating everything is unnecessary. Also, as the word "broom" is only used here as an example of a simile, there is no need for a 20-minute lesson on what a broom is, what its translation is, how students might use it in a sentence, and so on. By showing students that they can make sense of text without understanding every word, we apprentice them into the generative practices of language development that will serve them their entire lives. We show them that if they can figure out enough of the main ideas in a text and tolerate the ambiguity of not understanding everything, they can make educated guesses based on what they understand. Over time, their guesses will become more accurate.

Just as in the Preparing Learners Moment of the lesson, the flow of tasks during the Interacting with Text Moment is crucial to students' engagement and understanding of key concepts. This task (Task 9: Character Description Matrix) was preceded in this second Moment of the lesson by two other tasks, which, in turn, followed eight additional tasks in the initial Moment of the lesson. When students are first introduced to the text, they are not asked to analyze the author's craft by pointing out simile. Initially, they engage in a task called Reading Aloud With a Focus in which they listen to the teacher read aloud as they work together to try to understand the overall message of the text as a whole, once again reinforcing the notion that key ideas are the most important part of a text, not understanding every word. Next, they engage in a task called Reading Aloud in Four Voices, in which the text is strategically and deliberately "chunked" by the teacher so that as students read it (and hear it) aloud they hear how the author organized her thoughts (for a more thorough explanation of this task see Chapter 6). Only after engaging in these two tasks are students asked to take a deeper dive into the strategies used by the author to communicate her message. Because they have been supported step-by-step up to this point in understanding the main "gist" of the vignette and its organization, they are able to engage with one another in analyzing it deeply. This final task of Moment Two is also a step in preparing students for the final Moment of the lesson, in which they will use their analyses of the text to create their own.

It is also important to note the importance of dynamic assessment (introduced in Chapter 2), which occurs from Moment to Moment as students engage in the tasks. The teacher must be deliberate in monitoring what students are doing and saying so that she can evaluate what is beginning to become clearer for students, what they have already apprenticed, and where they are struggling. Many teachers of Newcomers struggle with the desire to ensure that all students master content before they move from one task to another. Of course, with the urgency for students to learn in deep and accelerated ways, especially at the secondary level, there is no time to spend hours and hours on one task. The teacher then must not only understand the core purpose of each task and how it moves students forward, but she must also pay close attention to what students do so that she can know when they have constructed just enough new knowledge to move on to the next task. Continuous dynamic assessment is the mechanism to do just that. Also, when lessons are designed in spiraling ways, students return many times to ideas and practices they will need throughout the lesson and units, making it unnecessary for them to understand everything the first time around.

Extending Students' Understanding of the Concepts

In the culminating Moment of the lesson, students will be asked to take everything they have been discussing, writing down and questioning as they support one another to understand and use it to create something new. As the name of the Moment, Extending Understanding, suggests, students will now use what they encounter in the text to show that they have begun to appropriate the practices identified in the goals and objectives of our lesson.

The lesson was designed by first thinking about this Moment and how students would be supported in getting there. As mentioned earlier, the culminating task for this lesson is a writing activity in which students describe their family members, applying all the skills and language they have been using along the way. However, because expressing ourselves in writing can be a complex task for anyone—even in one's first language—students are offered two more tasks to help them organize their original thoughts before they put pen to paper. In the first, students revisit the character of the mother in paragraph two and are asked to work together to include a picture, a symbol, an original phrase, and a quote that represents her. By engaging in this deep character analysis, students are supported in seeing how comparisons and description can tell a reader much more than what is explained explicitly in a text. In the following task, students are given a matrix very similar to the one they completed about the characters in the text in the previous Moment of the lesson. This time, however, they are asked to describe and make comparisons about people in their own families.

Now, when students arrive at the final writing activity of the lesson, they have rich ideas, experiences, and language to look back on and help them make an original composition about something very deep and important to them. However, because it is the first time they may be writing in such a formalized way, we offer them a structure to support them with the organization of ideas and linguistic structure of paragraphs.

CONCLUSION

This lesson is driven by the high expectations needed in ESL classrooms today to prepare Newcomer multilingual students for the demands of the 21st century. These high expectations of students are demonstrated by planned and dynamic, contingent support—not simply a series of exercises to build a lexicon of "survival" English vocabulary that will be added to other words until students are "ready" for a "real" English class. The lesson illustrates how teachers can invite Newcomers to participate in carefully scaffolded tasks that engage them in real academic work, weaving in deeper and deeper practices as they progress through the unfolding lesson. It also shows how teachers can treat English Learners as young scholars capable of grappling with deep concepts and rigorous ideas. The lesson—with its rigorous conceptual and language goals—allows teachers themselves to enact roles beyond simply providing language exercises, fun games, and new words until students are ready for "real work." Like their colleagues in the other disciplines, teachers of ESL can apprentice students into becoming accomplished readers, writers, and thinkers.

Using the Three Moments Architecture of a lesson, students move toward development of the critical skills they need. This does not mean that every student in the class understands perfectly every part of the text or its analysis. At this point in their educational careers, beginning English Learners are just beginning to be apprenticed into these new practices. As the year progresses, the teacher will offer them numerous additional opportunities to engage with one another, complex texts, and rigorous concepts in much the same way. Through the constant weaving of these processes throughout the year, students simultaneously appropriate the conceptual, analytic, and language practices they need. The teacher not only sees what her students are capable of during this lesson, but also anticipates what they are capable of by the end of the year and far into the future. We trust in students' potential, confident that they can and will be successful.

As we know, Newcomer students bring with them immense potential for growth, a wealth of life experiences, and complex linguistic knowledge. It is our duty as their educators to offer them quality opportunities to learn that will take them from where they are now to where we know they can be. Unfortunately, in many classrooms designed to support Newcomer multilingual learners, students are offered activities that are not challenging, rich, or meaningful. They are treated as though they are incapable of engaging in higher-order thinking because they cannot yet express themselves using complex language. But how are they to develop such complex language without conceptual understanding and analytic practices? Not only does that kind of treatment not honor who they are as people, it condemns them to a trajectory of becoming trapped in the designation of English Learner and, ultimately, the label of Long-Term English Learner.

The support students need to excel in school begins with the planning of lessons. Teachers must act in deliberately reflective ways to design lessons that allow students to learn in the ambitious ways described in this book, while observing what happens during the implementation of those lessons through dynamic assessment, and then making changes based on the information they receive. This cycle of design, implementation, and reflection allows teachers to develop their capacity to invite their students to go deeper and deeper in their learning and apprenticeship.

REFERENCES

Bunch, G. C., Walqui, A., & Pearson, D. P. (2014). Complex text and new common standards in the United States: Pedagogical implications for English learners. *TESOL Quarterly, 48*(3), 533–559. https://doi.org/10.1002/tesq.175

Cisneros, S. (1984). *The House on Mango Street.* Arte Público Press.

Common Core State Standards Initiative. (2010). *Common Core State Standards for English Language Arts and literacy in history, social studies, science, and technical subjects.* National Governors Association and Council of Chief State School Officers. https://learning.ccsso.org/wp-content/uploads/2022/11/ADA-Compliant-ELA-Standards.pdf

Office of English Language Acquisition. (2023, June). *Newcomer toolkit.* U.S. Department of Education. https://ncela.ed.gov/educator-support/toolkits/newcomer-toolkit

Umansky, I., Hopkins, M., Dabach, D. B., Porter, L., Thompson, K., & Pompa, D. (2018). *Understanding and supporting the educational needs of recently arrived immigrant English Learner students: Lessons for state and local education agencies.* Council of Chief State School Officers.

Valdés, G. (2018). Analyzing the curricularization of language in two-way immersion education: Restating two cautionary notes. *Bilingual Research Journal, 41,* 1–25.

Walqui, A., & Heritage, M. (2018, Fall). Meaningful classroom talk. *American Educator.*

Walqui, A., & van Lier, L. (2010). *Scaffolding reframed. Scaffolding the academic success of English Language Learners: A pedagogy of promise.* WestEd.

Part III

IMPLEMENTATION AND DEVELOPING TEACHER EXPERTISE

CHAPTER 11

Where the Rubber Meets the Road

What Teachers and Students Report When Implementing High-Quality Learning Designs for Multilingual Learners

George C. Bunch, Heather Schlaman, Sara Rutherford-Quach, Shirley Feldman, and Aída Walqui

Is pursuing the kind of amplified instruction envisioned in the previous chapters possible, especially after years of reductive approaches to language and literacy for multilingual learners? What can multilingual learners achieve when engaged in classrooms that follow the tenets and design features discussed in Chapters 2 and 3? What challenges do they and their teachers face in implementing curriculum designed to provide simultaneous engagement in rigorous and well-supported disciplinary practices, invitations to dialogue meaningfully with their peers around critical issues, and opportunities for language development?

In this chapter, we discuss several classroom implementations of amplifying the curriculum for multilingual learners. First, we share what students and teachers in three U.S. cities had to say about the challenges and opportunities they experienced when implementing a 4- to 5-week pilot unit exploring "persuasion" in various historical and contemporary contexts. That unit was designed to illustrate how teachers and schools could support English Learners to meet the same high expectations called for by the then-new Common Core Standards.[1] We then turn to reactions by teachers during the piloting of a subsequent, more ambitious three-unit sequence (approximately 12 weeks of instruction) designed as part of a national initiative to improve education for secondary English Learners.[2] That sequence was linked by a powerful question: "How have human beings across time searched for explanations, change, and control?"

PERSUASION ACROSS TIME AND SPACE

The 7th-grade English Language Arts unit *Persuasion Across Time and Space: Analyzing and Producing Persuasive Texts* was designed for the Understanding Language initiative by Aída Walqui, Nanette Koelsch, and Mary Schmida (2012) at the Quality Teaching for English Learners (QTEL) initiative at WestEd (see also Bunch et al., 2015; Kibler et al., 2015).[3]

Grounded in approaches consistent with the tenets discussed in Chapter 2 and developed using the Three Moments Architecture outlined in Chapter 3, the unit was created to illustrate how such a curriculum could be designed to provide rich learning opportunities for multilingual learners and their monolingual peers. Although this particular unit was developed for multilingual learners at or beyond the intermediate level of English language proficiency, the underlying principles and design features are applicable to students at more beginning stages of English language proficiency as well.

The unit was developed just after the Common Core Standards had been adopted by most states and as they were starting to be implemented. Because the new standards called for a departure from prevailing assumptions about learning for all students, with implications for rethinking language development and instruction for multilingual learners, the unit was designed to illuminate a number of theoretical and pedagogical shifts in the design and enactment of learning opportunities for multilingual learners (Bunch et al., 2015; Kibler et al., 2015; Walqui et al., 2012). Among the shifts exemplified in the unit are those that embody the notion of *amplification* discussed in this book, for example shifting from instruction centered around isolated ideas or texts to considering ideas and texts as interconnected, and moving from the use of simplified to more complex texts. A number of shifts also relate to specific tenets discussed in Chapter 2, as shown in Table 11.1.

* * *

The Persuasion unit is comprised of five lessons of approximately 1 week each, as shown in Figure 11.1. Each lesson contains a number of pedagogical tasks that support multilingual learners as they engage in making meaning of historical speeches, such as President Lincoln's *Gettysburg Address*, Dr. Martin Luther King Jr.'s *I Have a Dream*, and Robert Kennedy's *On the Assassination of Martin Luther King*.

In the introductory lesson, students engage with a variety of media to examine the use of emotional appeal in advertisements to interest readers and persuade them to take action. The second lesson takes students deeper

Table 11.1. Tenets and Shifts Enacted in Design of Persuasion Unit

Tenets Discussed in Chapter 2	Related Shifts Illustrated in *Persuasion Across Time and Space*
Development emerges in social interaction and is a consequence of, not a prerequisite for, learning.	From considering language acquisition as an individual process to understanding it as apprenticeship in social contexts.
Quality learning is deliberately and contingently scaffolded.	From activities that preteach content or simply "help students get through texts" to those that scaffold students' development and autonomy.
During learning, multilingual learners simultaneously develop conceptual, analytic, and language practices.	From identification of discrete structural features of language to exploration of how language is purposely patterned to do rhetorical work.
Quality school learning focuses on substantive and generative disciplinary practices.	From separate "content" and "language" objectives to objectives that highlight the role of language in engaging with disciplinary practices.
When it comes to the development of language practices, quality learning opportunities for multilingual learners selectively focus on form in contextual, contingent, and supportive ways.	From viewing language acquisition as a linear process aimed at accuracy, fluency, and complexity to understanding it as a nonlinear and complex developmental process aimed at comprehension and communication.

into analysis of persuasive techniques through close reading of and interaction with the *Gettysburg Address*. In the third lesson, students learn Aristotle's Three Appeals (ethos, pathos, and logos) and use this knowledge to critically analyze three Civil Rights–era speeches. In the fourth lesson, students collaboratively analyze the structural, organizational, grammatical, and lexical choices made in Barbara Jordan's *All Together Now* (1994) in order to examine how authors construct persuasive texts at both macro and micro levels. Finally, in the fifth lesson, students demonstrate their learning by analyzing a more recent address delivered to the United Nations by a 12-year-old and by writing their own persuasive texts.

Consistent with the notion of *spiraling* presented in Chapter 3 and used throughout this book, the arrangement of the lessons and activities is designed to provide iterative opportunities for students to discuss, read, and write about common themes throughout the unit to recursively develop deeper understandings.

Figure 11.1. The Persuasion Unit's Spiraled Design

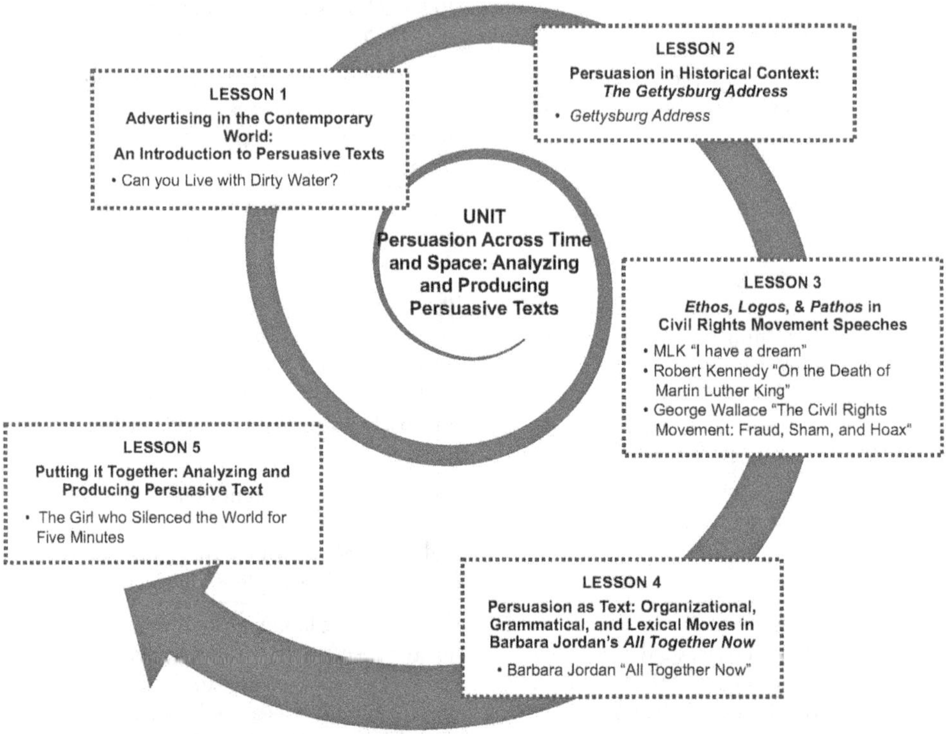

Source: Walqui, Koelsch, & Schmida (2012).

The unit provides various levels of scaffolding (Walqui & van Lier, 2010). At the *macro* level, the spiraled lessons allow students to move from analyzing persuasive discourse in forms with which they are more likely to be familiar, such as advertising, to genres that are less familiar to them, such as historical and political speeches. At the *meso* level, each lesson's tripartite structure allows students to (1) prepare to engage with upcoming texts by activating and building background knowledge, (2) interact with those texts in various ways, and (3) connect what they are reading and discussing to texts from other lessons, units, and courses, as well as to their lives and the larger world (see Figure 3.2). Finally, various interactive activities at the *micro* level provide opportunities for students to engage with each other and the teacher in collaborative tasks that they might not initially have been able to do by themselves. Suggestions for differentiation are provided, based on the level of scaffolding (light, moderate, heavy) needed for students to make meaning from a text.

* * *

After feedback on a draft of the unit was collected from teachers at several school districts across the United States, and after parts of the unit were "prepiloted" by a group of summer school teachers in Oakland and New York City, three urban school districts were chosen to pilot the full unit.[4] The districts were chosen based on the large numbers of EL-classified students they served, as well as the geographic and demographic diversity that the districts represented. One district was in a large Midwestern city with a long history of immigration and where EL-classified students represented 20% of the district's student population. Another was in a Southwestern city with almost 40% of students classified as English Learners. The third district was in a city in the South with a smaller, but dramatically increasing, EL-classified population.

Sixteen teachers in nine schools piloted the unit. Two days of professional development designed by the creators of the unit allowed teachers to learn about its theoretical underpinnings, experience several lessons as students, and discuss potential challenges that might arise in their classrooms. All classrooms participating in the pilot had at least 25% EL-classified students.

Two or three times during implementation of the unit, project staff visited pilot classrooms, video recording lessons and meeting with teachers to plan and debrief as well as discuss challenges and opportunities as they arose. Midway through the unit's implementation, web conferences were held for participating teachers to share questions, concerns, and successes across the three piloting districts. Teachers were not, therefore, implementing the unit without guidance and support. At the same time, this was not a "laboratory" setting or one that featured unusual levels of outside intervention, and teachers faced challenges common in many schools attempting to implement new initiatives.

The pilot was designed as an initial exploration to gauge the feasibility of the unit's approach to instruction and to address several questions: How would teachers and students experience the unit? How would students manage the increased demands? How effective would teachers perceive the supports to be? How would teachers embody the conceptual and pedagogical shifts? What implementation challenges would present themselves, and could these be overcome?[5]

Overall, teachers reacted positively to the unit. In their post-unit responses, almost all teachers expressed higher levels of comfort addressing the Common Core Standards with EL-classified students than they had had before teaching the unit. Teachers stated that the unit contained helpful models for providing scaffolding, differentiating instruction, and supporting multilingual learners' access to complex, rigorous texts. Participating teachers also highlighted ways that their teaching would change in the future as a result of the unit.

Students talked about the unit in positive terms as well, highlighting their engagement in the activities and noting the benefits of working collaboratively with their peers. Both teachers and students also described implementation challenges, some related to the shifts called for by the unit and others associated with institutional barriers to changing practice. Notably, many teachers expressed surprise at what their students, especially those classified as English Learners, were able to do, given the difficult texts at the heart of the unit.

We next share teachers' and students' comments about specific practices that students were able to engage in and develop during the unit and then turn to their perspectives on features of the curriculum itself.

What Students Were Able to Do

During and after implementation of the unit, teachers and students consistently reported their satisfaction with both the substance and processes of students' engagement and learning. As articulated in this section, participants highlighted the quality of the ideas multilingual learners and their classmates addressed together, their use of language to codevelop understandings of complex text, and their persistence and sense of agency as they tackled the challenging curriculum.

Students Engaged With Complex Texts and Themes. Consistent with the goals of the unit, teachers expressed satisfaction with the ways that students, including those classified as English Learners, were able to engage with complex texts. Several acknowledged that they were initially concerned about the complexity of the texts and skeptical that students would be able to read them without more explicit instruction. Typical was the response of one teacher who said that, initially, "We thought . . . we're never going to be able to do the *Gettysburg Address.*" But this teacher's expectations were exceeded once students began engaging with the unit activities: "Some of the things they're saying about it are amazing."

Teachers expressed surprise at their students' ability to understand the central concepts of the unit, including the persuasive appeals of ethos, logos, and pathos, and to recognize and apply those understandings across texts. One teacher said, "You never thought you could bring Aristotle into the 7th-grade classroom and they'd be just rolling it off the tongue." A number of teachers also noted the connections students made among texts, among subject areas, and between the unit concepts and their own lives.

Many teachers were impressed with what previously "struggling" students were able to accomplish during the unit. One teacher said,

> I really do think that each student walked away with something, whether or not they got the big picture of everything. I still think that even my students who struggle the most will walk away from that unit remembering something about persuasive speeches, and . . . that was kind of surprising to me.

Several teachers specifically pointed out that the unit was accessible to and effective for students of varying English language proficiency levels. As one teacher noted, the unit helped *everyone* to "elevate" their thinking and language.

Students Collaborated Constructively on Challenging Tasks. A prominent theme in the reflections of both teachers and students concerned the value of student collaboration, despite inherent challenges. Although students reported finding the texts (e.g., *The Gettysburg Address*, Martin Luther King's *I Have a Dream*) to be linguistically demanding, they spoke positively of the expectation that they present to peers and work collaboratively to decipher and use the texts' language and ideas. One student commented, "I think it's different because . . . we used to work independently. . . . We were working alone and now we work in groups . . . and now [our teacher] trusts us more." Although the expectations for collaboration stretched their capacities, students recognized the experiences as educative and believed their presentation skills had improved. As one student commented, "Group is good because the first one, he knows something, and another person, he knows another thing. We, you know, combined we formed the speech."

Teachers reported that they observed students in groups collaborating purposefully, not just "socializing." Several teachers commented that it was challenging for students to contribute verbally and be accountable for listening to and learning from their peers. Yet many teachers reported being surprised at how confidently and productively students communicated their learning with each other. These teachers observed students relying on one another, providing mutual scaffolding as they deciphered the language of the text.

Students Produced Oral and Written Language in New and Elaborated Ways. Both teachers and students discussed how students took up opportunities for language use and development provided by the unit's activities. Teachers talked about students' enhanced language use in terms of increased quality and quantity of conversations, arguments, presentations, writing, and engagement with texts.

One teacher pointed out that students moved beyond the procedural language she had often heard in group work previously (e.g., "How do I fold this paper?" and "Where do I draw this line?") to now include "purposeful" language, such as what kinds of symbols students should use to represent

George Wallace's ideas on a collaborative poster about Civil Rights–era speeches. According to the teacher, along with these kinds of discussions came opportunities for attention to language: "They're pushing each other's language. I mean, if you can hear them, 'No, . . . it's said like this' or 'Maybe there's another word for it.'" The teacher further explained with an example:

> Like today, I was just watching one of my students and he was struggling, but he was having a tremendous discussion at a very high level about something that was quite meaningful to him. I believe . . . it's the structure of the collaboration, and . . . it's just really wonderful hearing my kids talk again in class, . . . [to] have it so purposeful, and to push that language.

A number of teachers were impressed with students' conversational engagement during group activities and the depth of their textual discussions. Referring to an activity during which students analyzed advertisements for different persuasive techniques, one noted, "They were arguing with each other: 'No, this is the hard sell 'cause it has this.' 'No, this is the soft sell.' So they were really actively engaged . . . in helping each other learn through the process." The animation in students' discussions pleased teachers because they felt it reflected and led to new understandings.

Teachers reported that throughout the unit students became more confident not only in their ability to deconstruct complex texts, but also in their capacity to understand and use the language and ideas of the assigned texts. One teacher described her surprise at not having to unpack textual language herself as much as she had anticipated:

> I thought for sure I was going to have to go back and help out with the language in terms of what was a hard, medium, and soft sell. But because that was laid out for them and we had done so much work prior to that, they took to it immediately.

During the unit, students were asked to write short, paragraph-length responses and analyses throughout each lesson, a page-long reflection at the end of each lesson, and a longer persuasive piece at the end of the unit. According to teachers, most students' writing reflected their understanding of the unit's texts and elements of persuasion. One teacher described a particularly impressive piece of student writing: "It was something we had read and she just pulled out right away: 'This is pathos and this is why.' And I hadn't even instructed her to do that." Teachers also noted that students, in their own writing, utilized specific persuasive strategies that they had seen in the unit's texts, including strategic repetition, logical and emotional appeals, and counterargument.

Additionally, teachers reported that students were frequently using core conceptual terminology. Several teachers admitted being "surprised" or "amazed" by students' academic vocabulary use, and that students were appropriately "using words that they didn't know a few weeks before." Students themselves also highlighted how the unit texts and structure promoted vocabulary growth. As one student explained, "I'm learning more English because of the speeches and everything; they're using more big, fancy words." Another student said, "Big words get smaller for me now."

Students Demonstrated Persistence, Confidence, Maturity, and Leadership. Finally, teachers expressed a belief that students demonstrated significant personal growth in several other areas over the course of the unit, including maturity, independence, persistence in the face of difficulty, and confidence, particularly with respect to reading and speaking. One teacher noted that students' skills and confidence in language production grew after completing the unit:

> I feel like the confidence level of my ESL students has grown just by being required in a way, to talk about things out loud. So now, for example, 4 weeks after we finished, they're volunteering to read passages when they would have never volunteered to speak out before. . . . Their confidence is growing. That means that their language ability and their confidence in reading and speaking is growing.

Teachers and students indicated that students demonstrated more ownership over the curriculum during this unit than they had previously, noting that students regularly challenged each other's claims, language, and actions. Students appeared to be learning from each other and engaging in more authentic, academic, free-flowing conversations—what one teacher called the "freedom to talk."

Teachers' Successes and Challenges With an Amplified Curriculum

Teachers and students attributed students' success to the unit's overall design and the structure of specific activities. Not surprisingly, both teachers and students also experienced challenges related to the rigor of the unit and to the instructional shifts it required. In many cases, as will become clear throughout this section, the challenges were what led to the successes. Some teachers also identified limitations of the unit, such as lack of guidance for evaluating the progress of individual students. In response to their concerns, teachers described adaptations they had made during the unit or offered suggestions for future iterations. In this section, we discuss the specific features of an amplified curriculum that teachers and students highlighted as contributing to their experiences enacting the unit, as well as modifications that teachers made in relation to their own contexts and concerns.

Engaging Themes and Texts. Students said that the overall theme of the unit resonated with them, pointing out that learning how to persuade someone else about something was a useful skill, both in school and in life. They also said they were interested in the unit's texts, including speeches about race and the environment, videos exploring contemporary notions of body image, and historical speeches like the *Gettysburg Address*. Students indicated that the materials connected with their lives in powerful ways, particularly around issues of race, civil rights, and equality. One student commented,

> I think that in these speeches . . . it [doesn't only] teach you about . . . racism and everything, you actually get into it. You wonder what would happen if [struggles against] racism wouldn't have happened. We would probably be separated. We wouldn't have had friends to hang out with. . . . That's the great thing about this. It actually makes you interested in what you are learning.

Several teachers noted a correlation between the use of texts related to students' lives and their increased language use. As one teacher explained,

> They're very interested in the rights of minorities. Because [the] focus of all the readings . . . [was] around that, I heard a lot of discussion from their own personal lives, that they have experienced a time that they felt they weren't being treated equal[ly] or a time that their parents [or grandparents] shared with them.

Teachers also argued that many students who had been disengaged or even excluded from prior conversations about texts were revived by these materials. Collectively, students' and teachers' comments indicate the importance of the selection of interesting, compelling, meaningful, and relevant themes and topics around which to design learning opportunities—for multilingual learners and all students. Many teachers noted that suspending the notion that every student had to master every element of lessons freed them to recognize what each student was able to gain from engaging in the texts, topics, and themes at the heart of the unit.

Unit Structure and Spiraling. As teachers reflected on the unit before, during, and after implementation, they highlighted positive aspects of its sequencing and structure. Several commented on the value of inviting students, in the first lesson, to analyze persuasive elements of visual and print advertisements, including public service announcements, before moving on to the *Gettysburg Address* in the second lesson: "It started out very visually and, on the same theme throughout the unit . . . I really liked . . . starting with the hook of the video, and the visual, and something that's very relatable to the students." Another pointed out that "getting the kids interested visually first, rather than through [written] text . . . kind of sold them" on the type of analytical work they would be doing with the more difficult historical speeches.

Teachers also discussed how the unit was structured to provide students just enough supportive background information in advance of reading texts. The activities, according to teachers, facilitated comprehension without removing the challenge of grappling with the meaning of the texts once students began reading them. In the words of one teacher, "That was a good model for me, to see . . . the balance there of giving them background information, but letting them struggle to pull out some of the bigger ideas and vocabulary throughout the text."

One teacher highlighted the importance of the activities that allowed students to activate and build background information, pointing out how critical it was to get students' "prior knowledge enacted." Another said that it was "eye opening" to watch students struggle with text and "really think about things," and that providing some background information provided the opportunity to apply and synthesize what students had learned to the text itself:

> Watching them struggle with texts that were hard and the answers weren't right there in front of them, like, 7th-grade texts, like in a textbook, [where it] might be a lot easier to find answers. . . . for them to have to struggle and . . . really think about things, read the background information and apply that information, and do all that synthesis was really impressive for me—to see that they were capable of doing it and thrived on it.

Finally, one teacher pointed out that the process of engaging students with difficult text served not only to help "level the playing field" for students with different amounts of background knowledge, but also to introduce students to a process for approaching difficult texts in general:

> I think the biggest thing was the ability to analyze the mentor texts. And then, for them to see, I think in sort of a meta way, the steps that it takes for them to prepare for such a thing. So that it's not just about putting a document like the *Gettysburg Address* in front of you, but it is about the process that you take, with which to make it have . . . meaning. And the documents that they read leading up to it, how that helps to build their schema, I think is really important

for all the students, because then it sort of gave them a level playing field with which to engage the text.

When discussing the unit's implementation, teachers across multiple school sites discussed the spiraling embedded throughout the unit as one of the more important and helpful elements. Some teachers highlighted as helpful the opportunities students had for "listening/viewing multiple times with a different purpose each time," pointing out that asking different questions each time they watched a single video led students to new understandings each round and prevented boredom. Many teachers also discussed the importance of spiraling for increasing students' ability to read, comprehend, and analyze difficult texts. They pointed out the benefits for multilingual learners when students were invited to engage with a single text multiple times in different ways, as well as to spiral back on themes with texts in different genres, time periods, and social contexts. One teacher put it this way:

> Having . . . a central theme made [the lessons] consistent and purposeful as opposed to: "We're going to learn about persuasion and here's eight different speeches and this has this and this has this." [Instead, the texts] were linked together and . . . it was clearer that there were connections between them. And that helped them build their confidence and [ability] to analyze from text to text: "Oh I got this in the *Gettysburg Address*" and "Oh I see the same thing." So I feel like . . . the purposeful nature of it was helpful for them to make those deeper connections to the text.

Teachers also highlighted the importance of spiraling for students' writing. One teacher explained,

> It was good being able to say to the kids you know when it comes to your own writing . . . let's think back from day one . . . and they were able to. Let's go back to the advertising, let's go back to—I mean I could say to them, "What did . . . all of the writers do that was the same?" And they would know. . . . [T]he spiraling of everything really worked for them.

A few teachers worried that multiple activities around a single text challenged some students' stamina and may have been repetitive for more advanced readers. But others mentioned that the spiraling approach featured in the unit was something that they would apply to their future teaching and would share with other teachers. One teacher reported, "I can't picture going through another year without [using] the spiraling technique that's going on here." This particular teacher also mentioned that others implementing the unit at this school had talked about "how much this could affect [the] rest of our staff when we start sharing this."

Promoting and Supporting Student Collaboration. Teachers found that the collaborative nature of the unit, especially the structures calling for students to work with each other in groups of various sizes, placed more responsibility for learning on the students and less on teachers in their traditional roles at the front of the classroom. One teacher described this new role for teachers as "more of a facilitator" than the "leader." Some teachers found it challenging to relinquish control, knowing that not all groups would arrive at the same interpretations of the texts, or even gain complete comprehension. One teacher described the challenge of not "giving [the students] everything they need" but instead "trusting" the collaborative process. At the same time, most teachers recognized the value of turning the reading and analysis of texts over to students in this collaborative setting. One teacher described the benefit of allowing students to "struggle" rather than stepping in as the teacher to "remedy" the problems a group was encountering. Teachers agreed that, in the words of one of them, "letting go of [the feeling that] I have to be up there" resulted in deeper learning and more genuine engagement for students than would have been the case with solely teacher-directed reading and discussion.

Although most of the teachers had prior experience asking students to engage in collaborative work, several of this unit's activities engaged students in ways teachers had not seen before. One teacher suggested that the intentional structure of the tasks led students to work together rather than allowing one or two students to complete all the work for the group. A different teacher noted that when students had information that they were responsible for sharing with the rest of the group, they "took that very, very seriously." In fact, teachers at several schools commented positively on these "Jigsawed" activities (see Chapter 2), highlighting how this structure helped build students' background information, promoted collaboration, and led to student agency. This teacher pointed out that having students focus on different texts allowed them to become experts in a particular area, giving students "a sense of agency or purpose within that unit."

From students' perspectives, working collaboratively was challenging but allowed them to get feedback from others, support each other in the readings, and share ideas to arrive at understanding together. One student commented, "We can't just depend on the teacher to give us the answers to everything. We have to work together to actually do the work."

To be clear, fostering the desired levels of collaboration was not easy or automatic. Some teachers said that the student collaboration presented behavioral challenges, and many noted that it would have been helpful for students to have engaged in the kinds of collaboration called for by the unit earlier in the year. One teacher specifically noted frequent interpersonal conflicts among students that made forming groups challenging. Another teacher mentioned the tendency for "middle school drama" to interfere with students' ability to focus on the academic tasks. Teachers also noted in some cases that students found ways around genuine collaboration, for example by copying each other's graphic organizers rather than sharing information verbally and discussing it. One teacher commented that some students tended to work ahead, completing the work on their own rather than staying on pace with the group, and had to be reminded to collaborate. This teacher acknowledged that collaboration can feel less "efficient" than individual work. But she also acknowledged that "It's a good lesson to learn that even though you can do it more efficiently that's not really the point."

The sheer amount of collaboration was also identified as a challenge in one of the teacher focus groups. Teachers commented that they felt the group work needed to be interspersed with independent work and, in the words of one teacher, "periods of quiet reflection too" to help students remain focused. One teacher commented on the challenge of keeping students focused when there was no "output" in the form of an individual product to be turned in.

But in contrast to some teachers' comments about collaborative work increasing the number of behavioral problems, many students indicated that each individual's unique responsibility for the group tasks actually made it *easier* for them to stay on task. One student mentioned that, prior to the unit, "Some people in our class were usually, you know, with their head down and stuff. But now with the activities that they made us do . . . in groups, [those students] were able to participate a bit more . . . and understand the content a bit more." Another student commented, "In a normal English class, they can get away without doing anything."

One student noted increased participation among students classified as English Learners specifically: "Before the unit, when we used to work . . . the people that couldn't speak English would want to play around. But now [in this unit] they learned a lot and they participate in group work and everything." Another student put it this way: "I think it was better than just any other language arts class. We got to work with our . . . friends, so we got more work done, and we understood more."

Scaffolding and Differentiation. The unit prompted some teachers to rethink their conceptions of "differentiation" for students from a variety of linguistic and academic backgrounds. Teachers highlighted challenges in meeting the individual needs of their students, who were diverse in terms of their English language proficiency, academic backgrounds, and learning needs. But they also discussed ways in which the unit attended to some of those challenges—not by assigning different tasks to students at different levels of competence, as is often done based on traditional notions of differentiation, but rather by offering different levels of scaffolding within each task to support students' engagement and learning within the central endeavors of the unit (Walqui et al., 2012). As one teacher put it,

> I thought it was interesting just being more aware of minimal scaffolding versus maximum scaffolding. And I feel like, no one's ever kind of separated those two for me. It's always been like, "scaffold or differentiate!"

Several teachers in at least two different schools discussed how teaching the unit helped them understand that, in classes with mixed levels of language and academic proficiency, it was possible to present challenging material in ways that benefited all students, albeit perhaps in different ways for different students. One teacher said that, before teaching this unit, she was afraid to "push the rigor" for "ESL kids":

> Through some of these lessons where there are some difficult questions . . . I know that all levels of students in my class aren't necessarily going to get each little part of it, they're gonna get a part . . . I think the way that this [unit] is developed [helps]—everybody's getting something out of it.

A teacher at a different school said that the biggest lesson from the unit was that "Not everyone has to know everything. . . . You can be an expert in one area. And allowing that person to become the expert gives them a sense of agency or purpose within that unit. So that seemed to help quite a bit." This teacher remarked that in this unit, "I wasn't, you know, beating the heck out of it by trying to get everybody to comprehend every single speech, every single reading piece."

Some teachers noted that the unit's approach to scaffolding made it possible for students to benefit from individual supports that did not remove them from experiencing the challenging texts and conversations engaged in by their classmates. For example, one teacher commented that, rather than being responsible for a holistic understanding of an entire textual passage the first time students read it, each student was only responsible for focusing on one aspect of the text and completing one assigned piece of a graphic organizer during a Jigsaw reading activity. But in the group discussion that followed, each student then benefited from hearing from others who had been assigned to the other sections. All students were responsible for taking notes on the missing sections on their own graphic organizer as they listened to their colleagues who had been assigned the other sections. This approach contrasts sharply with some approaches to differentiation that might have separated EL-classified students or students at lower reading levels from their more proficient peers and assigned them a simpler text or less demanding discussion questions.

Teachers' Adaptations

Teachers themselves adapted the unit's tasks and materials to respond to several common challenges they encountered along the way.

Responding to Group Work Challenges. Teachers responded to the variety of challenges that collaborative work presented by grouping students strategically—both to avoid interpersonal conflict and behavior problems and to ensure that students who needed the most support were grouped with students who could provide it. Some teachers and students also commented on the fact that the collaborative nature of the unit presented challenges in terms of students' different speeds in completing activities. One teacher mentioned that the unit did not provide guidance for what some groups should do while waiting for others to complete the activities. To address the challenges of keeping students on task and ensuring effective collaboration, teachers suggested adaptations such as setting firm time limits to keep students focused, using a prop that students could pass around to establish who held the floor, and assigning roles for each student to ensure equal participation. One teacher added independent reading time at the beginning of each class period to help students gain focus before moving into the group activities.

Evaluating Individual Students' Learning. Another concern that arose from teachers about the collaborative nature of the unit was that it was often difficult to determine how well individual students were learning the concepts and when some might have been struggling. These teachers' comments on assessment point to the size of shifts they were being asked to make, the challenges inherent in formatively evaluating students' group conversations for evidence of student progress, and the need for more explicit tools and guidance for teachers in these areas. Their comments also point to the institutional pressure teachers often feel to justify their own performance by producing evidence of individual student outcomes.

Collaborative activities call for a focus on learning processes instead of products and suggest that the social context of learning and assessment should be inseparable from one another. Thus, they disrupt traditional conceptions of assessment, which evaluate the oral or written output of individual students often working alone. Instead, these activities require teachers to look at student growth in the context of interaction with peers. But without explicit evaluation tools, some of the teachers found it challenging to examine and determine the language and disciplinary practice development that was taking place when students were engaged in shared endeavors with peers. They also wondered how to document how this engagement supported individual students' overall growth.

In response, some teachers created their own strategies for evaluating what students were learning during the interactive activities. Some used formative assessment practices such as exit slips or miniessays to evaluate what individual students were learning each day as well as to guide their modifications of the lessons, grouping strategies, and their teaching to address individual student needs. One teacher described her formative assessment process:

> The biggest thing for me was whether or not the students actually were understanding what they [were] writing. Because so much of it was collaborative groups, I did a lot of exit slips and entrance slips (just quick, you know, put your poster up, a quick check board), so that I knew that they remembered what was going on early in the week. And then at the end, [if there was] someone in a group that wasn't paying attention . . . I could pull them, and give them a little bit of extra guidance the next day.

Another teacher described using miniessays to formatively assess students for strategic grouping purposes. As she explained,

> I had them write these miniessays. . . . It gave me something to fall back on. Like, to go back and say "Okay, where does this person get it and maybe I should group these two together?" It helped with the grouping. To see where, where they would go next or . . . taking into consideration the next lesson, "How am I gonna group you?"

Given the teachers' comments, it is clear that more support for their evaluation practices would be helpful, both in the unit itself and in larger efforts at professional development. In the spirit of the tenets discussed in Chapter 2, particularly helpful would be guidance and tools that prompted teachers to use diagnostic formative assessment practices to evaluate content knowledge, disciplinary literacy practices, and language competence. Such assessments would need to be framed in a way that view the three as developing interdependently, but also provide important information about individual students' progress along the way. As mentioned in Chapter 3, artifacts that provide students clear examples of high-quality work (prior student examples, rubrics, self-reflection tools) can also be used for students to evaluate their own work, increasing their agency and autonomy.

Promoting Accessibility for Students at Lower English Proficiency and Reading Levels. Despite their overall appreciation of the unit's approach to scaffolding, some teachers and students pointed out that challenges remained, even with different levels of scaffolding. One explained:

> Some of the reading levels [of the texts] were just [challenging to] . . . some of my students, about five of my students. . . . So that's where I had to use guided reading, to fold that in and make sure that we [were] able to do some reading, where they . . . could break it down into smaller chunks.

Although the unit was not designed for students classified as beginning-level English Learners, in some cases they were indeed enrolled in the classes piloting the unit, including ESL, sheltered, or even mainstream English Language Arts classrooms. Several teachers pointed out the challenges facing these students and detailed the types of adjustments to the curriculum they made. Teachers' adaptations included individually working with students to decipher texts, grouping students who speak the same home language but have various English proficiencies together, and encouraging students to translate for each other. One teacher was adamant that while she did have to make some changes to the curriculum, this unit met the needs of her linguistically heterogeneous class much better than any other she has taught, noting:

> I have not seen any unit in over 20 years that . . . addresses English language learners and their need for discourse, their need for real juicy material to talk about, [with] the rigor that this provides. . . . Constantly, we had to make some adjustments, but nowhere near the adjustments I've had to make in past units.

DESIGNING AND IMPLEMENTING THEMATIC UNITS: LESSONS LEARNED

Subsequent implementations in diverse schools around the United States of units such as the one discussed in the prior section of this chapter, and the one of the power of youth protest in change in Chapter 3, were so successful that the QTEL ELA team (Lee Hartman, Mary Schmida, Shirley Feldman, and Aída Walqui) wrote several other units following the same design.[5] In this section we (Aída and the QTEL team) report on the iterative design and implementation of a sequence of three units, each with three lessons, which we were able to follow and study. The units respectively explored mythology, pandemics, and street art (Figure 11.2) and used multimodal texts and a wide variety of dialogic activities organized

Figure 11.2. Three Spiraled Units

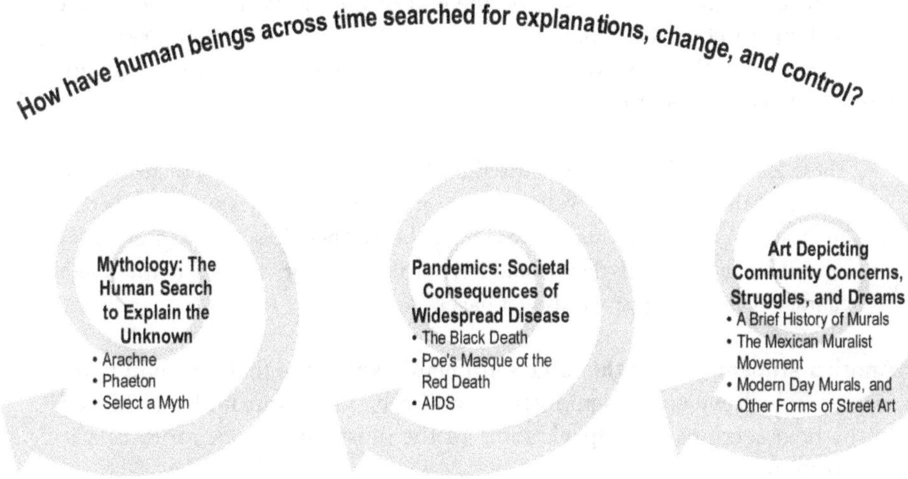

around the Three Moment Architecture that has been discussed throughout this book (see Figure 3.2). These units were piloted in full by teachers twice in Los Angeles Unified School District, in 2021 and 2022, during which they were iteratively refined four times. Additionally, the authors taught the units ourselves during an intensive summer academy in 2022 for 8th graders in three different New York City boroughs. We tried to replicate in time and intensity the 12 weeks during a one period a day, 60 hours of an academic year.

In this section, we discuss some of the evidence that emerged from those implementations, the advantages they presented for teachers and students, and the tensions that arose during the implementation of these new units. We received feedback from preparation workshops, classroom observations, written and oral reflections, interviews, panel discussions, and our own teaching logs. Here, some of that feedback is briefly presented from three perspectives: *students* (what they experienced and commented upon); *teachers* (what they said during preparation for the implementation during the three-day professional learning sessions, our observations of their teaching, and interviews with the teachers); and *designers of the lessons* (see Walqui, 2024, for a fuller report on these experiences).

What Students Experienced

Students overall were extremely receptive of the materials. They actively engaged in interactions with each other, jointly and then individually reading and writing, even when some had initially confessed they did not enjoy talking in class, reading, or writing. At the end of the 12 weeks, and when we asked them to compare what they had initially written in their preassessment, and what they ended up writing, they manifested surprise at the difference. As one student mentioned,

> These lessons make you put yourself in the circumstances of characters in the text, and there is no way you cannot react. In other classes we are asked to analyze characters, but not to wear their shoes. These lessons asked us to say or write what we think they would have at the moment. These activities made characters real, not just words in a paper.

Another student echoed the same sentiment, explaining that "we had many ways in which we could demonstrate, and even grow, our understanding." In the next sections we unpack some of the most salient categories of student responses.

Themes Were Relevant and Enticing. At the end of each unit's implementation, students commented that they really appreciated that topics were significant for them. For example, many mentioned that in the mythology unit, the lesson of Phaeton helped them connect personally to the issues being presented. As adolescents, they face questions of identity, some of them have a father who is mostly absent from their lives, they are stubborn, they face some teasing and sometimes even bullying. Reading about a teenager, although somebody from the times of the ancient Greeks, who went through the same situations made them feel that the lessons addressed their concerns. But it was not just the topic of the text. They appreciated the activities that made them discuss, play act, interpret, and together come up with solutions to everyday dilemmas that spoke to their own contemporary concerns.

A unit that explored pandemics—what the state of knowledge at the time made them think and believe, how they addressed the situation from the health point of view and societally—afforded students the opportunity to see that in history several interpretive patterns reoccur time and again. A young girl in the Bronx wrote, "Who could think there were the same ignorance, prejudices, discrimination, and suffering during the Black Death, the AIDs epidemic and now during COVID?" Another one wrote, "When I first saw Poe's story (The Masque of the Red Death) I thought there is no way I am going to read this, the language is so strange. But, after we engaged in reading and acting up parts of the text, I actually even re-read almost the whole story several times." This clearly suggested that if pedagogical activity prepares students, engages them with enticing activities, and invites them to see human concern interrelationships across a wide variety of texts, then they will engage and as a result develop deeper understanding and the ability to talk, read, and write about it.

Key Ideas Were Explored in Several Lessons. It was quite a realization for students to find that there were multiple connections made across lessons referred to above. David, a 9th grader, said, "To me, if one idea appears three or four times, it must be important. I like that. It is like my mother, reminding me of important things to watch out for, but every time it is in a different situation, and using different words. I like that."

Indeed, if we want to develop deep, robust, interconnected and generative conceptual understanding, curricula should offer students ways of weaving key ideas through many different applications of those ideas across contexts. Besides clarifying and making the idea robust, this approach also contributes to building language memory and the ability to use it. Isolated teaching of one idea after another leads to superficial and inert learning. Students appreciated the reappearance of key concepts and words.

In the unit focused on Public Art, some themes students are not necessarily keen on studying are presented time and again through three lessons that ended up captivating adolescents' spirit of justice and pride for ancestors. Everyday conversations of young people do not always include what counts as art; how it manifests interpretations of life, the beliefs, hopes, and dreams of people; and art as a subversive activity. But, after reading about and watching videos exploring the work of the Mexican muralists and studying everyday murals in their own cities, graffiti, and asphalt art in Lesson 2, what students know and express expands. They develop a new lens, new language, and critical perspectives. In the words of one student,

> When I first read about that muralist called Orozco and how he said that the purest form of art is displayed on walls for everybody to see, and not locked up in museums where you have to pay to see it, I did not understand what he was saying. Now, after having read, discussed, and viewed how Mexican painters like Diego Rivera for the first time painted native people and their history in walls, I love those guys and I agree with Orozco's words.

We have commented in this book that when education is done right, it appeals to students' sense of justice and contributes to building critical and engaged citizens. That result was clearly evident in students' growth and ability to perform during these units.

Invitations to Engage in Activity Offered Students Options. Students appreciated the fact that many tasks were flexible and enabled them to choose what aspects they wanted to explore, although responding to the same general guidelines and content. As an interviewed student commented, "We are not asked to all of us say the same thing. That makes the work uninteresting. We decide what we say, of course, we have to pay attention to the ideas, we cannot just make up absurd things. It ends up being really fun when we can compare what we say to what other students say." Another student added, "Sad, but in other classes we all have to say the same thing, why bother to listen to your classmates?" This affordance (the same sensory environment offers students the opportunity to perceive what attracts them most, interpret it, and act, in this case, write their reaction) is clearly illustrated in Chapter 3, with the Silent Graffiti activity (Photos 3.1 and 3.2). A similar activity, which invites students to explore their diverse reactions to events in a text, is illustrated in the Collaborative Dialogue Writing. For this task teachers have to break down a text into its meaningful components and describe the starting and ending points of the segments selected. Different segments are assigned to students so that they collaboratively write the dialogues they imagine took place at that moment of the story. Students have to use text, what they know about the context, and their assumptions of what characters in that situation would say. Each group makes a decision as to what to write. They all work together suggesting ideas, weighing them, and making decisions. If in a team of four there is a student who offers fewer ideas, that student gets to develop ideas and practices since he, as every other member of the team, needs to keep a full script. Furthermore, they will rehearse their script, and they may be called on as a team to perform their production in front of peers. For example, in Poe's *Masque of the Red Death*, a group received the following segment:

> *Group 1:* Prince Prospero tries to convince his friends to join him in his well-guarded castle to escape the plague.

The group of students who was assigned this dialogue wrote, rehearsed, and then performed the following script:

> *S1:* Come to the palace and hide with me. I have plenty of food for all of us. We will live well here, and we will have fun.
> *S2:* Prince Prospero, thank you for inviting us to this ball.
> *S3:* But Prince Prospero, how can we have fun inside when there is a lot of people suffering and dying outside. Shouldn't we be concerned about them?
> *S1:* I don't care about them, that is not my problem.

S2: Prince Prospero, but what would happen here if someone is affected here? We can all die from the red death. I am not sure this is a good idea.

S1: Don't worry, we are all safe here. The red death will not reach us here.

S3: OK, if you say so. I guess we are all safe and can have fun, but I am still worried about those who do not have our protection. What will become to them? (Walqui, 2024)

Through critical dialogic encounters, students both enjoy working with each other and seriously contemplate the connections between something that happened in the Middle Ages and what was happening in their own environment at the time of reading the piece. After all, this lesson was part of the unit on pandemics that was written during the COVID-19 pandemic. At the end of the performances one student commented, "I watched the news last night and they said that the prime minister in England had invited his friends to his mansion to have a party in the middle of the epidemic." A discussion ensued as to whether rich people today and through history were protected from epidemics because of their wealth, garnering interest for the study of the next two lessons on AIDS and COVID-19 and their societal impact.

Addressing this notion of tensions embedded in civic preparation, van Lier (2001) wrote, "In the social setting of the classroom, interaction among participants takes place against a backdrop of constraints and resources that are in some way different, in some ways similar, to those that characterize other settings" (p. 92). Diversity of perspectives, and the ability to compare them in reasoned ways is essential. In this sense, the classroom is seen almost as a preparation for life as a citizen and as a communicator. While in the classroom, what students express needs to align with the theme under discussion and certain guidelines, with everybody sharing their unique points of view. This then enables them to learn varying perspectives and rationales others may have about those same issues.

Michelle, a student from our summer implementation said, during an interview at the closing of the second week: "I really like the way we are doing things this summer. We compare things to other things, we look at details and then at the big picture, and back again. We also talk more in the classroom to each other, not just in response to the teacher." This student continued:

> In other classes we just write in response to questions. Here we are invited to write about our own ideas, what and why we think the way we think, how

> we interpret things. For example, during the Talk Show [an activity that asks students to pretend they are interviewing a character from a text that has been read, who then needs to respond] we got to pick which character to work on, which person you get to ask questions of. We chose Prince Prospero from *The Masque of the Red Death*. While at first nobody in class thought this would be fun, we actually liked reading about some rich dude who thought he could escape the plague. Just like us, we have to be very careful not to get covid. That Talk Show helped us get to places we had not intended to, which is really good.

What Teachers Experienced

When teachers we worked with first saw the three units, they were enthusiastic. However, during preparation for the implementation, they shared that the units and lessons were too ambitious. Their students did not like to talk, they had become used to using their Chromebooks in class and did not even look at each other because they liked to work by themselves. Our idea of a highly interactive class would not render results. In the next section we will discuss three main challenges in the implementation of dialogic pedagogy and how much we were able to gain in terms of changes in teacher perspective.

"Our Students Do Not Like to Talk." Teachers were concerned that "this generation likes to interact with technology, not with people." This issue, of course, has become part of a larger debate in society. However, we pointed out to teachers that as students left the room and walked to their next class, most of them were in groups chatting along. Our job partly consisted of showing them that students not only can enjoy talking, but that this is the way in which they learn best. As we wrote elsewhere, and as the student quotes above support, "The way in which students apprentice into critical academic practices in school is by being invited to participate with others in critical dialogic activity. Talk is rigorous, it focuses on central ideas related to the text and offers students opportunities to reflect on how those ideas connect to build larger ELA-specific, individual and social understandings" (Walqui, 2024, p. 30).

Our observations indicated that teachers did not clearly understand that a dialogic interaction in class needs to be supported by a clear *structure* that students follow initially, which can be varied once students have appropriated it. Without that, there is no good interactive *process*.

When teachers understood the need for the structures, they were then pleasantly surprised by the results. Our materials for teachers had notes on structure, rationale, what benefits each task afforded students, and suggestions for how to respond if students needed further support. However, planning took time, and all teachers we worked with felt overwhelmed by their courses, by demands in each class, and, in the case of some, by having to have another job to run to at the end of the school day because their pay was too limited.

"Students Love This Activity, So I Let Them Work on It Longer Than Advised." We visited teachers three times, each time for 3 days, to observe how teachers interpreted the curriculum and to talk with them and students. As we observed, one of our most salient realizations was that although we had suggested 15 or 20 minutes for an activity, such an activity often took far longer. For example, the Talk Show was supposed to be written jointly by four students, each of which kept a script during 15 minutes, with 5 minutes to rehearse and then share their presentations. In some cases, the Talk Show had been extended over three and even four class periods. The rationale? Students were so engaged in working on their scripts that teachers let the activity continue.

We explained that if what teachers were after was engagement and appropriation of concepts, analytic practices, and language use, that was promoted through the nine lessons. Furthermore, in response to their concern that students "do it right," we tried to explain that this is precisely the advantage of a spiraling curriculum, one that deepens and expands understanding of key disciplinary practices over several lessons, each time enhancing student clarity on practices and interconnections among them. There is a serious preoccupation that every piece the student produces be grammatically correct. Particularly problematic are outdated notions that students' grammatical errors will become "fossilized" if they are not immediately corrected, a notion that needs to be dispelled.

Pacing is one of the most pressing problems in classes with multilingual learners. If we work on some aspect of class until it is perfect, that exercise will isolate pieces of language or knowledge, and in the process will make classes unenticing for students. This is one of the advantages of spiraling thematic units: Students do not need to be "perfect" at once. They gradually apprentice into efficient readers and writers, as invitations to work dialogically revisit key themes from diverse perspectives.

Teachers Need Opportunities to Continuously Learn. It is unrealistic to expect that the time preservice teachers spend preparing to teach will be sufficient to support their development of deep, generative understanding of the subjects they will teach and the best ways to teach those subjects. Teachers feel they do not have time to plan, to learn. To address this issue, in one school we worked in, the principal had scheduled a common planning period for ELA teachers who taught the same class. Unfortunately, the reality of their daily lives distracted them from common planning, and not once during our visits did we see our teachers working together. They would each be in their classrooms working on what they individually needed to do.

The Tyranny of Discrete Tests. A teacher wrote in his reflection: "Something that keeps being brought up to me while being observed is, What are your criterias (sic) of success for these activities? For example, in reference to the partner discussion activities, how would I grade the students on these activities? At the moment I'm mostly keeping track of students that are participating and giving them credit/no credit." While discussing performance and dynamic assessment is beyond the realm of this chapter, it is important to note that in schools, still today, there is an overemphasis on grades, rather than the quality of performance students demonstrate over time.

A related theme is the interpretation and dominance of the phrase "data driven decision-making" in schools. Instead of interpreting the construct as dictionaries do, as facts and numbers that provide information and make decision-making possible, in education there is the tendency to correlate data to numerical information. The ability of teachers to observe their students, appreciate what and how they are learning, along with their preferences is not addressed in this approach. As Mercer (2019) wrote:

> It is only by pursuing the trajectory of students' learning over time that an analysis can begin to recognize the potential significance of the apparent repetition of certain actions (such as procedures in an investigation) as part of the learning process. The same act repeated, cannot be assumed to be 'the same' act because it builds historically on the earlier event . . . Teachers need to learn to observe and keep track of their students' development over time, not just in one isolated instance in time which may or may not reflect growth. (p. 192)

It is encouraging that, in the field of assessment, there is a resurgence of focus on performance, for example, in essays, debates, and talk shows through which students demonstrate their knowledge and skills (see, for example, Maier et al., 2020). This focus on assessing students' performance is, in fact, what we encourage teachers to do as they offer invitations to their multilingual learners to participate in purposeful, structured activities.

What Curriculum Designers Learned

Our experiences in the last few years have reaffirmed a number of our postulates and made it possible for us to redirect others. In the final part of this chapter, we highlight the four most salient lessons that have been guiding our work for the last 2 years.

Teachers Can Learn to Implement Rigorous, Well-Scaffolded Materials If They Are Offered Coherent Apprenticeship Opportunities. If we offer teachers opportunities to apprentice into new pedagogical practices, there have to be accompanying supporting structures and events that help them practice, reaffirm their implementation, and make them increasingly expert at the new direction. Teachers have gone through what Lortie called "the apprenticeship of observation" (1975; 2002), which he defines as the multiple years of their own schooling when they experienced and absorbed the practices of a transmission-oriented system of teaching and passive learning. Three days of professional development cannot turn around that experience for most. Apprenticeship takes time, good models, practice, support, self and other assessment, and above all, tracking of "the seeds of time" as Mercer (2019) referred to development over time.

Teachers implementing the three units on mythology, pandemics, and street art developed experience in running classes. A pivotal moment in their development occurred when the team decided to ask teachers if they wanted us to teach one of their periods, so that they might observe how instructions for activities are offered and how, even if not all students understand completely what is being done, teachers move on to the next activity. They began to appreciate the advantage spiraling curriculum offers, and they also began to observe that what was not learned deeply by students in the first lesson would be revisited again and again, each time affording students increasing opportunities to learn.

Schools Need to Provide Structures for Teachers to Work and Learn Together That Foster Their Internal Accountability. If schools provide common planning periods for teachers who teach the same class, there has to be some orientation and follow-up to the work. In fact, teams of teachers should coplan and demonstrate and analyze student products to assess quality and determine where to go next. That reciprocal sense of accountability, tied to the vision for the types of learning that everybody is headed to, and a critical analysis of the steps taken to get there, can help—ideally with the assistance of more expert others—strengthen weak aspects. In our experience, nothing motivates teachers more than to learn more deeply about the topics they have to teach and have their students enthusiastically engaged.

However, as we coached the teachers, we saw that they often tried to combine pedagogical concepts and approaches that were fundamentally incommensurable. Given lack of time and understanding, they sought materials that were ready to implement, even if those materials did not logically cohere. They also asked us for additional support. One teacher in an interview said, "When are you going to give us more materials because my students really love these kinds of interactive activities?" As a result, we have included educative notes (Davis et al., 2017) intended to develop teacher expertise, in which we explain the goal of lessons, the Three Moment architecture, the role of tasks as structure and process, and how to understand and respond to student work. These notes are to be read, discussed, and implemented by teachers during their common planning time.

In Education, Less Is More. After reviewing existing curricula, we ascertained that while the invitations suggested for teachers to engage students in substantive activity were lacking, many, in fact, had a broad array of good texts. Our suggestion to teachers is that they do not cover all the texts in a book, but that they work with those that initially speak more to them. If they are excited about working with a text, they will be able to communicate that enthusiasm to their students. Following pedagogical advice, similar to that contained in this volume, they can jointly create activities that are interlinked coherently and that take students into deep discussions and applications of text.

As the old dictum says, less is more. However, that less needs to be substantive, well explored, and should invite students to see literature and other texts both as mirrors to understand themselves better and windows to see, critique, and appreciate the world.

Use Consequential Themes to Organize Units and Essential Questions to Organize Clusters of Units. The more work is interconnected, the more it will make sense to students. Curriculum designed to spiral themes and practices builds in students' depth of understanding, and makes their own apprenticeship into academic work meaningful and easier.

Consequently, we propose units that, for example, address public art from the perspective of four interrelated lessons; use a wide variety of multimodal texts: essays, pictures, videos, and music; and explore from lesson to lesson the same considerations: how we define art, how murals and other public art capture societal perspective, and the like. Figure 11.3 illustrates this organization.

As we looked at the three units, we realized they all addressed the same human experience; thus, we decided to unite them under an essential question, and now propose that ideally teachers organize their lessons along macro concerns that give pedagogical work in the classroom life and intellectual productivity.

The Successful Implementation of Ambitious Curricula Requires Comprehensive Support and Pedagogical Coherence. After an initial introduction to the curriculum, to structures and processes it contains, support does

Figure 11.3. Public Art Unit With Four Lessons

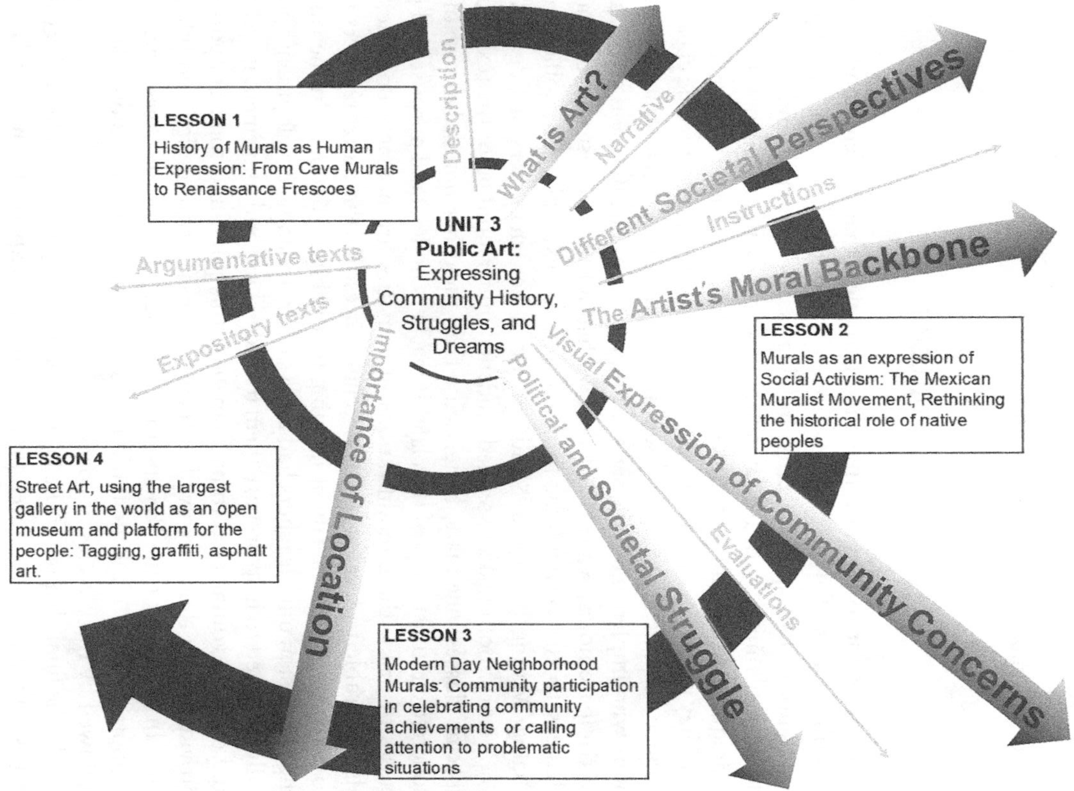

not need to come from the curriculum designers. Working together, teachers can review, plan, and then compare notes on implementation to decide what needs to be refined in the future. In fact, this type of collaboration among teachers is the most productive since it presents them with a domain to be learned (how to teach these units), a set of practices (plan, rehearse, enact, reflect), and the organic building of a community of practice that over time begins to share norms, values, and expertise (Lave & Wenger, 1991).

CONCLUSION

It is important to reiterate that the instruction that students and teachers describe in this chapter did not happen without preparation and support. As mentioned in Chapter 2, scaffolding is both planned and contingent. Iterative planning is ideal to produce best results with students. Each class is unique, and thus adjustments need to be made to tried and true lessons so that they meet the concrete expectations and interests of a specific class. This became very clear during our summer in New York City. When the three of us who implemented the series of units met in the afternoon after classes to compare notes, we realized that we had all made consistent but varied changes to the curriculum. In one class, for example, the Collaborative Dialog Writing became a Mind Mirror of key characters in Edgar Allan Poe's story. Both tasks extended students' understanding of the text, but in specific classes, one made better sense than the other option because of the concrete circumstances of the class. If teachers understand purpose and processes of tasks, these modifications of activities are not only possible, but also desirable to meet students' circumstances. Furthermore, teachers need to be prepared to implement learning that is highly dialogic. In the case of the Persuasion unit, teachers had 2 days of professional development specifically designed to help prepare them to understand and implement it. Schools and districts volunteered to participate in this pilot, and some support was provided from those involved in the broader efforts to design and pilot the unit. In the case of the IES-sponsored cluster of units, teachers were given support prior to implementation through 3 days of professional learning, followed by three cycles of coaching.

In the final chapter of the book (Chapter 12), we conclude by discussing issues surrounding the development of teacher expertise that enables teachers to create and enact the kind of ambitious and supportive instruction discussed in this chapter and throughout the book. That learning for teachers begins as early as the first years of teacher education and extends continuously throughout their careers. Achieving education systems that effectively provide support for continuous development of teaching that enables the success of multilingual (and all) learners requires the involvement and commitment of many in those systems, as we will explore in the next chapter.

ACKNOWLEDGMENTS

Pia Castilleja, Rob Lucas, Lydia Stack, Aída Walqui, and Steven Weiss were instrumental in the implementation of the pilot of the Persuasion unit. The Understanding Language initiative, cochaired by Kenji Hakuta and Maria Santos, was funded by the Carnegie Corporation and the Bill and Melinda Gates Foundation. Understanding Language's ELA Work Group, which included George Bunch, Martha Castellón, Susan Pimentel, Lydia Stack, and Aída Walqui, provided guidance and input throughout the development of the unit. We also wish to acknowledge Rebecca Greene, Eduardo R. Muñoz-Muñoz, and Renae Skarin for their contributions to the data analysis, and the Council of Great City Schools for helping to select the districts that piloted the Persuasion unit. We also wish to thank Dr. Helyn Kim at the Institute of Education Sciences (IES) for her continuing and critical support.

NOTES

1. We have been engaged in this work in different ways. George Bunch chaired the working group that initially invited Aída Walqui and WestEd to produce the unit, and he reviewed several drafts of the unit during its conception. The three first chapter authors contributed to the analysis of the data and the writing of this part of the chapter.

2. This project was conducted as part of the work of the National Center for Research and Development to Improve Education for Secondary English Learners, funded by the Institute of Education Sciences. Grant # R305C200008.

3. The Persuasion unit is available in its entirety on the Understanding Language website, including some videos of class implementation in one of those cities. (https://ul.stanford.edu/resource/persuasion-across-time-and-space-instructional-unit) and classroom vignettes of its implementation can be accessed on the Teaching Channel website (https://www.teachingchannel.com/k12-hub/blog/video-playlist-english-language-learners).

4. During the pilot, we videotaped selected lessons, collected student work, interviewed and surveyed teachers, collected pre- and post-implementation questionnaires, and facilitated student and teacher focus groups. We systematically coded the data using both *a priori* and emerging codes.

5. These units are part of the design and implementation portolio of studies of the National Research and Development Center to Improve Education for Secondary English Learners.

REFERENCES

Bunch, G. C., Walqui, A., & Kibler, A. K. (2015). Attending to language, engaging in practice: Scaffolding English Language Learners' apprenticeship into the Common Core English Language Arts standards. In L. C. De Oliveria, M. Klassen, & M. Maune (Eds.), *The Common Core State Standards in English Language Arts for English Language Learners: Grades 6–12*. TESOL Press.

Davis, E. A., Palinscar, A. S., Smith, P. S., Arias, A. M., & Kademian, S. M. (2017). Educative curriculum materials: Uptake, impact, and implications for research and design. *Educational Researcher. 46*(6), 293–304. https://doi.org/10.3102/0013189X17727502

Jordan, B. (1994, July/August). All together now. *Sesame Street Parents Magazine*.

Kibler, A. K., Walqui, A., & Bunch, G. C. (2015). Transformational opportunities: Language and literacy instruction for English Language Learners in the Common Core era in the United States. *TESOL Journal, 6*(1), 9–35.

Lave, J., & Wenger, E. (1991). *Situated learning: Legitimate peripheral participation*. Cambridge University Press.

Maier, A., Adams, J., Burns, D., Kaul, M., Saunders, M., & Thompson, C. (2020, October 13). *Using performance assessments to support student learning. How district initiatives can make a difference*. Learning Policy Institute. https://learningpolicyinstitute.org/product/cpac-performance-assessments-support-student-learning-brief

Lortie, D. (1975/2002). *Schoolteacher*. University of Chicago Press.

Mercer, N. (2019). The seeds of time. Why classroom dialogue needs a temporal analysis. In N. Mercer, *Language and the joint creation of knowledge: The selected works of Neil Mercer* (Chapter 9). Routledge.

van Lier, L. (2001). Constraints and resources in classroom talk: Issues of equality and symmetry. In C. Candlin & N. Mercer (Eds.), *English language teaching in its social context. A reader*. The Open University & Routledge.

Walqui, A. (2024). The role of curriculum in the development of teacher expertise to enact critical dialogic education. In F. Karam & A. Kibler (Eds.), *Critical dialogic TESOL teacher education: Preparing future advocates and supporters of multilingual learners*. Bloombury Academic.

Walqui, A., Koelsch, N., & Schmida, M. (2012). *Persuasion across time and space: Analyzing and producing complex texts*. Center to Support Excellence in Teaching, Stanford Graduate School of Education. https://ell.stanford.edu/teaching_resources/ela

Walqui, A., & van Lier, L. (2010). *Scaffolding the academic success of adolescent English Language Learners: A pedagogy of promise*. WestEd.

CHAPTER 12

Developing Teacher Expertise to Design Amplified Learning Opportunities for Multilingual Learners

Aída Walqui and George C. Bunch

This book has provided a framework for teachers to design powerful, exciting, and challenging learning opportunities to engage and support multilingual learners (and all students) in the concepts, analysis, and language at the heart of disciplinary inquiry and critical dialogue. We have argued that moving away from *simplification* toward *amplification* as an overarching guiding principle is necessary for recognizing and building on the resources multilingual learners bring with them, for maximizing their immense potential, and for envisioning them as both critical contributors to and beneficiaries of a more equitable, just, and sustainable 21st-century world. We have also shown how amplification enhances, rather than restricts, opportunities for the development of literacies and languages alongside other disciplinary practices and content. We have provided elaborated examples of such designs in various disciplines, in different grade levels, and in two languages. We have walked the reader through the kinds of decisions teachers face when developing lessons and units that follow the proposed tenets, and we have shared teachers' and students' reflections in classrooms where such designs are being used.

However, as is well-known by both teachers and those who work to prepare and support them, designing and implementing high-quality instruction—for any students, but especially for multilingual learners—requires more than access to a rationale, a framework, and examples, no matter how compelling they may be. Accomplished teaching is a remarkably complex achievement—one that teachers need to envision and apprentice into deliberately over extended periods of time. The ability to construct coherent and engaging lessons or units is a necessary component of this teaching expertise, but it is not sufficient for negotiating successful implementation of high-quality instruction in complex classroom environments. Teacher expertise is the knowledge teachers have plus their ability to successfully implement it in situated contexts, a notion that Lee Shulman once described as "the most complex, most challenging, and most demanding, subtle, nuanced, and frightening activity that our species has ever invented" (Shulman, 2004).

The key to teachers' long-term success, for both developing amplified learning designs and implementing them, is supporting the gradual apprenticeship of deep pedagogical expertise as a lifelong activity. In fact, studies demonstrate that when teachers do not have a deep and sophisticated pedagogical understanding, they may unwittingly transform innovative lessons into traditional instruction, maintaining core elements of the very instruction that the design was attempting to transform (Wilson & Berne, 1999). That is, teachers may selectively take up innovative ideas and implement them in shallow or incoherent ways (Coburn & Stein, 2016; Walqui, 2024), or they may adopt only surface-level features of the design and ignore those that are most important to the approach (Spillane & Zeuli, 1999).

And there is evidence that the curricular materials teachers are often provided may be working against efforts to realize the visions laid out in this book. For example, a review of currently used, commercially published English Language Arts materials (Walqui, 2024) reveals that they share seven key limitations:

1. A monolingual and essentialized student audience: School curriculum publishers, in spite of the fact that multilingual learners comprise an increasingly larger proportion of all the student population, still direct textbooks to students who are English-only speakers. Whenever specific notes suggesting how to work with multilingual learners are presented, they assume a monolithic population and recommend simplification.
2. A linear progression: The materials often assume that multilingual—and other—students learn practices once, when they are taught, and thus they do not merit being discussed from a different perspective later on.
3. Extensive and superficial coverage: Many lessons touch on important concepts once, with an abundance of "teaching" points.
4. Lack of academic rigor: When a lesson is rigorous, it focuses on key ideas and interconnections. Students are invited to work collaboratively and critically through several explorations of the theme, and thus what they learn over time becomes generative. In

contrast, available published curricula for the most part present lessons in piecemeal and superficial ways.

5. Activities that promote a transmission-based pedagogy: There is sometimes lip service paid to "have students work in groups," but the materials do not suggest how conversations may be structured so that all students participate and thus they all learn. In most curricula, students are asked to work alone or as a whole class, or to "turn and talk" as if this was the way in which human beings naturally interact.
6. Absence of intellectual challenge matched by high levels of pedagogical support: Curricula ask students to repeat what is on the page, and copy that information, but not to analyze it and use it in critical and creative ways.
7. Focus on language as structure, not as action, as demonstrated throughout this book.

The realization that published materials—no matter how good (and these are few and far between)—need to be modified by teachers to satisfy the needs of their specific classes and students is becoming increasingly evident. Javeria Salman (2024), writing about this topic in the Hechinger Report, quotes Chris Dier, Lousiana teacher of the year in 2020, as saying, "In 14 years of teaching, I have never had a curriculum provided by my school district that I can use without making significant adaptations." Although Mr. Dier did not specifically teach multilingual learners, adaptations are absolutely essential for those who work with these students. Salman adds that many teachers she interviewed commented that curricula weren't especially relevant to students or inclusive of their diversity. The teachers also believed that their materials did not prioritize students' perspectives, ability, and experiences, and that they appeared to be created by those without involvement in current classrooms.

We devote this final chapter, therefore, to exploring the complex nature of the expertise that teachers need to develop over their careers to most effectively design and implement the kind of amplified learning for multilingual learners, and all students, discussed throughout this book. To be clear, however, our message is *not* that only the most accomplished teachers who have undergone years of development have a chance at successfully designing and implementing amplified curriculum. We strongly believe in the power of apprenticeship over time, and such apprenticeship begins with where teachers are right now. Our view is proleptic; it focuses on what teachers will develop, not on what is missing now. So, we begin by offering concrete suggestions for what practicing teachers, regardless of their backgrounds, can do *immediately*, with their colleagues, to leverage and build their collective expertise as they engage in the kind of design we advocate for in this book. We then discuss the nature of the relevant expertise that teachers develop over the course of their careers. We conclude with how those who offer professional development can facilitate the development of this expertise, and what preservice teacher educators can do to help lay the foundation for the development of expertise that will come throughout teachers' careers.

WHAT TEACHERS CAN DO RIGHT NOW

What can teachers themselves do to develop their capacity to design and implement the kinds of learning opportunities introduced in this book? In this section, we provide some immediate guidance for the question most frequently asked by teachers: Where do teachers start, especially if they do not have access to professional development initiatives to help support them? In fact, even teachers who do participate in such initiatives face the moment when the workshop is over and they begin to tackle the hard work of developing and implementing their own learning designs. We paraphrase here high school teachers' responses to a recent professional learning session that Aída conducted as part of the implementation of a replacement 8th-grade curriculum, a component of the portfolio of work the National Research and Development Center to Improve Education for Secondary English Learners program is carrying out, and that is discussed in the prior chapter. We suppose that these sentiments might be shared by other teachers reading this book:

> The lessons, which are part of the three units we are pilot testing are highly motivating for our students. As we engaged in implementing the designs proposed, we ourselves were motivated and engaged. However, as we reflect on the lesson and its deliberate architecture, we see big differences between the proposed curriculum and our regular materials. Our own organization of curriculum is typically framed around individual (one-period) lessons, formulaic standards and objectives, scripted lesson plans, and/or periodic district testing goals. Given these contextual constraints and tensions, *where and how do we begin* to refocus planning and implementation of units and lessons to shift design and instruction to this architecture?

Indeed, this is the predicament in which many teachers find themselves. How do teachers break out of it? Part of the answer is "assertively," "ambitiously," and "holistically"—not in piecemeal ways. Another part is to understand and know how to oppose the status quo, explaining why practices in published materials need to change. Thirdly, we suggest working with a colleague who teaches the same assignment. Working collegially is not only more productive, it also builds community and support. Here, we offer specific suggestions for how teachers, working in collaboration, may proceed based on the conceptual tenets and design principles discussed throughout the book and linked to the model of teacher expertise to be described later in this chapter:

- Start with the end in mind: What conceptual, analytic, and language disciplinary practices do you want your students to begin to develop? Remember that you are not after mastery, but gradual development. What kinds of relevant, interesting, and consequential questions do you want your students to dialogue about?
- Choose texts, problems, or phenomena that represent robust, consequential, and enticing vehicles for the development of proposed practices. Use the overarching theme as an organizer. Read texts carefully and discuss together with colleagues which concepts, analytic practices, and disciplinary language you want your students to practice throughout. Remember that sometimes good texts can be found in bad textbooks, and there is no reason that teachers can't appropriate these texts as part of an amplified curriculum.
- Begin planning the itinerary. This begins by knowing where you are headed. The destination determines the road to be taken from where students find themselves. That, of course, includes understanding who the travelers are. It also includes a clear statement of what they will have accomplished when they reach the destination, albeit in diverse degrees and in different ways.
- Next, it is time to follow the Three Moment Architecture presented in Chapter 3 and used throughout the book. Start by considering how you might *prepare students* so that they are ready to get the most out of the text and goals. Then decide what tasks will help your students *interact with and make sense of the ideas and* text central to the lesson. Then, of course, decide how you will invite students to *extend their understanding* and apply what they learned in novel situations. Throughout, think of engaging students in substantive interactions. This planning is going to take you several hours, but it will offer you a week's work of instruction.
- Share with your fellow designer your reflections on the implementation of the lesson, including which tasks seemed to work well in the design and why, which seemed to create difficulties, and what students' participation and work indicate.

Take notes immediately after implementation, since a semester or a year later, many of your good ideas for improvement may not be as salient as in the moment.

- If you have a supportive principal, ask your principal to substitute for one of you for a couple of periods so you can visit each others' classes. Ideally, reflect together on tasks and other arrangements that will be kept or need to be redesigned.
- Refine the lesson based on your reflections.
- Continue working on your old lesson plans, superimposing on them the three-part lesson architecture and beginning to create spiraled units. You may discover that the texts you use do not support a high challenge/high support design, in which case it is time to replace these texts with rich, complex, alluring ones. Using potent, compelling texts is not only important for students. It is important for you, because if you cannot be excited about what you are teaching, your students will not be enthusiastic about learning.
- A month later, work with your colleague on another lesson, or on the original lesson as part of a larger, spiraled unit that invites your students to deepen and expand practices from other perspectives on the same theme. Follow the same process outlined above. Over a few years, you will have developed your own powerful curriculum. At the same time, you will have strengthened your own expertise to amplify future learning opportunities for English Learners and other students—part of the long-term development of teacher expertise to which we turn next.

THE NATURE OF EXPERTISE IN TEACHING: COMPLEX, INTERSECTING, AND CONTINUOUSLY DEVELOPING DOMAINS OF UNDERSTANDING

As we discussed earlier, teacher expertise entails both the knowledge and dispositions needed to teach plus the ability to translate them into fruitful action. More specifically, efforts to advise, prepare, and support teachers to fulfill the vision of designing the amplified curriculum presented in this book must be based on a clear and coherent understanding of the knowledge and actions that underlie effective teaching. And these efforts must be based on the understanding that effective teaching is always situated in particular disciplines with particular students.

To help both teachers and teacher educators understand the different interrelated components that comprise expertise, we present a model that has been helpful in the Quality Teaching for English Learners (QTEL) initiative as we have engaged in our own work with teachers at various stages of their career

In 1995 Lee Shulman, working on a project that considered what was required to support practicing teachers in communities of learners as they developed their situated expertise, developed a very useful and comprehensive model of teacher understanding. Because Shulman's original model was not specifically developed taking multilingual learners into account, Walqui (1997, 2007) adapted it to consider this important student population. Before proceeding further in describing the adapted model, we want to underscore two foundational notions from Shulman's original proposal: the consideration of teachers as professional lifelong learners, and the belief that this knowledge develops not in isolation, but in community, with the goal that teachers' autonomy, through collaboration and apprenticeship, emerges over time. Readers of this book will recognize important parallels between this conception of teacher development and the tenets regarding student learning introduced in Chapter 2 and illustrated throughout the other chapters. Teachers develop agency as professionals in ways that mirror the development of students' autonomy and agency as learners.

Walqui's adaptation of Shulman's model, as shown in Figure 12.1, presents six interrelated and mutually impacting domains of understanding: vision, motivation, knowledge, reflection, context, and practice, all of which develop, to various degrees, synergistically as a result of preparing to become teachers, and all of which either continue to grow or begin to stagnate during the years of professional practice. As will become apparent, the model is not set up in such a way that simple causal relations can be adduced, such as "first teachers develop motivation and then they craft a vision." Instead, the relationship is envisaged as a complex, dynamic one in which all domains play a crucial role in mutually strengthening or debilitating others, and development is organic rather than linear or modular.

Vision

The domain of vision, essential for teachers to be able to develop learning opportunities that are truly *amplified* for multilingual learners, has two main components. The first is teachers' conceptualization of how capable their students are and who these students can become in the short term (as the result of the course the teacher is teaching), midterm (as a result of their whole schooling), and long term (in their lives as adults in society). The second is teachers' understandings of the types of opportunities students will need to develop that capability, the learning activities they need to be invited into to keep growing. Teachers need to envision what optimal learning with

Figure 12.1. A Model of Teacher Understanding

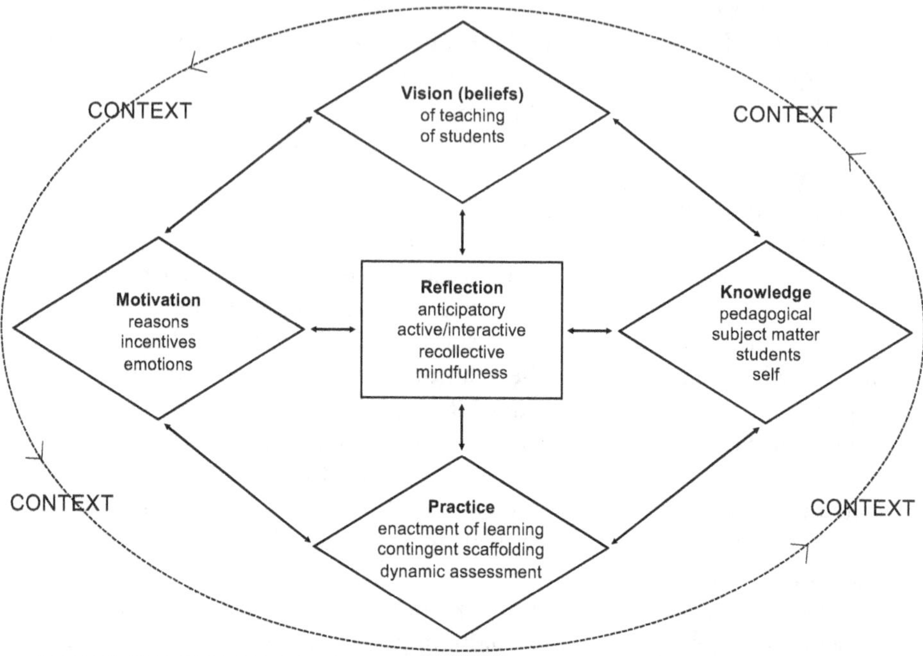

Source: Walqui (1997), adapted from Schulman (1995).

their students consists of, they need to understand that underlying that conceptualization are tenets of learning (discussed in Chapter 2) and lesson and task design (unpacked in Chapter 3). This vision includes a recognition that building what has not grown in students yet is the result of teachers' increasingly professional and intentional work. As we saw in Chapter 11, sometimes that vision derives from the assistance of others modeling the types of instruction that are being promoted, a role that instructional coaches can perform when there is an established and respectful collaboration between teachers and coach.

Motivation

Of course, to do the work we are proposing teachers do with multilingual learners, motivation is essential as well. This domain is composed of the reasons teachers go into teaching and remain in the field, and the incentives they derive as they carry out their work. As with the others, motivation is not a fixed domain, one that teachers have or do not have. Motivation is enhanced or diminished as a result of professional trajectories. At the beginning of their educational studies, most teacher candidates motivated to become teachers are moved by one or more reasons: their passion for a particular content area; positive experiences working with children and youth as tutors, coaches, or babysitters; a desire to make a difference in the lives of young people; and commitment to contributing to a more equitable and just world. These reasons can also include being inspired by good teachers in their own schooling who had a big impact in their lives or, on the other hand, their frustration with the lack of such teachers in their past.

As they begin their teaching, experiences at work strengthen or debilitate their motivation. For example, when teachers have the opportunity to work alongside colleagues in the design of lessons, to share experiences and student artifacts resulting from their enacted plans, and to focus on what worked or didn't work in order to improve future lessons, they find that these interactions strengthen their desire to teach. These opportunities also enhance teachers' joy in working with colleagues productively and develop teachers' professionalism. On the other hand, if teachers work in an environment where they are left on their own, behind closed doors, afraid to share experiences or worried that asking for help might signal a personal weakness, then their initial motivation will be eroded. Multiple other factors affect motivation, such as what teachers see as excessive emphasis given to testing that uses valuable time on preparing students for tests instead of engaging them in interesting subject-specific activity. Mandated pacing, with strict adherence to superficial lesson plans, is equally demotivating.

Knowledge

Shulman (1986) distinguished three areas of teacher knowledge, all central to the design and implementation of successful learning opportunities: subject-matter knowledge, general pedagogical knowledge, and pedagogical subject-matter knowledge (which he also referred to as pedagogical content knowledge). From the perspective of working with students classified as English Learners, Walqui added three other crucial components: knowledge of English Learners, pedagogical language knowledge (teachers' understanding of the role of language in teaching and learning), and knowledge of self. We discuss each of these components briefly.

Subject-Matter Knowledge. Teachers need deep understanding of the subject matter they teach when designing and implementing curriculum for multilingual learners. They need to know what it is about a particular concept, theme, or text that is essential and consequently needs to be focused on, and what, although interesting and valuable, is not indispensable for students who may be learning English to grasp during a first learning encounter. When they guide students in simultaneously developing conceptual understandings, analytic, and language practices, teachers need to know how to streamline these in order to focus on the most generative, productive ones first. Teachers also need to understand which key conceptual relationships students will be initially invited to work with as they develop their knowledge of the discipline, and which others will be built later on as the curriculum spirals to revisit, deepen, and expand concepts. Once again, knowledge of the discipline—while essential—is not a fixed state, nor something that is acquired exclusively before or during preservice education. In addition to teachers' own ongoing personal explorations and development of their content knowledge, opportunities to design lessons or units, whether introduced in preservice teacher education programs or further developed once teachers have their own classrooms, serve as opportunities to deepen subject-matter understanding.

Pedagogical Knowledge. This kind of knowledge refers to general ideas about how to invite students into learning opportunities. Pedagogical knowledge can include the architecture of lessons, the role of tasks, how to structure units of study, and the importance of providing students with substantive opportunities to talk, ask each other questions, and respond to interlocutors' ideas. It can also include teachers' knowledge of the value of wait time, the notion of scaffolding, and the types of scaffolding that exist for different purposes. All these ideas are important for teachers, but, as we will discuss next, they need to be implemented in specific classes with concrete and unique groups of students.

Knowledge of Students. Growing knowledge of the students, including multilingual learners, who are going to be the agents of learning in the classroom is equally important when designing opportunities to learn. In the same way in which a master tailor does not cut and sew a suit destined for a person without knowing and measuring the future owner to determine what may both suit and fit them, lessons are designed to suit and fit the learning needs of specific students. Various kinds of knowledge are critical to creating learning environments and lessons that are equitable and that invite and support every student to grow. These include knowledge of who the specific students in a class are, how they learn, what topics attract them, what they find enticing, how much English they know at the moment, where they seem to be progressing well, where growth needs to be scaffolded, and what barriers they may have to overcome (e.g., being painfully shy). This knowledge, which begins to develop in preservice programs (e.g., through reflection and discussion on readings as well as candidates' own case studies of students that can be tied to teachers' visions and motivation), is ultimately derived from teachers' keen observation in the classroom as students engage in activity. It certainly goes beyond students' test scores, since these scores may actually obscure what students are capable of accomplishing. In fact, during the lessons we have proposed in this book, whenever students are actively learning with each other, it is possible for teachers to observe students (rotating their focus as needed) to take notes that will later be useful during their lesson design. After all, as we established in Chapters 2 and 3, a lesson needs to be placed beyond students' ability to work on their own in order to spur their growth, and the support offered varies as students' self-regulation continuously expands.

Knowledge of students includes developing dynamic answers for questions such as the following: Why do particular students react the way they do? How should teachers deal with oppositional responses from students? What should teachers do when they are tempted to give up their high expectations and design simpler lessons for their students? How are students developing, and how are they different than when they first entered the classroom?

Pedagogical Language Knowledge. Galguera (2011) proposed this important component of teacher expertise, which was later elaborated by Bunch (2013, 2022), to refer to teachers' knowledge of the role of language in teaching and learning in the various subject areas. Such knowledge includes, for example, how to structure learning activities that invite students to experience and unpack how explanations work in history or in science, what their purposes are in the different disciplines, and what general organization different kinds of disciplinary explanatory texts tend to follow. The notion of *pedagogical* language knowledge challenges the idea that content-area teachers need to "teach English" in didactic and atomistic ways, whether for multilingual learners or any other students. For example, we disagree with current proposals that lessons for students classified as English Learners should start with the presentation of lists of vocabulary items (the "front-loading" of vocabulary) contained in the lesson. While explicit focus on vocabulary can be helpful at various points in teaching content-area lessons (including sometimes early on), it must always be approached in ways that support rather than curtail English Learners from developing larger and more important understandings of language. (For example, during an Anticipatory Guide, key terms students do not know may be introduced in context.) Language is a way of acting in the world, and as such, *what is accomplished by using it* needs to be the entry point for explorations of language.

Pedagogical Subject-Matter Knowledge. This area comprises the knowledge of how to build disciplinary understandings for all students in a class, emphasizing, especially for multilingual learners, how key ideas are advanced in specific types of text in English, while ensuring throughout that all learners are being challenged and supported. The chapters in this book illustrate this process in diverse subject-matter areas. It stands to reason that although subject-matter and general pedagogical knowledge begin to develop in preservice education, pedagogical subject-matter knowledge unfolds as a result of practice, deep self-knowledge, and constant reflection.

Self-Knowledge. An often-neglected aspect of teacher knowledge, one not usually associated with curriculum development, is *knowledge of self*. To envision and enact successful learning designs, teachers need to understand and consider themselves as simultaneously knowledgeable and in the process of learning. It is not possible for any teacher to know everything they need to know at any moment of teaching, but it is important for them to prepare with their best current knowledge for most every teaching event, and to keep their eyes open so they can learn from observing their students. Teachers also need to have a sense of humor about their own limitations and model for students the practices to repair whatever did not work optimally in a lesson. We often hear from students that they appreciate teachers saying, "I really do not know the answer to that question, but I will find out and report on it later on," and then coming back at a later point with a response. For students, it constitutes an example both of intellectual integrity and curiosity on behalf of their teachers.

Reflection

The domain of reflection for teachers is most typically considered an area of expertise that involves reviewing their teaching to identify what succeeded and what didn't—as a way of improving and refining lessons for individuals or for groups of students. This looking into the past to learn for the future has been part of educational theory since Dewey (1925) and, following van Manen (1991), we call it *recollective reflection*. Van Manen proposed three other types of reflection that are especially useful and that Walqui (1997) added to Shulman's model. *Anticipatory reflection*, directly related to design, refers to the deliberation among alternatives that teachers engage in as they select future pedagogical courses of action. Van Manen adds two other types of reflection to teachers' deliberations. One, related to enactment, is the deliberation that teachers engage in contingently as the lesson is proceeding. As teachers observe how invitations to engage in action are being interpreted by students, "on their feet" they contemplate appropriate additions or deletions to their original plan. This essential component of any good teaching is *interactive reflection*. It makes teaching contingent, responsive to the moment and to students' evolving needs. In current educational formulations, this reflection is called Formative or Dynamic Assessment (Grapin & Llosa, 2022; Heritage et al., 2015).

Finally, van Manen (1991) introduces the concept of *Mindfulness*, which refers to the ability to exploit the pedagogical moment, to act thoughtfully, to have "pedagogical tact" in less intentional ways than in interactive reflection. We could say that the cumulative goal of reflective activity in the classroom is to arrive at teachers' developing pedagogical tact, where their vast knowledge, built on constant reflection of practice, has led them to develop a presence of mind that leads them to do the right thing at the right moment in a class. In our model, reflection is at the center of all other domains because it is the engine that drives teacher expertise.

Context

That context matters for teachers is almost self-evident, especially now, when as discussed in Chapter 1, standards, accountability, and testing are an ever-present reality. The COVID-19 pandemic introduced a number of new tensions in schools, as virtual lessons for part of the year gave way to the generalized use of computers in classrooms. If face-to-face student interaction was difficult before to orchestrate, today the presence of electronic devices in class makes eye contact and kinesics more effortful than it used to be. Knowledge of the context is essential because it helps teachers anticipate possible barriers in class and prepare to dismantle them. Contextual knowledge entails the norms of society, requirements by school authorities, new educational mandates, new curricula, conflicts in the surrounding environment—and how to navigate them for the ultimate benefit of all students, with multilingual learners at the center of our focus.

The contexts within which teachers operate are especially important to consider in the development of their expertise. Beginning with the school, and moving beyond to the district, state, and national policy mandates, all these arenas of decision-making impact teacher expertise. For example, Walqui (2000) studied high school contexts that supported the intellectual, moral, and civic growth of multilingual learners. In one of the schools highlighted, The International High School at La Guardia Community College in New York City, the care invested in the building of productive contexts was exemplary. Teachers worked in cohorts that taught the same two groups of students for 2 years. Time was created during the school day for teams of teachers to collaborate with each other. Teams of teachers hired new colleagues and supported and assessed them. The universal definition of the principal by teachers was "he is a buffer for us"—meaning that he fought the necessary fights, such as creating time, to support teachers' work in the service of their students. Such a context promotes the development of teacher expertise, and educators need to see how to recreate it in their own venues.

Practice

We address teacher practice as the last domain in teacher expertise because knowledge alone does not a good teacher make. Expertise resides in the artful enactment of knowledge in classrooms that becomes the mark of a good teacher. Practice is the one domain that cannot be developed in isolation. Coaching, or what Latin Americans call "el acompañamiento de maestros" (accompanying teachers), is indispensable. Coaching represents opportunities for teachers to enact a lesson that has been either designed jointly by teacher and coach, or at least discussed by coach and teacher prior to implementation and observation. Coaches and teachers need to share a common understanding of how students learn, of lesson goals, lesson design, and the appropriateness of tasks. Only then can coaches serve as mirrors for teachers, helping them see what is working according to plan and what needs to be refined. Over time, teachers appropriate the stances of coaches, and, like accomplished ballerinas, can practice and use imaginary, internalized mirrors to enhance their implementation.

Often a good lesson design can go wrong during its implementation because certain aspects of the lesson have not been completely understood, and a teacher may not observe the confusion and frustration building up in some students and be able to respond contingently. As a result, good designs are derailed or misinterpreted (Anderson, 2017; Coburn, 2003). Vision, motivation, knowledge, and reflection are all required to offer real students in a specific class powerful learning opportunities that build on what they know to push and support their development. The never-ending process of planning, enacting, reflecting, and redesigning, along with the evolving expertise of teachers, enriches the lives of students as well as teachers' own professional lives.

SUGGESTIONS FOR PROFESSIONAL DEVELOPMENT AND TEACHER PREPARATION

How might teachers at various stages—not only along their journeys as teachers but also in terms of their experience with the concepts discussed in this book—be supported in developing the knowledge, dispositions, and teaching practices described in this chapter? We first discuss what those who engage with teachers in professional development initiatives can do to support the development of teachers' expertise. We then address what can be done in preservice teacher education programs to lay the groundwork for the development of teachers who will be able to amplify instruction for English Learners in the ways we have discussed.

Guidance for Professional Development

Professional Development for Groups of Teachers During Workshops or Institutes. When groups of teachers enroll in professional development sessions, they deserve the best professional experience, one that honors their interest to grow, recognizing where their points of departure are. Then, in planned and contingent ways, ideas and practices can be modeled and debriefed. During professional development sessions, teachers need to participate *as students* and then reflect *as teachers* on the lesson enacted. Teachers also apprentice and apprenticeship occurs through modeling, planned and contingent support, and anticipatory and recollective reflection. A survey was given to teachers who participated in a 4-day consecutive institute in San Antonio led by Aída on how to design and enact quality learning opportunities for multilingual learners. Two teachers' comments represent participants' general feeling that theory is important for their craft:

> It was awesome. We got to actually participate, experience, and analyze the activities . . . extremely well modeled, justified, and implemented strategies. I also enjoyed the fact that we planned activities and lessons for when we go back to school . . . understanding theory helped my excitement to implement.

> A good combination of theory, explaining why certain processes and activities work in learning content through a second language, implementation of those activities . . . analysis of structures and processes are the ingredients of a good professional development.

Ongoing Professional Development at the School Site. Many schools have sponsored professional learning communities (PLCs), groups of teachers who jointly study problems of practice in their context and propose solutions. Practicing teachers take real-life issues and questions of immediate importance to PLCs. Often, they want to know how they can improve their practice—and their lessons for tomorrow. While honoring and responding to these needs, those designing professional development initiatives also must attend to the fact that the future is most productively built thoughtfully and gradually as well as tooled with the best understanding. However, sometimes the goals of the professional learning opportunity are not met. With that tension in mind, we offer a few guidelines for professional developers as they guide teacher learning sessions on lesson design based on the QTEL team's extensive experience working with teachers.

- Before tackling lesson design, teachers need to experience and analyze lessons that model the structures and processes proposed in this book. This mirrors children taking ballet lessons, who need to have an idea of what accomplished ballet dancing is before they engage in the exercises that will eventually lead them to apprentice into ballet dancing. Good educative materials that both model and discuss purposeful lesson architecture and decision points made along the way are essential in this task of creating visions of good lessons and their components.
- It is helpful if professional developers, hopefully developing deep disciplinary expertise themselves, work with subject-specific groups of teachers. In this way the work, including analyzing the conceptual, analytic, and language practices at the heart of each discipline, can be carried out with the whole group and with teams of two or four. These teams work on the same lesson, albeit bringing their own choices and creativity to the lesson within the same pedagogical parameters. An advantage of this approach is that the professional developer can have groups compare their proposed lessons, drawing generalizations that would be appropriate for the whole group.
- Once teachers select objectives for the lesson, choose standards, and have a clear idea of where the lesson is headed, what follows is the decision of which text or texts (written, electronic, pictorial, etc.) will be used. Not every team needs to use the same texts; in fact, it is quite productive to get to the same pedagogical destination via alternative lesson routes.
- Next comes the analysis of the text, a central endeavor for good lesson design. Aída likes to call this part of lesson planning during teacher professional learning "x-raying the text." The point is to read the short story, essay, novel, and so on, and decide what core ideas (the backbone) and relationships (the system and interrelationships, how key bones connect and articulate to give movement to the body) the text presents to then select which ones the lesson will seek to invite students to understand. As discussed throughout this book, not all information presented in a text merits being the focus of a first encounter with the text, but if that first encounter makes the work rewarding for students, chances are that when they have an opportunity in the future, they will revisit the

text. In our experience, teachers enjoy the opportunity to discuss with peers which ideas they find essential in selected texts and the rationale for their choice. It is advisable that teachers read texts prior to the session and come ready to review their notes and begin the collaborative work.

- After that, teachers need to decide how students will demonstrate what they have been able to develop through the lesson, the culminating task. For example, Ms. Glick's students wrote essays about their research of Youth in Prison, calling attention to reasons, processes, and possible solutions to the situation. Because this exercise was going to be exhibited, students were especially careful that their work met the highest standards. Demonstrations, in their multiple formats, not only provide students with one more opportunity to present what they learned, but they strengthen student agency and voice.
- Then it is time to revisit—and perhaps readjust—the objectives of the lesson, refining initial work and agreeing on what conceptual (ideas), analytic (the operations ideas will be put through), and language practices constitute the chosen lesson objectives.
- Design teams of teachers present their lessons, discussing the rationale for their choices. As they listen to each other, teams take notes about specific task choices they like and can replace tasks in their lessons.

Laying the Foundation in Teacher Preparation Programs

What can preservice teacher educators do to begin to lay the groundwork for developing the knowledge, dispositions, and practices needed to create amplified learning opportunities for multilingual learners and other students? One answer, of course, is to provide novice teachers with authentic, supported contexts to do the kind of lesson planning and enactment—with real students in real classrooms—advocated for in this book. This is possible when multiple aspects of the teacher education program are aligned. Ideally, teacher candidates have access to student-teaching placements where the regular classroom teachers themselves have developed such understandings and practices—or at least are open to the student teachers' designing and implementing amplified lessons. Also ideal are programs where other important elements of the teacher preparation program (coursework, field supervision, teacher evaluation mechanisms) are aligned enough so as not to send mixed messages to candidates. Unfortunately, given the challenges facing teacher preparation programs, including the multitude of "moving parts" influenced by a wide range of conceptual, pedagogical, financial, and political factors, true alignment throughout a candidate's teacher preparation program is difficult to achieve.

These limitations do not mean, however, that individual teacher educators cannot introduce teacher candidates to important ideas relevant to amplifying instruction for multilingual learners. Indeed, it is possible to have these candidates engage in activities that will make those ideas "come alive" in ways directly related to their development of the elements of professional practice described above. After some initial introduction to the rationale, conceptual grounding, and design architecture for amplified instruction, courses in teacher preparation programs can incorporate many of the approaches described in the professional development section above. These courses can ask candidates to analyze and discuss model lessons such as those presented in this book; meet in disciplinary teams to discuss the target disciplinary practices embodied in those lessons or others they observe in their fieldwork (or, less ideally, the "counter-examples" they observe); and, with the support of classmates and the instructor, begin to design their own lesson (hypothetical or real, depending on the context). Given the limited real-world experience most teacher candidates initially have in designing or implementing *any* lessons, what teachers produce and how they reflect upon it will obviously differ from the lessons and reflections of more experienced teachers. But such "approximations of practice" can provide important contexts for further reflection and development of practice that amplifies learning opportunities for multilingual learners (James, 2024).

One advantage teacher preparation programs have in terms of the model of teacher expertise presented earlier in this chapter is the time and space they have to engage teachers in the *reflection* that is at the center of the model and connected to the other domains. Teacher preparation coursework, and mentoring in student teaching classrooms, can provide spaces for novice teachers to reflect on the *knowledge* they are developing and the *practice* they are observing and beginning to engage in themselves. Teacher educators can also provide opportunities for those entering the profession to reflect on their *motivation* and *vision*, including teachers' own upbringing and education, the reasons they decided to become teachers, differences between the ways that they were taught and the teaching practices to which they are being introduced, and the implications of teaching students who may be different from themselves in multiple and significant ways. Increasingly, teacher preparation programs, either on their own or because of state requirements, include courses on multilingual learners that can develop teachers' knowledge of the range of backgrounds, characteristics, strengths, and needs of students from multilingual backgrounds, as well as to help teachers understand the need for support for these students while simultaneously challenging them to amplify rather than simplify learning opportunities.

Courses focused on multilingual learners can also introduce practices that are central to amplifying the curriculum. For example, George has developed an assignment in one such course to introduce teachers to the notion of scaffolding—a key component of designing the kinds of lessons described in this book. The course is designed for secondary teacher candidates in various content areas who are in early stages of their yearlong combined master's and teacher credential program. The course comes early in the program year, when candidates have just begun to spend time in their student teaching placements, observing their cooperating classroom teachers, and beginning to participate marginally in instruction (working with individual or small groups of students or perhaps teaching part of one of the cooperating teacher's lessons).

After reading an introduction to scaffolding (Walqui & van Lier, 2010) that is consistent with our discussion of the concept in Chapters 2 and 3 and the examples throughout this book, students are asked to discuss how the reading challenged their previous notions of "scaffolding." Invariably, candidates discuss having heard the term used ubiquitously during their previous coursework but primarily as a synonym for the general concept of "help" (Bunch & Lang, 2023). Examples they provide of what they have heard called "scaffolding" thus include using visual cues to help English Learners' comprehension (e.g., writing things on the board or using pictures or graphic representations), "frontloading" or "preteaching" key vocabulary terms, providing students with sentence frames for writing products, or providing clear instructions and examples before asking students to complete assignments by themselves. In class, we discuss the fact that each of these may provide some basic support for English Learners. However, by themselves, none of them represent *scaffolding* in the service of amplification as described by Walqui and van Lier (2010) and as elaborated upon in this book.

After discussion of the reading and viewing videos of some compelling examples from practice similar to those featured in this book, candidates are asked to work together in small groups over several weeks to design an activity for multilingual learners to engage in disciplinary practices valued in the target content area—and to either teach and record it in one of their "real" student teaching placements (not feasible in all cases), or to lead our class in a simulation of the activity. After students show their video or conduct their simulation, we discuss as a class the structures and processes observed, the planned and unpredictable aspects of the activity, and what might be done in future iterations to improve the activity. Candidates complete the assignment by writing an individual reflection on the goals of their activity, the elements of scaffolding it entailed, and learnings that they might take with them for future planning.

We also discuss the fact that the assignment itself is designed to model key aspects of the vision of scaffolding that we are trying to help candidates develop and enact. For example, the assignment provides a clear structure (the requirement to work in small groups to design and teach a learning activity, clear evaluation criteria, etc.). It is designed to lead to unpredictable outcomes (the activities that each group ultimately designs and presents). It also provides opportunities for various kinds of contingent supports along the way: as candidates of relatively equal strength work through their ideas together, groups check in and receive suggestions from the instructor as they develop their plans, and students receive feedback from their classmates and the instructor after they implement their activity. We also discuss that the assignment models the kind of "handover" from the teacher and "takeover" by the students that ultimately moves toward student autonomy.

As might be expected with novice teachers who have not yet even begun to do any independent student teaching, the quality of the designs produced is varied, as is the extent to which they represent the intended understanding of scaffolding. But part of the learning is in reflecting on what didn't quite work and engaging in discussions on how the activity could be redesigned to better match the key elements of scaffolding we are emphasizing. An examination of preservice teachers' writing after completing the learning activities showed that most candidates discussed agency and autonomy as goals of scaffolding, described interactive structures as key components of scaffolding, and highlighted the importance of creating tasks that ask students to engage in tasks with open-ended, unpredictable outcomes (Bunch & Lang, 2023).

Another option, to be implemented either in conjunction with or instead of the example provided here, would be to ask teacher candidates to carefully observe, over time, the classes they are working with, recording examples of various kinds of student support and identifying the presence or absence of the elements of scaffolding proposed by Walqui and van Lier (2010). Such an activity could also be scaffolded for teacher candidates, so that they see models of how the instructor would conduct such an observation, do the observations in pairs or small groups so as to benefit from working with peers of various strengths, and move toward independent, autonomous observations by the end of the quarter. Whichever version is implemented, these examples show how the notion of "scaffolding" can itself be scaffolded; that is, how one of the key conceptual foundations necessary for the kind of lesson and unit development portrayed in this book can begin to be laid, albeit in modest ways, even in the earliest stages of teachers' journeys.

CONCLUSION

As we conclude this chapter and the book as a whole, we acknowledge that there is still much more to be said regarding how to best prepare and support *all* teachers to transform their practice from *simplification* toward *amplification* as the guiding principle, for the education of both multilingual learners and other students. For example, as we have noted but not had the space to fully address, schools, teacher preparation programs, and inservice professional development initiatives can all be better structured to create optimal conditions for teachers—throughout their careers—to develop the expertise necessary to do the difficult work discussed throughout this book. Structuring schools so that they become true communities of practitioners is essential, but unfortunately beyond our scope. And further research is necessary to better understand the promise, possibilities, and challenges in preparing teachers to design instruction with amplification as its goal. Nevertheless, we trust we have offered enough guidance for teachers to begin the ambitious work of designing learning opportunities of the highest quality for multilingual learners. We also believe we have offered productive suggestions for those involved in teacher preparation and professional development to support teachers in this work throughout their careers. Amplifying the curriculum is not easy, but the enormous potential that multilingual learners offer, both for their own development and for their contributions to solving our collective challenges, make these efforts both absolutely essential and eternally rewarding.

REFERENCES

Anderson, E. R. (2017). Accommodating change. Relating fidelity of implementation to program fit in educational reform. *American Educational Research Journal, 54*(6), 1288–1315.

Bunch, G. C. (2013). Pedagogical language knowledge: Preparing mainstream teachers for English Learners in the new standards era. *Review of Research in Education, 37*, 298–341.

Bunch, G. C. (2022). What do we mean by "language"? And other key questions related to building a language-related knowledge base for teachers. In L. H. Seah, R. E. Silver, & M. C. Baildon (Eds.), *The role of language in content pedagogy: A framework for teachers' knowledge.* Springer. https://doi.org/10.1007/978-981-19-5351-4_12

Bunch, G. C., & Lang, N. W. (2023). Scaffolding "scaffolding" in pre-service teacher education. In L. C. de Oliveira & R. Westerlund (Eds.) *Scaffolding for multilingual learners in elementary and secondary schools* (Chapter 13). Routledge. http://doi.org/10.4324/9781003196228-16

Coburn, C. (2003). Rethinking scale. Moving beyond numbers to deep and lasting change. *Educational Researcher, 32*(6), 3–12.

Coburn, C., & Stein, M. K. (2016). Key lessons about the relationship between research and practice. In C. Coburn & M. K. Stein (Eds.), *Research and practice in education: Building alliances, bridging the divide.* Rowman & Littlefield.

Dewey, J. (1925). Experience and nature. In J. A. Boydston (Ed.), *John Dewey: The later works, 1925–1953* (Vol. 1). Southern University Press.

Galguera, T. (2011). Participant structures as professional learning tasks and the development of pedagogical language knowledge among preservice teachers. *Teacher Education Quarterly, 38*(1), 85–106.

Grapin, S., & Llosa, L. (2022). Dynamic assessment of English Learners in the content areas: An exploratory study in 5th grade science. *TESOL Quarterly*, *56*(1), 201–219.

Heritage, M., Walqui, A., & Linquanti, R. (2015). *English Language Learners and the new standards: Developing language, content knowledge, and analytical practices in the classroom.* Harvard Education Press.

James, B. M. (2024). *"Collaboration, It's for the kids and for us": Pre-Service teachers' shifting orientations to language and scaffolding in collaborative video analysis* [Doctoral dissertation, University of California, Santa Cruz]. ProQuest Dissertation & Theses Global.

Salman, J. (2024, July 23). *Should teachers customize their lessons or stick to the 'script'?* The Hechinger Report. https://hechingerreport.org/should-teachers-customize-their-lessons-or-just-stick-to-the-script/

Shulman, L. S. (1986). Those who understand: Knowledge growth in teaching. *Educational Researcher, 15*(2), 4–14.

Shulman, L. S. (2004). *The wisdom of practice: Essays on teaching, learning, and learning to teach.* Jossey-Bass.

Shulman, L. S., & Associates. (1995). *Fostering a community of teachers and learners* [Unpublished progress report]. Mellon Foundation.

Spillane, J. P., & Zeuli, J. S. (1999). Reform and teaching: Exploring patterns of practice in the context of national and state mathematics reform. *Educational Evaluation and Policy Analysis, 21*(1), 1–27.

van Manen, M. (1991). Reflectivity and the pedagogical moment: The normativity of pedagogical thinking and acting. *Journal of Curriculum Studies, 23*(6), 507–536.

Walqui, A. (1997). *The development of teacher understanding. Inservice professional growth for teachers of English language learners* [Unpublished doctoral dissertation]. Stanford University.

Walqui, A. (2000). *Access and engagement: Program design and instructional approaches for immigrant students in secondary school.* Center for Applied Linguistics and Delta Systems.

Walqui, A. (2007). The development of teacher expertise to work with adolescent English Learners: A model and a few priorities. In L. Verplaetse & N. Migliacci (Eds.), *Inclusive pedagogy for English Language Learners* (pp. 107–129). Lawrence Erlbaum Associates.

Walqui, A. (2024). The role of curriculum in the development of teacher expertise to enact critical dialogic education. In F. Karam & A. Kibler (Eds.), *Critical dialogic TESOL teacher education: Preparing future advocates and supporters of multilingual learners*. Bloomsbury Academic.

Walqui, A., & van Lier, L. (2010). *Scaffolding the academic success of adolescent English language learners: A pedagogy of promise.* WestEd.

Wilson, S., & Berne, J. (1999). Teacher learning and the acquisition of professional knowledge: An examination of research on contemporary professional development. *Review of Research on Education, 24,* 173–209.

Index

Italiicized page numbers indcate text in Spanish.

About the Editors and Contributors

Aída Walqui directs the National Research and Development Center for Improving the Education of Secondary English Learners funded by the Institute of Education Sciences and housed at WestEd. There she started the Quality Teaching for English Learners (QTEL) Initiative focused on the development of teachers and educational leaders' expertise to support elementary and secondary English Learners' conceptual, analytic, and language practices in disciplinary subject-matter areas. Walqui taught in elementary and high schools, and in the Education Department at the University of California, Santa Cruz, and at the Stanford University School of Education, as well as in universities in Perú, Mexico, and the UK. A native Peruvian, she received an MS in Sociolinguistics from Georgetown University, and her PhD in Language, Literacy, and Culture from Stanford University. Throughout her long and productive career, Walqui's work has been funded by the MacArthur, Spencer, and Hewlett foundations as well as many others. Walqui is the author of multiple articles and several books including *Scaffolding the Academic Success of Adolescent English Language Learners: A Pedagogy of Promise; English Language Learners and the New Standards: Developing Language, Content Knowledge, and Analytical Practices in the Classroom;* and the recently coedited volumes *Reconceptualizing the Role of Critical Dialogue in American Classrooms* and *Equity in Multilingual Schools and Communities.*

George C. Bunch is professor of education and department chair at the University of California, Santa Cruz. An experienced K–12 teacher and teacher educator, he holds a PhD in Educational Linguistics from Stanford University and an MA in bilingual education and TESOL from the University of Maryland Baltimore County. His research, focusing on curricula, policies, and teacher preparation initiatives designed to serve multilingual learners in K–12 and higher education, has been funded by the Institute of Education Sciences, the National Science Foundation, the Spencer Foundation, the Hewlett Foundation, and multiple University of California research initiatives. He was a founding partner of the Understanding Language Initiative and received a Spencer Foundation midcareer grant to serve as a visiting scholar at the Carnegie Foundation for the Advancement of Teaching. He is a former National Academy of Education/Spencer Postdoctoral Fellow and a recipient of the Midcareer Award from the Second Language Research Special Interest Group of the American Educational Research Association.

Peggy Mueller is a lifelong educator who has supported efforts to achieve quality education for all for more than 50 years in multiple capacities: elementary, secondary, and college teaching; teacher preparation for urban teaching; education philanthropy; policy and research; curriculum development; and professional development. Most recently she worked with Quality Teaching for English Learners (QTEL) as a senior policy associate at WestEd and prior to that as senior program officer in education at The Chicago Community Trust for 17 years, program officer at The Spencer Foundation for 6 years, and teacher education coordinator for the Urban Education Program of the Associated Colleges of the Midwest for 16 years. Peggy holds a doctoral degree in Administration, Planning and Social Policy (Harvard University Graduate School of Education) and graduate degrees in Curriculum and Philosophy of Education (University of Illinois Chicago), Administration and Policy (Harvard University Graduate School of Education), and Human Development (Governors State University). She has coauthored curriculum publications supported by Fulbright and U.S. Japan Foundation grants and led teacher groups on Fulbright study seminars in India. Her most recent publication includes with Aída Walqui: "Language Education Policy and Practice in the U.S.: Emerging Efforts to Expand All Teachers' Understanding About Language Development and Learning" in *Language Policy and Language Acquisition Planning,* M. Siiner, F. Hult, & T. Kupisch, Eds. (2018).

Elsa Billings is a senior program associate at WestEd, where she works with schools, districts, and state and federal agencies to deepen the expertise and capacity of educators to improve the educational equity, access, and success of multilingual learners. Prior to joining WestEd, Billings was a coadvisor for the Council of Chief State School Officers' English Learner Collaborative; served as a professor in the College of Education at San Diego State University; and was a consultant for Stanford University's Understanding Language. She started her career as a preschool teacher before becoming a bilingual elementary teacher. Billings has earned a PhD in Language, Learning, and Policy from Stanford University, in addition to an MA in Language, Literacy, and Culture and an MA in Policy Analysis and Program Evaluation with a minor in Organizational Behavior, also from Stanford University.

Haiwen Chu is a research director for English Learner and Migrant Education Services at WestEd. Chu serves as coinvestigator of the Reimagining and Amplifying Mathematics Participation, Understanding, and Practices (RAMP-UP) Study, part of the portfolio of the National Research and Development Center to Improve Education for Secondary English Learners, funded by the Institute of Education Sciences. His work draws upon his experience teaching recent immigrants high school mathematics and integrating language development with curriculum design. He designs and conducts mixed methods research in partnership with districts to improve policy, programs, and praxis for English Learners. He holds a PhD in Urban Education Policy from the City University of New York Graduate Center.

Shirley Feldman is a senior program manager with English Learner and Migrant Education Services at WestEd. Ms. Feldman supports educators of English Learners through professional development, classroom coaching, and curriculum design. She leads professional development institutes for teachers and their support in practice so that they develop situated expertise to work with multilingual learners to simultaneously develop content knowledge, analytic, and discipline-specific language practices. She also designs curriculum that is used in classrooms to engage students in rigorous, challenging, and well-supported work as they develop their oracy skills and multiliteracies working in collaboration. Ms. Feldman is also a researcher on the English Language Arts team for the National Research and Development Center to Improve Education for Secondary English Learners housed at WestEd and is currently working on research on the impacts of teacher and student educative curricula for classified Long-Term English Learners in middle school.

Viviana Galdames is a highly experienced Chilean language teaching specialist, a policymaker, an author of multiple volumes, and a sought-out international consultant. She received a master's degree in Education from the Universidad Católica de Chile as well as a master's degree in Applied Linguistics from the University of Paris. She has had experience at all levels, having worked as an elementary teacher, a teacher educator, a member of the Chilean Ministry of Education, and a specialist in intercultural, multilingual education in Africa and Latin America. Ms. Galdames has written multiple articles and books in the field of intercultural, multilingual education, main among them *Taller de Lenguaje*.

Leslie Hamburger is Vice President, K–12 Systems at West Ed, where she leads a portfolio of K–12 research, development, technical assistance, and professional learning teams focused on improving K–12 education systems to achieve equitable outcomes for diverse student populations. As a leader in the Quality Teaching for English Learners (QTEL) initiative, she assists states, districts, and schools in the development and implementation of exemplary educational programs for multilingual learners and conducts professional development to enhance the expertise of educators to promote the development of disciplinary, analytic, and language practices in tandem. She serves as coinvestigator of the Reimagining and Amplifying Mathematics Participation, Understanding, and Practices (RAMP-UP) Study for the National Research and Development Center to Improve Education for Secondary English Learners (Contract # R305C200008).

Lee Hartman is a senior program associate on WestEd's English Learner and Migrant Education Services team. He is also an English Language Arts and English language development specialist on the Educative English Language Arts Curriculum Materials study at the National Research and Development Center for the academic success of Secondary English Learners. He creates and implements learning experiences for ELA and ELD educators in 4th- through 12th-grade schools through professional development and curriculum design. Previously, he served as an ESL instructional coach to teachers working with English Learners and was responsible for creating and implementing secondary ELA and ESL curricula. A former teacher of secondary Newcomer students, he specializes in the education of students recently arrived in the United States.

Daisy Martin, PhD, is the founding director of The History & Civics Project at the University of California, Santa Cruz. She previously cofounded the Stanford History Education Group, served as the Director of History Education for the National History Education Clearinghouse, and was a senior researcher in charge of history/social studies student assessment at the Stanford Center for Assessment, Learning and Equity. She has been teaching for several decades, and currently prepares teachers in the Masters of Arts/Teaching Credential Program at the University of California, Santa Cruz. Dr. Martin holds a CA Single Subject California Teaching Credential in history/social acience.

Sara Rutherford-Quach is a principal researcher and codirector of the multilingual learner program area at SRI Education. She is also the former director of Academic Initiatives and Research for Understanding Language at the Stanford University Graduate School of Education. A former bilingual teacher, she received her PhD in Linguistic Anthropology of Education from Stanford University. Her work focuses on language and literacy practices across content areas, particularly with respect to multilingual students and their educators.

Heather Schlaman is the Language and Literacy Coordinator at the Yolo County Office of Education and a lecturer in teacher education at the University of California, Davis. She holds a PhD in Education from the University of California, Santa Cruz, where she studied school leaders' roles in shaping the education of multilingual learners. A longtime high school English teacher and administrator, Heather now provides professional development for teachers and leaders focused on high-quality language and literacy instruction across disciplines.

Mary Schmida is a senior research associate with the Quality Teaching for English Learners (QTEL) initiative at WestEd. She develops instructional materials and designs and facilitates professional development nationally to enhance teacher knowledge in the areas of secondary English Language Arts teaching and pedagogy. She received a PhD in Education in Language, Literacy, and Culture from the University of California, Berkeley. Her research focused on the complex linguistic, academic, and social realities of Long-Term English Learners.

Tanya Warren is a program associate for secondary science on the English Learner and Migrant Education Services team. She creates and implements learning experiences for secondary science educators through professional development, lesson design, and content coaching. Previously she served as a K–12 science coordinator and as a secondary ESL specialist. She was also a classroom teacher for 17 years specializing in secondary ESL and science.

Lyn Westergard is a program associate at WestEd. Drawing on over 15 years of teaching experience and expertise in instructional design, her work focuses on creating impactful learning experiences for both educators and students. She earned a doctorate of Education from the University of Colorado–Denver's Leadership for Educational Equity program. Her expertise centers on multilingual education focusing on research, professional learning design, and developing innovative educational content.